GERMANIC KINSHIP STRUCTURE

Studies in Law and Society in Antiquity
and the Early Middle Ages

by

Alexander Callander Murray

This book is a major reevaluation of the traditional view of early Germanic kinship structure and the large body of evidence from Antiquity and the early Middle Ages which has long been thought to support its major assumptions. The book is about kinship, but also, directly and indirectly, about other aspects of the period: law, association and social organization, family institutions and the barbarian and Roman heritage of the early Middle Ages. It is its principal aim that from a re-examination of kinship will come a greater understanding of some of the central documents of barbarian social and legal history.

The studies presented here fall into three parts. In Part One the major theories of Germanic kinship structure and development are examined and subjected to a critical analysis based upon a modern anthropological understanding of kinship systems. Part Two examines the assumption that early Germanic society was constituted of unilineal clans and lineages, a view founded upon the classical accounts of Caesar and Tacitus and the *vicini*, *farae* and *genealogiae* of the early Middle Ages. Although this evidence is shown to have little bearing on the clan of traditional historiography, it does tell us a considerable amount about the ancient ethnographic traditions regarding the Germanic and non-Germanic north, the nature of kinship in barbarian society, and various forms of association in Antiquity and the early Middle Ages.

Almost half of the book (Part Three) is taken up with a consideration of the kinship texts of the Frankish legal collection *Lex Salica*, the interpretation of which has often suffered severely in the past from traditional assumptions about Germanic kinship structure and society. The conclusions offered in these studies concern not only Frankish kinship, but also property holding, association, the legal capacity of women, and the textual history of *Lex Salica* itself.

STUDIES AND TEXTS 65

GERMANIC KINSHIP STRUCTURE

Studies in Law and Society in Antiquity and the Early Middle Ages

BY

ALEXANDER CALLANDER MURRAY

PONTIFICAL INSTITUTE OF MEDIAEVAL STUDIES

ACKNOWLEDGMENT

This book has been published with the help of a grant
from the Canadian Federation for the Humanities,
using funds provided by the Social Sciences
and Humanities Research Council of Canada.

CANADIAN CATALOGUING IN PUBLICATION DATA

Murray, Alexander C., 1946-
  Germanic kinship structure

(Studies and texts, ISSN 0082-5328 ; 65)
Bibliography: p.
Includes index.
ISBN 0-88844-065-0

1. Civilization, Germanic.   2. Germanic tribes - Social conditions.
3. Kinship - History.   I. Pontifical Institute of Mediaeval Studies.   II. Title.
  III. Series: Studies and texts (Pontifical Institute of Mediaeval Studies) ; 65.

CB213.C34   943´.02   C83-094013-8

PRINTED BY UNIVERSA, WETTEREN, BELGIUM

To Joan

Contents

Acknowledgments IX

Abbreviations XI

Introduction 1

Part I

The Nature and Development of
Germanic Kinship Structure

1 Theories of Germanic Kinship Structure in Antiquity and the
   Early Middle Ages 11

Part II

Was Early Germanic Society
Clan- and Lineage-Based?

2 Introduction and the Indo-European Background 35
3 The Views of Antiquity 39
   A. Caesar's *Bellum Gallicum* 42. B. Tacitus' *Germania* 51.
4 The *Vicini* of the *Pactus Legis Salicae* and the *Edictum Chilperici*   67
5 The *Fara* 89
6 The *Genealogia* 99
7 Conclusion 109

Part III

The Early Middle Ages:
Frankish Kinship and *Lex Salica*

8 Kinship and *Lex Salica* 115

9 The Bilateral Kindred as a Personal Group I: Feud and
   Compensation 135
   A. The Paying and Receiving of Compensation: LS 62, *De
   conpositione homicidii* and LS 68, *De homine ingenuo
   occiso* 135. B. Compensation Liability: LS 58, *De chrenecruda* 144. C. The Abrogation of Relationship: LS 60, *De eum
   qui se de parentilla tollere uult* 150.

10 The Bilateral Kindred as a Personal Group II: Oathhelping in *Lex
   Salica* and the *Formulae* 157

11 Kinship Categories I: LS 44, *De reipus* 163

12 Kinship Categories II: An Introduction to Frankish Inheritance 177

13 Frankish Inheritance: The Period of the *Formulae* 183

14 Frankish Inheritance: The Sixth Century 193
   A. *Decretio Childeberti* (596) 193. B. *Edictum Chilperici*
   (561-584) 195. C. Gregory of Tours' HF 9.33 and 10.12: The
   Inheritance Right of the Mother in Frankish Law 197.

15 Frankish Inheritance: LS 59, *De alodis* 201

16 The Structure of Frankish Kinship: Conclusion 217

Conclusion 221

Appendix I. The *Mater* and *Soror matris* texts of LS 58.3 225

Appendix II. Herold and C6a on LS 59 231

Appendix III. The Succession Right of the Mother in Roman, Visigothic and Burgundian Law 235

Bibliography 243

Index 253

Acknowledgments

This book was originally submitted to the University of Toronto as a doctoral dissertation in 1976 under the title "Studies in Germanic Kinship Structure and Society in Antiquity and the Early Middle Ages." A work such as this comes at the end of a long, and it seems, fortuitous process. That I was sufficiently encouraged to set out on this course in the first place I owe in no small measure to kindnesses over the years which I have not forgotten, particularly from Diane Hughes and Angus Cameron. As far as the book is concerned, and more besides, thanks are due to Fathers Ambrose Raftis and Michael Sheehan. I would especially like to thank Walter Goffart, my thesis supervisor, whose sense of direction was right from the beginning and who permitted me to find that out for myself. Whatever the merits of the book may be, his advice and criticism have made it much better than it might otherwise have been.

Abbreviations

BG	C. Julius Caesar, *Commentarii de Bello Gallico*, ed. Fr. Kraner and W. Dittenberger, 20th ed. by H. Meusel, 3 vols. (Berlin, 1964)
Boretius	*Capitularia Regum Francorum*, MGH LL 2, I-II, ed. A. Boretius (Hanover, 1883-1893)
CE	*Codex Euricianus: El código de Eurico*, ed. Alvaro D'Ors, Cuadernos del Instituto Juridico Español, 12, Estudios Visigoticos, 2 (Rome, 1960)
CJ	*Codex Iustinianus*, ed. P. Krueger, in *Corpus Iuris Civilis* (Berlin, 1877), 2
CT	*Codex Theodosianus*, ed. Th. Mommsen (Berlin, 1905)
DRG	Heinrich Brunner, *Deutsche Rechtsgeschichte*, 2nd ed., Systematisches Handbuch der deutschen Rechtswissenschaft, 2, 1, 2 vols. (Leipzig, 1906-1928)
F	*Formulae Merowingici et Karolini Aevi*, MGH LL 5, ed. K. Zeumer (Hanover, 1886)
And.	*Formulae Andecavenses*
Arv.	*Formulae Arvernenses*
Big.	*Formulae Salicae Bignonianae*
Lin.	*Formulae Salicae Lindenbrogianae*
Marc.	*Marculfi Formulae*
Merk.	*Formulae Salicae Merkelianae*
Sen.	*Cartae Senonicae*
Tur.	*Formulae Turonenses*
G	*Cornelii Taciti De Origine et Situ Germanorum*, ed. J. G. C. Anderson (Oxford, 1938)
Geffcken	Heinrich Geffcken, *Lex Salica zum akademischen Gebrauche* (Leipzig, 1898)
HEL	F. Pollock and F. W. Maitland, *The History of English Law*, 2nd ed., 2 vols. (1898; rpt. Cambridge, 1968)
Hessels	*Lex Salica: The Ten Texts with Glosses and the Lex Emendata*, ed. J. H. Hessels (London, 1880)
HF	*Historiae Francorum*: Gregory of Tours, *Libri Historiarum X*, MGH, *Scriptores Rerum Merovingicarum*, I, 1, ed. B. Krusch and W. Levison, 2nd ed. (Hanover, 1951)
HRG	*Handwörterbuch zur deutschen Rechtsgeschichte*, ed. Adalbert Erler et al., 2 vols. (Berlin, 1971-1978)
Inst.	*Institutiones*: of Gaius, in *Fontes Iuris Romani Antejustiniani*,

	ed. J. Baviera, 2nd ed. (Florence, 1940), 2; *Inst. Iustiniani,* ed. P. Krueger, in *Corpus Iuris Civilis* (Berlin, 1872), 1
LA	*Lex Alamannorum,* in *Leges Alamannorum,* MGH LL 1, V, 1, ed. K. Lehmann (Hanover, 1926); 2nd ed. by K. A. Eckhardt, 1966
LB	*Lex Burgundionum,* in *Leges Burgundionum,* MGH LL 1, II, 1, ed. L. R. von Salis (Hanover, 1892)
LBai.	*Lex Baiwariorum,* MGH LL 1, V, 2, ed. Ernst von Schwind (Hanover, 1926)
Lewis and Short	C. T. Lewis and C. Short, *A Latin Dictionary* (Oxford, 1879)
Li.	Laws of Liutprand, in *Leges Langobardorum,* MGH LL, IV, ed. F. Bluhme (Hanover, 1868)
LRB	*Lex Romana Burgundionum,* in *Leges Burgundionum,* MGH LL 1, II, 1, ed. L. R. von Salis (Hanover, 1892)
LRib.	*Lex Ribvaria,* MGH LL 1, III, 2, ed. F. Beyerle and R. Buchner (Hanover, 1954)
LRV	*Lex Romana Visigothorum,* ed. G. Haenel (Berlin, 1849)
LS	*Pactus Legis Salicae,* MGH LL 1, IV, 1, ed. K. A. Eckhardt (Hanover, 1962), for redactions A, 'B', C, K, H; *Lex Salica,* MGH LL 1, IV, 2, ed. K. A. Eckhardt (Hanover, 1969), for redactions D, E, S.
LSax.	*Lex Saxonum,* in MGH LL V, ed. K. von Richtofen (Hanover, 1875-1889)
LTh.	*Lex Angliorum Werinorum Hoc Est Thuringorum,* in MGH LL V, ed. K. von Richtofen (Hanover, 1875-1889)
LV	*Lex Visigothorum,* in *Leges Visigothorum,* MGH LL 1, I, ed. K. Zeumer (Hanover, 1902)
MGH	*Monumenta Germaniae Historica*
AA	*Auctores Antiquissimi*
LL	*Leges;* where appropriate, *sectio* is indicated by an initial arabic numeral.
Niermeyer	J. F. Niermeyer, *Mediae Latinitatis Lexicon Minus* (Leiden, 1976)
Nov.	*Novellae,* ed. R. Schoell in *Corpus Iuris Civilis* (Berlin, 1895), 3
NTh.	*Novellae Theodosii II,* in *Codex Theodosianus,* ed. Th. Mommsen (Berlin, 1905)
PS	*Pauli Sententiae,* in *Fontes Iuris Romani Antejustiniani,* ed. J. Baviera, 2nd ed. (Florence, 1940), 2
Rechtsquellen	R. Buchner, *Die Rechtsquellen,* supplement to W. Wattenbach and W. Levison, *Deutschlands Geschichtsquellen im Mittelalter: Vorzeit und Karolinger* (Weimar, 1953)
Ro.	Laws of Rothair, in *Leges Langobardorum,* MGH LL, IV, ed. F. Bluhme (Hanover, 1868)
ZRG GA	*Zeitschrift der Savigny-Stiftung für Rechtsgeschichte, Germanistische Abteilung*

Introduction

For almost a century a theory on the nature and development of kinship among the Germanic peoples has shaped the attempts of scholars to describe the kinship structure of the barbarian peoples in Antiquity and the early Middle Ages and confounded efforts to interpret adequately a large body of evidence relating to a variety of social and legal forms in the same period. Like many comprehensive historical explanations the theory has never been monolithic and can take a number of forms. As is also to be expected, there have always been dissenters; at present, for instance, German scholarship, one of its major bastions in the past, seems on the point of jettisoning a number of the traditional elements. Yet the model of kinship development which the theory offers remains widely accepted. What makes its impact particularly profound is that many of its assumptions, which are not recognized as such or are left unexamined, have permeated standard interpretations of the legal, social, and political history of Antiquity and the successor kingdoms. These assumptions affect not simply notions about kinship or even the interpretation of particular texts, but also our ideas about the basic structures of barbarian and early medieval society and have, as a consequence, influenced to a considerable extent our perception of the origins of civilization in western Europe.

This book is an attempt to examine the theoretical and evidentiary foundations of the traditional view and to reinterpret and set in a clear context a body of evidence which has long been thought to support its major assumptions. If a theory is proven to be deficient one expects that another will be put in its place. To some extent this is done in the following pages. But the question arises whether there can ever be as comprehensive a model as was previously suggested. It is likely that we must be satisfied with less, but in so doing, we can also free ourselves to reexamine some of the basic sources for early medieval history. This is not a simple task nor one undertaken once and for all. I do not imagine for a moment that all the conclusions made here will settle matters which, despite the prevalence of the traditional view, have been simmering and occasionally bubbling over for many decades; nor do I think that the analysis of Frankish kinship offered in *Part III* can be simply transferred to the systems of other peoples. But I believe that the conclusions made in these pages will clear away some of the misconceptions which have obscured the few paths through the uncertainty of barbarian social and legal history, and also bring to the attention of historians, once again, a number of texts which, for all the frequent difficulty of their interpretation, deserve the scrutiny of all those interested in the foundations of early medieval civilization.

I have subtitled this work *Studies*, not because the various parts and chapters are unconnected, although some can be read independently and a number may engage the attention of those with no particular interest in kinship, but because it is impossible at this point to consider all the evidence pertaining to Germanic kin structure in the early Middle Ages. In particular, for reasons that will be plain enough, it has been necessary in considering the nature of the kinship systems of the various national groups to limit discussion to one people. On the other hand, all the major textual evidence for clan and lineage organization among the early Germans is surveyed, as is the classical evidence, such as it is, for kinship structure. In addition, as an historian, I have confined myself to the interpretation of historical texts. Linguistic, etymological and terminological considerations have been left, by and large, to the side, mainly because the historical sources are the primary and surest foundation for reconstruction and have too long been ignored.

Kinship is the province of the anthropologist and to talk of kinship inevitably means the use of a distinctive terminological and theoretical system with which some readers may be unfamiliar. I have decided not to append an extensive discussion of kinship classification and terminology for several reasons. Admirable and readable introductions to the subject from an anthropological perspective are readily available and do the subject far more justice than is possible here.[1] I recognize that such a discussion with reference to the notions and practices of modern historians of Antiquity and the Middle Ages would be salutary quite apart

---

[1] The best introduction is probably Robin Fox, *Kinship and Marriage* (Penguin Books, 1967); Roger M. Keesing, *Kin Groups and Social Structure* (New York, 1975) also offers a fine introductory perspective; both will direct readers to specialist literature. A useful compendium of examples is Ernest L. Schusky, *Variation in Kinship* (New York, 1974). Some of the broader issues of analysis and classification can be found in *Rethinking Kinship and Marriage*, ed. Rodney Needham, A.S.A. Monographs, 11 (London, 1971). A seminal article on cognatic kinship is J. D. Freeman, "On the Concept of the Kindred," *Journal of the Royal Anthropological Institute* 91 (1961) 192-220. Most anthropological literature lacks a European context, but see Robin Fox, "Prolegomena to the Study of British Kinship," *Penguin Survey of the Social Sciences*, ed. J. Gould (Penguin Books, 1965), pp. 128-143.

from the context of these studies. This subject is one I will probably return to elsewhere but consideration of it here would increase the volume of the book considerably, and such a discussion is not necessary to understand the conclusions drawn about the various texts considered below. The nature of the problems and the quality of the evidence for the period are such, I believe, that only a few basic concepts are absolutely essential and these can be pointed out in the introduction and in appropriate places in the body of the text. To begin with, then, I should state briefly the basic vocabulary to be used in the following pages, and indicate those ideas, some of them of recent vintage, which are crucial for analyzing kinship structure in the period under consideration.

Agnation, a term derived from Roman law, is used in its standard anthropological meaning to designate relationship through males. This sense roughly corresponds to the Roman meaning, which, however, could be more precisely defined depending upon its civil law context. Agnatic relatives include women, but not their offspring. A synonym of agnation is *patriliny*. Agnates or patrilineal relatives should not be confused with *patrilateral* kin, that is relatives on a person's father's side generally, since agnation is not inclusive of all these relations – for example, the son of one's father's sister can only be a patrilateral relative, not an agnate.

Matriliny also is used in the standard anthropological sense of relationship through females, and is the mirror image of agnation. Matrilineal relatives, therefore, include males but not their offspring; *matrilateral* kin, on the other hand, are simply a person's relatives whose relationship is mediated through his mother. Both agnation and matriliny, since they trace relationship through one line, either the male or female, are said to be *unilineal*.

Cognation, a term also derived from Latin, is used in the standard anthropological sense of relationship through males or females, in other words without regard to the sexual restriction which is found in unilinealism. Cognates, then, like the Roman *cognati*, are blood relations generally and cognatic relatives can be linked through males or females or any combination of the two. A synonym for cognatic is *bilateral*. It need not be characteristic of cognatic descent that relationship through males and females is always equally invoked; rather the circle of blood relationship created by bilateral descent creates a wider range of choice for the application of an individual's rights, claims, and affiliations.

Until fairly recently cognatic kinship was a much ignored area of anthropological research. While it was recognized that bilateral relationship was a feature to some extent of all societies, attention was largely directed toward unilineal systems, in which major corporate functions were carried out by descent groups. Cognation in a systematic sense was viewed mistakenly as unilinealism in transition or disintegration, particularly as there is sometimes a patrilineal or patrilateral bias to bilateral descent, or as a rare form of kinship affiliation. As more attention was turned upon cognatic systems, it was realized by the 1960s that a sizeable proportion of the world's societies fell into this category. The new awareness of the importance and possibilities of cognation, the recognition that it need not be unilinealism in disintegration, and the resulting understanding of the variety of factors which may constitute a kinship system are important for looking at the nature of kinship among the Germanic peoples.

Category is used to indicate a class of relatives who are defined for some purpose but do not act together as a group or have a sense of corporateness. Classes of relatives with inheritance rights (such as the Roman law *agnati* and *cognati*) are usually categories, if the heirs are normally called as individuals to the inheritance.

Group, on the other hand, implies a recognizable degree of corporateness, an existence in perpetuity apart from the life of an individual member, or some common activity among its members. Clans and lineages are *descent groups*. *Clan* and *lineage* indicate a group of kinsmen formed on the basis of descent from a common ancestor (*ancestor-focus*). When the genealogical relationship among the members is demonstrable and not simply assumed, the group is called a lineage; whether matrilineage, patrilineage, or cognatic lineage, depends upon the principle of relationship used in recruitment (a simple cognatic lineage, for example, is composed of the cognatic descendants of a common ancestor). Units of a higher order, which link a number of lineages or where genealogical relationship is assumed or fictive and cannot be demonstrated, are called clans. Until recently, descent groups, that is, clans and lineages, were seen only in terms of unilinealism, but now it is recognized that descent groups can also recruit on the basis of cognation, and that cognatic clans and lineages can exist and perform much the same functions as unilineal groups. This is of considerable importance for looking at the evidence for clans among the early Germans, since, previously, evidence for clans or lineages was taken automatically as evidence for unilinealism.

Unlike clans and lineages, which are based upon ancestor-focus, the *kindred* is based upon *ego*-focus. The kindred is defined by the common relationship all its members have with an individual (*ego*), who is the centre and raison d'être for the group; the members of a cognatic or bilateral kindred need not (and usually do not) all share descent from a common ancestor, but are simply related to *ego*. Since individuals are the focus of their own kindred and, in turn, belong to many other kindreds, bilateral kindreds endlessly overlap. While clans and lineages are descent groups, I follow the practice of calling the cognatic kindred a *personal group*, even though strictly speaking it cannot be corporate and permanent, but is rather a category of cognates out of which groups can be recruited from time to time.

Descent groups and personal groups can on occasion perform similar functions. Feud and compensation, for instance, can be the province of the lineage or the kindred. But clearly only descent groups can carry out those permanent, corporate functions which pertain to universal or constituent kinship groups of society. For example, the constituent settlement groups of society may be based upon lineage membership but not upon the kindred because of the overlapping nature of *ego*-focused systems.

Other considerations are worth keeping in mind when dealing with descent groups in the context of European history and historiography. Lineage structures, sometimes with a distinct corporate aspect and a unilineal bias, can form from time to time within segments of society – the nobility is a good example – while the prevalent forms of society as a whole are personal kindreds and cognatic descent. Societies with these limited and occasional lineage structures, which are common in European history, are to be distinguished from societies composed or constituted of lineages and clans, which have largely been the concern of anthropological research. This distinction between lineage and clan as occasional elements as opposed to constituent ones is important when considering attempts to reconstruct the foundations of ancient Germanic social and political life. Certain qualifications concerning the terminology of descent groups should also be noted. I have emphasized the corporate aspect of descent groups but common usage often applies the word 'lineage' to groupings with little corporate identity or to categories defined for some purpose on the basis of ancestor focus. It is unlikely this practice will change since it is rooted in the historical, as opposed to the artificial and technical use of the word and one can do no more than be aware of the range of meaning. Another range of meaning, which will be reflected in the following pages, involves the word clan. Traditional scholarship has regarded ancient Germanic society as composed of corporate descent groups of various dimensions to which the concepts of clan and lineage could apply. Precision here is not possible, and to avoid incessant repetition I will sometimes simply use the word clan to refer to these historiographical groupings.

Theoretically none of the principles of relationship or the groups described above are exclusive of one another. For the kinship system of a society can have more than one principle in operation, can even employ more than one dominant principle, depending upon the vantage point from which we view it and the particular functions under consideration. In some cases this has made the classification of societies and kinship systems a far more complicated problem than was first supposed. Usually, however, the major criterion in the classification of kinship systems has been the principle of descent used in the recruitment of corporate descent groups. Where corporate unilineal descent groups are not dominant or constituent features of society, cognation may be seen to have a broader functional role to play in the determination of categories and groups.

While this brief terminological and theoretical framework is sufficient for the task at hand, a few comments may help put it in perspective. Probably no one would be surprised to discover that it can undergo many refinements and variations, that anthropologists are not always unanimous in the detailed interpretation of its elements, or even that there are ways of looking at kinship systems other than in terms of descent; yet there is now a fair consensus on at least the formal meaning and application of the terms discussed above, even if their value is sometimes in dispute. What may be more disquieting for those dealing with the literature of historians is the variety of unexplained terminology in use which often represents imprecise or confused models. In general, where the underlying conception is clear, I have translated such terms into the standard vocabulary given above. Finally, the kinship wars of anthropologists and historians alike and the attention lavished on terminology and classification may seem to some an arid and abstract concern, but the implications can be profound. In the attempt to reconstruct early European societies, theoretical constructs, as will be clear in the following pages, have had a fundamental role to play in the formation of the traditional view of barbarian society. They will no doubt continue to have an important role, if only because we are all prisoners of conceptual models, whether or not we recognize them as such.

What remains to be done is to give some indication of the constitution and arrangement of this work. Simply put, the traditional view has rested upon two notions: first, that ancient Germanic society was based upon a clan and lineage system; second, that the ancient structure of kinship was unilineal. Consequently the largely kindred-based cognatic structure of the Middle Ages was viewed as the result of the breakdown of this extensive unilineal and highly corporate structure which originated in the prehistoric period, but which, it was thought, persisted recognizably into the early Middle Ages. *Part I* gives a brief survey of the theoretical and evidentiary foundations of this approach. The lineaments of the major theories are outlined and their main assumptions considered in the light of modern anthropological notions of kinship structure and development. The major theories clearly rest upon outmoded conceptions of the nature of relationship and the development of human societies; for that reason the cognatic factor in Germanic kinship has either been misunderstood or ignored. Part I should also serve as a guide to the reader who wishes to make his own way among the terminological and theoretical confusion of modern treatments of the subject.

The remainder of the book is concerned with studies of the principal evidence of kinship among the Germans with particular regard to the view that constituent clans and lineages lay at the foundation of society and that originally the structure of kinship was unilineal.

Part II examines the assumption that early Germanic society was clan and lineage-based, an interpretation founded upon the classical accounts of Caesar and Tacitus and the *vicini, farae* and *genealogiae* of the early Middle Ages. In fact none of this evidence supports the notion of the clan structure of barbarian society, but it does tell us a considerable amount about the ancient ethnographic traditions regarding the Germanic and non-Germanic north, the nature of kinship in barbarian society, and various forms of association in the early Middle Ages and late Antiquity.

Traditional historiography has regarded unilinealism as a necessary feature of the clan basis of Germanic society. This assumption and the notion that the clan and unilinealism must have disintegrated in the early Middle Ages have formed the basis for interpreting many texts touching upon the family institutions of the national groups of the successor kingdoms. In rejecting the hypothesis of the clan we can look at these sources in a new light. The kinship structure of one of the national groups that settled within the old Empire is examined in *Part III*, in order that we may perceive the diverse functions of kinship within a single system and, in particular, study the operations and interrelaton of kinship categories and groups and the principles of relationship. The Franks have been chosen owing to the early date of redaction of their law, *Lex Salica*, the wide scope of kinship related material it contains, and its importance among legal antiquities. The Frankish evidence has suffered severely from the traditional assumptions about Germanic kinship and society, but if we approach the evidence from outside this framework, a number of important aspects of Frankish law can be reinterpreted. Although much of Frankish kin structure must remain in darkness, it nevertheless displays a marked bilateral stamp; furthermore, nothing about the character of historical Frankish kinship patterns suggests that it is the result of devolution from a once encompassing unilineal system.

These studies show that there is no evidence for the idea that the society of the ancient Germans was rooted in a clan or extensive lineage structure. Moreover, the evidence of the classical sources and Frankish law, as well as the prevailingly bilateral character of medieval kinship structures, also brings into question the idea of the unilineal nature of the ancient kinship structure of the Germanic peoples as a whole. The universal group of the Germanic peoples of Antiquity and the Middle Ages appears to be the bilateral kindred. Although it is apparent various kinds of kinship differentiation were employed, cognation was pervasive and is best seen as an ancient and integral part of barbarian kinship structure, not as the result of a dissolving unilineal system. The implications of these views are of importance for our understanding of the social and legal order of ancient Germanic society, the polity of the migration period and earlier, and the integration of the northern cultures with the political and social forms of mediterranean Antiquity.

This book is about kinship, but it is also, directly and indirectly, about other things: law, association and social organization, family institutions, and the barbarian and Roman heritage of the early Middle Ages. The traditional views of Germanic kinship development were not simply abstract or accessory ideas concerned only with kinship. In the face of the quality and extent of the evidence from Antiquity and the early Middle Ages the nature of the ideas made them models which could be used as basic tools for interpreting texts. It is really the principal aim of this book, and I hope one of its merits, that from a reexamination of kinship will come a greater understanding of some of the central documents of barbarian social and legal history.

Part I

The Nature and Development
of Germanic Kinship Structure

1

Theories of Germanic Kinship Structure in Antiquity and the Early Middle Ages

When the state of the evidence permits a fairly comprehensive and detailed view of Germanic societies in the medieval period, observers have often been struck by the markedly bilateral or cognatic character of the kinship systems. To Bertha Phillpotts the general prevalence of the cognatic kindred in the original homeland and in the areas of later settlement suggested difficulties in the theory of originally agnatic lineages or clans among the Germanic peoples, and "these difficulties," she wrote, "increase in the light of our general review of the later evidence."[1] Her conclusion, based mainly on legal documents, came from an extensive consideration of the solidary aspects of kinship in Germanic areas of northern Europe, including northern France, the Low Countries, and Anglo-Saxon England. Approaching the problem from quite different viewpoints, more recent scholars stress the bilateral nature of medieval society in north-western Europe. The social anthropological approach of Lorraine Lancaster shows historical Anglo-Saxon kinship to be thoroughly imbued with the cognatic principle.[2] So, too, contemporary German research into the kin groupings of the Carolingian aristocracy emphasizes the fluid and optative features of bilateral relationship, and places in the eleventh century the genesis of the strongly dynastic structure characteristic of the later German nobility.[3] Marc Bloch in his classic study of feudal

---

[1] *Kindred and Clan* (Cambridge, 1913), p. 268. This is the classic account of the subject in English, which has recently been influential in the German reappraisal of the *Sippe* theory. See below, pp. 21-22.

[2] "Kinship in Anglo-Saxon Society," *British Journal of Sociology* 9 (1957) 230-250 and 359-377.

[3] The pertinent literature is reviewed in K. Leyser, "The German Aristocracy from the Ninth to the Early Twelfth Century: A Historical and Cultural Sketch," *Past and Present*, No. 41 (Dec., 1968), pp. 25-53. Some of this work is now reflected in the collection

institutions and society also concludes, after briefly considering the early medieval and prehistoric period: "But whatever one is to think of these problems of origins, it is at all events certain that in the medieval West kinship had acquired or retained a distinctly dual character";[4] indeed, Bloch would regard the bilaterality of society, and what he supposes is the consequent weakness of the kinship tie, as central to explaining the rise of feudalism itself.[5] Although agnatic categories are occasionally recognized for various purposes, medieval society has seemed cognatic to observers because the bilateral kindred is the prevailing constituent kin group and cognation legally and ideologically lies at the heart of the descent system.

But was this always the case? Can this judgment safely be applied to the migration and pre-migration periods? Or did these two earlier ages witness profound changes in the kinship fabric of western European society? The prevailing answer to the last questions is yes. Bloch, again, puts the matter succinctly:

---

translated by Timothy Reuter, *The Medieval Nobility: Studies on the Ruling Classes of France and Germany from the Sixth to the Twelfth Century*, Europe in the Middle Ages, Selected Studies 14 (Amsterdam, 1978): see esp. Karl Schmid, "The Structure of the Nobility in the Earlier Middle Ages," pp. 37-59. See also Leyser, "Maternal Kin in Early Medieval Germany," *Past and Present*, No. 49 (Nov., 1970), p. 126 and *Rule and Conflict in an Early Medieval Society: Ottonian Saxony* (London, 1979).

The same model has been applied to the French nobility: Georges Duby, *The Chivalrous Society*, trans. Cynthia Postan (London, 1977), pp. 98-103, and chs. 9-10. One should not draw too much from the author's rather loose use of the terms agnatic and patrilineal to describe the kinship structure of the new lineage-conscious nobility, for the cognatic structure of the descent system is still very much in evidence in the material he considers.

The notion of Léopold Genicot that in the early Middle Ages nobility may have been transmitted matrilineally is assuredly mistaken: "Was nobility transmitted by one's mother, or by one's father? By either? Or conjointly by both? The first hypothesis, seemingly the most astonishing, should not be excluded; it may even be the most plausible." ("The Nobility in Medieval *Francia*: Continuity, Break, or Evolution?" in *Lordship and Community*, trans. and ed. F. L. Cheyette [New York, 1968], p. 131). His examples simply suggest, not surprisingly, that transmission was cognatic: e.g. "Tetradia nobilis ex matre, patre inferiore," means "Since her father was of lower (or lowly) birth, Tetradia received her 'nobility' from her mother's side." One could claim status through either parent, or through both.

[4] *Feudal Society*, trans. L. A. Manyon (London, 1961), p. 137.

[5] "Yet to the individual, threatened by the numerous dangers bred by an atmosphere of violence, the kinship group did not seem to offer adequate protection, even in the first feudal age. In the form in which it then existed, it was too vague and too variable in its outlines, too deeply undermined by the duality of descent by male and female lines .... The tie of kinship was one of the essential elements of feudal society; its relative weakness explains why there was feudalism at all" (ibid., p. 142). Cf. Otto Hintze, "The Nature of Feudalism," in *Lordship and Community*, esp. pp. 26-28.

Vast *gentes* or clans, firmly defined and held together by a belief – whether true or false – in a common ancestry, were unknown to western Europe in the feudal period, save on its outer fringes, beyond the genuinely feudalized regions. On the shores of the North Sea there were the *Geschlechter* of Frisia or of Ditmarschen; in the west Celtic tribes or clans. It seems certain that groups of this nature had still existed among the Germans in the period of the invasions. There were, for example, the Lombard and Frankish *farae* of which more than one Italian or French village continues to bear the name; and there were also *genealogiae* of the Alemans and Bavarians which certain texts show in possession of the soil. But these excessively large units gradually disintegrated.[6]

Bloch sees the kinship system of the Germanic invaders as based upon an agnatic clan system, even though, as he later says, there is a trace of a submerged but once primary matriliny.[7] A number of features of Bloch's view are worth noting at the outset because they are commonplaces in the historiography of Germanic kinship: the dominance of the agnatic principle; the juxtaposition and similarity of the Roman *gens*, Ditmarschen *Geschlecht*, and Germanic clan or lineage; the identification of the Lombard and Frankish *farae* and Bavarian *genealogiae* with the agnatic clan, and the consequent persistence of the clan well into historical times; the characterization of the clan as a landholding and settlement group; and finally the notion that this agnatic group was not a relatively limited or restricted unit, but extensive in scope. A fairly comprehensive model for the development of kin structure is quite apparent, in which the age of the Romano-Barbarian kingdoms is the crucial period for the disintegration of the vast corporate *gentes* of the migration and pre-migration periods; in the wake of this disintegration society is seen to have reconstituted itself on a feudal pattern within the context of an emergent bilateral kinship structure.

The views of Bloch represent variations upon the old but prevailing matrilineal and patrilineal theories of Germanic kinship development; to some degree even Phillpotts is in reluctant agreement, although there is no talk in her pages of clans of any kind in the historical period, except for the Ditmarschen examples. Yet there are major difficulties with the picture these theories present of early society, whether in the *regna* or

---

[6] Ibid., p. 137.

[7] Commenting on the presence of 'spear' and 'spindle' kin he notes: "it was as though among the Germans the victory of the agnatic principle had never been sufficiently complete to extinguish all trace of a more ancient system of uterine filiation" (ibid., p. 137).

prior to the invasions, and with the comprehensive explanation they offer of changes in the social, legal and political structures from the prehistoric period through the early Middle Ages. For instance, the documentation which is offered, and which at first glance may seem impressive, is far less so when seen apart from the theoretical context which informs its interpretation. To evaluate the worth of the kind of model presented by Bloch and others, therefore, it is important to begin by examining the genesis and elaboration of the traditional theories, and by asking to what extent their theoretical foundations are justified. Such an inquiry seems all the more worthwhile when we consider the period in which the traditional theories were formulated, the changing perspective of anthropological thought,[8] and the subsequent historical interpretation of individual constituent elements of the complete formulations.

Kinship has been a neglected area in the study of the history of the early medieval period. Since the war, but particularly in recent years, there has been a quickening of research in the general area of family and kin in the Middle Ages, but for obvious reasons this has concentrated on periods with greater and less puzzling source material. Despite important studies, which have had some impact upon prevailing notions, the whole conception of the nature and development of early Germanic, and to a large extent Indo-European, kinship has reiterated, or at the least has rested, however uneasily, upon the ideas and research put forth over three-quarters of a century ago. The current relative quiescence was not always the case. In the late nineteenth century and in the period before World War I, the nature of Germanic kinship was a hot issue, debated by two contending schools. As it was then conceived, the question was the primary form of kinship, not only among the Germans, but also among the Indo-Europeans and their predecessors in Western Europe; either patriliny or matriliny was put forward as the principal historical fact of the kinship systems of the Germanic and other European peoples. Subsequent developments from prehistoric into historical times were seen in terms of the impingement of other kinship forms upon originally unilineal structures.

It cannot be said that the debate was ever completely settled. In Germany, by the turn of the century, the agnatic or patrilineal viewpoint seemed to prevail as far as Germanic kinship was concerned: the idea of the *Sippe* (a word with the principal meaning of clan or lineage but which is, unfortunately, extremely difficult to translate because of its various

[8] See pp. 2-6.

applications and associations) by 1906 had reached, if not its most elaborate, certainly its most influential and convincing expression in Heinrich Brunner's *Deutsche Rechtsgeschichte*.[9] A more recent German critic (1960) has written: "Till now, scarcely anything in this theory has been changed."[10] Perhaps this is something of an exaggeration, if only because the elements of the theory have been subject to great variation, but certainly the continued re-edition and, under new editors, the reworking of the legal handbooks, has run true to type. Even though the word *Sippe* was elsewhere adopted as a technical term, the patrilineal theory as a less formalized aspect of historiography was never simply an expression of German scholarship, as a perusal of French and Italian works will show. It was also well reflected among scholars writing in English, but while the less speculative aspects of late nineteenth-century Germanist research, through the works of Vinogradoff, Seebohm, and (in an English translation) Rudolf Huebner, have had influence, particularly on non-historians, in the English-speaking world for a variety of reasons the patrilinealists have not commanded the field.[11] To some extent this has been due to the remarkable vitality of the matrilineal viewpoint among British historians which persists to the present day. Elsewhere as well the matrilineal theory, while perhaps on the whole faring badly, has certainly not been submerged, partly because it is an element in Marxist historiography, and partly because it has been espoused by notable scholars such as Marc Bloch.

   While the matrilineal/patrilineal distinction reflects just one aspect of the problem of early kinship, nevertheless it was around this issue that the major theories and the controversies which accompanied them evolved. At the same time, although there was no satisfactory resolution to the question of the primacy of matriliny or patriliny, there still remained a residuum of common assumptions about which there was a considerable amount of agreement. Despite the differences, both theories were united in regarding unilinealism and descent groups as the basis of kinship development and in using these concepts as a means of reconstructing, not only kinship, but also some of the basic institutions of barbarian society. As a result, even if one can sometimes find apparent and understandable

   [9] See in particular DRG 1: 110 ff. and 324 ff., and compare the treatment of the *Sippe* in Jacob Grimm's *Deutsche Rechtsalterthümer* (1828), 4th ed. (Leipzig, 1899) 1: 642 ff.
   [10] Karl Kroeschell, "Die Sippe im germanischen Recht," ZRG GA 77 (1960) 13.
   [11] Paul Vinogradoff, *The Growth of the Manor* (London, 1911) and *Historical Jurisprudence* (Oxford, 1920-1922), 1; F. Seebohm, *Tribal Custom in Anglo-Saxon Law* (London, 1911); R. Huebner, *A History of Germanic Private Law*, trans. F. S. Philbrick, The Continental Legal History Series, 4 (Boston, 1918).

uneasiness when circumstance requires some statement as to the earliest
kinship structures of the barbarians, on the whole scholars have approached the problem by adopting some, often general, variant of the two
main theories.

The substance and implications of the patrilineal or agnatic viewpoint
can best be seen in the elaborations of German scholarship. There the
central distinction has been between what is called the closed or fixed kin
group (geschlossene or feste Sippe), and the open or shifting kin group
(wechselnde Sippe).[12] Other variations in terminology exist. Brunner, for
instance, also refers to the fixed kin group as an agnatic lineage (Geschlecht or agnatische Geschlechtsverband) composed of a number of
Hausgemeinschaften tracing their descent in the male line from a common
male ancestor (Stammvater); and he defines the shifting kin group as
Blutsverwandten, Verwandtschaft, or Magschaft, the whole circle of an
individual's blood relations. The word Sippe, he says, unavoidably has to
be applied to both these conceptions, although its primary and original
meaning applies only to the agnatic lineage (feste Sippe or Geschlechtsverband). It should be noted that Brunner at least properly confines the
designation of Verband to the fixed kin group, since only it can be,
properly speaking, a corporate group.[13] It is also thought that these two
kinds of kin groups and patterns of reckoning relationship are reflected
in the terms Schwert-, Ger-, or Speermagen, the sword or spearkin,
composed of male relatives of the male line, and Spindel-, Spill-, or
Kunkelmagen, the spindle kin, consisting of females or those related
through a female; another classification was current which simply divided
the Magschaft, or kindred, into Vatermagen and Muttermagen, relatives
whose relationship was mediated through one's father and mother
respectively. In the context of our earlier discussion of terminology,
clearly the shifting or open kin group corresponds to the English word

---

[12] Examples of the traditional teaching can be found everywhere in German (and
many non-German) historical works, legal and otherwise. Bibliography of the various
legal handbooks and some other works can be found in Felix Genzmer, "Die germanische
Sippe als Rechtsgebilde," ZRG GA 67 (1950) 34-49; K. Haff, "Der umstrittene Sippebegriff
und die Siedlungsprobleme," ZRG GA 70 (1953) 320-325; and Kroeschell, "Die Sippe im
germanischen Recht," pp. 1-25. Particularly noteworthy and basic are Heinrich Brunner,
DRG 1: 110 ff. and 324 ff. and S. Rietschel, "Sippe," in J. Hoops, Reallexikon der germanischen Altertumskunde (Strassburg, 1919), vol. 4.

[13] "Dieser [the shifting kin group] is selbstverständlich weiter als der Personenkreis
jenes Verbandes [the fixed kin group], da ja der einzelne sein Blut aus verscheidenen
Sippen herleitet, und schliesst eine genossenschaftliche Verfassung begrifflich aus, da er
sich regelmässig für jeden Einzelnen verschieden gestaltet" (DRG 1: 112).

kindred, the *ego*-focused personal group.[14] To the fixed group can be applied our terms lineage or clan, or rather agnatic lineage and clan. In many cases clan is a more suitable term since, from the frequent equation of the Caesarian *gens* (BG 6.22) to the Germanic *Sippe*, and the political, territorial and military functions often given to it, as well as the common origin sometimes attributed to the *Sippe* and the Latin *gens* and Greek *genos*, kin units of a higher order are meant, including major tribal divisions.

Attributed to the *Sippe*, whether as a bilateral kindred or as an agnatic clan or lineage, are a variety of functions. Now clearly, in considering the functions of kinship, care has to be taken in distinguishing those activities proper to descent groups such as a clan and those applicable to kindred organization. Failure to do this by some of the traditional teaching has resulted in confusion, as Felix Genzmer has noted.[15] Yet there is reason for this confusion, which springs not simply from misunderstanding, but from one of the fundamental notions of the theory, and one of the most important for understanding the treatment accorded cognatic relationship. While it is held that in the historical period and in our sources both kindred and clan organization exist, this co-existence, it is thought, was not always the case; for originally the only kinship group which the Germans had was the patrilineal clan. Consequently *all* the functions of relationship found in the historical period were at one time limited to the agnatic clan and manifestations of cognation with legal consequences had to postdate that of agnation. This element in the old theory had far-reaching results, and suggested that examples of cognatic relationship were innovations upon agnation and secondary to it; that agnatic forms of the historical period were mere traces of a once encompassing agnatic system. For example, the cognatic elements in the inheritance law of *Lex Salica* were seen as a relatively late and unstable innovation introduced into a basically agnatic structure. The result was a model which presented the legal development of Germanic, and indeed Indo-European, kinship as a passage from agnation to cognation.

Out of this theory another element central to the traditional teaching easily suggested itself, an element which had some support from the

---

[14] At times the description of the *wechselnde Sippe* suggests that the individual was less the centre pin of a circle of simple blood relationship, than the focus for the linking by cognation of a number of fixed kin groups; that is, that the *wechselnde Sippe* was brought temporarily into being by, and composed of, various *feste Sippen* linked through *ego*. See Rietschel, "Sippe," p. 182, and previous note.

[15] "Sippe als Rechtsgebilde," pp. 34-35.

earliest sources, which fitted well into current notions of the development of human society, and which supported certain academic, political, and social ideas on the nature and origin of Germanic society. Since the patrilineal clan as a discrete and fixed entity was capable of functioning as a corporate, particularly a political and land-holding unit; since certain collective and communal aspects of late medieval agrarian life were thought to be merely weakened survivals from the prehistoric and early medieval period; and since individual ownership of land was regarded as having been unknown among the pre-migration Germans, what unit served better as the agent and organ of the originally collective nature of Germanic society than the clan? In this way the strongly corporate nature of early kinship structure became a key element in the conception of the *Sippe*. Many of these aspects of the *Sippe* theory also seemed to find convincing support from the fact that Germanic kinship and society were not viewed in isolation; for the nature of the prehistoric kin group was put in the context of, and indeed explained by, the supposed kinship system of those inferential people, the Indo-Europeans. Agnation was regarded as a marked feature of all the Indo-European peoples, and the presumed agnatic system of the early Germans was viewed as a continuation of the original strongly 'patriarchal' or patrilineal organization of the Indo-Europeans as it was reconstructed by linguistic analysis.

Further implications and assumptions of the traditional teaching need to be considered, but let us first look a little more closely at the way in which the legal activities and functions performed by the early kin groups have been viewed. Although it was held that originally all legal functions applied only to the lineage or clan, it was recognized that in the early sources a number were applicable to the bilateral personal group. Foremost among these functions was vengeance and the payment and receipt of wergeld. The kindred, and originally the lineage, was thought to be obliged to go to feud in order to avenge a death or to seek compensation. Not merely the homicide but his whole *Sippe* was exposed to the vengeance of the deceased's kin; while a member of a *Sippe*, a man could not unilaterally conclude peace with the contending party; if compensation was to be given, payment was made by one *Sippe* to the other. The internal arrangements for the payment and distribution were believed to have been originally the affair of the lineage (*Geschlecht*), although the earliest sources show a fixed rule of apportionment. That the maternal kin in historical times might receive and pay less than the paternal kin, as was the case among the Anglo-Saxons, was thought to be an aftereffect of the originally exclusive right of the agnatic lineage. The kindred performed other roles in the legal process. In oathhelping procedure, for instance, a litigant required to take an oath might be supported as to its truth by a fixed number of oaths from members of his kindred. Originally oathhelping was supposed to be limited to lineage mates, then kinsmen generally, but it is conceded that insofar as the legal sources make any kinship requirement, relatives were drawn from the kindred although there might be a distinction between patrilateral and matrilateral kin. Other functions are attributed to the *Sippe*, involving inheritance, the guardianship of minors and women, marriage, the punishment of adultery, the support and burial of indigent kinsmen and the like, but sufficient notice has been taken here of activities concerned with a fairly wide circle of kinsmen who act, or were thought to act, together in some sense as a group, to indicate something of the tenor and method of the *Sippe* theory. At its heart lies the notion that the various functions were once limited to the lineage but were found in historical times, to a greater or lesser degree, among the kindred, even though, it is said, the agnatic group remained at the core of the kin structure and its functions.

Now there are other features which are thought to be characteristic of early Germanic kinship which can only apply to the lineage or clan. Of a territorial or corporate nature and thus unsuited to kindred organization, they are considered to be a much more vital and elaborated feature of pre-migration society than is the case later. Yet, they also are said to persist recognizably into historical times, or else to leave clear traces of their former strength in the legal sources. Foremost is the role of the clan or lineage as a military unit in the army (*Heeresabteilung*). Until fairly recently this was regarded as one of the most solid pillars of the *Sippe* theory. A statement of Tacitus is cited for earlier times and, for the period of the *regna*, support is found in a comment by Mauricius and in the *farae* of the Burgundians, Lombards and other peoples. Apart from the military functions, a number of views attribute to the clan characteristics which indicate that it was a territorial unit. The least documented of these regards the clan as lying beneath the real and imagined political and judicial divisions of the early Germans – the *pagus*, mark, and hundred. The idea that the Germanic nations were composed of clans – indeed were the result of the fusion of clans – is widespread, and common even among scholars who show little inclination to repeat the intricacies of the traditional teaching. With greater reason the clan is seen as a landholding corporate group. In this regard a passage of Caesar is cited for the earliest period, and traces are thought to persist in the *genealogiae* of the *leges barbarorum* and the *Markgenossenschaften* once believed to lie at the root of economic and political life. In the invasion of the Empire the various tribes were viewed as settling in clans. Thus the *Sippe* became a unit of settlement (*Siedlungsverband*). Among the proofs offered for this contention are the above-mentioned *farae* and *genealogiae* and the evidence of place names. Although the ending *-ingas* is no longer assumed to refer to original clan settlement, place-names in France and Italy formed from *fara* are still regarded as clearly indicating occupation of the soil by clans or lineages. In addition, the rights of neighbours (*vicini*) found in *Lex Salica*, and particularly the *Edictum Chilperici*, are often thought to reflect an original settlement by the *Sippe*.

Various additions and permutations could be added to this rough summation of the patrilineal clan theory as it appears in the *Sippe* of German historiography; the framework it offers has enabled scholars to add and subtract elements according to their lights, their interpretation of the sources, and their understanding of the social, economic, and political forms of barbarian society. If we put to one side some of its extreme or antiquated manifestations the main tenets are these: the division of early society into unilineal descent groups; the primacy of agnation in the constitution of these groups; the highly corporate nature of the lineage or clan; its disintegration in the historical period and gradual replacement by bilateral kindred organization; and, finally, the direct derivation of Germanic kinship from, and its essential harmony with, the patrilineal structure of the Indo-Europeans.

Not until after World War ɪɪ, and the publication of Felix Genzmer's "Die Germanische Sippe als Rechtsgebilde," was the dominance of the *Sippe* theory seriously challenged in Germany. Genzmer's has proved an influential critique,[16] although, paradoxically, apart from consideration of the *Sippe* as a *Heeresabteilung*, which dealt with early sources, his examination concentrated on the Icelandic *Grágas*. Mainly on the basis of this collection of legal texts Genzmer was led to deny the traditional teaching in regard to vengeance, feud and wergeld. From the standpoint of cultural history Genzmer believed that the *Grágas* in many respects

[16] See K. Haff, "Der umstrittene Sippebegriff und die Siedlungsprobleme," pp. 320 ff.; K. von Amira and K. A. Eckhardt, *Germanisches Recht*, 4th ed., Grundriss der germanischen Philologie, 5 (Berlin, 1960), p. vi; W. Schlesinger, "Randbemerkungen zu drei Aufsätzen über Sippe, Gefolgschaft und Treue," in *Alteuropa und die moderne Gesellschaft: Festschrift für Otto Brunner* (1963), rpt. in *Beiträge zur deutschen Verfassungsgeschichte des Mittelalters* (Göttingen, 1963), 2: 286-334. Karl Bosl, "On Social Mobility in Medieval Society: Service, Freedom, and Freedom of Movement as Means of Social Ascent," in *Early Medieval Society*, ed. and trans. Sylvia L. Thrupp (New York, 1967), p. 95, calls it "a devastating attack on the clan (*Sippe*), that showpiece of German legal and social history."

showed older traits than even the sixth century *Lex Salica*, despite the fact that the contents of the Icelandic texts postdated the Frankish collection by at least five hundred years. While conceding the importance of the agnatic line,[17] he concluded that blood relationship generally and also affinity operated strongly in the legal life of the historical Germans; moreover there was no fixed legal unit since the form and dimension of the kin groupings often varied in particular circumstances. In fact, Genzmer's disagreement with the older teaching is much less than it is made to appear; first, because sound proponents of the old theory conceded that in historical times the *feste Sippe* or lineage, particularly in regard to vengeance, feud and wergild, had been replaced by the kindred, even if emphasis within it sometimes fell on agnatic or paternal kin; second, because the *Grágas*, despite claims for the antiquity of its spiritual and social world, never constituted any basis for the *Sippe* theory as it applied to the early and pre-historic society of the continental Germans. The value of Genzmer's work really lay in his insistence on a clear distinction between the two types of *Sippe* when approaching sources, his emphasis upon the medieval use of the word *Sippe*, which simply does not reflect the meanings attributed to it by modern scholars, and his denial, based upon a review of Tacitus, that the *Sippe* formed a *Heeresabteilung*.

Less well received it seems, probably because it involves a profound departure from almost the whole of the *Sippe* theory, was the work of Karl Kroeschell. In "Die Sippe im Germanischen Recht" he attacked the dimension and structure attributed to Germanic kinship, the role it was thought to play in legal life, and the very concept of the word *Sippe*.[18] Kroeschell supported his views by pointing to what he saw as revisions of the traditional teaching and by considering the question of the kinless man in the Anglo-Saxon laws. As a critique, much of what he says is to the point, but the reliance upon Anglo-Saxon material throughout, and in particular to show the restricted nature of the kin group, has raised the criticism that the English material is a poor basis for generalizations on early continental conditions despite his claims to the contrary; it has been pointed out, for example, that British scholars, and specifically Phillpotts on whom he puts reliance, have regarded English kinship structure as a special case, much weakened from its earlier continental prototype.[19]

---

[17] Although this importance is not at all evident in the texts he considers.

[18] ZRG GA 77 (1960) 1-25.

[19] Schlesinger, "Randbemerkungen zu drei Aufsätzen uber Sippe, Gefolgschaft und Treue," pp. 292-293. See also the conclusion of H. R. Loyn, "Kinship in Anglo-Saxon England," *Anglo-Saxon England* 3 (1974) 208; but cf. Donald Bullough, "Early Medieval

It would appear that as a result of these recent reevaluations the traditional notion of the *Sippe* is in an unstable state.[20] Because the patrilineal clan theory has been made such a formalized, and even extreme, aspect of German historiography, it has finally become an obvious and identifiable object of revision, and it remains to be seen what will remain of it. What is perhaps surprising is that the criticism it has elicited has only begun to meet it on its own grounds and to explore its implications. For at its best, the traditional theory has rested upon a small number of theoretical suppositions and upon a range of continental evidence from Antiquity and the early Middle Ages. But the *Sippe* theory also goes beyond this, in that it has had a double existence. On one hand it has persisted in various forms as a model, supported by a corpus of texts, which linked prehistory and the early Middle Ages into a comprehensible unit; on the other, it has conditioned the interpretation of many sources which, in themselves, were never mainstays of the original model.

In opposition to the agnatic theory, another formulation exists which seeks to explain the nature and development of Germanic kinship on the basis of matriliny. The origins of this theory go back to the 1860s in Britain and Germany and the mutually independent work of Bachofen

---

Social Groupings: The Terminology of Kinship," *Past and Present*, No. 45 (Nov., 1969), pp. 14-15, who would regard the restricted nature of the English group as characteristic also of continental conditions.

[20] Cf. H.-R. Hagemann, "Agnaten" in HRG, 1: 61-63; the volume containing "Sippe" has not yet appeared. The re-editions of the legal handbooks which note the works of Genzmer and Kroeschell, and which I have consulted, seem to change very little, or else misunderstand their critiques. Cf. Haff, "Der umstrittene Sippebegriff," p. 320 and Hans Fehr, *Deutsche Rechtsgeschichte*, 6th ed. (Berlin, 1962); Schlesinger, "Randbemerkungen," esp. p. 288, n. 5 and H. Planitz and K. A. Eckhardt, *Deutsche Rechtsgeschichte*, 2nd ed. (Graz, 1961), pp. 51 ff. See also R. Wenskus, *Stammesbildung und Verfassung: das Werden der frühmittelalterlichen gentes* (Cologne, 1961), pp. 145-146, 300-305, 325-326, who accepts Genzmer's conclusions as to the historical *Sippe*, and gives the concept of *geschlossene Sippenverbände* a very minor role in the formation of the Germanic tribes. Yet the tribal consciousness itself is represented by him as an *Abstammungsgemeinschaft*: "Die germanischen Stämme sind aber nach dem Begriffsystem der deutschen Ethnosoziologie am ehesten endogame Klans" (p. 16). Genzmer and Wenskus lie behind the synthesis of Josef Fleckenstein, *Grundlagen und Beginn der deutschen Geschichte*, Deutsche Geschichte 1 (Göttingen, 1974), pp. 19-21, 23-26; English translation by Bernard S. Smith, *Early Medieval Germany* (Amsterdam, 1978), pp. 3-5, 7-10; which well illustrate the problem of the term *Sippe*, and its translation "clan," being applied to very disparate kinship (and non-kinship) structures.

Outside of Germany their reassessment seems to have made little impact. For a recent French work in which the clan plays a central role in Germanic society, see P. Ourliac and J. de Malafosse, *Histoire du droit privé*, 2: *Les Biens*, 2nd ed., Themis, Droit, 11 (Paris, 1971), 127 ff.

and McLennan.[21] Picked up by Marx and Engels, it has remained a sometime element in Marxist historiography ever since.[22] For a time it was a powerful force in German historiography, though it eventually faded before the agnatic theory. It has often had weighty proponents, particularly in Britain, where it has maintained its vitality up to the present day in the influential writings of Phillpotts, H. M. Chadwick and, more recently, E. A. Thompson: for this reason the following discussion of the matrilineal theory will be confined largely to the British school.[23] The matrilineal viewpoint is important, not simply because elements of matriliny may be applicable to aspects of Germanic kinship, or on account of the scholarly weight of its advocates, or because the matrilineal theory is still very much alive, but also because in itself it constituted a significant critique of the patrilineal theory; for despite its integration into Marxist historiography, it could also be a pragmatic response to the failings of the agnatic theory, and, given certain suppositions, be the only real alternative available at the time to a view which seemed to make light of some of the special features thought to be found in both late and early evidence of Germanic kin structure.

The matrilineal theory can take many forms. As we have previously seen it expressed by Bloch, and as it recently appears in the work of E. A. Thompson, it is integrated into the patrilineal theory, and in many respects is its mirror image.[24] According to Thompson, the various highly corporate and territorial features, which are generally attributed to the patrilineal *Sippe*, pertained first to matrilineal clans or lineages, then as the

[21] J. J. Bachofen, *Das Mutterrecht* (Berlin, 1861); J. J. McLennan, *Primitive Marriage* (London, 1865).

[22] Frederick Engels, *The Origin of the Family, Private Property, and the State* (New York, 1972). The result is often a great deal of vituperation. See, e.g., H. Galton, "The Indo-European Kinship Terminology," *Zeitschrift für Ethnologie* 82 (1957) 121-138.

[23] Quite apart from the history of the Germanic peoples, matriliny is an important element in British historiography: see for instance G. D. Thomson, *Studies in Ancient Greek Society* (London, 1949): "The task I have set myself is to reinterpret the legacy of Greece in the light of Marxism" (p. 7).

[24] See especially *The Early Germans* (Oxford, 1965), pp. 8-28, 48 ff., 63 ff., and note 26 below.

Thompson's views contribute to the Marxist account of Perry Anderson, *Passages from Antiquity to Feudalism* (London, 1974), pp. 107-109, and the Germanic background given in Suzanne Fonay Wemple, *Women in Frankish Society: Marriage and the Cloister, 500-900* (Philadelphia, 1981), pp. 9-15; his analysis of the changing pattern of Germanic society (though without reference to the principles used in clan recruitment) also seems to be influential in the accounts of Edward Peters, *Europe, The World of the Middle Ages* (Englewood Cliffs, 1977), pp. 32-33; and Malcolm Todd, *Everyday Life of the Barbarians* (London, 1972), ch. 2, although the clan has been dropped in Todd's *The Northern Barbarians 100 B.C.- A.D. 300* (London, 1975).

agnatic principle came to prevail, to agnatic descent groups. He regards the clan as the basic unit of the various tribes, as an agricultural group communally working the land and sharing the fruits, and as a unit of the army; these functions, originally fulfilled by matrilineal descent groups, had become, or started to become, transferred to agnatic clans by Caesarian times. The process in which matriliny was superseded by patriliny in historical times[25] occurred, Thompson believes, in a context of growing inequality of wealth and private property.[26]

A different approach is taken by Phillpotts, who does not try to tie the matrilineal and patrilineal theories together. As already noted, in her view, which has been influential in the recent critique of the *Sippe*, the cognatic nature of historical kinship suggested difficulties in the theory of agnatic clans in the primitive period.[27] "Yet," she goes on, "if the group of kinsfolk was originally a land-owning unit, as is usually assumed, the fluctuating kindred cannot be the original system of the Teutons, for such a group cannot hold land." For this reason, which is true enough, and because of what she calls "ample evidence from all parts of the world for transition from matrilinear to a partially or wholly patrilinear society," she concludes: "we must either deny that the primitive group was capable of holding land, or we must fall back on the theory, in favour of which other indications are not lacking, that membership of the primitive group was determined by descent through females."[28] Phillpotts' predicament is

---

[25] The implication would seem to be that cognation results from the transition from one unilineal system to another. The view that cognation results from the clash of disparate unilineal influences is common. For example, the effects of the supposed matrilinealism of the pre-Indo-European inhabitants upon the agnatic Germans are often seen as the cause of the cognatic structures of the historical period: e.g. H. Planitz and K. A. Eckhardt, *Deutsche Rechtsgeschichte*, pp. 51 ff.

[26] See also Thompson's "The Passio S. Sabae and Early Visigothic Society," *Historia* 4 (1955) 331-338, where the clan and the rot of private property, increasing since Tacitean times, are superimposed on Visigothic society. Stress is also laid upon the disintegration of the clans in the settlement of the Empire; cf. also his "The Barbarian Kingdoms in Gaul and Spain," *Nottingham Medieval Studies* 7 (1963) 14, 16, 20; *The Goths in Spain* (Oxford, 1969), p. 138; and *The Visigoths in the Time of Ulfilas* (Oxford, 1966), p. 63.

To describe the above unilineal groups, Thompson uses the terms 'kindred' or 'clan' interchangeably, which may have contributed to some confusion. For example, Donald Bullough ("Early Medieval Social Groupings," p. 14, n. 25) has taken Thompson to task for underestimating the functions and importance of kinship in the Romano-Germanic kingdoms, but their differing viewpoints probably stem from more than contrary perceptions of function since Bullough sees kinship in the *regna* in terms of personal groups or kindreds.

[27] Above, p. 11.

[28] *Kindred and Clan*, pp. 269 ff. Her ample evidence is presumably the writings of the nineteenth-century evolutionists, who, following in the tracks of Bachofen, McLennan and Morgan, saw matriarchy as a state of society prior to patriarchy.

instructive. She was faced by an ethnographical theory, existing till recently, which did not admit of cognatic descent groups as land-holding corporations. Confronted by the difficulties inherent in the evidence of kinship in historical times, and not quite willing to forego the idea of corporate kinship groups prior to the Middle Ages, Phillpotts fell back on her only alternative – matrilineal lineages or clans as the kinship unit of the early Germans. But Phillpotts' predicament is not ours: we are not compelled to regard highly corporate kin functions simply in terms of the unilineal principle, for we now know that groups recruited on the basis of cognation, or a combination of principles, can carry them out as well.[29] The whole question of extensive corporate kin groups – of whatever kind – is a matter which will be thoroughly examined at a later point in these studies. It is enough to note here that, if the earliest evidence for kin structures raises problems with the agnatic theory, and if we still wish to maintain, or at least consider, the possibility that early Germanic society was composed of extensive corporate kin groups, the possibility of cognatic clan structure is a solution which must be considered. Simply put, corporate functions carried on by extensive groups are in themselves no argument for unilineal kin structure.

H. M. Chadwick's discussion of matriliny also takes a distinctive form.[30] Relying on Tacitus and *Lex Salica* for the continental tribes, and mainly semi-historical and legendary material for Scandinavia and the north generally at a later period, he sought to counter "the prevalent view" that "the Teutonic family system was mainly agnatic from early times" and to show an underlying and once primary matriliny.[31] Nowhere does Chadwick claim to find documented a full-blown matrilineal system in operation; rather he regards the periods under consideration as ones of transition in which the remnants of a preceding matriliny are unmistakably visible. One other feature of Chadwick's approach to the characterization of kinship in the early period is worth

[29] Above, pp. 3-4.

[30] H. M. Chadwick, *The Origins of the English Nation* (Cambridge, 1907), pp. 145 ff., 303 ff., and *The Heroic Age* (Cambridge, 1912), pp. 345 ff. Notice has to be taken of the author's use of terminology, particularly *agnation* and *cognation*. Chadwick employs these words in a variety of ways: *cognation* can refer generally to blood relationship that is not covered by agnation, but is also used as a synomym for matriliny; *agnation* is used in its strict sense, but also, it seems, as a general term in opposition to strict matriliny.

[31] *Origins*, pp. 303-304. Chadwick also makes interesting observations concerning the role of women. As he admits, this in itself is no argument one way or the other for matriliny; yet he suggests that the early period saw to some extent the replacement of goddesses by gods, and priestesses by priests.

considering: he disavows the highly corporate and territorial nature of kinship structure, as well as everything that this implies for the importance of kinship as the foundation of political organization. This critique is not compelled by his espousal of matriliny, for, as we have seen, the highly corporate functions attributed to Germanic kinship fit as well the matrilineal as the agnatic theory. The idea that the tribe was an aggregate of clans, that the clan was intimately bound up with the village, and formed within the tribe what we can call a political or judicial unit, is denied by Chadwick simply because, in his view, there is no evidence;[32] he would see the kindred as the basic extensive kin group, and the military and lord/man relationship as the most potent political force. Chadwick's point is well-taken; there is a difference between seeing kinship as a kind of social grease – helping to keep the wheels of social (and thus political) life turning, facilitating all kinds of relationships within society, even constituting a critical factor in the operation of feud process and the judicial system – and seeing it as the basis of 'political' or 'tribal' organization and affiliation: one role is quite compatible with kindred organization, the other is compatible only with the clan.

In any review of the English literature on early and prehistoric Germanic kin structures the British school of matrilinealists, which constitutes a continuous thread stretching from the early years of this century and before to the present day, tends to stand out because, in part, it has remained a consistent and influential factor in historiography, and because scholars writing in English have tended to shy away from the question of early kin structure, or else have dealt with it fleetingly in terms of the Anglo-Saxon material. Whether born out of a more pragmatic approach to history or out of a vision directed primarily to insular problems and sources, this neglect may tend to overemphasize the importance of the matrilineal school. Yet there have been exceptions to the general neglect of kinship and to the matrilineal viewpoint: Seebohm and Vinogradoff, who have already been mentioned, and at an even earlier date, D. W. Ross;[33] at the present time the question whether

---

[32] Ibid., pp. 145-146, 303.

[33] See n. 11; D. W. Ross, *The Early History of Land-Holding among the Germans* (London, 1883). This has been called a "pioneer work," though not particularly in reference to kinship, by Carl Stephenson, "The Common Man in Early Medieval Europe," *American Historical Review* 51 (1946) 425, n. 18; see also an appreciation by Dopsch, *The Economic and Social Foundatios of European Civilization*, trans. M. G. Beard and N. Marshall, 1937, rpt. New York, 1969, p. 25.

originally Anglo-Saxon, and by extension Germanic, kinship was agnatic and lineage-based, has been raised again by T. M. Charles-Edwards.[34]

Another, rather distinctive exception, was F. W. Maitland.[35] Most views of Maitland are worth consideration, but particularly so in this case; based upon his deep distrust of easily penetrating beyond the historical period, on his reliance upon the evidence as it stands, and his profound knowledge – which was not limited to the Medieval period – of the process of legal development, his views ran counter to the prevailing theories of his day, as well supported as they appeared to be. Put simply, he would have no truck with either the matrilinealists or patrilinealists. At the time the English material formed an important element of the *Sippe* theory, but Maitland denied the existence of clans in England in the settlement period, and recognizing the bilateral and personal nature of the *maegð*, he disputed the Germanist notion that it was a corporation and a *gens*. He was also doubtful that the tendency in the historic period was toward the admission of the 'spindle-kin,' that is, increasingly toward cognation, and suggested that the opposite was true: a tendency towards the postponement of cognates by agnates. "This is what we see," he wrote, "so soon as we see our ancestors. About what lies in the prehistoric time we can only make guesses." Taking note of the matrilineal and agnatic theories, and the view that the migration period had made family organization extremely indefinite, he concluded: "What seems plain is that the exclusive domination of either 'father-right,' or 'mother right' – if such an exclusive domination we must needs postulate – should be placed for our race beyond the extreme limit of history."[36] Maitland's critique was couched mainly in the context of the English evidence, and he never brought himself to deny outright the unilineal clan theories as they pertained to continental conditions, although he firmly withdrew the Anglo-Saxon material from the arsenal of contention. He also appeared to avoid offering any counter theory – he said of his discussion of the 'antiquities' of family law that it would be filled with warnings rather than theories – probably because there was no really acceptable model available to him. But he well understood the need for some theoretical

---

[34] "Kinship, Status and the Origins of the Hide," *Past and Present*, No. 56 (Aug., 1972), pp. 3-33.

[35] HEL 2: 240-245; and cf. his *Domesday Book and Beyond: Three Essays on the Early History of England* (1897; rpt. London: Fontana Library, 1960), "Essay" 2, sec. 6.

[36] HEL 2: 243. 'Father-right' and 'mother-right' are synonyms for patriliny and matriliny respectively. Cf. the very similar concerns of Wenskus, *Stammesbildung*, pp. 302-305.

framework, and in effect he started to offer a tentative theory of the primary role of cognation in Germanic kinship.[37]

Maitland's doubts about unilinealism were well founded. For the patrilinealists and matrilinealists both misunderstood and ignored the nature and dynamics of cognation. In the present review of the contending schools, the question naturally arises whether both parties have mistaken the constituent cognatic elements of Germanic kinship for unilinealism in transition.

A few further observations should be made concerning the genesis, methodology, and implications of the traditional theories which will help account for the form they have ultimately taken. To do this is not to explain them, or explain them away, simply on the basis of the intellectual milieu in which they arose; nor is it to dismiss them on the basis of their ideological foundations instead of the sense they make of the source material. But it is worthwhile to consider the larger context which gave rise to them if we are to avoid unnecessary assumptions ourselves, and if we are to understand the exigencies and emphases of the theories and their treatment of the ancient and medieval evidence.

One of the most significant factors shaping the genesis of the traditional teaching was the proximity in time this development had to the very inception of the discipline of social anthropology. The same decades of the late nineteenth century which saw the first efforts at establishing a systematic and comparative study of kinship witnessed the birth of the fully elaborated theories of the nature and development of Germanic kin structure. This in itself would suggest there may be many difficulties in the traditional teaching. To give an important example: early anthropologists were greatly influenced by the principle of evolution, and much of their effort was directed at ordering human societies, institutions, and ideas, on an evolutionary pattern. These were thought to develop through

---

[37] "And yet so long as it is doubtful whether the prehistoric time should be filled, for example, with agnatic *gentes* or with hordes which reckon by 'mother-right', the interpretation of many an historic text must be uncertain" (HEL 2: 240). To the extent they have considered the matter, modern anthropologists, eschewing conjectural history, have regarded Germanic kinship as largely cognatic. Before the recent awareness of how widespread bilateral systems were outside of Europe, indeed cognation was regarded as a kind of 'Teutonic aberration'. See e.g. the "Introduction" by A.-R. Radcliffe-Brown to *African Systems of Kinship and Marriage*, ed. Radcliffe-Brown and Daryll Ford (Oxford, 1950), pp. 15-18; Keesing, *Kin Groups*, p. 91. As far as historical kinship is concerned, Maitland's view has frequently been followed by British scholars: see, e.g., Lancaster (n. 1 above), Bullough and Loyn (n.19 above).

a fixed series of stages, with certain institutions, social forms and ideas being proper to the various steps. Contemporary primitives were thought to illustrate the early stages to a greater or lesser extent, and even more developed contemporary and historical peoples were thought to preserve, often in a changed or weakened state, forms proper to an earlier stage of their development. Simple forms preceded in origin more complex, and so by isolating the various components of a given idea, organism, or institution, one could deduce, in effect, the stages of its historical development. This notion is still very common in the analysis of the origin of early Germanic institutions[38] and is, in fact, quite ahistorical, depending upon a kind of deductive process from given principles. It also permeates almost every aspect of the traditional teaching on kinship. We have seen, for instance, how the matrilinealists can offer no evidence for a full-fledged matrilineal structure, but on the basis of what is considered to be traces of such a system and an evolutionary pattern in which matriliny precedes patriliny, suppose it to have once been the dominant, if not exclusive, feature of the earliest Germanic kinship.[39] The same kind of assumption operates in the patrilinealists' contention that often weak agnatic, or even just patrilateral, features of historical times are the feeble remnants of a onetime exclusive agnatic system, a fact for which, amongst the Germans, there is not a shred of documentary evidence. Such a methodology means that very late documents can be used to explicate early and prehistoric times, that such documents in fact may be preferable to earlier ones, provided, it is thought, that they reflect or maintain more ancient features and conditions. Thus in Brunner's explication of kinship in the early period frequent, at times almost exclusive, reference is made to the Ditmarschen clans, the evidence concerning which comes mainly from the late Middle Ages.[40] Also springing from the idea that the simple and homogeneous precede the more complex, and combined with the idea of Germanic cultural unity,[41] is the supposition that behind that welter of

---

[38] A sophisticated example can be found in Walter Schlesinger's search for the origins of lordship among the Germanic peoples in "Lord and Follower in Germanic Institutional History," trans. F. L. Cheyette, in *Lordship and Community*, pp. 64-99, esp. p. 67.

[39] A more modern resolution of the matrilinealist's position, which is to say one maintained outside of the evolutionary framework, would probably claim a bilineal kinship structure for the Germans in which matrilineages and patrilineages coexist and perform distinct functions. But the quality of the historical evidence still places the existence of such groups in the realm of conjectural history.

[40] DRG 1: 110 ff.

[41] On which cf. the remarks by V. J. Goebel, *Felony and Misdemeanor: A Study in the History of English Criminal Procedure* (New York, 1937), pp. 3-4.

often divergent custom called the *leges barbarorum*, there lies at some point a common prototype of custom. With this conception, it becomes possible to put aside as secondary or additive all that does not conform to that pure strain, and to fuse together inextricably into a single thread what are really the independent variables of language, culture and race.

Arising when it did, the traditional teaching on kinship shared many of the assumptions of nineteenth-century Germanist thought, and was a significant feature particularly in the theory of *Markgenossenschaft*,[42] and all the accompanying speculation on the origins of associational life and the German state. So many of the elements of the mark theory – the primitive communism of the mark, its judicial and political functions, its character as a collection of free and equal warrior peasants and its existence within a relatively 'stateless' society – could only find their being in the principle of consanguinity: the *Sippe*. Even though with the disintegration of the clan as a fixed group the mark was thought to be based largely on vicinage, the agnatic clan or lineage was considered the germ and prototype for all associational life, gradually giving way to such alien principles as cognation, lordship and following, and private property. With an almost biblical sense of time, much of the development of human society as it was then conceived seemed to be crowded into the centuries from just before Caesar to Charlemagne. Perhaps not surprisingly, as the mark theory gave way before its critics, many of its elements remained relatively intact in the theory of the *Sippe*.

Related closely to the concept of the *Markgenossenschaft* another current idea helped shape the traditional teaching. Despite a fine, sometimes romantic, appreciation of the virtues of barbarian culture, scholars often saw Germanic society in its first entry into the light of history as quite primitive, with a minimal amount of political and administrative organization and little social differentiation – an impression increased by an inflated estimation of the Roman world. Did not Caesar, some thought, clearly support the belief that in the evolutionary scheme of things the Germans near the beginning of our era were still primarily in the pastoral stage? Not only did this almost demand a society based on clan and lineage organization but it readily explained the disintegration of such organization under the civilizing influence of the Empire and the social stress of kingdom-building in the migration period and after. In fact, such a view of early Germanic society does not require these conclusions

---

[42] See Dopsch, *Economic and Social Foundations*, pp. 1-29 and Stephenson, "The Common Man in Early Medieval Europe," pp. 419-438. Both deal very fleetingly and imprecisely with the role of kinship in the mark theory.

and one need not have a magnified impression of the sophistication of barbarian society with many centuries of agricultural, social and political organization lying behind it in order to question the assumptions of the traditional teaching as it developed in the late nineteenth and early years of this century. The following pages will suggest why, in the area of kinship structure, as with so many other features of early medieval society, the case for profound disruption and radical change is by no means convincing.

So brief a synthesis of the chief ideas which have defined approaches to the problem of early kinship structure has been largely confined to German and British scholars, though the same reliance on the traditional framework has characterized continental views of the subject. The present account has also concentrated upon major and explicit treatments; but shorn of detailed exposition, a number of the traditional notions, in part by dint of repetition, have become historiographical commonplaces,[43] although some scholars who repeat them would no doubt feel ill at ease with the theoretical constructs that originally accompanied them. As a result, while the evolutionary schemata which produced the debate over social evolution in the late nineteenth and early twentieth centuries are now widely rejected as comprehensive explanations of the development of human societies, descent groups and unilinealism, which were the accepted elements of the debate, are still thought to be valid concepts, in some cases rightly so, for the analysis of early societies, that of the Germans among them. The effect of the traditional theories, however, has gone beyond embedding unilineal descent groups in the historiography of the early Middle Ages; for the prevailing analysis, once disseminated and established, could not help but influence the interpretation of a whole host of texts which were never the principal supports of the original formulations. For these reasons, and despite criticisms and a variety of views on particulars, the opposing unilineal theories have remained at the

---

[43] The extent to which the idea that Germanic society in some way was composed of descent groups or clans has remained standard can be gauged from recent surveys: C. Warren Hollister, *The Making of England* (Boston, 1966), p. 19; A. H. M. Jones, *The Decline of the Ancient World* (New York, 1966), p. 11; and see note 24 above. Frequently a specifically political dimension is attributed to the clan. Typical is this comment by Robert Latouche: "It is important here to stress that the German ambition to assume succession of the Roman Empire and create in its place national states was feasible only within the framework of vast territories. Consequently, this involved the fusion of small clans – often numerous – of the same race, and the formation of extensive realms encompassing all these clans" ("Introduction" to Dopsch, *Economic and Social Foundations*, p. xv); this begs a number of questions apart from those of kinship.

foundation of our understanding of kinship in the prehistoric and early historic periods. Yet the problem remains, and because of its implications for our understanding of the social, spiritual, economic and political history of the Germanic peoples, is one which is fundamental to our conception of the origins of western European society. The nineteenth century saw this clearly, and however much we may differ with its interpretations and assumptions, we must recognize that it did offer a solution, although one which, based as it was upon a fixed evolutionary model, was too rigid and uncompromising. This feature above all must be replaced. Necessarily all extensive formulations of the nature of pre-historic Germanic family and kin structure must be hypothesis, and no amount of spade work, literal and otherwise, will change this. This is not a statement of despair, for if we cannot have firm foundations for our hypotheses we can at least be aware of the ground on which they stand: we can try to make them accommodating, principally to what we know, and then to what we suspect. Maitland has said that until we populate the prehistoric period with some definite kin structures, the interpretation of many an historic text must remain uncertain.[44] This may appear to be stated backwards: is not the key to the prehistoric period the correct interpretation of the earliest texts? To some extent, at least, the process must be reciprocal; both the texts and the hypotheses should suggest and confirm one another. Proponents of the traditional framework have always claimed to find significant confirmation in texts drawn from Antiquity and the early Middle Ages. Yet enough has been said about the genesis of the traditional theories to suggest that the cognatic factor of early kin structure has been overlooked and that perhaps the corporate lineage and clan has been accepted too uncritically as a necessary model for explaining the dynamics of early barbarian society. With this in mind we can begin to look at the evidence.

[44] See n. 38.

Part II

Was Early Germanic Society
Clan- and Lineage-Based?

2

Introduction
and the Indo-European Background

The previous discussion suggests that in order to reexamine the nature and development of kinship among the Germans we need to distinguish two broad areas of inquiry, each of which is concerned with answering separate but related questions. On the one hand, we must ask what principles of relationship defined the rights and obligations of kinship in Antiquity and the early Middle Ages; how these principles were applied in the legal and social framework of society; and whether any evidence suggests a shift in the balance and application of these principles through the course of this period. It has usually been claimed that, in the period considered here, cognation was increasingly altering an agnatic structure which had originally defined the major legal consequences of relationship. Now this is said of the Germanic people as a whole, but we must be careful not to assume that each of the various national groups will display precisely the same structural features and undergo similar transformations and permutations. While Tacitus – and among ancient sources he is unique in doing so – purports to give testimony concerning the functions of relationship among the west Germans as a whole, the examination of the systems of individual peoples must depend largely upon the evidence of the early medieval *leges barbarorum* and related contemporary documents. Such an examination will be undertaken below, in *Part III*, for the Franks.

On the other hand, we must ask if there are any grounds for supposing that in Antiquity and the early Middle Ages society was composed of extensive corporate lineages or clans. It will be remembered that clans have commonly been said to form the basic elements of early Germanic society, and to have disintegrated only in the course of the early Middle Ages. It is imperative that we be clear as to the quality of the evidence upon which this view of the foundations of north-western European civilization rests. The previous discussion has also suggested a number of points which must be kept in mind when examining the evidence for clan and lineage structure. In the past it has generally been assumed that if sources support the conclusion that major corporate functions were carried out by descent groups, then these groups perforce were unilineal. We now know this to be an unwarranted assumption, since cognatic or bilateral groups can perform the same functions as their unilineal counterparts. Consequently if, after all, a text is thought to testify to the existence of descent groups of some kind, we cannot automatically infer unilinealism, but must enquire what principles of relationship figure in their constitution. The distinction between societies with limited and those with constituent lineage structures should also be remembered. Occasional descent groups with varying degrees of corporateness existed throughout the Middle Ages and can be found to some extent in late Antiquity and even in modern societies. Such groups, of course, are not at issue: to justify the traditional model we must find good reasons to believe that society was constituted of corporate descent groups; that the structures and functions of kinship for society as a whole were fundamentally different from the prevalent forms of well-documented periods of the Middle Ages and after.

The Germanic clan has been said to be a political and territorial unit, a corporate land-holding group, a settlement group in the occupation of the Empire, and a military unit. The range of evidence that is adduced to document these contentions is not extensive, but it does come from the two main periods under consideration. From Antiquity there are two passages in the Germanic ethnographies of Caesar and Tacitus; from the early Middle Ages a number of texts dealing with *vicini, farae* and *genealogiae*. Although the point of view of these sets of texts is quite distinct and of varying value, they nevertheless constitute direct evidence of a kind. Before dealing with the testimony of these texts, however, it is well to consider the value of far more indirect evidence, which like an insubstantial spectre stands behind the traditional model.

Germanic kinship has often been seen as a reflection and extension of the system of the Indo-Europeans as reconstructed largely on the basis of linguistic analysis.[1] According to a common hypothesis Indo-European

---

[1] A good example of linguistics applied to the reconstruction of Indo-European society is Emile Benveniste, *Indo-European Language and Society*, trans. Elizabeth Palmer (London, 1973); also, see generally, R. A. Crossland, "Indo-European Origins: The Linguistic Evidence," *Past and Present*, No. 12 (Nov., 1957), pp. 16-46, and the references cited there.

descent was patrilineal, the original extended patriarchal households gradually evolving into agnatic lineages and clans. Quite apart from the question of whether we should assume a single culture, the reconstruction of the details of Indo-European society is a difficult and hazardous task, particularly when, as in the case of kinship, behavioral, sociological and ideological facts have to be extrapolated from linguistic facts.[2] The evidence can be, and has been, used to reach contradictory conclusions,[3] and moreover, has usually been seen in the confines of the simple matrilineal/patrilineal distinction. The kinship terms at our disposal for comparison refer to such a limited number of designated relatives that probably the most that can be inferred are residence patterns, not extensive kinship categories and groups. Even if we accept most of the common linguistic interpretations, scholars in speaking of 'patrilineal descent' appear to be indicating no more than patri- or viri-local residence; at the same time bilateral affiliation or bilateral kindreds are now suggested or conceded.[4] There is no evidence to speak of for clan and lineage organization[5] although it may very well have existed. The main problem with the Indo-European evidence is that it is doubtful that very

---

[2] The results can sometimes be Freudian: H. Galton ("The Indo-European Kinship Terminology," *Zeitschrift für Ethnologie*, 82 [1957]) suggests the evidence "yields a pretty grim picture of the I-E 'father' – a despotic and probably polygynous warrior patriarch who ruled with absolute power over life and death of the members of his family while he was strong. He probably monopolized as many women as he could and maybe his sons had to content themselves with the role of polyandrous husbands of a girl bought from another tribe, a foreigner to their clan" (pp. 129-130). To start the history of European family types from notions such as these contributes to a very definite, and often simplistically 'progressive' model of the development of family institutions.

[3] The problem is aptly put by anthropologist J. Goody, "Indo-European Kinship," *Past and Present*, No. 16 (Nov., 1959), pp. 88-91.

[4] A survey by G. S. Ghurye (*Family and Kin in Indo-European Culture* [2nd. ed., Bombay, 1962]) has concluded that the primitive Indo-European family was an extended family of three or four generations, patrilineal in descent, patrilocal in residence; there was bilateral recognition of kinship. The question is what exactly 'patrilineal in descent' means, apart from residence in an extended family which tended to be patrilocal. The Indo-European *Grossfamilie*, according to Benveniste, might include married daughters and their offspring (*Indo-European Language and Society*, p. 252), which would give it a cognatic character. P. Friedrich ("Proto-Indo-European Kinship," *Ethnology*, 5 [1966]), a strong supporter of patrilineal descent and agnatic clan structure among the Indo-Europeans, grants that the culture had bilateral kindreds as well (p. 22) and concedes that the Indo-European nomenclature by itself could be accounted for by the minimal assumptions of bilateral descent and extended patrilocal families (pp. 32-33, n. 11).

[5] Although some scholars continue to talk of (agnatic) clans, it has long been recognized that the invocation of the *gens/genos* (Goth. *kuni*, OE *cynn*) as an Indo-European clan is without foundations. Cf. e.g. V. Gordon Childe, *The Aryans* (New York, 1926, p. 82), and Ghurye, *Family and Kin*, p. 213.

comprehensive conclusions can ever be drawn concerning kinship. At any rate, although extensive reconstructions of Indo-European conditions have often been seen as the beginning of the European development, the question of the Indo-Europeans need not detain us. Whatever the merit of the theories about these peoples, there is really no reason to let the inferred family structure of Indo-European speakers of 2500 BC or earlier influence unduly our view of Germanic society over two millenia later.

Our understanding of Germanic kinship must depend therefore upon the interpretation of historical documents from Antiquity and the early Middle Ages. In the following pages the major documentation of the unilineal clan theory will be considered, beginning with the testimony of the ancient ethnographic tradition of Caesar and Tacitus.

3

The Views of Antiquity

The traditional teaching has always claimed that constituent clans and lineages were clearly documented in the writings of Antiquity. In the examination of these sources a major consideration is the distinctive approach they take to their subject. The earliness of the ancient material immediately suggests that it should be of unsurpassable value for questions relating to prehistoric social forms, but the date of this evidence, which brings us to the very threshold of the appearance of the Germans in history, should not obscure for us the real difficulties which arise from its point of view. That it offers the interpretations of foreigners commenting upon an alien culture accounts for its unreliability only in part, for such interpretations can be valuable, if based on sound observations. The main difficulty really arises from the often indiscriminate transference of north-ern, non-Celtic ethnography to Germanic culture, and the dependence upon prevalent ideas as to the evolution of human communities. The classical sources can be of use, but it must be realized that their contents are not all of equal value, and that the evidence they contain cannot be uncritically accepted without an understanding of the philosophical and ethnographic basis of classical speculation on barbarian and primitive societies.[1]

The two central works in all discussions about the reconstruction of Germanic kin structure and social organization are the ostensible

---

[1] Many of the texts illustrating such ideas can be found in A. C. Lovejoy and G. Boas, *Primitivism and Related Ideas in Antiquity*, Documentary History of Primitivism and Related Ideas, 1 (Baltimore, 1935). For their application in nothern ethnography, see G. Walser, *Caesar und die Germanen: Studien zur politischen Tendenz römischer Feldzugs-berichte*, Historia, Einzelschriften, Heft 1 (Wiesbaden, 1956); and J. J. Tierney, "The Celtic Ethnography of Posidonius," *Proceedings of the Royal Irish Academy*, 60 sec. C (1959-1960) 189-275, and the works cited there. See also Thomas Cole, *Democritus and the Sources of Greek Anthropology*, American Philological Association Monographs 25 (Western Reserve University, 1967).

description of Germanic mores in Caesar's *Bellum Gallicum*, and the ethnography of Tacitus' *Germania*. Two particular considerations must be kept in mind in dealing with both of these sources. First, neither source is a straightforward description based on the author's observations. This has always been recognized of Tacitus' work, and even though Caesar has been frequently treated as an eyewitness, the same is now recognized of the Gallic and Germanic ethnography of the *Bellum Gallicum*. Of prime importance for the evaluation of the reliability of the Caesarian and Tacitean accounts, therefore, is the nature and quality of the sources which lie behind their descriptions. Second, we must recognize that both ethnographies are cast in literary-historical forms which are deeply steeped in Greek conceptions of human history and of the place of barbarian peoples within it. Viewed from outside the mythological dimension which was frequently a part of the formulation, current society was regarded by the ancients as having gone through a number of stages. In the earliest, men existed in a state of nature and were simple food gatherers and then hunters. Gradually, with the domestication of animals, they entered a pastoral stage. Both phases were characterized by a primitive communism, and by a lack of private property, of fixed boundaries dividing up the land, and of significant social distinctions. This was the Golden Age of human history. Pastoralism, however, saw the turning of man's energies to war and bloodshed, and with the discovery of precious metals, to greed. The full introduction of private property and social distinction marked the final agricultural phase, in which the land was finally subjected to the surveyor's marks. In the Platonic and Aristotelian expression of this formulation, the sequence of social organization began with households, followed by consanguineous groups or clans formed into villages or larger communities and associations, and finally the city state.[2] The perception of this broad pattern was frequently accompanied by a primitivistic idealization: man's state was thought to have been happiest in former times, when he lived in greater harmony with nature, and consequently himself. In confronting contemporary barbarian peoples, the ancients, in much the same way as modern evolutionists, associated more primitive cultures with the levels through which they thought their own civilization had passed. Not only were poets, historians, and philosophers, prepared to use the customs of barbarians to prove or disprove primitivist notions, but at an early date they had a set idea of the customs and attitudes to expect among less

[2] *Laws* 3.681-682; *Pol.* 1252b.

civilized nations. The result was a stock collection of questions and answers and assorted ethnographic motifs, which, by mechanical transference, could be readily abused by the less able, and less patient, ethnographers. However, as a people was drawn into contact with the Mediterranean world, and became better known, the less liable were its culture and habits to be forced into the rigid preconceptions of the ethnographic-historical schemata. In considering the accounts of Caesar and Tacitus, therefore, it is crucial to examine the extent to which they were subject to the distortions of ancient ethnography and also to have an idea of the general state of contemporary knowledge about the Germans.

Without a doubt the *Germania* and *Bellum Gallicum* were affected by the undesirable features of the long ethnographic tradition which lies behind them. In cases suggestive of the transference of ethnographic motifs from one people to another, the problem is whether this resulted from an uncritical and mechanical transposition or simply the appropriation of a well-turned and suitable phrase. However one finally decides to treat the *topoi* found in Tacitus, there can be no doubt that much of his account is based on relatively sound sources and knowledge and that many of his descriptions receive confirmation from archeological, linguistic, or literary sources.[3] As will be suggested below, the same cannot be said for Caesar. Not only is his account rife with ethnographic commonplaces and motifs, but the more archaeological and literary evidence has been examined the more doubt has been cast upon the accuracy and sources of his Germanic ethnography.

In the case of the *Germania* and *Bellum Gallicum* a single passage in each work has been regarded as particularly indicative of the unilineal clan-basis of society. An examination of the role these passages have played in the traditional exposition of early Germanic kinship gives us an opportunity to consider the validity of the usual interpretation and also to consider the broader context of each account. In the case of Caesar it will

---

[3] See the remarks of J. G. C. Anderson, *Cornelii Taciti De Origine et Situ Germanorum* (Oxford, 1938), pp. xxvii ff., who perhaps overly plays down the distortion caused by transference. E. Norden (*Die germanische Urgeschichte in Tacitus Germania*, 4th ed. [Stuttgart, 1959]), who first highlighted the *Wandermotive*, did not thereby dismiss the work of the Tacitean ethnography. There is much in Tacitus' account which palpably has no connection with ethnographic *topoi*, much based upon the current known relations between the Romans and free Germany (e.g. his account of Veleda and other female seers). He clearly had reliable information on inner Germany about which we might be inclined to be sceptical if it were not on the whole verifiable; for example, his description of the north German fertility cult surrounding Nerthus, *terra mater*, which has analogies in the linguistic, literary, and archaeological evidence from Scandinavia, must be founded on a basically sound report, wherever it comes from.

be seen that all aspects of his ethnography are rooted firmly in the tradition of ancient ethnographic speculation. The passage of Tacitus usually regarded as showing the clan as a military unit is only one of several references to kinship in the *Germania*, so it is worthwhile considering the image of kinship that all this evidence suggests. Although the kinship evidence of the *Germania* cannot be verified, it does not partake of the obvious distorting elements of ancient ethnography.

A. CAESAR'S *BELLUM GALLICUM*

The *locus classicus* thought to indicate the presence of the unilineal clan as a land-holding corporate group comes from the Germanic ethnography of Caesar's *Gallic War*. In fact, Caesar actually gives two German ethnographies. The first one, in 4.1-3, concerns the Suebi and is relatively brief. The second, which repeats many of the details of Bk. 4, and in some cases expands upon them, occurs in Bk. 6, and is applied to the Germans as a whole. The second is part of a lengthier excursus contrasting Gallic (6. 11-20) and Germanic (6.20-28) mores. The inclusion of the Gallic and Germanic ethnographies at this point in the narrative is gratuitous; Caesar interrupts the account of his crossing the Rhine in search of the Suebi, enters a lengthy account of Gallic and Germanic customs and then concludes briefly with a report of the failure of his expedition. Possibly the ethnography is included here because this marks the end of his German campaigns; undoubtedly the emphasis upon the non-agricultural economy of the Germans in the ethnography was meant to explain his failure to penetrate Suebian territory, which he attributes to his fear of a shortage of grain.[4] Although the view that the ethnographic and geographic passages of Caesar's account are spurious interpolations is no longer widely held,[5] certainly the distinctive character of the ethnographies sets them apart from the rest of the commentaries. Norden emphasized that the ethnography of Bk. 6 was clearly a literary product,[6] and suggested that it was a literary expansion, intended for the reading public, of the official sketch of the Suebians originally given in the year end report of the fourth year (Bk. 4.1). There can be no doubt as to the literary character of the Germanic excursus of Bk. 6, and the mutual dependence of it and the Suebian ethnography of Bk. 4. The overall reliability of these passages will be discussed below, but it is necessary first

---

[4] BG 6.29: "Caesar ... inopiam frumenti veritus, quod ut supra demonstravimus minime homines Germani agri culturae student, constituit non progredi longius."

[5] Tierney, "The Celtic Ethnography," p. 211.

[6] *Die germanische Urgeschichte*, pp. 484 ff.

to be certain of the precise testimony they give as to the nature and role of kinship.

The passage interpreted as evidencing clan structure is found in Bk. 6.22 as part of Caesar's description of the economic foundation of Germanic society. A similar passage is found in Bk. 4. There the Suebi are said to practise agriculture[7] but "there is no trace of a system of private and separate land ownership among them nor is it permitted to stay in one spot for longer than a year for the purpose of cultivation" ("privati ac separati agri apud eos nihil est neque longius anno remanere uno in loco colendi causa licet").[8] In 6.22 a related passage appears. He says of the Germans in general that they do not apply themselves to agriculture, living mainly off milk, cheese, and meat; that each does not have a fixed portion of land nor his own boundaries. Each year the chiefs or magistrates are said to distribute the arable "gentibus cognationibusque hominum."[9] Precisely at this point the manuscript tradition shows signs of corruption and gives us the choice of "qui cum una coierunt" (α) or "quique una coierunt" (β). A variety of other possible renditions have been adduced, reflecting the general dissatisfaction with the manuscripts: for example, "qua tum," "qui una," "qui communiter," "quicumque una." These are all attempts to make *qui ... coierunt* describe the *gentes cognationesque hominum*; however, while "qui cum una" is not admissable as it stands, "quique" is perfectly acceptable usage.[10]

What concerns us is whether by the phrase *gentes cognationesque hominum quique una coierunt* Caesar intended to describe the basic units of society as property-holding unilineal descent groups. Those who think so point to the *gentes*. But as Brunner, an exponent of the agnatic clan theory, long ago admitted: "The juxtaposition of the *gentes* and *cognationes* causes difficulties."[11] Actually there are many different ways

---

[7] Speaking of the Suebi staying at home and going to war in turns: "Sic neque agriculturae nec ratio atque usus belli intermittitur" (4.1).

[8] This is the language of Roman polity which divided Roman territory, *ager Romanus*, into *ager publicus*, public property (which apparently is the only kind of property the Germans have) and *ager privatus*, private property and estates (which does not exist among the Germans).

[9] "Agri culturae non student maiorque pars eorum victus in lacte, caseo, carne, consistit. Neque quisquam agri modum certum aut fines habet proprios; sed magistratus ac principes in annos singulos gentibus cognationibusque hominum quique una coierunt quantum et quo loco visum est attribuunt atque anno post alio transire cogunt."

[10] "Die Lesart von α ist unmöglich; die von β ist tadellos ... ohne jenes *que* müsste man statt *qui* ein *quae* erwarten" (Kraner, Dittenberger, Meusel, *Commentarii de Bello Gallico*, 2: 525).

[11] "Schwierigkeiten macht die Nebeneinanderstellung der *gentes* und *cognationes*" (DRG, 1: 84, n. 10). This is Brunner's explanation: "Mit der gens ist zweifellos die agna-

to interpret the phrase in question, but what is clear is that, if descent groups of any kind are meant, this feature is indicated by the word *cognationes*; and it, in itself, among other things, can designate a unilineal or a cognatic group. The juxtaposition of *gentes* and *cognationes* in fact is not particularly strange when we consider that *gens* means 'tribe.' While *gens* can mean a unilineal descent group among classical writers, it is a particular lineage they have in mind – the ancient Roman *gens*, or agnatic clan of their own history, not the kinship organization of barbarian peoples. Applied to non-Romans, particularly barbarians, it means simply 'tribe' or people in an extensive or restricted sense.[12] The numerous instances where Caesar and other ancient writers refer to Germanic *gentes* clearly conform to these contexts. If Caesar therefore is referring to the situation where members of each of the extensive *gentes* of the Germans regarded themselves as related to one another, the resulting vast fictive descent groups are very likely to be cognatic.[13] There are other possibilities. If the 'tribes' are regarded as being composed of *cognationes*, nothing indicates the rules of descent; moreover the *cognationes* may be thought to be extensive, or they may simply represent the commonplace of shallow extended families. And in all of this, how are we to understand the phrase "quique una coierunt," for there are three distinct designations applied to the recipients of the land: 'tribes,' *cognationes*, and "those who

---

tische Sippe gemeint. Unter den cognationes hominum qui tum una coierunt, mag man kleinere gentes verstehen, die miteinander verschwägert oder verwandt waren und zu einer Wirtschaftsgruppe vereinigt wurden oder auch eingere Verwandtsgruppen von solchen gentes, die zu gross geworden waren, um einen einzigen Wirtschaftsverband zu bilden" (ibid.). Cf. n. 13.

[12] See the examples in Lewis and Short, and E. H. Merguet, *Lexikon zu Schriften Cäsars* (Jena, 1886), s.v.

[13] It is worth noting that the attribution of land to *gentes* and *cognationes* need not mean such units communally work the land or share the fruits, but simply that certain areas are ascribed to certain groups.

Interestingly, those who speculate on the nature of the groups of Caesar's description represent them as quite unlike the *agnatische Sippe* of the legal histories (thus, cf. even Brunner, above, n. 50), but rather as something approaching the fluid cognatic Highland clans: cf. J. M. Kemble (*The Saxons in England* [1849; rpt. London, 1876], pp. 56-57): "I represent them to myself as great family unions, comprising households of various degrees of wealth, rank and authority: some in direct descent from the common ancestor, or from the hero of the particular tribe; others more distantly connected, through the natural result of increasing population, which multiplies indeed the members of the family, but removes them at every step further from the original stock: some, admitted into communion by marriage, others by adoption, others even by emancipation, but all recognizing a brotherhood, a kinship or *sibsceaft** ... all known to themselves and to their neighbours by one name." Communion by marriage means cognatic descent through females.

have joined together"? Rather than pursuing numerous interpretations which attempt to make concrete and literal sense out of Caesar's wording, we could simply recognize the literary nature of the passage and regard it as an exercise in rhetorical circumlocution: the land is distributed "to the tribes and species of men and those who have joined together." This might merely indicate village communities – supposing of course that something real is being referred to. But herein lies the crux of the matter, for it is exceedingly unlikely that the actual social organization of Germanic society is being described. The indefinite nature of the passage is meant to suggest the types of simple groups of primitive peoples without actually describing them, and in fact is reminiscent of speculative ethnographic-historical passages in other authors.[14] This judgment seems all the more certain when we consider the nature of Caesar's Germanic ethnography as a whole.

Caesar's account of German mores has always given historians pause. As early as 1780 Möser, the founder of the *Markgenossen* theory, felt that the circumstance described could not have had general application but was the result of war conditions.[15] Even though the text has been frequently interpreted literally to show variously that the Germans were communistic or that they were not,[16] investigation over the years of the archaeological and the historical-ethnographic background of the account has cast ever greater doubt upon the validity of Caesar's remarks, which make it continually more difficult to find excuses for the reliability of his Germanic ethnography. Caesar draws a sharp distinction between the Gauls and the Germans, and their respective cultures, on each bank of the Rhine. On one side stand the Gauls, sedentary and agricultural; on the other the far more primitive Germans, not given to agriculture and private property, displaying the litany of primitive characteristics proper to the ancient conception of nomads or pastoralists. Archaeologically this distinction is completely false.[17] Quite apart from the fact that the account

---

[14] For examples, see n. 2.

[15] Dopsch, *Economic and Social Foundations*, p. 5. Cf. the remarks of Kemble, who introduced the mark theory to England: "But so deeply does the possession of land enter into the principle of all Teutonic institutions that I cannot bring myself to believe in the accuracy of Caesar's statement. Like his previous rash and most unfounded assertion respecting the German Gods, this may rest only upon the incorrect information of Gallic provincials: at the utmost it can be applied only to the Suevi and their warlike allies, if it be not intended to be confined to the predatory bands of Ariovistus encamped among the defeated yet hostile Sequani" (*The Saxons in England*, pp. 39-40).

[16] As to the latter, see Dopsch, *Economic and Social Foundations*, pp. 33-34; and at an early date D. W. Ross, *Land-Holding Among the Germans*, pp. 17 ff.

[17] For a recent review of the question, C. M. Wells, *The German Policy of Augustus*

of the *Bellum Gallicum* indicates that there were *Germani* on both sides of the Rhine, just as there were Gauls, and that Caesar's description of the supposedly Germanic Tencteri and Usipetes as farmers does not sit well with the ethnography of Bk. 6, the fact is that in all respects the culture on both banks of the Rhine is fairly homogeneous late La Tène. Recent surveys of this evidence regard Caesar's emphasis on the Rhine frontier as a politically motivated artificial distinction created to justify his operations in Gaul and his 'thus far and no farther' decision.[18]

It seems he also created an ethnography to match. He had to, because he was not an eyewitness of the trans-Rhenan culture; he had only a brief meeting with the troops of Ariovistus[19] and he never penetrated Suebian territory.[20] The questions that must be answered are what was the source of his ethnography and what was his method of compiling it? Did he carefully sift the reports of Gallic provincials concerning their neighbours? Or did he or his secretaries employ the accepted speculations on the nature of primitive customs and previous ethnographic material which had been applied to the area in which he now found the Germans? We

---

(Oxford, 1972), pp. 14-31. "The discrepancy between Caesar's evidence and that of archaeology is marked" (p. 24). There is little certainty about the obscure linguistic situation in the area either. For a salutary and highly sceptical view of the modern linguistic suppositions underlying the identification of 'Germans' in the Caesarian period, see Rolf Hachmann, *The Germanic Peoples*, trans. James Hogarth, Archaeologia Mundi (Geneva, 1971), pp. 11-81; fundamental is R. Hachmann, G. Kossack, and H. Kuhn, *Völker zwischen Germanen und Kelten* (Neumünster, 1962). In Kuhn's view (pp. 105-128), based on linguistic considerations, a third group, whose distinctiveness went unnoticed by the ancients, and whose speech was pre-Celtic and pre-Germanic, but still Indo-European, occupied the area between the Oise and Aller rivers.

[18] Wells, p. 30; Hachmann, *Germanic Peoples*, pp. 35-36. Wells does not consider the ethnographic tradition behind Caesar. Citing O. Klindt-Jensen, *Denmark Before the Vikings*, Ancient Peoples and Places, 4 (New York, 1957), for the general archaeology of the area Wells says that Caesar's descriptions may be suitable for the northerly lower Elbe and Jutland culture which, he suggests, the Suebi (as opposed to the other tribes Caesar calls *Germani*) preserved. The material culture does appear to be relatively poorer (particularly compared with the earlier Bronze age remains), but cf. Klindt-Jensen's description of the economy: "Both the sandy soil and the richer loamy soil was cultivated by the farmers .... A great number of so-called 'Celtic' fields have been found .... The fields are rather small and are square or rectangular in shape. They are surrounded by low banks of earth, and stone .... In some cases a large field has been divided into several smaller ones .... In whatever way we interpret these boundaries, they suggest that the people of the period possessed a strong sense of private property" (pp. 95-96).

[19] Of the tribes in Ariovistus' army, Suebi, Sedusii, Harudes, Marcomani, Triboci, Vangiones and Nemetes, the last three have Celtic names, as did apparently Ariovistus himself (Wells, *German Policy*, p. 22). His host appears to have been at least a mixed German-Celtic force.

[20] BG 6.29.

know that, even though he was in a position to acquire intimate knowledge about Gaulish custom, he relied heavily upon the earlier work of Posidonius, adding some details of his own.[21] The nature and quality of his Germanic ethnography is apparent from his treatment of the Germanic gods. Contrasting Gallic and Germanic religion, he says that the Germans worship only those gods whom they perceive and which are clearly helpful, namely the Sun, Fire and Moon; they have not even heard of other gods.[22] The idea that the Germans worshipped only those elemental forces has always seemed preposterous; it contradicts the evidence of Tacitus, which is in agreement with later literary and linguistic evidence,[23] and with the ritual remains of the Germanic regions from the Bronze and Iron Age. It is frequently supposed that Caesar has received misinformation from Gallic informants, but as Walser has shown, the source is ancient ethnographic-philosophical speculation. In the *Cratylus*, for instance, Plato has Socrates say that the only gods of the early inhabitants of *Hellas* were the Sun, Moon, Earth, Stars and Heavens, and that was still the case among many barbarians.[24] Walser in fact has shown the roots of Caesar's Germanic ethnography as a whole to be the ancient ethnography of the north, particularly that of the nomadic Scythian tribes;[25] and in his account Caesar himself says that he had consulted Eratosthenes and *quidam Graeci* on the trans-Rhenan area.[26]

[21] Tierney, "Celtic Ethnography of Posidonius," pp. 211 ff.

[22] BG 6.21: "Nam neque druides habent qui rebus divinis praesint, neque sacrificiis student. Deorum numero eos solos ducunt quos cernunt et quorum aperte opibus iuvantur, Solem et Vulcanum et Lunam, reliquos ne fama quidem acceperunt." The first part of this account is also false. We can accept the proposition that the Germans had no druids (or is Caesar trying to say they have no priests?), but not that they took no interest in sacrifices. Posidonius (via Strabo, 7.2.1,3) had already described certain women among the Cimbri sacrificing prisoners by cutting their throats over special cauldrons (one of which was apparently later given as a present of Augustus); Tacitus likewise mentions human sacrifice a number of times: G 7, 9, 40. The Danish and north German bogs have preserved vast amounts of ritual deposits including, without a doubt, human victims (the most famous example of which is the so-called Tollund man); later literary sources from late Antiquity through the Christianization of Scandinavia continue to associate sacrifice, human and otherwise, with Germanic paganism. The only defence of Caesar's statement is that he means to say only that, compared to the Gauls, the Germans sacrificed *less*; but in fact considerably more than this is said.

[23] G 9, 40; Anderson, pp. 73 ff.

[24] Walser, *Caesar und die Germanen*, p. 66. In the *Laws* 3.680 a similar comparison is made with regard to power vested in a lineage or clan chief.

[25] Walser, pp. 52 ff. Tierney comes to much the same conclusion: "The Celtic Ethnography," pp. 201, 216 ff., as does Hachmann, *The Germanic Peoples*, pp. 36-37.

[26] "... in Hercyniam silvam quam Eratostheni et quibusdam Graecis fama notam esse video, quam illi Orcyniam appellant ..." (BG 6.24). This is usually taken to mean that he had read Posidonius, and the Greek writers, including the great geographer Eratosthenes,

There is considerable justification for being cynical about Caesar's motives in describing the Germans the way he does, but there are a number of legitimate, if mistaken, factors which undoubtedly contributed to the pastiche he offers as a Germanic ethnography. Caesar appears to have been the first to stress in writing the distinction between Celt and German, although that fact was known before the *Bellum Gallicum*, but no sure information on the trans-Rhenan area or inner Germany became available until the Augustan wars. Like Posidonius, Caesar could only have had knowledge of the celticized cis-Rhenan tribes in settled conditions. However, before the Germans made their presence known, the ancients regarded the north as inhabited by the Celts and their neighbours, the largely nomadic Scyths, Getae and Mysians; the Scythians were regarded as extending north of the Celts to the Baltic and North seas. Little wonder that in knowing that the Germans were to be found where the Scyths and other tribes once stood, Caesar has attributed much of the generalized northern ethnography, particularly that of the nomad and semi-nomadic tribes, to the Germans beyond the Rhine.[27] The initial encounters of the Romans with the trans-Rhenan tribes in the Cimbric and Ariovistus campaigns probably helped to suggest this transference, since they appeared on the move, accompanied by their wives and children and wagons, which was an especial characteristic of the Scyths; we know from Strabo (7.2.2) that Posidonius thought that in the Cimbri he had found the ancient Cimmerians. Moreover, in ancient historiography the barbarian nomads had already been incorporated into the speculation on the development of human communities and the customs thought proper to the various stages of their evolution. Caesar in fact had at hand a vast amount of information which he no doubt thought could be used with some semblance of justification to contrast the Celts of Gaul and the Germans of the north, whom he regarded as far less civilized.

This is certainly the context which lies behind Caesar's account of the Germanic economy in 6. 22: the lack of boundaries and agriculture; the subsistence mainly on milk, cheese and meat; the distribution of the land to the various human groupings; and the yearly migration to new lands. Indeed the various aspects of Caesar's description of Germanic economic life can be found in ancient ethnography and literature attributed to the northern peoples (Scythians and Getae) or to the Golden Age when

---

(275-194 BC), quoted by him, on the area of the Hercynian forest: Anderson, p. xxii; Tierney, p. 218.

[27] Tierney, pp. 199, 201.

nomadic or pastoral communism prevailed. For instance, Caesar's statement that the Germans do not apply themselves to agriculture, or have a
fixed portion of land each, and their own boundaries ("Agriculturae non
student .... Neque quisquam agri modum certum aut fines habet
proprios"), can be compared with Trogus' description of the lack of
boundaries and agriculture among the Scyths ("hominibus inter se nulli
fines. neque enim agrum exercent"[28]). In descriptions of the Golden Age
the idea of lack of boundaries frequently symbolized both the nomadic-
pastoral and communistic state of society, the two concepts being
conflated.[29] The diet attributed to the Germans ("maiorque pars eorum
victus in lacte, caseo, carne consistit") is also characteristic of the Scyths;
Cicero, for instance (quoting a Greek source of probably the third century
BC) has a Scythian prince claim the same subsistence on milk, cheese and
meat ("lacte, caseo, carne vescor"[30]). The extraordinary statement of
Caesar that the Germans changed their lands and abode each
year – "neque longius anno remanere uno in loco colendi causa licet"
(4.1); "magistratus ac principes in annos singulos gentibus cognationibusque hominum quique una coierunt quantum et quo loco visum est agri
attribuunt atque anno post alio transire cogunt" (6.22) – has frequently
been interpreted as a mistaken impression of the simple rotation of land
under cultivation, although Caesar certainly implies far more than this.[31]
But similar practices were attributed to the Getae, whom Strabo, for
instance (7.3.1) thought were the neighbours of the Germans in the
Hercynian forest. Horace speaks of the Getae "immetata quibus iugera
liberas frugas et ceream ferunt/nec cultura placet longior annua" (whose
unmeasured – i.e. undivided – fields bear free fruit and grain, nor do they
care to plant for longer than a year).[32] One could attempt to relate these
descriptions to the known customs of other regions in later ages[33] but in
the ancient context there is no point in trying to determine if such customs
should be applied in reality to anyone, for they are based on speculation

[28] Quoted in Lovejoy and Boas, *Primitivism*, p. 327.

[29] Examples in Lovejoy and Boas, *Primitivism*, pp. 47, 63 (Ovid), 59 (Tibullus), 67
(Trogus), 149 (Maximus Tyrius), 232 (Lucretius), 329 (Horace).

[30] Ibid., p. 329.

[31] Anderson, p. 134.

[32] Lovejoy and Boas, p. 329. Cf. also Diodorus of Sicily's account of the Iberian
Vaccaei (5.34.3); among them there is a yearly division of the land; the fruits are the
property of all; and the death penalty imposed upon whoever appropriates some for
himself.

[33] Although with difficulty; but cf. the practice of partition among shallow lineages in
parts of Ireland during the sixteenth century: Kenneth Nicholls, *Gaelic and Gaelicized
Ireland in the Middle Ages*, The Gill History of Ireland, 4 (Dublin, 1972), pp. 60-64.

concerning the origin of greed, social distinction, and the relations of these facts of civilized life to private property and agriculture; such speculation was cast in the context of the Golden Age and also the culture of barbarian peoples who were thought to be near or entering the agricultural stage, which – the ancients knew – was the root of the problems of civilization. This is particularly clear in Caesar's case when he immediately goes on to give the reasons for the distribution of land by the magistrates and the yearly change of abode:[34] lest long attention to agriculture should weaken their warlike abilities; lest individuals should seek to expand their private property (*fines*) and the powerful drive the weak from their holdings; lest they indulge in more luxurious housing; lest the greed for money arise, which was the cause of civil strife and dissension; and finally, in order to keep the common people under control since each man sees that his wealth is equal to that of the most powerful. Each is a *topos* in the ancient analysis of the debilitating effects of civilization: with settled agriculture and private property come luxury, aggravated social distinctions, greed, the oppression of the poor by the wealthy, and civil dissension. There could be no clearer sign of the philosophical-ethnographical sources of Caesar's description of the economic foundation of Germanic society.

The foundation of the clan theory inexorably leads back to a mis-interpretation of Caesar's account and a misunderstanding of the value of his Germanic ethnography. The great irony is that the ancient philosophical-ethnographical notions on the nature and development of human societies, which are the shaping forces behind the customs Caesar attributes to the Germans, have also been in large part shared by modern historians, who supposed that their ideas were based upon scientific principles. When they thought they found in Caesar raw evidence for their theory of social evolution among the Germans they found only the ancient roots of their own speculation.

---

[34] "Eius rei multas adferunt causas: ne adsidua consuetudine capti studium belli gerendi agri cultura commutent; ne latos fines parare studeant potentioresque humiliores possessionibus expellant; ne accuratius quam ad frigora atque aestus vitandos aedificent; ne qua oriatur pecuniae cupiditas, qua ex re factiones dissensionesque nascuntur; ut animi aequitate plebem contineant, cum suas quisque opes cum potentissimis aequari videat" (6.22).

That Caesar actually attributes these reasons to the Germans themselves only emphasizes the unreliability of the account. Cf. Thompson (*Early Germans*, p. 10), who believes that "this penetrating analysis" was derived "from some of the clansmen themselves." These ideas are rife in ancient historical thinking; but even if this were not so, it would be very curious that such perceptions of civilization and its discontents came from men who supposedly were unfamiliar with it.

B. TACITUS' GERMANIA

In Antiquity the most extensive account of German mores and of the nature and function of kinship comes not, as we might have expected, from Caesar, who met the Germans in the field, nor from the Greeks, who fashioned and perfected ancient ethnography, but from the *Germania* of Tacitus, published in AD 98.[35] The unique status of the Tacitean account is not merely the result of the happenstance of survival (Caesar's descriptions after all survive intact); an important factor contributing to the relative fullness of the *Germania* was the increase in interest and knowledge about the Germans from the period of Posidonius and Caesar to the end of the first century AD. The Germans themselves were relatively new to the consciousness of the Mediterranean world, appearing first in the great Cimbric migration (ca. 120-102 BC). At the time they were thought to differ little, if at all, from the Celts, a view which persisted even in works of the historian of the Cimbric wars, Posidonius, whose work was published around 80 BC. It appears the identity of the Germans was recognized soon after this, but as far as we are concerned the first clear (and most certainly too clear) distinction between the two peoples was made by Caesar in the *Bellum Gallicum*. Although, as in the case of the initial encounter between the Romans and the Cimbri, Roman-German relations for the some five hundred years following Caesar's confrontation with the trans-Rhenan tribes were sporadically marked by fierce conflicts, even in the early years there are clear signs on the part of the Romans of an acceptance of the barbarian talents of the Germans and a conscious attempt to assimilate those tribes brought within the imperial orbit.[36] In the century and a half between the accounts of Caesar and Tacitus the Germans became a familiar and persistent consideration of Roman policy, and the Rhine frontier a common station for the officers and men of the imperial army.

---

[35] There are countless editions of the *Germania*. The standard English edition is that of J. G. C. Anderson, *Cornelii Taciti De Origine et Situ Germanorum* (Oxford, 1938). See also: K. Müllenhoff, *Die Germania des Tacitus*, Deutsche Altertumskunde, 4 (Berlin, 1900); R. Much and H. Jankuhn, *Die Germania des Tacitus* (Heidelberg, 1967); J. Lindauer, *Germania* (Munich, 1967); E. Fehrle and R. Hünnerkopf, *Germania* (Heidelberg, 1959); J. Forni and F. Galli, *Taciti De Origine et Situ Germanorum* (Rome, 1964).

[36] As early as the reign of Tiberius a German bodyguard protected the Emperor (Tacitus, *Ann*. 1.24); *Ann*. 11.19 gives a fine example of an attempt to assimilate the Frisians by the Roman commander Cn. Domitius Corbulo in AD 47: "natio Frisionum ... datis obsidibus consedit apud agros a Corbulone descriptos; idem senatum magistratus leges imposuit."

This situation is of some importance in evaluating the sources and reliability of Tacitus' account. For our purpose, a detailed discussion of the *Germania*'s sources[37] is beside the point; most are lost and of little help in attributing origins to the minutiae of Tacitus' references to kinship. It was suggested above that much in the Tacitean account is valuable and also that the author, or his sources, have shared in some of the distorting features of ancient ethnography. It is impossible to say with certainty to which category belongs each of the details of his observations on kinship. What can be said in their favour, however, is that, with one possible exception, they do not appear to be among the accepted *topoi* of ethnographers, and again, with the possible exception of the passage usually cited as indicating the role of clans in military organization, they are not used to prove moral or philosophical points. On the whole, in fact, the kinship references are rather down-to-earth. Their reliability must depend on how we evaluate the worth of Tacitus' sources in general; and these appear to have been largely worthwhile. The earliest is the writing of Posidonius on the Cimbri and Teutoni, but to what extent relied upon, particularly as to details must remain unknown, as the work is largely lost.[38] The other main sources are also lost, notably the work of Livy (Bk. 104), and, most importantly, the *Bella Germaniae* of the elder Pliny, who himself served on the Rhine.[39] Possibly to this body of information should be added oral material from soldiers and traders available to Tacitus in the years surrounding the composition of his treatise. Interestingly enough, little use is made of Caesar; the Tacitean treatment is quite independent and in important places differs from that of his predecessor. The *Germania*, then, is largely a compendium (Tacitus never claims to have been an eyewitness), and as such has its faults, notably a tendency to anachronism:[40] it does not give a picture of Germanic society at one moment in time and some of the observations may be of varying value. In

[37] The standard work is E. Norden, *Die Germanische Urgeschichte in Tacitus Germania*. See also Anderson, xix ff.; one can usefully consult J. J. Tierney, "The Celtic Ethnography of Posidonius," pp. 189 ff.

[38] Although Posidonius did not recognize there was a distinction between Celts and Germans, he apparently did treat of individual tribes who were later recognized as being Germans.

[39] R. Syme, for one, considers Pliny the main source. "That officer had served with the armies of the Rhine; he knew both Upper and Lower Germany from the sources of the Danube; and he had been on expeditions across the river into the lands of the free Germans. Pliny united relentless energy, encyclopedic tastes, and a keen faculty of observation. No better source could be imagined" (*Tacitus*, Oxford, 1958, 1: 127).

[40] For examples, see Syme, 1: 127 ff.

sum, the *Germania* does not by any stretch of the imagination present an account approaching modern ethnographic standards, but that could hardly be expected. Written by one of the lights of Roman historiography for a nation well aware of the German presence, and drawing upon competent sources, it represents, nevertheless, the closest we will come to a relatively sober presentation of the ancient world's view of German, mainly west German society, and consequently the functioning of kinship within it. From this standpoint alone the *Germania*-deserves attention.

There is another reason. The ethnography of Tacitus has long been used as a tool by historians of north European culture and of the early Middle Ages. Usually from the point of view of supposed later conditions, and more frequently on the basis of preconceptions about the nature of early Germanic society, much has been read into the Tacitean account, and probably just as much read out as error. It is true that in particular instances the subsequent situation – if in fact we are sure what that is – may be illuminating, although it proves little; and doubtless in some cases – on the basis of archaeological evidence for instance – we may have a better idea of what lies behind the text than the author himself. But we must still start from the simple presumption that Tacitus means what he says. We should try to read the language of the text as we may reasonably expect it was understood at the time of its publication, and try to consider its contents in the context of the interests and assumptions of a Mediterranean observer. When this is done very little seems to support the traditional teaching.

Of the references in Tacitus' work to kinship among the Germans and to their military operations, one brief passage has frequently been cited as showing that unilineal lineages and clans formed discrete units in the army (*Heeresabteilungen*). In G 7 he writes that it was not happenstance or chance grouping which made up the units of foot and horse but "familiae et propinquitates."[41] To Genzmer the passage indicated no more than that the Germans fought in groups composed of relatives, friends, and neighbours.[42] Clearly, this interpretation is as far as the Tacitean text will

---

[41] "non casus nec fortuita conglobatio turmam aut cuneum facit, sed familiae et propinquitates."

[42] "Die germanische Sippe als Rechtsgebilde," pp. 37-38; this is also his conclusion on the late sixth-century statement on the battle array of the western barbarians by Mauricius. He says no more than Tacitus because, as is clear from its structure and contents, the statement is simply a verbose paraphrase: τάσσονται ... εἴτε πεζῇ εἴτε ἐπὶ τῶν ἵππων, οὐ μέτρῳ τινὶ ὡρισμένῳ καὶ τάξει, ἢ ἐν μοίραις ἢ ἐν μέρεσιν, ἀλλὰ κατὰ φυλὰς καὶ τῇ πρὸς

take us. The audience of the *Germania* was familiar with the rationalized military organization characteristic of contemporary ancient communities; in contrast, Tacitus from a Roman viewpoint is alluding to the usages of barbarian warrior societies, where most freemen were expected to be able to fight, where a man fought along with family members, friends, relatives and neighbours, and where ties of kinship might contribute to the cohesion of military groups.[43] These features are as characteristic of societies with bilateral kinship and kindred systems as of those with unilineal organization.[44] Moreover, a much better idea of the basis for

---

ἀλλήλους συγγενείᾳ τε χὰι προσπαθείᾳ (*Arta Militara*, ed. H. Mihaescu [Bucharest, 1970]), 11.4. (Their foot and horse are arranged not in squadrons and lots of fixed measure and arrangement but in divisions [drawn up] in mutual relationship and affection.) Centuries later this learned conceit is taken over almost word for word by the Emperor Leo vi (886-911) in his *Tactica*, 18, and applied to the contemporary Franks (Migne, *Patrologia Graeca* 107: 966-967). These texts should not be taken seriously; cf. ch. 5, n. 20. For the full text of Tacitus, see below, p. 55.

Sometimes cited (e.g. Brunner, DRG 1: 118, n. 38; Franz Beyerle, "Das Kulturporträt der beiden alamannischen Rechtstexte: Pactus und Lex Alamannorum," in *Hegau* (1956) rpt. in *Zur Geschichte der Alemanner*, ed. W. Müller, Wege der Forschung C (1975) p. 140; and more recently Thompson, *Early Germans*, p. 64, n. 1) is the suggestion made by Lehman that the phrase in the *Pactus Alamannorum* (2.45; in *Leges Alamannorum*, MGH, LL, 1, v, 1) "in heris generationis" = "ante exercitum secundum familias ordinatum," i.e. before the *Heersippe*. This interpretation is out of the question. The phrase occurs in a condensed law dealing with the wrongful freeing of another's *letus* either "in ecclesia" or "in heris generationis." *Generatio* means simply *natio*, *populus*, or possibly more specifically, an armed host of the people. The law refers simply to public manumission in church or before the army. Cf. the Lombard agreement of 851 between Radelgisus and Siginulfus: "Nor with my subjects, nor with the Franks, nor with the Saracens, nor with any other *generatio* shall I ... withdraw [from the agreement] not assail it .... Through my land I shall not permit nor allow any *generatio* to come against the land and people of your region. I and my people shall resist this *generatio* ..." (in *Leges Langobardorum*, MGH, LL, IV, p. 221.

[43] Genzmer is trivializing, I presume, when he suggests that what is being described is no different from the grouping of friends and relatives together in units by the German command in the First World War. What we are really dealing with in the Tacitean text is a question of perception. Compare a modern historian's description of the fifteenth-century Swiss infantry: "There was no need to waste days in the weary work of organization when every man stood among his kinsmen and neighbours, beneath the pennon of his native town or valley" (C. W. C. Oman, *The Art of War in the Middle Ages A.D. 378-1515* [1885; rev. ed. Ithaca, 1953], p. 79). The relative point of view is similar, although Oman uses family and propinquity to explain the rapidity of Swiss mobilization, Tacitus to explain Germanic valour (see below, n. 46).

[44] See Freeman, "On the Concept of the Kindred," p.214. He cites the Iban, who in the early nineteenth and twentieth centuries mounted large and successful attacks on their neighbours on the basis of their kindred organization. Forces of hundreds or thousands were formed through the expedient of individuals recruiting kinsmen who in turn recruited their kinsmen, and so on through the greater part of the tribal area if the enterprise was thought worthwhile. Leaders were recognized on the basis of their ability

Tacitus' observation, and the motive behind it, can be gathered from the whole context of the passage. To the ancients, a characteristic of, first the Celts and then the Germans, was valour in battle. Roman observers were also struck by the occasional presence of women and children near the line of battle. Caesar mentions this, for instance, in the battle with Ariovistus (BG 1.51) and Tacitus in the revolt of Civilis (*Hist.* 4.18) and in G 8.[45] In the passage of the *Germania* under discussion, both these phenomena are the main objects of the account.

> Particularly conducive to the incitement of valour are the facts that neither chance nor accidental grouping makes up the troop of horse or foot but families and friends [or relatives or neighbours], and that a man's dear ones are at hand so that the crying of women and the wailing of children can be heard. They are the most holy of witnesses and the greatest bestowers of praise. The men bear their wounds to their mothers and wives; they in turn do not fear counting and examining the blows and bring food and encouragement to the combatants.[46]

What Tacitus is actually giving us is a partial explanation for German valour not a description of military organization at all. The casual allusion to the constitution of the host, which contributes to his theme, is a far cry from a statement that the organizational principle of Germanic armies was the agnatic clan acting as a discrete unit. And if nothing about the Tacitean description presupposes clans and lineages, just as clearly, if the assumption of clan organization is made, nothing suggests that these

---

and status as warriors, but had no institutionalized authority, and discipline was very poor. It is not to be suggested that this is exactly how German society operated but, if we accept the validity of the passages from Caesar and Tacitus below, the description suggests another paradigm in which the accounts of Caesar and Tacitus can be understood, which pulls together what we know of Germanic kindreds, the reported role of kinship in their forces, the role of warleaders, and the indiscipline of their armies: "Latrocinia nullam habent infamiam quae extra fines cuiusque civitatis fiunt .... Atque ubi ex principibus in concilio dixit se ducem fore, qui sequi velint, consurgunt ii, qui et causam et hominem probant" (BG 6.23); "Reges ex nobilitate duces ex virtute sumunt ... et duces exemplo potius quam imperio, si prompti, si conspicui, si ante aciem agant, admiratione praesunt ... non casus nec fortuita conglobatio turmam aut cuneum facit sed familiae et propinquitates" (G 7). For their indiscipline see remarks on the Chatti, G 30.

[45] See also Plutarch's account of Marius' battle against the Teutones based on Posidonius, where the women in desperation entered the fight. Cf. also Tacitus on the Britons (*Ann. 14.34*).

[46] "quodque praecipuum fortitudinis incitamentum est, non casus nec fortuita conglobatio turmam aut cuneum facit, sed familiae et propinquitates; et in proximo pignora, unde feminarum ululatus audiri, unde vagitus infantium. hi cuique sanctissimi testes, hi maximi laudatores: ad matres, ad coniuges vulnera ferunt; nec illae numerare et exigere plagas pavent, cibosque et hortamina pugnantibus gestant" (G 7).

would be based on the unilineal principle. Indeed when Tacitus' other references to kinship are considered it will be seen that he seems to stress cognatic relationships.

Inheritance, the giving and taking of hostages, the so-called avunculate, and feud are all matters in which Tacitus displays some interest, but it is also worthwhile noting what he does not say. Considering common views of early Germanic society, the silence on two matters is significant. First, in the discussion of what can roughly be called the political and administrative makeup of society, there is no hint that it was based in any way on a clan or extensive lineage system.[47] The same can be said of agricultural organization and landholding: a fair reading of the pertinent passages suggests rather a system of individual or family ownership.[48] The rules of intestate succession which will be considered below confirm this judgment, since they are, to use Maitland's word, individualistic.[49] Property is seen as belonging to an individual, and on his death other individuals, including cognatic kinsmen, succeed to it class by class. A similar picture appears in the description of succession among the Tencteri, who apparently practised primogeniture: the inheritance itself is

---

[47] Tribal states of varying dimension and autonomy are designated: *gentes, civitates, nationes, populi*. Within the tribe are smaller divisions: *pagi*. The major forces shaping political life were the *concilia, duces, principes, nobiles, proceres, primores, sacerdotes, reges*, and female seers.

[48] "Nullas Germanorum populis urbes habitari satis notum est, ne pati quidem inter se iunctas sedes. colunt discreti ac diversi, ut fons, ut campus, ut nemus placuit. vicos locant non in nostrum morem conexis et cohaerentibus aedificiis: suam quisque domum spatio circumdat, sive adversus casus ignis remedium sive inscitia aedificandi" (G 16); "ceteris servis non in nostrum morem descriptis per familiam ministeriis utuntur: suam quisque sedem, suos penates regit" (G 25); "agri pro numero cultorum ab universis in vices occupantur, quos mox inter se secundum dignationem partiuntur; facilitatem partiendi camporum spatia praestant. arva per annos mutant, et superest ager" (G 26); speaking of a select group of Chatti warriors: "nulli domus aut ager aut aliqua cura: prout ad quemque venere aluntur, prodigi alieni, contemptores sui ..." (G 31). C. 26 is probably the most debated of all passages in the *Germania*; the modern view is largely that followed by Latouche (based originally on an interpretation of Fustel) *The Birth of Western Economy*, pp. 30 ff. The old idea that this passage shows the Germans not to have had private property in the arable is less than fruitful. First, the existence at some level of a dependent estate system is implied in c. 25. Second, there is little point in measuring Germanic ownership by modern or by Roman standards. The fact that the villages as a whole, for very practical reasons, initially occupied large chunks of arable implies no lack of private property nor that ownership lay with the community. The important point is that this land is immediately divided into uneven individual plots. C. 31 shows that Tacitus imagined that normally individuals possessed (or would have liked to possess) a *domus* and *ager*.

[49] HEL, 2: 250.

designated as *familia et penates et iura successionum*.[50] Fustel long ago rightly pointed out that *familia* in this context is the standard legal usage of inheritance and means *patrimonium*.[51]

What the *Germania* appears to describe is a society in which bilateral relationship is a central feature of the kinship system. Unilineal categories or groups are given no special functions[52] and, outside the house community, the kindred defines those perquisites and obligations based on kinship. This is true not just of less tangible benefits, but also of significant legal or judicial processes such as inheritance and feud. The system of inheritance, for instance, is described in this way:

> heredes tamen successoresque sui cuique liberi, et nullum testamentum. si liberi non sunt, proximus gradus in possessione fratres, patrui, avunculi.
>
> (G 20)

> An individual's heirs and successors, however, are his own children, and there is no provision for a will. If there are no children the next degree to take possession are his brothers, then paternal and maternal uncles.

Preceding this passage the author has described the special role of the *avunculus* in Germanic kinship. Aware of the implications this might have for his readers,[53] he has taken care to specify that there is no intimation of matrilineal succession (hence the *tamen*). Without speculating on the answers to the many questions the pattern of inheritance given here has raised among modern scholars, nor upon possible proprietal distinctions which may be involved, we can at least be fairly certain of how the major lineaments of the system described here would be understood by Tacitus' readers.

---

[50] "inter familiam et penates et iura successionum equi traduntur; excipit filius non ut cetera maximus natu sed prout ferox bello et melior" (G 32).

[51] "Recherches sur cette question: les Germains connaissaient-ils la propriété des terres," in *Recherches sur quelques problèmes d'histoire* (Paris, 1885), p. 237. Cf. Gaius, *Inst.* 2.102: "familiam suam id est patrimonium suum" and the numerous laws on the *actio familiae erciscundae*. Anderson (p. 159) would limit it to slaves "who must have been exceedingly few (if they existed at all) in the primitive household of the ordinary German" since, according to the traditional teaching, there would be no patrimony beyond moveables and the dwelling house and the plot around it (*penates*). If this was really the system of the Germans, Tacitus and his readers were blissfully ignorant of it.

[52] *Agnatus* does appear ("numerum liberorum finere aut quemquam ex agnatis necare flagitium habetur": c. 19) but it is recognized (generally, see n. 35) that here it is clearly used in the specific technical sense of children who are born after one is already considered as heir.

[53] Ancient ethnography was aware of matriliny; see Herodotos 1.173 on the Lycians, and Polybius 12.5 on the Italian Locrians. The latter seem to have been a subject of debate as Polybius mentions the conflicting opinions of Timaeus and Aristotle on the origins of the institution among them.

The first to inherit are the *liberi*, the deceased's children. So unambiguous a statement might seem beyond dispute, but it is generally agreed that only *filii*, sons, are meant.[54] Apart from the fact that the other potential heirs are males, this interpretation is based on the idea that the limitations on female inheritance which sometimes appear in the later *leges* were once absolute; that what is regarded as the military nature of barbarian culture, and the originally patrilineal organization of the family structure, not only excluded females from all inheritance but even originally denied them the capacity to hold landed property.[55] Such a view is groundless. What is common in Germanic law is not the exclusion of women from landed inheritance and proprietary rights, but their postponement before males, particularly the postponement of sisters before brothers. The obvious meaning of the Tacitean expression must stand. If the author had intended to designate only sons we can reasonably expect him to have done so more explicitly, especially when we consider that, to Romans, *liberi* in this context is probably a technical legal usage[56] which might remind his educated readers of the first class of the praetorian system of intestate succession (*unde liberi*). The fact that only males are mentioned as the other potential heirs should cause no problem. This may simply be the result of schematization, or it may also have been intentional and as such would also have been understood by readers. The Romans were familiar with a system which limited the rights of female agnates more distant than sisters while it treated daughters and sisters on a par with their male counterparts.[57] It is not surprising that, in any system, natural affection should maintain the rights of close female relatives which, on account of other considerations, elsewhere waned or did not exist. Limitations upon female inheritance are by no means a sign of an earlier or more primitive social state; the Roman restriction upon female agnates, for instance, is not a legacy of the ancient civil law, which treated

---

[54] See n. 35.

[55] See, e.g., Anderson, p. 117. An original female incapacity in Germanic law is also unfortunately one of the starting points in Suzanne Wemple's *Women in Frankish Society* (Philadelphia, 1981), pp. 44-47.

[56] Cf. the use of *agnatus*, n. 52 and *familia*, p. 57.

[57] Classical Athenian law too limited the inheritance rights of women more distant than sisters. Interestingly, while a woman could not succeed to the estate of her cousin, for example, her son could (W. K. Lacey, *The Family in Classical Greece* [London, 1968], p. 139). The reasons for this kind of restriction undoubtedly lie in the fact that the civic and military burdens dependent on the *oikos* could not easily be performed by women (ibid., p. 99).

male and female evenhandedly, but can be traced to the late Republic[58] and was instituted probably as a result of rising fortunes. The Tacitean text, then, certainly must have been read as indicating that the first class to inherit among the Germans were the deceased's children. If we wish to relate this to later law it could be supposed that the daughters' rights were postponed to those of their brothers on the understanding that they would be provided with maintenance or a marriage portion from the family property; and that a system of more or less equal division prevailed.[59]

If there are no sons or daughters ("si liberi non sunt") the next class to inherit are, as we might expect, the deceased's *fratres*. If there are no brothers, the *patrui* and *avunculi* succeed. Whether or not the paternal uncle precedes the maternal uncle, or both succeed together to some division of the inheritance, it would be hard to imagine in so brief a sequence a clearer indication of the bilateral nature of the inheritance system.[60]

In light of the inheritance system, it would be expected that the rights and obligations involved in the feud process were defined in some fashion by the kindred, as was the case in the early Middle Ages and later. "It is necessary for a man to take up the feuds as well as the friendships of his father or near kinsman ... and the whole circle of relations involved receives compensation" ("Suscipere tam inimicitias seu patris seu propinqui quam amicitias necesse est ... recipitque satisfactionem universa domus") (G 21). Writing of cases in the assembly Tacitus notes: "part of the penalty is paid to the king or the state, part to the injured party or his near relatives" ("pars multae regi vel civitati, pars ipsi qui vindicatur vel propinquis eius exsolvitur") (G 12); payments to the injured party's *propinqui* would be for homicide. The language here is broad, probably intentionally so. There is little doubt that *propinquus* means 'a blood

---

[58] Possibly to the *lex Voconia* of 169 BC but probably later: "Feminae ad hereditates legitimas ultra consanguineas successiones non admittuntur: idque iure civili Voconiana ratione videtur effectum; ceterum lex XII tabulorum sine ulla discretione sexus adgnatos admittit" (PS 4.8.20); the Voconian attribution is disputed: cf. Gai. *Inst.* 3.14; *Inst. Iust.* 3.2.3; see any of the major Roman law handbooks; A. Watson, *The Law of Succession in the Later Roman Republic* (Oxford, 1971), pp. 177-178.

[59] Supposing that the custom of the Tencteri was exceptional. In the second part of the treatise, dealing with individual tribes, Tacitus indicates that primogeniture was the rule among these people (G 32). This is generally thought to be an unusual case. At any rate in medieval law primogeniture appears only under the influence of feudalism.

[60] Otherwise a radical alteration of the Tacitean text is needed: "*Avunculi*, if correctly added (which is doubted), could only come into account when there were no relatives on the father's side" (Anderson, p. 118); see also Müllenhoff, p. 324.

relation generally':[61] that, as in the case of inheritance, the circle of relatives involved comprised a category of cognates. The use of the word *domus*, which is merely a synonym for *propinqui* (cf. "pars ... propinquis eius exsolvitur"), does not alter this conclusion. In Tacitus it is often a word of wide application; a few lines preceding the passage under consideration, for example, it is used to embrace the relationship between an uncle and his sister's son.[62]

The system of kindred organization which has so far been indicated implies a relatively close bond between an individual and his mother's family. This feature is given particular emphasis in the description of the so-called avunculate, which has generally been regarded as puzzling, as a counterpoise to the supposed patrilineal nature of the kinship structure or as a remnant of a prior state of matriliny.

> sororum filiis idem apud avunculum qui ad patrem honor. quidam sanctiorem artioremque hunc nexum sanguinis arbitrantur et in accipiendis obsidibus magis exigunt, tamquam et animum firmius et domum latius teneant.
>
> (G 20)
>
> Sisters' sons derive distinction from their maternal uncle as much as from their father. Some think this blood tie more sacred and constraining, and make it a special requirement when receiving hostages, thinking thus to gain a firmer grip on the heart and a wider hold on the family.

The relationship between nephew and maternal uncle has frequently been noted in later sources. Yet, although Tacitus does take special note of the relationship between an uncle and his sister's son in his historical writings, nothing there nor in any other literary source, either early or late, stresses the relationship quite so strongly as G 20. It is probable that there is a certain amount of rhetoric in the passage; that Tacitus, or his source, familiar with the ethnographic convention of matriliny, and finding the *avunculus* playing a pivotal role among the Germans, have found the relationship worthy of special note. The particular hallmarks of the relationship are: special affection, the *honor* a sister's son received, and the stipulation of the relationship in the receipt of hostages. The last feature suggests that Tacitus was basing his observation on the activities of

---

[61] On this there is agreement – generally, see n. 35. Cf. G 20: "quanto plus propinquorum, quanto maior adfinium numerus," where blood relations are contrasted with affines. This is the standard usage throughout the *Historiae* and *Annales*. Note also this use of *proximus* in regard to the Germans: "Briganticus sorore Civilis genitus, ut ferme acerrima proximorum odia sunt, invisus avonculo infesusque" (*Hist.* 4.70).

[62] See immediately below, G 20.

noble and royal houses, and indeed there is enough in his writings about this stratum of society to suggest grounds for his remarks.

The word *honor* includes the ideas of a mark of honour or respect; a distinction or that which publicly distinguishes a man; a preferment or post. Tacitus speaks of the grant of arms in the assembly by a youth's father, *propinquus*, or a *princeps*, for instance, as the *primus iuventae honos*. This signified a youth's entry into adulthood and his participation in public life. As a ceremony taken by Tacitus to be analogous to the assumption of the *toga virilis* at Rome, its possible performance by the *avunculus*, as one of the closest of the *propinqui*, may have suggested the special relationship.[63] Another feature of the upper reaches of Germanic society helps explain this situation further. Tacitus says the assumption of arms was only the first *honor* or public distinction of youth; thereafter the well-connected or the exceptional joined a retinue, which required service in another's household. Many of the young of Germany who were, or hoped to be, somebody, served in this way, in expectation of reward and promotion within the *gradus* of the *comitatus*.[64] It is likely that, as later, kinship and lordship reinforced one another, and that the substantial rewards of service more often than not found their way into the hands of kinsmen and affines. Tacitus' description in fact suggests that the sponsorship of a youth by a *princeps* or *propinquus* may normally have signalled his enrolment into his sponsor's following. In an interlocking network of kinship and lordship, a youth's enlistment with his maternal relations, and in particular with his *avunculus*, would have been common enough. In his historical works Tacitus underlined this relation of maternal uncle and nephew in the political life of German princely families, and while the tie obviously interested him, the instances he cites present a more balanced view than that suggested by the *Germania*. He says that Civilis placed military command in the hands of his two sisters' sons.[65] He also noted, though, that Briganticus, also Civilis' sister's son,

---

[63] "Sed arma sumere non ante cuiquam moris quam civitas suffecturum probaverit. tum in concilio vel principum aliquis vel pater vel propinqui scuto frameaque iuvenem ornant: haec apud illos toga, hic primus iuventae honos; ante hoc domus pars videntur, mox rei publicae: insignis nobilitas aut magna patrum merita principis dignationem etiam adulescentulis adsignant" (G 13). *Arma sumere* is also on the analogy of *togam virilem sumere* (Anderson, p. 90).

[64] "Ceteris robustioribus ac iam pridem probatis adgregantur, nec rubor inter comites aspici. gradus quin etiam ipse comitatus habet, iudicio eius quem sectantur; magnaque et comitum aemulatio, quibus primus apud principem suum locus, et principum cui plurimi et acerrimi comites" (G 13).

[65] *Hist.* 4.33; 5.20.

In the legendary history of the Geats, an Anglo-Saxon poet represents Beowulf as serving in the troop of his maternal uncle Hygelac, and obtaining from his lord and

hated and fought against his uncle.[66] In AD 50, he points out, the sister's sons of the Suebic king Vannius deposed their uncle and divided up his kingdom.[67] What is of particular interest in this event is not so much the enmity between uncle and nephew, but the fact that maternal relationship was no bar to the accession of Vannius' nephews to the throne.[68]

Some other considerations which could suggest the special character of the avunculate are worth noting. The mother's brother was an important source of support against claims made by the *patruus* on his nephew's inheritance from his father; and he stood as the natural protector of his sister and her sons in cases of her husband's remarriage or where polygamy or concubinage was practised. Although polygamy appears to have been a relatively rare feature among the Germans, it, and doubtless concubinage , were certainly known among the upper levels of society.[69] Particularly in princely houses later analogy suggests that the relation of maternal uncle and nephew could appear to be based on a profound sense of affection, lacking as it did the obvious cause of friction which existed

kinsman, among other gifts, hereditary lands the size of a kingdom (*Beow.* 219 ff.; ed. Fr. Klaeber, 3rd ed. [Boston, 1922]). He later acted as guardian and protector of the person and kingdom of his maternal cousin and was offered the throne on Hygelac's death in preference to the king's own son because of fear of foreign aggression; declining it he supported the clearly more legitimate, if at this point unsuitable heir, and succeeded to the kingship only after the youth's death (ibid., 2369-2379).

Originally Beowulf had been placed in the household of king Hrethal, his maternal grandfather and the father of Hygelac. Interestingly, in words reminiscent of the rhetoric of Tacitus description, the poet has him describe his fosterage in the following fashion:

> Ic waes syfanwintre, þa mec sinca baldor
> fraewine folca aet minum faeder genam;
> heold mec ond haefde Hrethel cyning,
> geaf me sinc ond symbel, sibbe gemunde;
> naes ic him to life laðra owihte,
> beorn in burgum, þonne his bearna hwylc
> Herebeald ond Haeðcyn oððe Hygelac min.

(2428-2434)

(I was seven winters old when the lord of treasures, the kindly ruler of peoples, took me from my father. King Hrethel maintained me, and supported me, gave me treasure and feasted me, bore in mind our kinship. As a young warrior in his strongholds I was no less dear to him while he lived than any of his own sons, Herebeald, and Haethcyn, or my own Hygelac.)

[66] *Hist.* 4.70.

[67] *Ann.* 12.29,30.

[68] As also in *Beowulf*: see n. 34.

[69] "nam prope soli barbarorum singulis uxoribus contenti sunt, exceptis admodum paucis, qui non libidine sed ob nobilitatem plurimis nuptiis ambiuntur" (G 18). Ariovistus had two wives (BG 1.53).

between a son and his father,[70] and a nephew and his *patruus*.[71] It is perhaps significant that the avunculate remained a feature of European literature and folklore.[72]

All these considerations suggest that the Tacitean description of the avunculate is probably based partly on rhetoric and partly on real enough features of Germanic military and political life particularly among the aristocracy. It is best not to overemphasize it, make it something arcane, or try to limit its strongest expressions to particular tribes.[73] In his description of the avunculate Tacitus is emphasizing only one feature, though an extremely important one, of kinship among the west Germans; this is not surprising when we remember the optative features of bilateralism, especially in a society with a relatively low level of governmental and judicial sophistication, in which kinship ties are not merely beneficial, but necessary. The avunculate in the *Germania* is not evidence for a prior or existing matrilineal system, but seen in the wider context of

---

[70] An interesting example of the support of an *avunculus* for his nephew when the latter came into conflict with his father appears in the chronicle of Fredegar (4.55) for the year 627. At the assembly at Clichy, a feud broke out when the comptroller to Charibert, the son of king Clothar, was killed by the followers of Aighyna. Bloodshed would have ensued between Charibert and Aighyna but Clothar intervened to keep the parties apart. However, Brodulf, Charibert's *avunculus*, set about gathering together a force from all parts so that he and his nephew could prevail over the wishes of Clothar and take vengeance upon Aighyna. Clothar managed to keep the peace by relying on a third group, his Burgundian vassals.

[71] Compare the role of nephews and uncles in *Beowulf*: Beowulf, devoted retainer of his *avunculus* Hygelac, and protector of his lord's wife and son; Onela, brother of Ohtere, king of the Swedes, and slayer of his brother's son Eanmund; Eadgils, along with this brother Eanmund, excluded from kingship by his father's brother, Onela, whom he eventually slays; Hrothulf, nephew to his father's brother Hrothgar, the king of the Danes, seen as a clear threat to the security of Hrothgar's sons. The fact that a man's brother-in-law had no inheritance right could make him, among his sons' near relatives, a far safer repository for his son than his brother.

Obviously, though, the poet saw that tensions between brothers-in-law could bring about disaster. The Finn episode tells how Hnaef and the sons of his sister Hildeburh were slain when he visited the hall of their father Finn. The poet views the calamity from the point of view of Hildeburh, who had once known the greatest bliss in seeing her brother and her sons together. She gives orders that on the funeral pyre her dead sons are to be placed shoulder to shoulder with their uncle.

[72] See, for example, March Bloch, *Feudal Society*, p. 137, among others, and the works there cited. Somewhat earlier than the earliest *chansons* is *Beowulf*: see nn. 65, 71.

[73] *Quidam* is sometimes taken to refer to "certain tribes" (Anderson, p. 117, Müllenhoff, pp. 321-322; Forni and Galli, p. 122).

Cf. *quidam*, c. 2.4, in reference, it seems, to Greco-Roman antiquaries (Anderson, p. 41). R. Much (p. 20) suggested its use in c. 20 referred to *reges* and *principes* of individual tribes. While I think they were the basis of Tacitus' remarks, it must have been read more indefinitely.

Tacitus' description and known features of historical kinship, appears to be merely one of the optative features of a system of cognation.[74]

The treatise of Tacitus is the fullest account of a Mediterranean view of Germanic society and kinship, and is the only account which attempts to depict the functioning of various features of kinship within barbarian society. That there was a great deal more to Germanic kinship is obvious enough. Probably even the collector(s) of the material which appears in the *Germania* knew more than appears there; but whatever other features were known, either Tacitus or his source saw no reason to bring them to the attention of the Roman public. We must accept the evidence for what it is, and largely as it stands, or else reject it in its entirety as inadequate. Without the confirmation from Antiquity or, as we shall see, from the early Middle Ages of extensive unilineal descent groups, either individually or in combination, as constituent elements of society, the evidence as it stands indicates a kinship system based upon bilateral kindreds and thoroughly imbued with the cognatic principle, though this does not exclude the recognition of unilineal categories for some purposes. In inheritance at an early stage we find the participation of the mother's brother, who inherited either alongside the *patruus* or directly after him. Likewise the relatives involved in the feud process undoubtedly constituted a cognatic category. The same principle is important when we see the effect of kinship on social, political and military life. In the giving and taking of hostages the inclusion of relatives related through females was a prime consideration. In the interrelation of kinship and lordship, maternal relations probably played an important role, and in the case of the *avunculus* perhaps a dominant role. These circumstances make it even more likely that Tacitus' remark concerning the composition of the battle line only refers to the fact that families and kinsmen fought together, that considerations of kinship as well as lordship were an important element in the grouping of the host. To stress the kindred and the cognatic features of Germanic society is not to say that kinship was weak or unimportant. We can still state, to use a current phrase, that society was kinship articulated, possibly more so at this period than later. Kinship was a crucial factor in all aspects of barbarian activity, but its uses and groupings were fluid, and probably on the whole not long lasting. Here the optative element of bilateral relationship came into play. If kinship groupings or kinship-based groups lay behind many political, military and social institutions, these were groups leavened not merely by blood relationship and lordship but by a strong dose of personal preference and allegiance, and economic and

[74] As far as a bilineal resolution is concerned see ch. 1, n. 39.

personal interest. It was a situation which offered mobility and choice, and which at times would result in the conflicting claims and obligations which are the stuff of epic.

The reservation voiced at the conclusion of *Part I* that perhaps the clan has been too readily accepted as a means of understanding the world of the early Germans is amply confirmed by the present review of the ancient evidence, for there is no clear documentation of the clan as a basic unit of society in the ancient sources. The ethnographic commonplaces put together by Caesar can no longer be accepted as a sound description of Germanic society and Tacitus takes no explicit notice of its supposed clan-basis. The latter's account is best understood as a description of a society with bilateral kindreds in which cognation plays a critical role in the descent system; at the very least, this interpretation is the most economical and one which is in harmony with the evidence from the Middle Ages. It might be objected, however, that the ancient sources are too brief and inadequate, and that possibly descent groups as a major feature of social and political organization have gone unrecorded, or lie behind the descriptions which Tacitus chose to illustrate his account of the west Germans. Such an objection would be valid from the standpoint of historical reconstruction only if the extensive sources from the early Middle Ages bore witness to the existence of descent groups in something of the dimension and role attributed to them by the clan theory. Whether they in fact do so is the subject of the following pages.

Since the existence of corporate lineage and clan structure is not immediately apparent in the sources of the early Middle Ages, the traditional view regarded the hypothetical descent groups of Caesarian and Tacitean times as having eventually broken down in the new milieu of the successor kingdoms, although not before a few clear traces of their existence had been left in the legal and narrative sources of the period. A small number of texts dating from the sixth to the ninth centuries refer to a series of groups variously associated with landholding, inheritance and military organization. These are the functions, of course, which traditional historiography has attributed to the ancient Germanic clan. Consequently, these early medieval groupings, called *vicini*, *farae* and *genealogiae*, have generally been interpreted as showing the persistence of ancient Germanic social forms, in particular the survival of the hypothetical clans of the period of Caesar and Tacitus. As will be seen, a thorough reexamination of the constitution and functions of these groups and the principles used in recruitment leaves little room for the traditional interpretation; at the same time it enables us to establish for them a proper place within the framework of late ancient and early medieval society.

4

The *Vicini* of the *Pactus Legis Salicae* and the *Edictum Chilperici*

Two laws of the Salian Franks, ᴌs 45 and the *Edictum Chilperici*, which mention the rights of *vicini*, 'neighbours,' have been the subject of much speculation concerning the nature of early Frankish and barbarian society. These two provisions lie at the heart of modern theories about Frankish kinship, inheritance, and property-holding. The dominant idea shaping interpretations of the *vicini* is that they are a reflection of the supposed collective, communal, or clan basis of barbarian society and, as such, represent a common feature of primitive Germanic social organization quite foreign to conceptions of Mediterranean civilization. In ᴌs 45, *De migrantibus*, one of the *vicini* of a villa, by objecting, can have a new settler (*migrans*) expelled from their midst. The *migrans* himself is the subject of two other Salic provisions, which established penalties for assailing him or for opposing his settlement if he bears a royal writ (*preceptum regis*). The provision of the *Edictum Chilperici* (561-584) sets out a statutory order of succession to the *terrae* of a deceased person who also has *vicini*. The first to inherit are the sons "sicut et lex salica habet"; then the daughters; next, the brother of the deceased, not the *vicini* ("frater terras accipiat, non vicini"); thereafter the deceased's sister succeeds to the lands. This explicit exclusion of the right of the *vicini* has continually been seen as reflecting the communal aspects of ancient Germanic village life. In the traditional view of Germanic kinship development it forms a significant feature on two counts. First, the apparent inheritance right of the *vicini*, seemingly being abrogated here, has commonly been regarded as a sign that the Franks settled in clans or lineages and that these groups had very important inheritance rights to the lands of their members. Second, the provision is regarded as emending the inheritance sequence of the Franks as found in the *Pactus Legis Salicae*, in which, it is imagined, women were completely excluded from inheriting land.[1]

A better indication of the context for these related provisions was given some time ago by Dopsch.[2] He suggested that an analogy to the so-called *Vicinenerbrecht* could be found in Roman and Byzantine law. The *vicini* had a preferential right (προτίμησις) as a consequence of ἐπιβολή or *iunctio*. "If adjoining neighbours on great Roman estates were compelled to take over uncultivated land as part of their taxes," he wrote, "it is quite comprehensible that such an advantage in inheritance would fall to their lot."[3] Likewise he believed the the situation behind *De migrantibus*[4] could

[1] Variations on the above views can be found throughout the literature as the *vicini* are one of the cornerstones of the mark theory, with or without a kinship element. For the older literature see Geffcken, pp. 172 ff., 269 ff. Some recent treatments of *De migrantibus* are considered by Franz Staab, *Untersuchungen zur Gesellschaft am Mittelrhein im Karolingerzeit*, Geschichtliche Landskunde, 11 (Wiesbaden, 1975), pp. 254 ff. See also n. 38 below. Representative of the traditional view is this statement by Vinogradoff (*Historical Jurisprudence*, 1: 335): "In Frankish law a curious manifestation of communal ownership by neighbours has been preserved by an Edict of King Chilperic (AD 571). The right of the neighbours, which is abrogated by the Merovingian king, as it is connected with succession, was obviously derived from the settlement of a kindred." More recently see, for example: Walter Schlesinger, "Lord and Follower," p. 76; J. Balon, *Traité de droit salique: Étude d'exégèse et de sociologie juridiques*, Ius Medii Aevi, 3 (Namur, 1965), 2: 569, where the *vicini* of the *Edictum* are regarded as *proximi* and members of a "groupe clanique," and *Les Fondements du régime foncier au moyen âge depuis la chute de l'empire romain en Occident: Étude de dogmatique et d'histoire du droit*, Anciens Pays et Assemblées d'États, 7 (Louvain, 1954), p. 23; Ourliac and Malafosse, *Histoire du droit privé*, 2: 130, 132, 134.

[2] Dopsch, *Economic and Social Foundations*, pp. 148-149: translated from the German 2nd ed. published in 1923-1924; the 1st ed. was published in 1918. For a recent, non-traditional interpretation see Staab, *Untersuchungen*, pp. 257 ff. See also nn. 4 and 5.

[3] Ibid. "The edict is actually concerned with land belonging to seigneurial estates and not with free mark-associations ..." (p. 149).

[4] An interesting explanation of *De migrantibus* similarly based on tax considerations was given by F. Thibault ("Observations sur le titre 'De migrantibus' de la loi salique," *Revue Historique de Droit Français et Étranger* 45 [1921] 448-458) a short time after the appearance of the first edition of Dopsch's book. According to Thibault, *De migrantibus* was intended to combat fraud whereby a tax-exempt Frank settled land of a Gallo-Roman on conditions advantageous to both. The other *vicini* were given the right to reject the fraudulent settler because the taxes on the now exempt land would be shifted on to them. See note 5, below, for imperial constitutions seeking to check this kind of abuse. The Salic vicinage rights as a whole are, I think, more broadly based.

Also of interest is an interpretation by J. J. Rabinowitz, "The Title *De Migrantibus* of the *Lex Salica* and the Jewish *Herem Hayishub*," *Speculum* 22 (1947) 46-50. According to him a virtually identical provision existed among the Jews of Germany and France in the Middle Ages for barring the settlement of a stranger in the community. His suggestion that the Salic rule was the direct result of Jewish law and was designed for only a small group of the population in order that Jewish merchants might limit competition is without foundation. Rights of exclusion are not peculiarly Jewish, just as they are not peculiarly Germanic. See nn. 5 and 30, below.

be similarly explained by ἐπιβολή.[5] Despite a lack of response to his suggestion[6] Dopsch was undoubtedly correct in recognizing that the clues

[5] Although Dopsch cites no texts illustrating a *Vicinenerbrecht* in late Antiquity, he does refer to some imperial provisions cited by Zachariä v. Lingenthal (*Geschichte des griechisch-romanischen Rechts*, 3rd ed. [Wurttemburg, 1955], pp. 236 ff.) to explain the veto power of the *vicini* found in *De migrantibus*. The pertinent passages are as follows.

Referring to an old law, probably of Constantine, abolished in 391: "Dudum proximis consortibusque concessum erat ut extraneos ab emptione removerent neque homines suo arbitratu vendenda distraherent." (CT 3.1.6; see Pharr, *The Theodosian Code* [Princeton, 1952], p. 64, nn. 15, 16; Zachariä v. Lingenthal, *Geschichte*, pp. 237-238.) *Interpretatio*, LRV: "Prior ordinatio legis fuerit ut, si unus ex consortibus pro quacunque necessitate rem vendere voluisset, extraneus emendi licentiam non haberet." This refers only to a preferential right of purchase to property held in common, or undivided, which is now abolished. K. S. Bader, *Dorfgenossenschaft und Dorfgemeinde* (Weimar, 1962), pp. 135-136, suggests the *Interpretatio* was the direct model for the Salic redactor of *De migrantibus*, who adapted it to Frankish circumstances by changing the prohibition against sale to one against donations to outsiders. The adaptation, if such it was, goes well beyond this since the provision of the CT and LRV explicitly abolishes the old law against sale to outsiders. The late imperial context of *De migrantibus* is far more general than a specific text of Roman law. What is more to the point is that the CT shows there need be nothing peculiarly 'Germanic' about the Salic provision. Cf. also n. 30, below.

CT 11.24.6 (*De patrociniis vicorum*) a. 415: "Metrocomiae vero in publico iure et integro perdurabunt, nec quisquam eas vel aliquid in his possidere temptaverit nisi qui ante consulatum praefinitum coeperit procul dubio possidere, exceptis convicanis, quibus pensitanda pro fortunae conditione negare non possunt."

CJ 11.56 a. 468: "In illis quae metrocomiae communi vocabulo nuncupantur, hoc adiciendum necessario nostra putavit humanitas ut nulli extraneo illic quoquo modo possidendi licentia tribuatur: sed si quis ex isdem vicanis loca sui iuris alienare voluerit, non licere ei nisi ad habitatorem adscriptum eidem metrocomiae per qualemcumque contractum terrarum suarum dominium possessionemque transferre."

These last two laws ably illustrate the nature of the legal ties and mutual rights that could bind *vicani* together. The aim of, and the conditions giving rise to, the above provisions are quite different from the situation prevailing in the Salic laws and the other imperial constitutions quoted below. The above are not encouraging the *vicani* of free villages to refuse legitimate settlers, for usually quite the opposite was the intent of the government. Rather, they are seeking to stop patronage, that is, the buying up or acquisition by other means, particularly in Egypt, of the freehold *metrocomiae* by powerful landowners and officials: lands so acquired and their cultivators would then be protected from government taxation. Cf. CJ 11.54.2: "Nequis vicanis patrocinium polliceatur neve agricolas suscipiat redituum promissionem vel aliud lucrum pro eo accipiens" (the original is in Greek; the Latin is that of the Kreuger ed.). See also A. H. M. Jones, *The Later Roman Empire, 284-602: A Social, Economic, and Administrative Survey* (1964; rpt. Oxford, 1973), 2: 776.

[6] As far as I can tell, it is not that his conclusions are explicitly gainsaid, but that they are passed over. See, for instance, the work of Beyerle and Buchner, cited below, n. 38, and Schlesinger, Balon, Ourliac and Malafosse, above, n. 1. The list could go on. A typical account is that of R. Koebner ("The Settlement and Colonization of Europe," in the *Cambridge Economic History*, edd. J. H. Clapham and E. Power [Cambridge, 1941, unchanged in 2nd ed., 1966]), where, however, there is no trace of the clan: "The *Pactus Legis Salicae* ... in its *Titulus de Migrantibus* (45) pictures a vivid scene from the times of

for understanding the *vicini* and the vicinage rights of Frankish law lay in late Roman social and fiscal organization. When in the course of the following pages the imperial constitutions regulating ἐπιβολή and the acquisition of *agri deserti* are looked at, it should be clear that the ancestry of the *Edictum Chilperici* and the Salic provisions concerning the *vicini* and *migrantes* do not lead back to Germanic custom but to conditions prevalent in late Antiquity. Not hypothetical clans, nor primitive communal associations, but the kinds of ideas found in the policies of the later Emperors for settling veterans, federates, and others, on vacant private and public lands, and for regulating the rights and obligations of vicinage groups for fiscal purposes, most readily explain the peculiar features of the Frankish laws. These imperial constitutions once and for all remove the Frankish *vicini* from the hypothesis of the Germanic clan; they also shed some light on the dark question of the nature of the Frankish settlement of Gaul, and the principles behind it, and necessitate a reevaluation of the importance of the *Edictum* for understanding Frankish inheritance.

We are able to get some idea of those aspects of imperial rural organization which pertain to the rights of *vicini* largely because of the concern of the later emperors about vacant and ownerless lands and farms (*vacantes terrae, agri deserti*).[7] Such lands, whether private or part of the

---

the wandering in which the 'Tacitean' village springs to life. ... The wording makes it clear that we are not dealing with a big village community. ... We found the free German proprietors scattered over the land in just such groups in Tacitus' time. ... The grouping was now reproduced by the Franks on Roman soil" (p. 34). Cf. the remarks of Latouche (*The Birth of Western Economy*, p. 79), who, while denying the foundations of *De migrantibus* in primitive Germanic communism, nevertheless passes over the imperial antecedents: "In an age when rural law and order were still rudimentary, villagers had to take matters into their own hands, and the arrival of a stranger was inevitably a source of anxiety. For further proof of this we have only to glance through the numerous clauses in barbarian laws devoted to the suppression of theft, assault and battery, and homicide. The lawmakers thought it wise to give villagers some means of defence against the intrusion of suspicious strangers." No doubt the rights of the *vicini* served this purpose, but the basis of their rights is not Frankish criminal law; moreover, this explanation makes little sense of the *Edict of Chilperic*.

Recently in Germany the reevaluation of Bader (see n. 5) has occasioned interest and some support. Cf. Staab, *Untersuchungen*, pp. 254 ff., and Ruth Schmidt-Wiegand, "Die volkssprachigen Wörter der Leges barbarorum," *Frühmittelalterliche Studien* 13 (1979) 61.

[7] On which, generally, see Jones, *Later Roman Empire*, 2: 812-823 and the texts given there. *Deserti* need not be uninhabited, but rather lacked *domini*; see W. Goffart, *Caput and Colonate: Towards a History of Late Roman Taxation* (Toronto, 1974), p. 67, n. 4: " 'deserted' was the legal term for land whose owner or registered taxpayer could not be located."

imperial estates, were incapable of producing revenue either by way of public taxes and services or by rents. If these difficulties are inherent in any system of taxation based on land, the situation was doubtless exacerbated by an oppressive tax system which forced small proprietors to insolvency or rendered the returns minimal for many lands, and in affected areas, by the results of unrest and military incursions. In order to render these properties productive, or to continue to exact the taxes and rents formerly owed from them, the later emperors resorted to two main methods. If the old owners could not be located and forced to take over their responsibilities, new owners were sought to take up the estates, frequently with offers of temporary remissions of taxes and of various immunities. An obvious source of new landholders was veterans, and consequently we find a number of constitutions seeking to encourage them to take over abandoned farms, with the added enticements of initial capital and immunities.[8]

The second major expedient was to require neighbouring landholders, generally members of the same fiscal unit, to take over the abandoned land and its tax liability (ἐπιβολή, *adiectio sterilium*).[9] In Justinian's time we find ἐπιβολή applied to two different categories of property, although the precise principles of apportionment proper to each are a little unclear, particularly before the sixth century. Ὁμόδουλα were properties which at one time had belonged to, or constituted, one great domain. This collection of individual estates continued to be regarded as one fiscal unit for purposes of taxation. Abandoned property was liable to be assigned to the owner or owners of property which had once been a part of the abandoned land. Ὁμόκηνσα were individual properties which had never

---

[8] CT 7.20.3 a. 320: "Veterani iuxta nostrum praeceptum vacantes terras accipiant easque perpetuo habeant immunes."

CT 7.20.8 a. 364: "Omnibus benemeritis veteranis quam volunt patriam damus et imunitatem perpetuam pollicemur. Habeant ex vacantibus sive ex diversis ubi eligerint agros ... amplius addentes, ut etiam ad culturam eorundem agrorum et animalia et semina praebeamus .... Si quos etiam veterani servulos familiasve ad agrum duxerint, immunes perpetuo possideant"; cf. *Ro.* 177, below, Ch. 5, n. 19.

CT 5.11.7 a. 365: "... < em > eritis veteranis vel gentibus dividamus ...," evidently in reference to ownerless or deserted lands.

CT 7.20.11 a. 370: "Conmoneat tua sinceritas hac sanctione veteranos ut loca absentium squalida et situ dissimulationis horrentia de solida fructum indemnitate securi ... exerceant."

[9] On what follows see Jones, *Later Roman Empire*, 2: 814-815; J. B. Bury, *History of the Later Roman Empire from the Death of Theodosius I to the Death of Justinian* (1899; rpt., New York, 1958), 2: 444-445. For a discussion of the pertinent literature, see P. Charanis, "On the Social Structure of the Later Roman Empire," *Byzantion* 17 (1944-1945) 44-45 and n. 25.

formed a single domain. Etymologically the word refers to properties on the same census list. These too formed a single fiscal unit, and abandoned lands were assigned to neighbouring proprietors, following, it seems, some principle of proximity. It is not surprising that within these groups of *convicani* and *vicini* – the word is found in CT 13.11.13[10] – a sometimes complicated network of mutual rights and obligations was recognized as regards the lands which formed the fiscal unit of the large estate or the territorial group inscribed in the census.

This system of rights and obligations remained a factor in Roman rural organization to the time of Justinian and beyond, that is, well into the period of the Frankish occupation of Gaul; and we know now that in the east ἐπιβολή continued to be practised long after the sixth century.[11] In Gaul it is fair to assume not only that the problems of rendering unproductive land productive did not go away with the coming of the Franks but that, despite the influx of new cultivators, the troubles of the fifth and sixth centuries could only have aggravated the situation. That elements of the old imperial system would have been maintained by the Frankish kings seems likely even if no other evidence were available to us, but seems especially so when we consider that these same kings made an effort to preserve the imperial legacy of taxation.[12] What the *Pactus Legis Salicae* and the *Edictum Chilperici* show is that, whether or not ἐπιβολή was a vital element of the public law, the complex of mutual rights and obligations among neighbouring property-holders which are revealed in the imperial legislation on ownerless and abandoned lands persisted after the Frankish occupation.

I

LS 45, *De migrantibus*,[13] considers the case of an individual's settling upon a *villa* already occupied, in part at least, by other landholders.

---

[10] Considered below, p. 81.

[11] At least to the eleventh century. The old view of Monnier that ἐπιβολή was abolished by Tiberius (578-582) has proved to be wrong. Some of the literature on the question is given by Charanis, "Social structure," p. 45, n. 25; see also J. Karayannopulos, "Die kollektive Steuerverantwortung in der frühbyzantinischen Zeit," in *Vierteljahrschrift für Sozial- und Wirtschaftsgeschichte* 43 (1956) 289-322.

[12] For the texts showing the continuation of the Roman tax system, see E. Chenon, *Histoire générale du droit français public et privé des origines à 1815* (Paris, 1926-1929), 1: 298 ff. and Dopsch, *Economic and Social Foundations*, pp. 306-307, 237 and esp. 377-378.

[13] The nature and editions of the compilation are discussed extensively below in ch. 8. A brief note should serve for the following discussion: Eckhardt refers to the editor of the

Si quis super alterum in villa migrare uoluerit si unus uel aliqui de ipsis qui
in villa consistunt eum suscipere uoluerit si uel unus exteterit qui
contradicat, migranti ibidem licentiam non habebit

If anyone wishes to settle upon another's [property] in a *villa* and one or
any number of those who reside in the *villa* wish to accept him, he shall not
have the leave to settle there if there is even one resident who objects[14]

If the new settler persists and remains, then in an established procedure
the *vicinus* who objects must make formal complaint with witnesses every
ten days over a period of thirty days, calling upon the *migrans* to vacate
within the ten day period. The resident may then summon him to court,
and, if he fails to show, have the *migrans* expelled by the local count. If
such a recourse is required the settler must not only lose the fruits of his
labour but also undergo a thirty *solidi* penalty.[15]

Si uero quis migrauerit et infra xii menses nullus testatus fuerit, securus
sicut et alii vicini maneat.

But if anyone has settled and within twelve months no one has opposed
him, let him remain as secure as the other residents.

For our purposes there are a number of notable features to this law.
Firstly, a settler from outside (*migrans*) has come and attempted to take up
residence in the *villa*. *Migrare* in the language of the period can mean
simply *ambulare*, but in the legal literature it contains two related ideas:
that of leaving a place, and that of establishing oneself in another. It is the

---

recent critical edition of the MGH; Hessels to the editor of the old standard edition. The
accepted date of the A redaction is 507-511, although it just as likely dates from up to a
few decades later; C is dated at some point later, though probably still Merovingian; D is
early Carolingian, though perhaps earlier; K is Carolingian.

[14] The text followed is that of A1. There is little variation among the other codd.

[15] "Si uero contra interdicto unius uel duorum in uilla ipsa adsedere praesumpserit,
tunc ei testare debet. Et si noluerit inde exire, ille qui testat cum testibus sic ei debet testare.
Hic tibi testo in hac nocte proxima in hoc quod lex saliga habet sedeas et testo tibi ut in x
noctes de uilla ipsa egredere debeas. Postea adhuc post decem noctes iterum ueniat ad
ipsum et ei testet ut iterum in decem noctes exeat. Si adhuc noluerit exire item tertio
decem noctis ad placitum suum addatur ut sic xxx noctes impleatur. Si nec tunc uoluerit
exire tunc maniat eum ad mallum et testes super singula placita qui fuerunt ibi praestos
habeat. Si ipse cui testatum est noluerit inde exire et eum aliqua sunnis non tenuerit et ista
omnia quae superius diximus secundum legem est testatus. Et tunc ipse qui testauit super
furtuna sua ponat et roget grafionem ut accedat ad locum ut eum inde expellat. Et quia
legem noluit audire quod ibi laborauit demittat et insuper mal. vui drisittolo hoc est IMCC
din. qui f. sol. xxx culp. iudic." The only emendation is that, in conformity with A2, "est"
which comes between *lex* and *saliga* in line 3 has been omitted. This section of the
passage is found only in A1 and A2. The C redaction adds a provision fining whoever
invited the *migrans* before agreement had been reached among the *vicini*.

latter idea which predominates, and so *migrare* can best be translated as
"to establish oneself" or "to settle in some place."[16]

Secondly, the settlement of the newcomer takes place *in villa*. This term
has been variously interpreted as 'village' or as 'domain,' 'estate.'[17] In the
context of LS 45 there is no need to choose. As an estate, the *villa*,
elsewhere sometimes called a *fundus*, was a unit, often bearing a single
name; it could be owned or held by one individual, but frequently it was
divided among several who might hold farms of varying sizes.[18] These
might be owned outright or be holdings on leases of various kinds, some
conferring virtual ownership. As we have noted, in late Antiquity and on
through the Byzantine period these estates composed of a number of
smaller estates or farms and the *vicini* who held them were regarded more
or less as a unit for fiscal purposes. Thus it makes no difference whether
villa is understood as 'village' or 'estate' – that is in the sense of a domain
held by a number of owners. In LS 45 *villa* is the legal abstraction denoting
a large unit supporting a number of landlords.

Thirdly, the settlement takes place on properties within the *villa*;
specifically *super alterum*. Again this term has been variously understood.
Probably it means 'upon the land or holding of another';[19] but it may

---

[16] See the discussion and texts given by N. D. Fustel de Coulanges, "Recherches sur
quelques points des lois barbares," in *Nouvelles recherches sur quelques problèmes
d'histoire* (Paris, 1891), pp. 340-341.

[17] In the latter sense by Fustel, "Recherches," pp. 341 ff. Cf. Bader, *Dorfgenossenschaft*, p. 133.

[18] Fustel, pp. 341 ff. See also ch. 6, n. 5, below; cf. the *participes villae* in HF 7.47.

[19] Stephenson, "Common Man," p. 434: "upon the land of another." The view (see J.
M. Pardessus, *Loi salique* [Paris, 1843], p. 389) that *super alterum* = *contra voluntatem
alterius, nolente alio* was undermined by Fustel ("Recherches," pp. 342 ff.). Aside from
the fact that the phrase is never found elsewhere with the meaning attributed to it by
Pardessus and others, a number of texts clearly indicate the meaning given above. Cf. LS
66 and, in particular, LS 47: "Si quis seruum aut caballum uel bouem aut qualibet rem
super alterum agnouerit" (A1); in other codd. *super* is replaced by *cum, apud*.

Fustel, however, mistakenly suggested that *super alterum in villa* simply equals *in
villam alienam*, meaning that *super alterum* refers to the proprietor of the *villa*. Among all
the manuscripts only A4 has: "Si quis alienam uillam migrare uoluerit," but this was not
part of the original redaction and is the result of interpretation or contamination. Cf. LS
14.6; the addition in the C redaction of LS 45.3; and the D and K redactions of LS 45. At
any rate *alienus* can mean not only 'another's' but also 'that which is not one's own,' or
'that to which one does not belong,' 'foreign.'

Fustel also put too much stock in the capitulary of Louis the Pious which emended
the Salic provision. "De eo qui villam alterius occupaverit. De hoc capitulo iudicaverunt,
ut nullus villam aut res alterius migrandi gratia per annos tenere vel possidere possit; sed
in quacumque die invasor illarum rerum interpellatus fuerit, aut easdem res quaerenti
reddat aut eas, si potest, iuxta legem se defendendo sibi vindicet" (Boretius no. 142, c. 9,
p. 293). The opinion is general that this is a poor guide to the meaning of the original Salic
provision. The capitularies of Louis emending the old Salic law were called into being not

simply strengthen *migrare* in order to emphasize the meaning 'leave one's own place and settle, or take up residence, in another.'[20] Nevertheless, the gist of the provision is clear: an outsider is relocating in the *villa* and taking up a holding, that is, he is attempting to join the ranks of the landlords within the *villa* ("securus sicut et alii vicini"). This suggests that he is taking up vacant land, possibly undeveloped waste shared by the *vicini*, but also more likely properties abandoned by their owners, who perhaps have fled, given up cultivation, or on whose decease no heirs could be found. Certainly in the case of the *migrans* with the *preceptum*, as Stephenson noted,[21] we are dealing with a person who is interested in the portion of a *villa* which still has buildings, slaves, and *coloni*. Roman and Byzantine law did not regard the farms as ownerless because of their abandonment, for the obligation to pay rents or taxes still pertained to the real owners if they could be found.[22] If failure to induce the owners to return occurred then the lands might be added to the assessment of neighbours or the other residents of the estate (*vicini*) or given over to strangers willing to take over the cultivation and burdens (*peregrini volentes*).[23] suitably protected after a period of time.

Fourthly, the settler takes the land normally with both the consent and approval of the *vicini*. If one objects, however, he can be removed. This has always been the most curious feature of the law and the one which lent credence to ideas of mark associations and kin groups. But if instead of looking to the hypothetical agricultural arrangements of the early Germans, we once again consider this characteristic in terms of late

---

because the ancient law in its entirety was still valid or because it was even understood in anything near the same terms as the early sixth-century redactors intended, but because the proliferation of manuscripts at this period had made it a novel, disputatious, and poorly understood addition to the common law. An echo of *De migrantibus* can perhaps be found in a later ninth-century fragment of Frankish law in Italy: "Non potest homo migrare nisi convicinia et herbam et via... (text breaks off)" (*Extrav.* B, 11; Hessels, 421). This may have been intended as an interpretation or revision of *De migrantibus*, or may have nothing to do with it at all. Cf. Bader, *Dorfgenossenschaft*, p. 137.

There are two distinct ideas in *De migrantibus*. (1) The settlement is made on the property of another which constituted part of the *villa* as a whole. (2) The *migrans* is a stranger to the *villa* – a *peregrinus volens* or *alienus* of Roman law – that is, he is not one of the *vicini*.

[20] Cf. *alibi peregrinare*, below, n. 39.

[21] "Common Man," p. 437.

[22] CJ 11.59.11, a. 400: "Locorum domini intra sex menses edictis vocati revertantur. qui si adfuerint et propria teneant et ea quae ex praeterito contraxerint debita redhibere cogantur." See also CT 5.11.11; 5.11.12; 13.11.13.

[23] CT 13.11.13. This important text will be considered further below.

Roman legislation, it is clear that we are dealing simply with the commonality of late Antiquity.

Many problems could arise when either an outsider or a neighbouring
landholder occupied vacant land, since the various interests of individuals,
vicinage fiscal units, and the state apparatus, were involved. For instance,
after the settler had brought the land into cultivation, the old owner might
return and claim his land and the crop on it, or a rent for its use
(*agraticum*). A constitution of Valentinian and Valens (a. 370) indicates
that this was sometimes a deliberate ploy, and takes care to protect
veterans in particular from "those who customarily lie in wait for the
harvest time."[24] Efforts were made to recall the former owners before
others were given properties "de iure dominii et perpetuitate securus."[25]
In 391 the period in which the old owners could claim was set at two
years, and compensation had to be made to the settler who had taken up
the farm.[26] This was reduced in 400 to six months.[27]

When deserted land was to be taken up, preference was given to
neighbouring land owners. The general nature and extent of this right
as against *peregrini* comes out in a constitution of 386 concerning
patrimonial, that is, imperial *fundi*, which bears directly upon *De migrantibus*. Clearly the state preferred that if someone wished to take up
deserta he do so in his own district; this helped to ensure that bad fields
were taken with good, and that the responsibilities of the landholder could
be kept track of more easily, since his estate would be contiguous or at
least in the same census district. According to the law a person must take
special care to take lands which are neighbouring to his own (*vicinae
possessiones*) and in the same territory (*in eodem territorio*). In this
circumstances he would receive protection against any objection to his
acquisition. If no such land was available, he might take property
elsewhere, once again taking care that the lands as much as possible were
contiguous. But here a problem arose, for now the rights of the
neighbours of the deserted property located in another district must be
confronted:

> [possessiones] pro modo et aequitate suscipiat ut consensu omnium fiat
> quod omnibus profuturum est.

---

[24] "... nihilque illis qui messium tempus adsolent aucupari agratici nomine deferatur"
(CT 7.20.11).
[25] CT 5.11.11. See also n. 22, above.
[26] CT 5.11.12.
[27] CJ 11.59.11.

Let him take up such lands with moderation and equity so that what is to the benefit of all is done with the consent of all.[28]

Consensus omnium expresses succinctly the principle at work in *De migrantibus*,[29] and it is not really surprising when we consider the responsibilities of the various rural groupings, their treatment by the late Roman state and their absolute necessity for the maintenance of the imperial tax structure.

Although most of the precise internal arrangements for the allocation of vacant lands and the exact rights of the vicinage groups, however defined, whether territorially by their enrollment on the census or by their possession of a once homogeneous estate, remain largely outside the purview of the imperial constitutions, a number of features are clear: that the deserted fields were still considered to have an owner whom efforts were made to recall and compel to pay his taxes; after a period variously defined he lost any claim to his property; that, since the primary liability for taxes fell on the vicinage members if the owner failed to show up, the initial right to claim the land also pertained to them; and that, at least on the imperial estates, this preference was expressed through a *consensus* of the *vicini*, which was needed to permit a stranger to take up vacant land. Presumably the *vicini*'s preferential right, like that of the original owner, must have had to be exercised within a stipulated time; in *De migrantibus* after twelve months the *migrans* became a secure resident of the vicinage

---

[28] CT 5.14.30 = CJ 11.59.7 a. 386: "Quicumque defectum fundum patrimonialem exercuerit instruxerit fertilem idoneumque praestiterit salvo patrimoniali canone perpetuo ac privato iure defendat velut domesticum et avita successione quaesitum sibi habeat, suis relinquat... Nemo tamen qualibet meriti et potestatis obiectione submoveatur quominus ad dicatochiae vicem defectas possessiones patrimonialis iuris accipiat earum tributa et canonem soluturus: illud speciali observantia procurans ut primum vicinas et in eodem territorio sortiatur; dehinc si neque finitimas neque in iisdem locis reppererit constitutas tunc demum etiam longius positas sed in quantum fieri valet pro interiecto spatio sibimet cohaerentes pro modo et aequitate suscipiat ut consensu omnium fiat quod omnibus profuturum est." Cf. CJ 11.56, n. 5, above.

[29] This idea of *consensus* and *consensus omnium* appears a number of times in the imperial constitutions in reference to the various associations. Some examples: 1. A breadmaker once assigned to the guild shall not be granted the opportunity to withdraw "etiamsi ad absolutionem eius pistorum omnium laboret adsensus, et consensus convenisse videatur" (CT 14.3.8); 2. breadmakers shall not be allowed to change status by marriage even with the *adsensus omnium pistorum* (CT 14.3.14); 3. curials who have become clerics can keep their property, provided they are sincere and "adsistente curia ac sub obtutibus iudicis promente consensum ... maxime si totius populi vocibus expetetur" (CT 12.1.49); 4. exemptions granted by the *consensus civium* are not to be valid (CT 12.1.17); 5. apparitors shall be allowed to transfer themselves to the clerical state as long as they have fulfilled their duties and "sub notione iudicum, officiis consentientibus" (CT 8.4.7).

fiscal unit: "securus sicut et alii vicini." In this overall context there can hardly be doubt that the Salic provision reflects the same conditions which are perceptible in the late Empire and continued long afterwards in the east. That there was some Frankish adaptation of imperial precedents is not unlikely. It is because of the burden of ἐπιβολή that the rights and obligations of the vicinage groups surface in the imperial constitutions; what should be emphasized in the Frankish case is the continuing concern of the state to maintain the integrity of the rural units and, ultimately, its own resources.[30]

The associational aspect which is so often considered a feature, sometimes a peculiar feature, of Germanic law, was a central characteristic of late Roman social organization and can be found not merely among the rural and food-producing population but also among soldiers, traders, tradesmen, state officials, and city councillors (*curiales*). The state sought to protect them by excluding those who would destroy their public functions,[31] and by making these functions hereditary. It also sought to ensure the performance of public duties by making them the joint responsibility of the group's members. Joint responsibility also meant that a network of rights peculiar to the group operated among its members – preferential rights to property for instance and even, as we shall see, inheritance rights to the estate of a member. Moreover, since the public functions depended not simply upon the number of members but upon the resources of the unit, the preferential right, which however had to be exercised within a given time, was readily recognized as the power of excluding newcomers. The *vicini* of *Lex Salica*, responsible for rents or tax, or whatever other burdens pertained to them,[32] therefore had the right as a group to accept or reject newcomers who wished to enter the *villa* and join their ranks as landlords.[33]

[30] Cf. remarks of Ernst Levy, *West Roman Vulgar Law: The Law of Property* (Philadelphia, 1951), p. 119. He regards the rigorous exclusion of outsiders from the village communities as being prompted by an attempt to compensate them for the imposition of ἐπιβολή and *peraequatio*, yet also considers that the right of preemption may have had its origins in local usages unfamiliar with these institutions. This is worth noting for the late Roman state may have been forced to recognize provincial practices which it would earlier have suppressed (cf. cj 4.52.3). Quite apart from ἐπιβολή authorities of one kind or another may also have recognized that the protection of rural resources could be furthered by supporting local claims of neighbourhood. See also LB 84.2.

[31] See above, n. 5.

[32] Cf. LB 38.4.5, where the landlords of a *villa* are jointly responsible for providing fodder and for compensating one of their fellows who had to expend hospitality on a foreign legate.

[33] One might question whether the *vicini* need only be seen in terms of public law since the Salic provisions may be regulating the possessors of patrimonial or public

Once this context of *De migrantibus* is understood, the other Salic provisions (LS 14.5,6) concerning *migrantes* fall into place. These fix penalties for anyone attacking or opposing the settlement of a *migrans* with the royal *preceptum* if he has shown his authorization in the public *mallus*.[34] The last is interesting since it shows that there were two different classes of settler: the simple *migrans* who on his own, or at the invitation of the énhabitants of a *villa*, undertook to take up vacant private or public lands, and thus as *De migrantibus* reveals, was subject to the approval of the local *vicini*; and the settler who arrived with special authorization from the king and whose right to take up properties no one could dispute. By this series of laws on *migrantes* and *vicini* the Frankish kings, following procedures already recognized by their imperial antecedents, sought to accomodate the continuing settlement and relocation of Franks (and probably non-Franks) and to protect, at the same time, the rights and resources of the vicinage groups.

II

In the *Edict* of King Chilperic there occurs reference to the rights of the *vicini* in the case where a fellow *vicinus* had died. The text of the *Edict*,

---

estates. It will be noted that the *consensus* of neighbouring landholders in Roman law is found in a constitution concerning holders of imperial *fundi*. Dopsch cast the *vicini* in a seigneurial context, though 'seigneurial' is a term describing a level of the social scale below the landlords of portions of *villae* in *Lex Salica*, or their counterparts in the Burgundian law, both Roman and Burgundian, who possess their own slaves and *coloni* (LB 38.4-11).

[34] LS 14.4 (A1): "Si quis hominem qui migrare uoluerit et de rege habuerit preceptum et abbundiuit in malum puplico et aliquis contra ordinationem regis testare praesumpserit, VIIIM din. qui f. sol. CC culp. iud."

LS 14.5 (A1): "Si quis hominem migrante adsalierit quanti in contubernio uel superuentum, mal. texaga hoc est, IIMD din. f. sol. LXIII culp. iudc." The other codd. which contain the provision (with the exception of A3) give a 200s. penalty, which is adopted by Eckhardt in his reconstructed text. This may very well be right. Yet A3 also prescribes a 63s. penalty, which Eckhardt regards as a result of conflation with the following provision concerning attacks on a *villa*, although an abbreviated text is often characteristic of A3. 14.5 is also one of the "fliegende Satzungen" which may have started as a gloss (see p. 125, below) variously incorporated in the text. If the *migrans* of 14.5 was thought to be the simple settler without the royal *preceptum* 63s. may be a likely penalty since this is the sum imposed on each despoiler of a freeman (14.1, 2), or attacker of a *villa* (14.6). The 200s. penalty levelled against the individual in 14.4 who objected to the settlement is appropriate since the objection is made against the *ordinatio regis*.

which has only barely managed survival and transmission, is in bad shape and, in parts, probably fragmentary.[35] C. 3 reads:

> Simili modo placuit atque conuenit ut si quicumque uicinos habens aut filios aut filias post obitum suum superstitutus fuerit, quamdiu filii aduixerint terra habeant sicut et lex salica habet. et si subito filii defuncti fuerit, filia simili modo accipiat terras ipsas sicut et filii si uiui fuissent aut
> 5 habuissent.
>
> Et si moritur frater, alter superstitutus fuerit, frater terras accipiat, non uicini. et subito frater moriens, frater non delinquerit superstitem, tunc soror ad terra ipsa accedat possidenda.

Despite a number of syntactical difficulties, the tenor of the law is clear enough:

> Likewise it is resolved and agreed that if either sons or daughters survive anyone who has *vicini*, let the sons have the land for as long as they live as is Salic law. And if unexpectedly the sons have died, in the same way, let the daughter take those lands just like the sons if they had lived and possessed them.
>
> And if a man dies and another brother survives him, let the brother take the lands, not the *vicini*. And if he dies, and does not leave a brother to survive him, then let the sister accede to the possession of the land.[36]

---

[35] It survives only in one manuscript of the later Carolingian redaction of *Lex Salica* (K17). A1 lists it in the table of contents but it is not to be found in the text. Generally, see F. Beyerle, "Das legislative Werk Chilperichs I," ZRG GA 78 (1961) 1-38. It is printed there with commentary and suggestions for reconstructions, and can be found also, among other places, in Eckhardt, and Boretius. For a clear and accurate understanding of the state of the text in manuscript Hessels' edition must be consulted (numbered as LS 78).

[36] Although the manuscript does not set the provision off from the preceding law with a new paragraph at *Simili modo* (line 1), new paragraphs are indicated at *et* (line 3) and *et* (line 6).

si quicumque, line 1: the manuscript reads *sicumque*; the emendation adopted here is the usual one but Beyerle ("Das leg. Werk," p. 5) suggests *cuicumque*, which is also possible.

advixerint, line 3: unaccountably Beyerle emends this by dropping the *ad*, and wonders perhaps if it should be read *adhuc vixerint*. The word is perfectly good as it stands however: see, e.g., Lewis and Short, s.v., 2, which gives the meaning: 'to live on', 'continue to live', citing examples from the *Vulgate* and the *Digest*. For examples in the *formulae* see the index, s.v., of Zeumer's edition.

aut, line 4: I have tried to render some sense into this above. Hessels notes the word is superfluous and Beyerle and Eckhardt drop it, which may be advisable. Beyerle suggests that *antehabere* = prefer makes good sense (p. 12) but this is exceedingly rare.

frater[1], line 6: following Beyerle and Geffcken, I have placed the comma after *frater*, not before as is usual: literally, "If a brother dies and another brother survives...." The comma, though, is unimportant. The paragraph now concerns collateral inheritance.

possidenda, line 8: immediately following this word, without a break in the text, as if part of the preceding sentence, we find: "det illi uero conuenit singula de terras istas qui si adueniunt ut leodis qui patri nostro fuerunt consuaetudinem quam habuerunt de hac re

At first glance it may seem curious that the *vicini* would be mentioned in a regulation ostensibly concerned only with inheritance. Yet in considering the role of neighbours in the fiscal arrangements of late Roman law it is apparent that as soon as an estate became vacant for whatever reason – though the death of the proprietor or though abandonment – the *vicini* might be made liable for the burdens devolving from the land, or alternately, if the estate was worth it, might claim the property on the basis of their preferential right of vicinage. The sequence for this imposition and preferential right was, first, the heirs, then the *vicini*, and finally a willing and financially capable outsider. This comes out plainly in a constitution given at Ravenna in 412, which also succinctly illustrates a number of the connections which we have already made between late imperial and Frankish practice in regard to *deserta*. In districts (*loca*) which cannot meet their tax payment an adjustment and equalization of assessment is ordered:

> Et primo quidem veteribus dominis adscribi praedia ipsa conveniet; quorum si personae eorumve heredes non potuerint repperiri, vicinos vel peregrinos volentes, modo ut sint idonei, dominos statuendos esse censemus.

> First, let the estates be assigned to the old owners; if their persons or their heirs cannot be found, we decree that the *vicini* or willing outsiders must be established as proprietors, provided they are solvent.[37]

What we have in Chilperic's *Edict* is simply a provision that the preferential right of the *vicini* should not usurp that of the statutory heirs; put another way, that the heirs must take up the land and its burden before the *vicini* – one's perspective depends upon whether the property and its liability are worth it. That the *Edict* has not been seen this way is the result of the neglect shown its imperial antecedents, and of its association with Germanic custom; it is due also to the role the *Edict* has traditionally played in the exposition of Frankish inheritance. In considering this further we can get a better idea of the context of Chilperic's legislation and what it has to tell us about the Frankish inheritance sequence.

---

intra se debeant." This is always considered to be a new chapter. Kern's suggestion (for which see Hessels) that *det illi = De tilli, tilli* being the same as O. Fris. *tilathe, acquisitio* has generally been followed; it is thought, then, that a distinction is being made between patrimonial estates and acquisitions. For an attempt to make some sense of this passage, see Hessels. Beyerle prints the passage not as a unit but as a series of words and phrases followed by lacunae.

[37] CT 13.11.13.

To the present, four ideas have formed the accepted interpretation of the *Edict*:[38] (1) that the *Edictum Chilperici* principally concerns inheritance, in particular the reformation of the old law; (2) that it constitutes an abrogation of the rights of the *vicini*; (3) that the emendation pertains to the rules found in ls 59; and (4) that the innovation of Chilperic for the first time preferred daughters, brothers, and sisters, over the *vicini*, and constituted the first recognition of women to inherit *terra*.

That the *Edict* concerns inheritance is obvious enough. But, we should not imagine from this that it must be innovative and that the innovation touches upon the sequence of the heirs. The provision is not concerned with Frankish inheritance as a whole but only with succession to members of a vicinage unit (*quicumque vicinos habens*). Curtailing abuse of the inheritance sequence within vicinage groups is sufficient to explain mention of the *vicini* alongside the other heirs; indeed, all the emphasis of the provision concerns the *vicini*. When we have come across the *vicini* elsewhere in Roman or Frankish law the context has been the maintenance or augmentation of the rural unit so that its ability to produce revenue was increased or, at least, not diminished. Ultimately this too is the purpose of the *Edict*. I would suggest also that its association with King Chilperic, called the Herod of his time by Gregory of Tours, points to a specific context for the provision. A good deal of Chilperic's bad reputation comes from the severity of his tax measures. According to Gregory, the oppressiveness of his new tax assessments made throughout his kingdom caused many to flee their possessions and kingdom, thinking it better to migrate and take up land elsewhere (*alibi peregrinare*) than remain.[39] In these circumstances it is not at all unlikely that Chilperic, like

---

[38] There is little point in mentioning the older literature. These ideas also prevail among contemporary historians; see, e.g., Beyerle, and Buchner, in their commentary to the *LRib.* 57, *Lex Ribvaria*, MGH, LL, 1, III, 2 (Hanover, 1954) 157; Beyerle, "Das legislative Werk Chilperichs I," pp. 30-31; H. Conrad, *Deutsche Rechtsgeschichte: Frühzeit und Mittelalter* (Karlsruhe, 1954), p. 218; D. Herlihy, "Land, Family, and Women in Continental Europe, 701-1200," *Traditio* 18 (1962) 90-91; Ourliac and Malafosse, *Histoire du droit privé*, 3: 338; Wemple, *Women in Frankish Society*, p. 46. Again, this list is by no means exhaustive. Cf., too, Dopsch (*Economic and Social Foundations*, p. 157) who also regarded the *Edict* as abolishing the hereditary right of the *vicini*: "It was replaced by a law which shows the great importance of the new German arrangements – hereditary rights were now extended to collateral relations, especially brothers, thus strengthening the right of possession of individual peasants against the oppressive authority acquired by the great estates in late Roman times."

[39] "Chilpericus vero rex discriptiones novas et gravis in omne regno suo fieri iussit. Qua de causa multi relinquentes civitates illas vel possessiones proprias, alia regna petierunt, satius ducentes alibi peregrinare quam tali periculo subiacere, statutum enim fuerat ut possessor de propria terra unam anfora vini per aripennem redderit. Sed et alii

his imperial predecessors, would attempt to ensure that taxable property had owners and would require a precise and fixed succession – whether from within the vicinage unit or without – of the revenue-producing properties.

We have already noted the generalized sequence of this procedure required by Roman law: first, *heredes*, then, *vicini*, and finally *peregrini*. This sequence is part of a pattern found throughout Roman society. Estates of a deceased intestate decurion for instance went first to the *liberi*, then *gradu proximo heres*, then to his *curia*.[40] The great problem with curial property was that an heir might be immune from municipal burdens and thus the obligations would be thrown back on the council. Plainly in some cases it was in the council's interests to keep *alieni* out of the inheritance, either to protect its own resources or to add a rich prize to the municipal estates. When a curial became a cleric the kinsman who took over his property was required to assume the responsibilities, but even so CT 12.1.49, a. 361, still felt the need to make the explicit provision that the kinsman of the deceased need not have formerly served the council.[41] Similar patterns can be found among the armourers, swine collectors, bakers,[42] and soldiers. By a law of 347 which has found its way into the *Breviary* Constantius provided that when soldiers died without statutory heirs their property went to their unit.[43] A similar law applied to those receiving imperial properties as a group: when two individuals had

---

functionis infligebantur multi tam de reliquis terris quam de mancipiis; quod implere non poterat. Lemovicinus quoque populus, cum se cernerit tali fasci gravari, congregatus in Kalendas Martias Marcumque referendarium, qui haec agere iussus fuerat, interficere voluit; et fecisset utique, nisi eum episcopus Ferreolus ab inminente discrimine liberasset. Areptis quoque libris discriptionum, incendio multitudo coniuncta cremavit. Unde multum molestus rex, dirigens de latere suo personas, inmensis damnis populum adflixit suppliciisque conteruit, morte multavit. Ferunt etiam tunc abbatis atque presbiteros ad stipitis extensus diversis subiacuisse tormentis, calumniantibus regalibus missis, quod in siditione populi ad incendendus libros satellitis adfuissent, acerbiora quoque deinceps infligentes tributa" (HF 5.28). See also 5.34, 6.22 and 7.15, 9.30, 10.7.

[40] CT 5.21 = LRV 5.2.1.

[41] "... ut per propinquos, si tamen curiales sunt aut etiam si curiae numquam antea obsequium praebuerant, praebeatur susceptis facultatibus obsequella." For curial inheritance and attempts to solve the problems of the *alienus* succeeding, see, CJ 10.35.1, 3; *NTh* 22.2 = LRV 11.2; *Nov. Iust.* 38, 87, 101.

[42] *NTh* 5.1; CT 14.4.5, 7; 13.5.2.

[43] CT 5.6.1 = LRV 5.4.1: "Universis tam legionibus quam vexillationibus comitatensibus seu cuneis insinuare debebis, uti cognoscant, cum aliquis fuerit rebus humanis exemptus atque intestatus sine legitimo herede decesserit, ad vexillationem, in qua militaverit, res eiusdem necessario pervenire." *Interpretatio*: "Milites si sine legitimo herede intestati decesserint et proximos non habuerint, eorum bona qui in eodem officio militant vindicabunt."

acquired a grant from the State, a constitution, probably of roughly the same date, permitted the one to succeed the other if the deceased left no will and no offspring.[44] Both these provisions suggest an interesting possible connection to the vicinage right of Frankish law if we assume, as Beyerle does for instance, that the *vicini* were Frankish settlers who formed the military backbone of the Frankish Neustrian settlement.[45] Certainly the norms of Roman or Romanized military law and estate practice could be merged when troops were settled, but it is very uncertain that the *vicini* of the *Edict* and the *Pactus* were all Franks. Nothing indicates that the *vicinus* was specifically a military colonist; and we have already seen that the peculiar features of the Frankish vicinage regulations can be found not simply in Roman military law but in various areas of Roman associational law. In a phrase reminiscent of *De migrantibus* the Burgundian law speaks of the inhabitants of a *villa* (*consistentes intra terminum villae*) as being both Burgundians and Romans.[46] Most likely *vicini* was a generic name for the members of vicinage groups however they happened to be composed, whether Gallo-Romans, Franks, or a mixture of both.

Inheritance rights were just one of a number of interrelated character-istics which pertained to the associations. Not only could the associations

---

[44] CT 10.14.1 = LRV 10.6.1; and CT 10.14.2. The law presumably would also apply to a group receiving a grant, with the group succeeding to an intestate childless member.

[45] "Tief in die überkommene Nachfolgeordnung in Liegenschaften schneidet c. 3 [of the *Edict*] ein. Nach LS 59.6 sollten ... sich die Ländereien ... nur im Mannesstamm weiter vererben. Aus diesem auf der Heerverfassung fussenden (weil eine lebensfähige Krieger-schicht sichernden) Ordnung klammert nun Chilperich das von Natur kognatische Band.... Die Landnahme muss wohl derart erfolgt sein dass zur Behauptung der fränki-schen Herrschaft in sich geschlossene Gebürschaften gebildet wurden – sei's dass sie ihre Ansiedlung gemeinschaftlich in Angriff genommen hatten oder sie doch gemeinschaftlich verwalteten und verteidigten, wogegen ihnen dann vakante Höfe samt den Ländereien heimfielen.... Mit dieser (wenn das Wort erlaubt ist) kolonisatorischen Ordnung stand und fiel im späten 5 und frühen 6 Jh. offenbar die fränkische Herrschaft über Neuster" ("Das leg. Werk," p. 30). There is no mention of the imperial antecedents for such a type of settlement.

Beyerle regards the *Edict* as not only emending LS 59, but also as affecting the rules found in LS 45, *De migrantibus*, and LS 46, *De acfatmire*. The latter he regards as being designed for the introduction of a son- or brother-in-law into a position to inherit for the brotherless daughter or brotherless sister. However he considers that *De migrantibus* shows that such an acquirer of an estate by marriage could still be ejected by each of the *vicini*. According to Beyerle Chilperic now excluded this danger for the brotherless daughter or sister by reserving the landed estate to these women, thus also making the transference of goods to the son- or brother-in-law superfluous (ibid., pp. 30-31). Although an ingenious explanation, there is no direct indication of this in any of the above provisions.

[46] LB 37.4.5; these are landlords with their own slaves and *coloni*; see LB 37.11.

inherit, but their members, unless with special sanction, were fixed to their occupation for life, or at least a prescribed period until their full services were completed. Among the rural population free proprietors might be subject to recall if they left their land, although it was usually expedient only to try to restore coloni.[47] In addition, the functions of the various groups such as soldiers, armourers, breadmakers, swine collectors, shipping masters, government officials, and city councillors (*curiales*) were made hereditary on their offspring, particularly their sons. It followed from this that the state had the power to recall not merely delinquent performers of their duty but also descendants and other kinsmen similarly bound – a power which existed side by side with the right of forcible enrolment of other citizens with sufficient property qualification. The numerous provisions repeatedly recalling decurions to their functions even after many years are well known.[48] It is likely that many of these were being summoned by their councils to take up what one law calls *res familiares*, that is, family property bound to public burdens,[49] which they now were in a position to inherit. A law which forbade the alienation of *praedia rustica vel urbana* held by bread makers *iure privato*, permitted gifts to sons, grandsons and other kinsmen, because they were compelled by the right of succession to undertake the public services.[50] The same applied to other groups. In 389 it was pointed out to the Prefect of Rome that the resources of the swine collectors were collapsing because their *fundi* and *alia praedia* were being alienated to *extranei*. Instructions were given that the estates be recalled to the original owners, or that the current owners, if they refused to give them up, had to assume the burdens; otherwise their kinsmen could be compelled to take over the name and public burden of swine-collectors.[51]

---

[47] A. H. M. Jones, "The Roman Colonate," *Past and Present*, No. 13 (April, 1958), pp. 4-6, and *Later Roman Empire*, 2: 796, esp. n. 62. On the question of *de facto* and *de iure* mobility among the agricultural population in the early Byzantine Empire, see Charanis, "Social Structure," pp. 44-45. In both periods it seems a certain amount of mobility was tolerated but was always subject to revocation, as in Egypt in 415.

[48] CT 12.1, passim.

[49] CT 12.1.63.

[50] CT 14.3.3. Transfers to *extranei* were not valid unless they voluntarily assumed the burdens.

[51] CT 14.4.5: "Consanguineos quoque eorum vel originales ut memoratorum nomini functionique iubeas adiungi plenum et aequitatis et iuris est." The meaning of *consanguineus* here is doubtful. At times it seems to retain its old civil law meaning of siblings of the same father (CT 2.19.2 = LRV 2.19.2 and *Interpretatio*) but can also refer to kinfolk in general (CT 5.1.9) or close agnatic relatives (CT 3.17.2; 5.1.1).

Only with difficulty did the late Roman state balance the rights and duties of association and of kinship along with the needs of the state. In this context two complementary aims can be suggested as lying behind the *Edict*. First, Chilperic is requiring, possibly only in reference to public lands, that in the case of undesirable farms the near relatives of the deceased[52] must undertake their cultivation; and second, presumably in cases of wealthy farms, he is most certainly seeking to exclude premature claims by the *vicini* who may be trying to exclude the rightful heirs, particularly if they are alien to the vicinage unit.

Consideration of the other traditional suppositions concerning the *Edict* confirms the likelihood of the above suggestions. LS 59 will be discussed more fully elsewhere, but it is enough here to note that this law provides not for the exclusion of women but for their postponement before their brothers, which is indeed what we find in the *Edict*. Whether "sicut lex salica habet" refers to LS 59 makes little difference, but it should be noted that c. 59 is not a direct parallel since it deals with intestate succession to a childless individual and thus the rules governing the succession of the deceased's children are taken for granted; in any case, not every reference to *lex Salica* must refer to the *Pactus*, for Salic law was composed of much more than specific written provisions.

Not every statement of law is a statement of innovation. Unfortunately nowhere has this fact been so readily forgotten as in the interpretation of the phrase "frater terras accipiant, non vicini" as indicating that for the first time daughters, brothers, and sisters excluded the *vicini*,[53] and that thereafter the vicinage right was abrogated.

> Hereditatem defuncti filius, non filia, suscipiat.[54]
>
> Pater et mater defuncti, filio, non filiae, hereditatem relinquent.[55]

No one would interpret these passages from the Anglian and Saxon laws as showing that according to former law daughters postponed sons to the

---

[52] The *Edict* as it stands indicates that these are the descendants of the deceased's father, presumably the former holder of the farm. More may have been said on this subject since the law appears to be fragmentary and may have run on further; see above, n. 36.

[53] Within the old interpretation there are a number of internal inconsistencies (especially if LS 59 is considered) which need not be dealt with here except to note: the phrase *non vicini* occurs not after the mention of the *filia* but of the brother and so should indicate that only the collateral succession was new; the fact that the *frater* and *soror* precede the *vicini* should not mean that the vicinage right was abrogated as is often said, but merely that it was postponed before heirs of the second parentela.

[54] *LTh.* 26.

[55] *LSax.* 41.

inheritance. These are attempts to reestablish norms, and curb either a growing tendency for daughters to inherit alongside their brothers, or else the idea that this should be acceptable. In the same way Chilperic is attempting to maintain and require the statutory heirs in the face of the claims and obligations of vicinage members. The *Edict* does not indicate either the postponement or abrogation of the vicinage right, but shows its continued vitality throughout the sixth century.

5

The *Fara*

The institution of the *fara* is one of the central supports of the unilineal clan theory, and to most authors the agnatic clan or extensive lineage and the *fara* are synonymous.[1] The famous gloss of Paul the Deacon: "faras hoc est generationes vel lineas"; and the presence of *fara* as a place-name element are the usual basis for the claim that the *fara* or clan formed a military unit and a settlement association in the occupation of the conquered lands. This is thought to be particularly true of the Lombards, Burgundians, and Franks, among whom the presence of the word *fara* is attested; among the Burgundians, for instance, we find freemen called *faramanni*, a term which Marc Bloch, among others, renders as "clansmen."[2]

The only real support for this view is Paul's gloss. This may appear to some extent to be an unambiguous enough confirmation, although there is nothing in the passage to suggest the nature and range of the family or kin groups involved. In any case there is more to Paul's reference to the Lombard *fara* than this usually truncated quotation suggests. And, there is also a body of evidence from other sources which by no means confirms the usual interpretation of the passage. For the Lombards, apart from the *Historia Langobardorum* of Paul, there is the testimony of the *leges* (*Ro.* 177), the chronicle of Marius of Avenches for 569, and the record of toponymy; for the Burgundians also, there is their national law (54.2,3) and the Chronicle of Fredegar (4.41,44,55); for the Franks, it is supposed

---

[1] L. Musset, *Les Invasions: les vagues germaniques*, 2nd ed., Nouvelle Clio, L'Histoire et ses problèmes, 12 (Paris, 1969), p. 237. English translation by Edward and Columba James, *The Germanic Invasions* (University Park, Pennsylvania, 1975), pp. 173-174. See also below, nn. 6, 7.

[2] "Une Mise au point: les invasions," *Annales d'Histoire Sociale* (1945), rpt. in *Mélanges historiques*, Bibliothèque Générale de l'École Pratique des Hautes Études, sect. 6 (Paris, 1963), 1: 133.

that there is only the evidence of toponymy; recourse is also had to the later continental survival of the word, and most importantly, its etymology. To this accepted body of evidence we must add a perfectly clear, if somewhat oblique, reference in Gregory of Tours' history of the Franks, and we might also note the occurrence of the word in Anglo-Saxon, where its usage and the sequence of its meanings are unambiguous and completely consistent with the continental evidence. Taken together, these sources are at odds with the traditional view, although, rather than contradicting the meaning of Paul's gloss, the material clarifies it and puts it in perspective.

The most influential revision of the idea of the *fara* has been that of the noted specialist on the Lombards, G. P. Bognetti, in his treatment of the influence of Roman military ideas upon Lombard institutions and the development of Lombard law.[3] Following in the footsteps of a number of scholars, including Franz Beyerle, he accepted and elaborated upon a more technically military interpretation, based, first, upon the most obvious etymology. *Fara* comes from *faran, fahren*, and means a wandering, or migration. In reference to a nucleus this presupposes a separation or detachment from the larger whole. In Bognetti's presentation, then, *fara* is the *expeditio* itself, or the company of the *expeditio*, whether in reference to detachments or the migration of the whole army. This accounts for the phrase (with, note, *fara* used in the singular) of Marius of Avenches: "Alboenus ... cum omni exercitu reliquens atque incendens Pannoniam suam patriam cum mulieribus vel omni populo suo in fara Italiam occupavit." At the same time it explains the presence of *fara* as a place-name element in localities where detachments settled, and thus even the application of the term to a *castrum*, such as that of Bergamo. The Burgundian *faramanni*, as a synonym for free warriors, is consequently brought into line with the Lombard freemen, the *arimanni, exercitales*. According to Bognetti, in Paul's gloss, the equation of the *farae* with "le genti," refers only to isolated, although still military, migrations, and the final incarnation or fragmentation of the *fara* as a whole.[4] Owing to the military character of the Germans this final military group can coincide with a family, whether a *famiglia naturale* or *gruppo gentilizio*.[5]

---

[3] "L'influsso delle istituzioni militari romane sulle istituzioni longobarde del secolo vi et la natura della 'fara'," in *Atti del congresso internazionale di diritto romano e di storia di diritto*, 4 (1953), rpt. in *L'età Longobarda* (Milan, 1967), 3: 3-46.

[4] Ibid., p. 13.

[5] Ibid., pp. 35, 39.

The main thrust of Bognetti's view is correct, but the important question of the relation of the *fara* and the clan remains, even though the old simple etymological equation has been undercut. For as just noted, the view represented by Bognetti still regards extensive agnatic groups (*le genti, gentes*) as bearing the name *farae*. Beyerle, for instance, who endorses the etymology of *fara* from *faran*, still believes that the Lombard clans bore the name *farae*, and changed from migratory associations into village associations in the occupation of the land.[6] In looking at the sources we must explore this possibility and try to determine the nature of the groups which lie behind references to the *farae* in the barbarian kingdoms.

The starting point inevitably is etymology,[7] but although it is the necessary first step, by itself it does not really get us very far. The obvious etymology is also the correct one: *fara* comes from *faran*, to go, travel, wander. The sequence of meanings which this might give comes out clearly in Anglo-Saxon, although it is obscure in the scant and diverse continental survivals. OE *faru*, from *faran*, has as its primary meaning: way, going, journey, expedition.[8] It can refer to the body of people who go with a person: train, followers, troops, *comitatus*; thus too, family, household, moveables, livestock. This pattern explains why later isolated continental survivals are of little help in interpreting specific early texts. If

---

[6] *Gesetze der Burgunden* (Weimar, 1936), p. 190. Cf. Musset (*The Germanic Invasions*, p. 174): "All this hardly justifies a comprehensive theory of kinship, and we cannot know for certain whether French and Italian place-names which include the word *fara* indicate colonization by family groups, or military settlement." But this caution is not typical. See Florus van der Rhee, *Die germanischen Wörter in den langobardischen Gesetze* (Rotterdam, 1970), p. 49, where *fara*, with the meaning *Fahrtgenossenschaft*, is regarded as a term for the *Sippe*. C. G. Mor, "Fara," HRG 1: 1074-1077 also maintains the association of the clan and the *fara* without, seemingly, the old etymologies, although it is said that Paul the Deacon "nennt uns die eigentliche Bedeutung dieses Wortes;" a number of meanings are acknowledged but "in ihren Ursprüngen ist die [Fara] ein Zusammenschluss von Familien, die durch Sippenzugehörigkeit verbunden waren und auf freiem Land angesiedelt waren." Cf. also J. M. Wallace-Hadrill, *The Barbarian West A.D. 400-1000: The Early Middle Ages* (New York, 1962), p. 46, who appears to share similar views.

[7] For various etymologies, see Brunner, DRG 1: 118, n. 37. For the *fara/faran* etymology, see R. Henning, "Die germanische fara und die faramanni," *Zeitschrift für deutsches Alterthum und deutsche Litteratur* 36 (1892) 316-326; Florus van der Rhee, *Die germanischen Wörter*, pp. 48-50.

[8] See Bosworth and Toller, *An Anglo-Saxon Dictionary* (Oxford, 1898), *Supplement* (Oxford, 1921), s.v.; quotations here cannot always be trusted without reference to the texts themselves; see n. 21, below. Cf. also *faer, for*. Except for Henning, scant attention has been paid to the Anglo-Saxon material because of the incontrovertible derivation of OE *faru* (= *fara*) from *faran*.

fara has been adopted by non-Germanic speakers with a familial meaning,[9] it also survives in Lyonnais meaning 'wanderer' and 'knight'[10] – all quite consistent with the etymology from *faran*, but each a poor basis in itself for interpreting the Burgundian *faramanni* or French and Italian place-names. *Fara* can mean many related things. Particular usages can only be determined by careful comparison and strict attention to textual context. Moreover if we are interested in the evidence of its usage in the period of migration and occupation, we must employ one of the most basic tools of historical research, a strict regard for chronology.

Among the Burgundians there are two main pieces of evidence. The earliest is a law in the *Lex Gundobada* which can be dated to about the first fifteen years of the sixth century.[11] Here the term *faramanni* is applied to the barbarian 'guests' of the Roman landlords (*possessores*). Nothing suggests 'clansmen.' Literally the *faramanni* are the "men of the *fara*."[12] Beyerle suggests that in this context the *faramanni* are the participants in the expedition which led to the occupation, who have received *hospitalitas* or grants from the king.[13] In view of the fact that the *expeditio* was decades removed from the law in question, the *faramanni* at this point must be the descendants of the original settlers who received *hospitalitas* and grants, that is, those Burgundians whose properties and positions are derived from the occupation.

---

[9] "Geschlecht": Schlesinger, "Randbemerkungen," p. 294; Mor, "Fara," 1075.

[10] Beyerle, *Gesetze der Burgunden*, p. 190.

[11] LB 54: "De his, qui tertiam mancipiorum et duas terrarum partes contra interdictum publicum praesumpserint.

Licet eodem tempore, quo populus noster mancipiorum tertiam et duas terrarum partes accepit, eiusmodi a nobis fuerit emissa praeceptio, ut quicumque agrum cum mancipiis seu parentum nostrorum sive nostra largitate perceperat, nec mancipiorum tertiam nec duas terrarum partes ex eo loco, in quo ei hospitalitas fuerat delegata requireret, tamen quia complures comperimus, inmemores periculi sui, ea quae praecepta fuerant excessisse, necesse est, ut praesens auctoritas, ad instar mansurae legis emissa, et praesumptores coerceat et hucusque contemptis remedium debitae securitatis adtribuat. Iubemus igitur: ut quidquid ab his, qui agris et mancipiis nostra munificentia potiuntur, de hospitum suorum terris contra interdictum publicum praesumpsisse docentur, sine dilatione restituant.

De exartis quoque novam nunc et superfluam *faramannorum* conpetitionem et calumniam possessorum gravamine et inquietudine hac lege praecipimus submoveri: ut sicut de silvis, ita et de exartis, sive anteacto sive in praesenti tempore factis, habeant cum Burgundionibus rationem; quoniam, sicut iam dudum statutum est, medietatem silvarum ad Romanos generaliter praecipimus pertinere: simili de curte et pomariis circa *faramannos* conditione servata, id est: ut medietatem Romani estiment praesumendam." Italics added.

[12] Cf. Lombard *arimanni* (*ari* = Ger. *Heer*), *exercitales*.

[13] *Gesetze*, p. 190.

At least a century and a half after the *Lex Gundobada*, *fara* appears in a different compound. In the Burgundian-based chronicle of Fredegar several passages refer to *Burgundaefarones*. There can be no doubt that the aristocracy or some portion of it is meant. On the one hand the *Burgundaefarones* have been seen as the native Burgundian nobility[14] and as the lords created by the occupation.[15] On the other, Fustel de Coulanges regarded *farones* as a Burgundian equivalent of *leudes* – not in the sense of dependents generally, but of the group of notables, vassals, and officials directly connected to the king and summoned to his court. Possibly these two views are not completely exclusive of one another; however a comparison of the relevant texts confirms the interpretation of Fustel that, most simply, the *Burgundaefarones* were the Burgundian *leudes* of the Frankish king.[16] Much the same connotation appears in the Frankish material.

Gregory of Tours tells what he considers a humorous story concerning the downfall of Clovis' relative and kingly colleague, Ragnachar, king of the Franks at Cambrai; the point of the joke depends upon a pun on the proper name Farro and the *fara* or *leudes* of the king. According to Gregory,[17] Ragnachar was guilty of the considerable fault of parsimony

---

[14] E. Zöllner, "Die Herkunft der Agilofinger," *Mitteilungen des Instituts für Österreichische Geschichtsforschung* 59 (1951) 247.

[15] Beyerle, *Gesetze*, p. 190.

[16] *The Fourth Book of the Chronicle of Fredegar*, ed. J. M. Wallace-Hadrill (London, 1960): "Burgundaefaronis vero tam episcopi quam citeri leudis timentis Brunechildam et odium in eam habentes, Warnachario [mayor of the palace] consilium inientes...." (a. 613, 4.41); "Anno xxxiii regni Chlothariae [616] Warnacharium maioris domus cum universis pontificibus Burgundiae seo et Burgundaefaronis ... ad se venire precepit. Ibique cunctis illorum iustis peticionibus annuens preceptionebus roborauit" (4.44); in the year 627 when a feud broke out on the occasion of any assembly of the "pontificis et universi proceres regni sui tam de Neuster quam de Burgundia ... Chlotharius ad Burgundefaronis specialius iobet ut ..." (4.55); cf. "omnes pontefecis et leudis de regnum Burgundiae" (4.56); "omnes leudis de Neuster et Burgundia" (4.79); "Nantildis regina ... omnes seniores, ponteueces, ducebus et primatis de regnum Burgundiae ad se venire precepit" (4.89); "collictis ... pontefecis et ducibus de regnum Burgundiae" (4.90). Concerning these usages Fustel notes (*La Monarchie franque*, 2nd ed., Histoire des Institutions Politiques de l'Ancienne France, 3 [Paris, 1905]): "sous des formes diverses elles présentent le même sense, elles indiquent les mêmes catégories d'hommes ... les *farones* étaient les grands, les leudes du pays" (p. 633, n. 1). We cannot see here only the native Burgundian nobility if we mean by this only those who could trace their origins to the occupation.

[17] HF, 2.42: "His habebat Farronem consiliarium simili spurcitia lutolentum, de quo fertur, cum aliquid aut cibi aut muneris vel cuiuslibet rei regi adlatum fuisset, dicere solitum, hoc sibi suoque Farroni sufficere. Pro qua re Franci maxima indignatione tumibant. Unde factum est, ut, datis aureis sive armellis vel baltheis, Chlodovechus, sed totum adsimilatum auro – erat enim aereum deauratum sub dolo factum – haec dedit leudibus eius, ut super eum invitaretur. Porro cum exercitum contra eum commovisset, et

towards his followers; but he had a counsellor called Farro upon whom
he lavished favours, "concerning whom it was said that when food or a
gift or any property whatever was brought to the king, he was
accustomed to say that it was sufficient for him and his Farro." On
account of this the Franks under Ragnachar became disaffected and
Clovis, taking advantage of this fact, bribed Ragnachar's *leudes*. As
Clovis' army closed in and Ragnachar asked his scouts the strength of the
enemy force, they would reply: "It is a great sufficiency for you and your
Farro." It is generally a thankless task to explain a joke, but the story
really makes sense only in terms of a Farro/*fara* pun, where *fara*, as in
the case of the Burgundian evidence, stands for the king's *leudes*, those
who normally expected to be recipients of the royal munificence, on the
one hand, and who were the backbone of his military power on the other.

The material considered thus far – all of which dates from the sixth and
seventh centuries – aptly agrees with the etymology of *fara* from *faran*.
Its usages have centred around the meaning *expeditio*, or the following or
leudes of the head of the *expeditio*. None of it has remotely suggested
agnatic clans or extensive lineages, or even, in an exclusive sense,
families.

Next we must consider the Lombard evidence. The earliest, to which
we have already referred, comes from the chronicle of Marius of
Avenches for the year 569, describing Alboin's abandonment of Pannonia
and conquest of Italy *in fara*: "Along with his army Alboin left and
burned his native land Pannonia, and with his wives and all his people in
a migratory expedition (*in fara*) took Italy."[18] Since Avenches is located in
the northeastern corner of the Burgundian kingdom, we may feel sure the
chronicler well understood the expression he used, although for the same
reason it may reflect a Burgundian perception of the nature of the
Lombard invasion. Undoubtedly Lombard usage is the expression *cum
fara sua migrare* of Rothair's edict published in 643. The law prescribes
that if a freeman who has royal permission to migrate with his *fara* no
longer wishes to remain with his lord he must return to him or his heirs
any property formerly granted.[19] As it stands, the passage is open to a

---

ille speculatores plerumque ad cognuscendum transmitteret, reversis nuntiis, interrogat,
quam valida haec manus foret. Qui responderunt: 'Tibi tuoque Farroni est maximum
supplimentum....'"

[18] "Alboenus ... cum omni exercitu reliquens atque incendens Pannoniam suam
patriam cum mulieribus vel omni populo suo in fara Italiam occupavit" (MGH AA, XI,
Chronica Minora, 2, ed. Th. Mommsen, Berlin, 1894).

[19] *Ro.* 177: "Si quis liber homo potestatem habeat intra dominium regni nostri cum
fara sua megrare ubi voluerit – sic tamen si ei a rege data fuerit licentia – et si aliquas res ei

number of interpretations, but the least likely is that *fara* refers to an agnatic clan or extensive lineage of which the freeman is a member.[20] It is the freeman as an individual who has the power of going wherever *he* wishes, who decides to stay with his lord or not, and who receives and returns the benefice granted him; whatever the *fara* is, he is at the head of it and it is dependent on him. All this implies, in fact, that *fara* here means some variation on family, in a relatively narrow sense, or household moveables; the *fara* may include of course the freeman's personal followers and may even, in part, constitute a very shallow lineage if, as was sometimes the case, sons and grandsons stayed within the household of the grandfather.[21] It is all that circle of human dependents and property which is not attached to the benefice and which will go with him when he moves. On a smaller scale it is similar to the description of Alboin on the march: "cum omni exercitu ... cum mulieribus vel omni populo suo in fara."

The final evidence for the *fara* among the Lombards is the famous gloss of the late eighth-century historian Paul the Deacon. It is worth stressing that Paul wrote well over a century to two and a half centuries after the sources which have been discussed up to this point. The succinct neatness of the gloss has meant that it has almost always been quoted quite apart from its full context. A better idea of what Paul understood the sixth-

---

dux aut quicumque liber homo donavit, et cum eo noluerit permanere, vel cum heredes ipsius: res ad donatorem uel heredes eius revertantur."

[20] This view is recently repeated by Charles-Edwards, "Kinship, Status and the Origins of the Hide," p. 32 and n. 54, who appears to view it as having a possible depth of seven generations; see also Mor, "Fara," 1077. Musset (*The Germanic Invasions*, p. 174) seems to accept *fara* in this context as one of the basic units of the army. His invocation of the Greek tacticians here is misguided: see above, ch. 3, n. 42.

[21] The sense of moveable goods is given in the gloss of the tenth-century *Cod. Matritensis* (in *Leges Langobardorum*, MGH, LL, 4: 651): "fara, id est rebus"; and may not simply be a stab in the dark. Cf. the Anglo-Saxon *Earlier Genesis*, ca. 700 (*Die ältere Genesis*, ed. F. Holthausen, Alt- und mittelenglische Texte, 7 [Heidelberg, 1914], lines 1130-1131): "gewit þu nu feran 7 þine fare laedan, ceapas to cnosle" (go now forth on your journey and lead your *faru*, the cattle or possessions for your progeny). The Anglo-Saxon equivalent of *migrare cum fara, feran mid fare* appears in Aelfric's translation of the *Heptateuch* (*The Old English Version of the Heptateuch*, ed. S. J. Crawford, Early English Text Society, Original Series, No. 160 [Oxford, 1922]): "Abram ða ferde of Aran ..., 7 Loth ferde mid him, mid ealre fare 7 mid eallum aehtum" ("Egressus est itaque Abram ... et ivit cum eo Lot ... Tulitque Sarai uxorem suam et Lot filium fratris sui, universamque substantiam quam possederant, et animas quas fecerant in Haran"), Gen. 12.4, 5; "Abram ða ferde of Egipta lande mid ealre his fare" ("uxorem illius et omnia quae habebat"), Gen. 12.20; see also: "God ða gemunde Noes fare 7 ðaera nytena" ("Recordatus autem Deus Noe, cunctorumque animantium et omnium iumentorum"), Gen. 8.1.

century *fara* to be can be gleaned not only from the gloss but also from the passage as a whole. Paul describes how Alboin, after taking Venetia, wondered to whom he should grant this first of the conquered provinces of Italy. He decided upon his own nephew Gisulf, master of the horse. But Gisulf declared he would not undertake the task unless Alboin granted him those *farae* of the Lombards which he himself wished to pick. It was done, and with the king's consent he took the chief families (*praecipuae prosapiae*) whom he had chosen to stay with him.[22] As Paul refers to them, the *farae* are neither clans nor even the minor family units of Lombard society as a whole. They are the *praecipuae prosapiae*, the noble or magnate houses commanding their own *expeditiones*, and the mainstay of Alboin's army. Gisulf, faced with holding down Venetia either with his own *expeditio* or with the aid assigned him by Alboin, would only take the job if he had the discretion of picking for himself the magnate families who would support him.

Paul's description can take us in two main directions. If one wishes to accept it as a basically sound description of sixth-century conditions, it suggests powerful houses which possessed considerable lordship and following and formed a significant counterforce to the royal power. Subsequent Lombard history suggests this anyway. Shortly after the conquest, some thirty-six *duces* are found ruling the Lombards, and some two years after Alboin's death, with the assassination of Cleph, the ducal houses decided to go it alone without any monarchy whatsoever.[23] Considering when Paul wrote, however, it is wiser to emphasize the retrospective character of his description, and suggest that in describing the *fara* he is transferring the eighth-century conditions with which he was familiar onto the sixth-century occupation, and explaining, after the fact, the founding of the houses of the Friuli nobility.

[22] *Historia Langobardorum*, 2.9 (in MGH, *Scriptores Rerum Langobardicarum*, ed. G. Waitz [Hanover, 1878]): "Igitur dum Alboin animum intenderet quem in his locis ducem constituere deberet, Gisulfum, ut fertur, suum nepotem, virum per omnia idoneum, qui eidem strator erat, quem lingua propria marpahis appellant, Foroiulanae civitati et totae illius regioni praeficere statuit. Qui Gisulfus non prius se regimen eiusdem civitatis et populi suscepturum, nisi ei quas ipse eligere uoluisset Langobardorum faras, hoc est generationes vel lineas, tribueret. Factumque est, et annuente sibi regi quas optaverat Langobardorum praecipuas prosapias, ut cum eo habitarent, accepit."

[23] For emphasis on the particularism of the Lombards, see Bognetti, "L'influsso delle istituzioni militari romane," *passim*; and for the idea of traditionally powerful allegiances and lordships held by powerful families quite apart from the royal house, Schlesinger, "Lord and Follower," esp. pp. 71-74, 76-79; Leyser, "The German Aristocracy," pp. 31-32.

Implicit within the word *fara* are a number of related conceptions: the idea of a basically artificial grouping of persons organized for the purpose of a military expedition; the idea of dependents or followers; of property or moveable goods which can accompany a person; and finally the idea of family, household, or even line of descent. None of these senses, of course, need appear exclusively in any particular usage, but it is worthwhile to note where the emphasis has lain in the evidence which we have considered. In the earliest material the overriding context is the artificial, mainly military, grouping, whether in the sense of *expeditio* or *leudes*. To a large extent this meaning remains firmly rooted in all the evidence, whether late or early. By the mid-seventh century in the *Edict of Rothair* we find an added family dimension; but this is just one element among several, including household, dependents, and moveable property, and indicates 'family' in a relatively narrow sense. Finally in the late eighth century we find the word applied to the Friuli magnate houses and their *expeditiones*. Whether the evidence is taken together or singly it is indeed clear that the word *fara* is a poor basis for any comprehensive view of the nature and development of kinship. It should be eliminated once and for all as evidence that in the ancient period Germanic society was composed of extensive unilineal and corporate clans and lineages.

6

The *Genealogia*

A small number of references in Bavarian and Alamannian sources of the eight and ninth centuries to *genealogiae* have frequently been cited as evidence for the clan structure of early Germanic society; moreover the *genealogiae* have been understood to show that the Germans settled in the Empire in agnatic clan or lineage groups, that the *vici* were in origin clan settlements, and even that the clan practised common cultivation.[1] The Bavarian evidence for these ideas consists of a reference in the *Lex Baiwariorum*, dating from 741-743, to certain named noble families (*genealogiae*) which, like the ducal house of the Agilofings, are conceded higher wergelds. There is also a charter of 750 in which members of two *genealogiae* donate *deserta* to the church of Freising. Finally, in a *formula* of the mid ninth-century Passau collection, *genealogiae* is used as a territorial designation. The Alamannian evidence is a single law of the *Lex*

---

[1] For an account of these views which are found throughout the older literature see Brunner, DRG, 1: 117-118. It is to be noted that the *genealogiae* are connected with the groups and agricultural practices thought to prevail in the time of Caesar. For instance, although Huebner, *History of German Private Law*, pp. 115, 139 ff., deals extensively with various communities of heirs common in the medieval period, he yet associates the *genealogiae* with what were thought to be the clans (*gentes*) of the Caesarian period; see also Bloch (*Feudal Society*, p. 137) who does the same and Beyerle, "Das Kulturporträt der beiden alamannischen Rechtstexte: Pactus und Lex Alamannorum," p. 141. Even Dopsch, who prefers to emphasize the role of followings, and rightly cautions that the eighth-century date of the *Lex* means that it "can be used only with considerable caution for earlier times" shares some of these views (*Economic and Social Foundations*, pp. 114, 117); for instance, he writes: "When we consider the oft-quoted passage in the *Lex Alamannorum* about the strife of the *genealogiae* over their boundaries ... we may not be able to deny that clans [*Sippen*] played a part of some importance in the settlement" (p. 114).

Against these views of the *genealogiae*, see Kroeschell, "Die Sippe im germanischen Recht," p. 10, n. 41, who emphasizes their aristocratic character; on which see below, n. 12.

Alamannorum, which dates probably from around 730, concerning a boundary dispute "inter duas genealogias."[2]

Various aspects of the word *genealogia* are reflected in these sources. That in each case there was a familial or kinship content, in origin at least, seems clear enough, but this in itself is not enough to postulate a unilineal clan as the basic unit of society or as a settlement group in the *Land-nahme*. The distinctive features of the evidence which need comment are the facts that a group with a family or kinship basis (*genealogia*) acted as a unit with regard to *deserta* and estate boundaries, and that a familial term (*genealogia*) was applied to a territorial unit. These features can be thought to be characteristic of a system of clan or extensive lineage organization, but it is important to realize that they are also applicable to other forms of early medieval (and late ancient) society, particularly the rather common inheritance communities. When each of the texts is examined in turn it will be apparent that it is, in fact, the commonplace of medieval and ancient society, and not the hypothetical constructs of German prehistory, which confront us in the Alamannian and Bavarian sources, and that the *genealogiae* will tell us nothing about the apportionment of the soil during the *Landnahme*. Some preliminary observations will help to underscore such an interpretation.

At the outset the date of the texts mentioning *genealogiae* must be stressed. As evidence coming from the eighth and ninth centuries they have to be used with discretion to explicate conditions of several centuries earlier; indeed there must be compellingly good reasons to use them at all. What we have in the Alamannian and Bavarian documents are the results of settlement and not the process itself. For this reason, when members of family groups – although it will be seen that the *genealogiae* need not always to be exclusively such – are found acting in concert in specific instances and treated by the law as entities, we must be prepared to ask whether associations of this type arose naturally over the course of time after the occupation of the soil or whether such groups were present from the beginning as the agents and units of settlement.

It is worth noting too that the *genealogiae* do not in any way lie at the heart of the legal and proprietal foundations of Alamannian and Bavarian law. This is clear enough from the small number of times they are mentioned in the sources. Scholars have long recognized that the system of property and inheritance in both laws is individualistic and, to that

---

[2] On the dating of the laws and *formulae* cited in this chapter, see Buchner, *Rechts-quellen,* under the appropriate heading.

extent, at one with the other *leges*:[3] for instance, the laws show that a man's landed inheritance was to be divided on his death amongst his children – daughters, incidentally, inheriting if there were no sons.[4] To maintain the *genealogiae* as clans or lineages in the highly corporate sense of traditional historiography, one must imagine their existence in the eighth century either as only shadows of their former selves, or as archaic islands standing apart from the legal structure of Alamannian and Bavarian law. Neither supposition is necessary, however, if we consider the estate division and inheritance practices common to Roman and medieval law, because here is found the recognition of not only individual rights but also the legal entity of individuals formed into voluntary associations.

The domain of ancient and early medieval rural organization (called a *villa* or *fundus* among other designations)[5] normally possessed a name, based upon the personal name of a past owner. This name, and the extent and configuration of the domain, frequently persisted – even over centuries – long after the owner who had originally given his name to the unit was dead and forgotten.[6] The domain continued to be regarded as an entity even though its actual ownership might be divided among a number of individuals through the natural process of inheritance, sale, and exchange. In one sense therefore, the domain might be fragmented, its ownership and possession divided among a number of individuals; in another sense, frequently as a complex and interrelated arrangement of arable, vine, and orchard, of undivided pasture, forest and waste, of demesne and dependent tenancies, it remained a discrete, and named, entity, with external boundaries. When this unit was possessed by owners unrelated to one another, large stretches of pasture and waste frequently remained undivided. On occasion even the arable, vine and orchard might be kept undivided among owners, particularly in the case where co-heirs

---

[3] See Dopsch, *Economic and Social Foundations*, pp. 115 ff.

[4] *LBai.* 2.7; 15.9, 10; LA 55, 85, 89.

[5] In using the word domain, *villa*, we can no longer have the idea that in the early Middle Ages this referred only to vast estates divided into demesne and tenancies. On the various forms the *villa* could take, see Latouche, *The Birth of Western Economy*, pp. 63 ff. "In reality a wide diversity of types was concealed under one comprehensive term.... In the northwest most of the great estates must still have been, in part at least, waste land" (ibid., p. 68). By domain we mean simply property that was regarded by its owner or owners as a unit and was so designated – whether developed or largely undeveloped, or used as a hunting preserve.

[6] See Fustel de Coulanges, *L'alleu et le domaine rural pendant l'époque mérovingienne*, Histoire des Institutions Politiques de l'Ancienne France, 4 (Paris, 1889), pp. 15 ff., 220 ff. Cf. Paul Vinogradoff, *The Growth of the Manor*, pp. 63-64.

together maintained their inheritance, or part of it, intact. The community of heirs in various forms was known to Roman law throughout the whole history of its development, the archaic *consortium* giving way to the *communio pro indiviso* of the classical period and after.[7] The community of heirs was also a feature of medieval law.[8] In the *leges barbarorum* it is explicitly mentioned in the laws of the Alamannians and Lombards,[9] although as a voluntary, and largely private, alternative to dividing the inheritance, it certainly existed everywhere.

The inheritance communities of the early Middle Ages, like their Roman counterparts, were voluntary associations whose dissolution could occur at any time. The co-proprietorship held by their members might be extended to the entire inheritance or only part of it. In the case of a patrimony inherited by co-heirs the co-ownership of the undivided share might extend to the arable as well as the waste – which there was often little point in dividing in any case – and to the demesne and dependent tenancies; but it also might be decided to divide only part of the inheritance and hold the rest jointly. An early eighth century law of Liutprand, for example, regulates the procedures to be followed when after forty years parts of an inheritance still remain to be divided among sons and grandsons.[10] Because of their private and voluntary nature inheritance communities in Antiquity and throughout the Middle Ages existed in a legal framework of individualistic property holding and inheritance. They were not clans in the traditional sense nor the remnants of corporate clan and lineage organization. But because the co-heirs were frequently siblings or cousins, the community might constitute a shallow descent group – a *genealogia*, to use the terminology of the Alamannian and Bavarian law. Finally, even though the form of inheritance communities was ancient – going back to Roman law and beyond, and probably also to prehistoric Germanic practice – it is apparent that the communities were not long-lived, but owing to the exigencies of inheritance and division, were continually dissolving and being reconstituted.

Starting with the Bavarian evidence we can now look at the *genealogiae*. Title 3 of the *Lex Baiwariorum* regulates the compensation to be paid to the duke and the ducal house of the Agilofings, as well as to five

---

[7] These are considered by most of the major handbooks; in particular, M. Kaser, *Roman Private Law*, trans. R. Dannenberg (Durban, 1968), pp. 99-100, 187 ff., 310-311.

[8] Its various forms in German lands are conveniently outlined by Huebner, *History of German Private Law*, pp. 139 ff.

[9] LA 55; *Ro.* 167; *Li.* 70, 74.

[10] *Li.* 70.

noble families (*genealogiae*) called the Hosi, Drazza, Fagana, Hahilinga, and Anniona.[11] These five families have often been interpreted as being the remnants of the *altgermanische* nobility or Bavarian *Uradel*, or even as the descendants of old Swabian royal families, although these are suppositions for which there is no evidence.[12] For our purposes it matters little whether the roots of these families go back to the period of migrations and settlement or not, because the concession by the Frankish crown of a double compensation to a number of Bavarian noble houses says nothing about the kinship structure of Bavarian society as a whole, and nothing about the occupation of the land. However, the remaining Bavarian evidence differs in context from *LBai*. 3, and, because the word *genealogia* is associated in it with land-holding and territorial units, deserves closer consideration.[13]

A charter of 750 records a donation *pro anima* acquired by Bishop Joseph from Duke Tassilo for the Church of Freising.[14] The donation

---

[11] "De genealogia qui vocantur Hosi Drazza Fagana Hahilinga Anniona: isti sunt quasi primi post Agilofingos qui sunt de genere ducali. Illis enim duplum honorem concedamus et sic duplam conpositionem accipiant.

Agilofingi vero usque ad ducem in quadruplum conponantur quia summi principes sunt inter vos.

Dux vero ... ille semper de genere Agilofingarum fuit et debet esse, quia reges antecessores nostri concesserunt eis....

Et pro eo quia dux est, addatur ei maior honor quam ceteris parentibus eius sic ut tertia pars addatur super hoc quod parentes eius conponuntur...."

[12] A fact emphasized by the most recent treatment of their distribution and connections: W. Störmer, *Adelsgruppen im früh- und hochmittelalterlichen Bayern* (Munich, 1972), pp. 90 ff. See also H. L. Günter Gastroph, *Herrschaft und Gesellschaft in der Lex Baiuvariorum*, Miscellanea Bavarica Monacensia 53 (Munich, 1974), pp. 105 ff., 137 ff.

[13] Kroeschell ("Die Sippe im germanischen Recht," p. 10, n. 41) rightly dismisses the *genealogiae* as evidence for *Sippensiedlung*; the reason he gives is that the concept of *genealogia* did not apply to any "Sippe" but only to the powerful "Adelsgeschlechter" and the areas ruled by them. Perhaps. The word is certainly applied to noble lineages in *LBai*. 3 but it seems to me that it should not be limited as a term of nobility. The evidence is sparse, but where applied in a proprietal context (see below) *genealogia* designates not only the Fagana who are mentioned in *LBai*. 3 but also another group which is not. It is a term, therefore, applied outside the five *primi post Agilofingos*. Moreover nothing in the Alamannian law about *genealogiae* suggests limiting the designation to 'nobility'. The term is also used in the Bavarian law in the sense of 'descent': *secundum genealogiam suam*, regarding compensation to be paid to monks (1.8), and to those killed by someone committing *scandalum* in the army (2.4), and in reference to the *dos* to be paid a dismissed wife (8.14); also "mulieres ... totae libere ... de genealogia sua" (15.9). Again in this context it is not limited to 'nobles'. In the *Formulae Imperiales* (ca. 830) we find a woman and her *genealogia* – namely her brothers – wrongfully reduced to servitude (no. 51).

[14] "Dum in dei nomine ego Josephus episcopus ... in castello nuncupante Frigisinga dum erga eodem loco conexae arve ducali pascua non sufficerant, appetivi locum ad

consists of a *locus* called Eriching, composed of waste land (*inculta atque deserta*). This land was held by a number of owners (*possessores*), who had come by their possession through inheritance ("appetivi locum ad proprios heredes") and whose consent to the gift, as well as that of Tassilo, their overlord, is recorded in the charter of donation.[15] Eriching was divided between two groups of owners. Part belonged to the Ferings (this time a family and not a place name), identified as Alfrid and his brothers. They agreed to the donation along with their *participes* and *consortes* in the waste; the remainder belonged to members of the *genealogia* Fagana – one of the noble families of *LBai. 3* – namely, Ragino, Anulo, Wetti, Wurmhart, and all their *participes*.[16] As a consequence of the donation, Eriching, composed of the properties of both *genealogiae* ("fines utrorumque genealogiarum") was to be transferred to the church of

---

proprios heredes quo vocatur Erichinga et ibidem pro necessitate domos construxi quia antea iam temporibus plurimis inculta atque deserta remansit. Omnes autem possessores huius loci prumptis viribus donantes atque tradentes pro remedium animarum suarum: imprimis gloriosissimus Tassilo dux Baioarorum quicquid ad Feringas pertinebat pariter ipsis consentientibus Alfrid cum fratribus suis et participibus eorum atque consortiis, reliquas autem partes quicquid ad genealogiam quae vocatur Fagana pertinebat tradiderunt ipsi, id sunt Ragino, Anulo, Uuetti, Uurmhart et cuncti participes eorum, donantes atque transfundentes seu firmitatem secundum ius Baioarorum facientes ut ipsaque huius loci, id est Erichiga fines utrorumque genealogiarum sine fraude ditionibus beate praedicte dei genetricis Mariae consistere in perpetuum firma permaneat, ut nulla requisitio ab heredibus vel futuris prolibus eorumque qui firmitatem nectebant adesse debeat, ut si quis contra haec firmitatis epistolam fraudare conaverit, cum praedictam dei genetrice Mariam communicet causam..." (*Die Traditionen des Hochstifts Freising*, ed. T. Bitterauf, Quellen und Erörterungen zur bayerischen und deutschen Geschichte, NF 4, 5 [Munich, 1905] 1: no. 5).

[15] The precise relation of Tassilo to the two main groups of owners is a bit difficult to fathom. He certainly appears to be the overlord of the Ferings and stands for them in the donation. The wording suggests the Fagana stood for themselves. Yet at the beginning of the donation the properties in question appear to be designated as ducal ("ducali"), suggesting that both the Ferings and Fagana held a stretch of pasture land from the duke. Possibly the lower station of the Fering brothers explains their closer association with their overlord Tassilo.

[16] See Störmer, *Adelsgruppen*, p. 113. The older literature regarded the donation as being made by the Agilofings (of whom Alfrid and his brothers are members) and the Fagana. I follow Störmer here in seeing the role of Tassilo as that of overlord, and the major parties as the Ferings and the Fagana. Alfrid and his brothers are not Agilofings: "quicquid ad Feringas pertinebat ... *ipsis* consentientibus Alfrid cum fratribus." Possibly of course there may be connections between the Fering brothers and the Agilofingian Tassilo, but I cannot see that the suggestion that the Ferings are a secondary line (*Nebenlinie*) of the Agilofings gets us very far; quite pointless are suggestions that both names are synonymous, or that the Agilofings formed a "Herzogsippe innerhalb der Grossfamilie, des 'Stammes' der Feringen" (see Zöllner, "Die Herkunft der Agilofinger," p. 249).

Freising and no claim was to be made on this land by any of the present heirs or future offspring of those agreeing to the donation. Clearly in this document we are looking at the private arrangement of inheritance communities concerning waste land and not clans and clan lands. Eriching has been inherited by two groups of co-heirs belonging to two families (*genealogiae*), the Ferings and Fagana, whose members have kept their portions undivided. It is problematic who the *participes* and *consortes*, that is the other partners in the waste, are. Possibly they may be kinsmen and co-heirs of the individuals named in the donation, but it is far more likely that they are simply unrelated (and inferior) *possessores* holding Fering or Fagana land, who have rights in the waste of Eriching.[17]

In the Freising charter *genealogia* still appears to be used in the strict sense of family or lineage. However it is a simple matter of transference to indicate a unit held by a *genealogia* as a divided or undivided inheritance by the name of the *genealogia* itself, that is, to turn *genealogia* into a territorial designation. This is what has happened in the final piece of Bavarian evidence found in the Passau *formulae*. Once such a transference has been made it no longer matters whether any descendants of the original group of co-heirs are in possession of property in the *genealogia*, for the name will continue. In this respect the name Eriching in the Freising donation is worth noting: presumably called after a former holder of the unit, the area has maintained its name and integrity even though its ownership has been divided among members of two different families. The mid ninth-century *formula* from Passau was intended to record the exchange of properties between a certain bishop, representing his church, and a layman. The properties transferred by the bishop are said to be "in the *vicus* and the *genealogia* which are designated at the juncture of such-and-such a stream and such-and-such a river."[18] This method of location and phraseology, so far as I am aware, is unique, and

[17] Cf. LRB 17.5.

[18] "... vir venerabilis illius eclesie episcopus ... cum quodam viro – *nomen* – pro communi utilitate et compendio de quibusdam rebus commutationem fecisset, datis scilicet a parte eclesie suae eidem viro – *nomen* – ad suum proprium ad habendum in vico et genealogia quae dicuntur ubi rivolus ill. intrat in ill. flumen, curtiles 2 et aforis a terra arabili iurnales tant. et de pratis ad carradas tantum et molendinum 1. Et econtra in compensatione harum rerum dedit memoratus vir..." (no. 5). "In vico et genealogia quae dicuntur" is the traditional form in which this text is quoted (the MGH has a comma after "dicuntur") the implication being that "quae dicuntur" stands in place of one of the usual formula for indicating proper names. However this is most peculiar usage for the *formulae*. Even in the text in question care has been taken to supply the usual *ill.* or space has been left for a name. Rather "dicuntur" is to be taken with "ubi."

makes it difficult to be certain of the nature of the *vicus* and *genealogia* and their relation to one another.[19] If the *vicus* and *genealogia* are one and the same unit, that is are coterminous, it would appear that the *vicus* had once been held by a community of heirs, and that at some point part of it had been alienated to the church represented by the bishop. However it is probable that *vicus* and *genealogia* indicate distinct, if related, units.[20] Conceivably, then, the *vicus* forms part of the property (*genealogia*) once held by, and named after, a family of co-heirs; but, again it is more likely that this property (*genealogia*) is being located with reference to a neighboring *vicus* ('township,' parish) with which it is associated.[21] In any case the text does not justify the conclusion that the *vicus*, village, originated as a clan settlement centuries before the Passau formula, and that the same was true in general of other Bavarian village settlements.

The Alamannian evidence consists of a single entry in the *Lex Alamannorum* (c. 81). It is roughly contemporary with the earliest Bavarian material, predating the *Lex* by about ten years and the Freising charter by about twenty. The Alamannian law regulates the procedure to be followed when contention arises between two *genealogiae* (*inter duas genealogias*) as to the location of the boundary between them.[22] After the various formalities conducted before the local count the issue is to be

---

[19] The word *vicus* can mean a number of things. Most frequently it means 'village', of greater or lesser extent, whether free or unfree. However it can also indicate a domain (see R. Latouche, *The Birth of Western Economy*, pp. 64 ff.); and terms like *locus, villa, curtis* and *vicus*, might be used interchangeably (Dopsch, *Economic and Social Foundations*, p. 107). In Frankish sources the *vicus*, as a village, appears to be habitually associated with a church, and therefore might serve as a term for parish (Latouche, pp. 64, 65, n. 3).

[20] Commonly the *formulae* locate properties by two or more designations, but these are not synonyms: cf. in the same document "in pago ill., in villa vocabulo ill.," and in the one following, "in pago ill., in marcha ill., in loco ill."; usually the greater unit precedes the lesser.

[21] On the location of *villae* by their proximity to *vici*, see Latouche, p. 69.

[22] "Si quis contentio orta fuerit inter duas genealogias de termino terrae eorum, unus dicit: 'Hic est noster terminus', alius revadit in alium locum et dicit: 'Hic est noster terminus', ibi de praesente sit comis de plebe illa, ponat signum ubi isti voluerint et ubi alii voluerint terminos, et girent ipsam contentionem. Postquam girata fuerit, veniant in medium et de praesente comite tollant de ipsa terra quod Alamanni 'corfo' dicunt et rama de ipsis arboribus infigant in ipsa terra quod tollunt et illas genealogias qui contendunt levent illa terra praesente comite et comendant in sua manu. Ille involvat in fanone et ponat sigillum et comendet in manu fidele usque ad constituto placito. Tunc spondeant inter se pugna duorum. Quando parati sunt ad pugnam tunc ponat ipsa terra in medio et tangant ipsa terra cum spatas suas quos pugnare habebunt et testificent Deum creatorem ut cui sit iustitia illi donet Deus victoriam et pugnent. Qualis de ipsis vicerit ipse possedeat illa contentione et illi alii praesumptione quare proprietate contradixerunt cum 12 solidis componant."

decided by duel between two individuals representing each of the parties.[23] While the context of the dispute is clearly domanial, nothing in the law tells us precisely about the nature of the *genealogiae* or the properties which are held by their members. But we can safely eliminate the idea that we are dealing with clans and clan lands, considering the contemporary Bavarian evidence and the nature of inheritance and property-holding otherwise found in Alamannian law. The real question is whether the *genealogiae* of the *Lex Alamannorum* represent actual communities of heirs sharing to some extent inherited land, or neighbouring territorial units designated *genealogiae* as in the Passau *formula*. Either meaning is possible and perhaps either is meant, although it should be noted that direct evidence for the territorial designation comes a century after the accepted date of the redaction of the Alamannian law. In the situation envisaged by the provision it is apparent that the land shared by each of the *genealogiae* could take a number of forms. As an inheritance community each might share among its members a common inheritance in the arable, or (and this applies also to the *genealogia* as a territorial unit) simply the waste. It is well to recall the situation of the Eriching donation. There the Fering brothers and the Fagana along with their *participes* happen to appear amicably donating their waste land to the church at Freising, but one can easily imagine them, in other circumstances, as the principals in the kind of dispute found in the *Lex Alamannorum*.

At no point in this survey of the *genealogiae* did the evidence bring us close to the realm of clans and clan lands as these have been represented in traditional historiography, or of extensive unilineal groups as the constituent units of society: what we have found are the commonplaces of the early Middle Ages and late Antiquity. In view of the usual treatment of the term *genealogia* a number of results concerning its relation to property and land-holding are worth stressing in conclusion.

In the first place, the *genealogiae* tell us nothing about the *Landnahme*, least of all that the settlement of the land took place by *Sippen* (however that word is understood) or extended families. One reason is that the evidence is centuries removed from this event. The other reason is that the *genealogiae* do not tell us about settlement at all, but about the practice of inheritance. These are quite distinct activities. Probably the ancient

---

[23] Cf. the boundary dispute between two *conmarcani* in *LBai*. 12.8, 9 also settled by duel if there is no clear proof of possession.

Germans on occasion left the inheritances of their father and grandfather intact, but this certainly does not mean that the descent groups which resulted packed up and resettled again as a group. Descent groups of co-heirs as we find them in the early Middle Ages and Antiquity exist simply because of inheritance and continually arise, after the original occupation, acquisition, purchase or inheritance, of property by an individual.

The evidence of the *genealogiae* does not indicate community property. Rather it shows undivided inheritances – specifically undivided waste – shared by members of the *genealogia*, or, where the term is used as a territorial unit, a domain in the possession of a number of property holders.

Finally, *genealogia* used in reference to groups possessing property, or to the property itself, was in origin a term indicating a descent group of co-heirs. But it is also apparent that, probably also from the beginning, the property of the *genealogia* might be shared by others who were not part of the descent group, because the co-heirs were liable to grant, alienate, sell, or exchange parts of their inheritance portion. Furthermore, the *genealogia* as a descent group sharing certain undivided properties might contain women and the offspring of women, since by Alamannian and Bavarian law women were free to possess and inherit landed property, and daughters succeeded after sons to their father's estate.

7

Conclusion

Despite the extent to which the clan and lineage have figured in modern attempts to describe the social, military and political life of the early Germans, none of the evidence documents extensive unilineal, or for that matter cognatic, descent groups as the constituent kinship groups of society. The clan as a political division, a primitive economic association, an agent of settlement in the successor kingdoms and a military unit fades away before a critical examination of the sources which have long been thought to lend support to its existence.

The major supports for the unilineal clan-basis of society before extensive contact with Mediterranean civilization and the establishment of the successor kingdoms were thought to have brought about its disintegration are the accounts of Germanic society by Caesar and Tacitus. In different ways they do have much to tell us about the ancient world's understanding of the barbarian north, but nothing to tell us about its supposed foundation upon a clan and lineage system. Caesar's Germanic ethnography has long been something of a puzzle to historians. Our new understanding of the artificial ethnographic tradition behind it, which shows it to be a pastiche of speculative *topoi* on barbarian and primitive people and the evolution of human societies, finally means it can no longer be read as a sound description based upon observation or carefully weighed reports. Influenced by the learned theory that contemporary barbarians reflected a social stage through which advanced civilizations had already passed, Caesar attributes to the Germans institutions thought to be appropriate to their primitive level of development. Moreover, although he did not have accurate information on the trans-Rhenan Germans, whom he had never seen in the settled conditions of their homeland, he did have at his disposal spurious ethnographic motifs which had been applied to the non-Celtic north and trans-Rhenan area (though not specifically to the Germans, who were a novelty) with which he was able to flesh out the ethnography that was expected to accompany his German campaign. The traditional misunderstanding of the value of Caesar's ethnography lent credence to the notion that the clan must lie behind the description of the west Germans in Tacitus' *Germania*, but only one passage, which contains an oblique allusion to the composition of the host, has any direct bearing on the question of the clan-basis society. In it, however, Tacitus does not tell us that kin groups of any description formed discrete units in the army, as the traditional teaching maintains; indeed, he does not give a description of military organization at all, but rather merely touches on conditions which he felt helped explain Germanic valour. His reference to family members and neighbours fighting together is as characteristic of societies in which extensive descent groups have no major role to play as it is of those composed of clans and lineages. Tacitus' other remarks about kinship conform hardly at all to the corporate, clan and agnatic view of the kinship system.

As far as the early Middle Ages are concerned, an examination of the small number of texts referring to various groups associated in some fashion with military organization, settlement and landholding again fails to find the clan of traditional historiography. The rights of the *vicini* in sixth-century Frankish legal texts, so often seen as reflecting the hypothetical conditions of Germanic prehistory, are already perceptible among the vicinage groups (called *vicini* as in the Frankish sources) of the late Empire. The term *fara*, as found in continental texts from the sixth to the eighth centuries, has probably been the mainstay of the view that the clan constituted a widespread military and settlement group among the invading Germans. Burgundian, Frankish and Lombard sources show it applied to a range of groupings with the basic and original meaning of *expeditio* and following. The artificial, largely military nature of the *fara* predominates in the earliest sources, but the term could also be applied to households and their dependents. Only in the very late gloss of Paul the Deacon was a definite lineage dimension attributed to it; yet even in this context Paul was not describing the constituent kin groups of society, but was taking a retrospective look at the Friuli magnate houses, which owed their position to the conquest under Gisulf. Finally, with the *genealogiae*, which eighth- and ninth-century sources show associated with landholding, we indeed meet a term which in origin at least indicates a descent group. The characteristics of the *genealogiae* as revealed in the sources show them to be nevertheless the commonplace inheritance communities of medieval landholding, not the hypothetical corporate *gentes* of Caesarian times with whom they have so often been linked.

The rather small body of texts surveyed here has long constituted the textual foundations for the clan theory of Germanic society. The brevity and nature of the classical evidence may tempt some to suppose that the clan's existence somehow went unrecorded in Antiquity, although it should be clear by now that there is no justification for assuming that recruitment was based only on unilinealism. But as regards the early Middle Ages, the quality and the amount of the evidence from the successor kingdoms renders such an expedient impossible. For both periods, however, if history and historical hypotheses are to be based upon the evidence of texts, and not upon preconceptions regarding the nature of social evolution, we should remove the idea of the clan from the historical treatment of the Germans.

In doing so, we eliminate far more than a particular feature of kinship from the question of the origins of northern European civilization. For, as has been indicated, modern historiography has utilized the clan and lineage as a conceptual framework which was intended to explain the very heart of the legal, social and political basis of Germanic society. It became a way to link Antiquity and the early Middle Ages, to explain the evolution of law, kinship, social structure and tribal polity from pre-historic times to the period of the *regna* and beyond. Each one of these areas, therefore, must be cast in a framework radically different from the one that has been commonly propounded.

As the consideration of various texts above has shown, the conception of the clan and lineage has become a stumbling block in the interpretation of many sources and features of social organization. This will be evidenced again in *Part III*, which concerns the second broad area of our enquiry – namely the role of kinship in the legal framework of the *regna*; for the clan is intimately connected with the prevailing ideas on how the principles of relationship defined the rights and obligations of kinship. Because the clan was thought of only as a unilineal group, it was assumed that the rights and obligations proper to cognatic categories in the early Middle Ages once pertained solely to agnates. As the agnatic clan survived into the *regna*, so too, it was thought, did the primary, unilineal nature of kinship; cognation was regarded as a secondary, additive feature to the structure of relationship. This is the framework which has been imposed upon many texts of the early Middle Ages, just as it was imposed upon the evidence of Tacitus. As we will see, again, in considering the specific instance of the Franks, more often than not it has been a poor fit.

Part III

The Early Middle Ages:
Frankish Kinship and *Lex Salica*

8

Kinship and *Lex Salica*

From the standpoint of historical reconstruction, the question whether early Germanic society was constituted of clans must be answered in the negative on the basis of the available evidence from Antiquity and the relatively extensive sources of the early Middle Ages. If we go beyond that conclusion and attempt to reconstruct a detailed picture of kinship structure at the time of the barbarian settlements, we shall find that the evidence is accompanied by limitations that are often severe. At the heart of the problem is the lack of a sufficiently broad and wholly reliable ethnographic sample in the modern anthropological sense. However, that is only to say that we are dealing with historical, not contemporary, documentation and must base our conclusions upon sources of varying value, and in various states of preservation, whose information is fragmentary or disjointed; these difficulties concerning kinship, in fact, are not extraordinary and are just a specific instance of the general situation with which all historians of the period have to deal. The particular limitations of the evidence considered up to this point, especially the synthetic account of the west Germans by Tacitus, suggest that at least we should look for material which not only is of an early date but also, to some degree, meets two criteria. First, it should present a view from within, which is to say that, as much as possible, it should reflect the ideas and emphasis of the society in question. Second, it should be evidence which reveals the operation of the rules of kinship in some diversity – most of all, it should encompass the recruitment of kin groups as well as the determination of kinship categories. The earliest sources which can meet these criteria to some extent are the *leges barbarorum* and related documents of the successor kingdoms. However, a large number of problems must be confronted which are peculiar to these legal collections.

At present we are far from fully understanding the nature and complexity of the so-called barbarian laws.[1] If we ask ourselves precisely what these collections are, the answer must depend upon many aspects of their constitution and development. The reason for the compilation of a code in the first place, the origin of the social and legal elements making it up, the relation of the written law to the legal and administrative apparatus of the kingdom as well as to the law in practice and customary law, the internal and external history of the collection, and its relation to the other collections, both as individual laws and as a body of legal thinking, are all problems whose resolution greatly affects our understanding of the barbarian laws. Nor should we expect all these aspects to be the same for each of the collections; for if the barbarian laws are clearly an interrelated body of literature, they are also, just as clearly, frequently diverse in the substance of their contents, their application, and internal development. A number of these features will recur in the treatment of *Lex Salica*, but for the moment it is necessary to point out one approach to the nature of the provisions of the *leges* which is central to any understanding of them as compilations of national law.

Although the intimate connection of the barbarian laws with Roman law has been recognized for a long time, this aspect has been largely ignored in favour of extracting the 'Germanisms' or supposed Germanisms from them. The question of the *vicini* illustrates the limiting effect of this effort which has been based to a large extent on wishful thinking. Consideration of the available sources makes it plain that, for completely practical reasons, the genealogical examination of the elements of the *leges*, if it is to be founded on documentary evidence and not on largely hypothetical constructs of prehistory, must first explore the avenue of late Roman law.[2] This approach is not as restrictedly legalistic as it may first

---

[1] Some important observations are made by Patrick Wormald, "*Lex Scripta* and *Verbum Regis*: Legislation and Germanic Kinship, from Euric to Cnut," in *Early Medieval Kingship*, ed. P. H. Sawyer and I. N. Wood (Leeds, 1977), pp. 105-138; cf. remarks by J. M. Wallace-Hadrill, *Early Germanic Kingship in England and on the Continent* (Oxford, 1971), p. 36. See also Clausdieter Schott, "Der Stand der Leges-Forschung," in *Frühmittelalterliche Studien* 13 (1979) 29-55; the various *leges* entries in HRG; and n. 2, below.

[2] This change in approach was required by Ernst Levy's *West Roman Vulgar Law* (1951) which clearly showed the connection between the *leges* and the vulgar law of the late Empire. For a survey of legal developments in the late Empire and the pertinent literature, see Wolfgang Kunkel, *An Introduction to Roman Legal and Constitutional History*, trans. J. M. Kelly (Oxford, 1966), ch. 10, who concludes: "The question of Roman influence on the Germanic law of the early Middle Ages must now be posed anew as a result of this research on late Roman vulgar law" (p. 140); and cf. Hermann Nehlsen, *Sklavenrecht zwischen Antike und Mittelalter*, Göttinger Studien zur Rechtsgeschichte 7 (Göttingen, 1972).

appear. Late Roman legislation, whose sources have largely moved beyond the narrow traditions and interests of one class in one city, can often be seen to illustrate the experimentation and commonality of late Antiquity. If the result of viewing the barbarian laws in the context of the concerns and tendencies of the late Empire is to 'de-Germanize' a lot of what we find, this in turn does not simply lead to 'Romanizing' it. In the period being considered here 'Roman' and 'Germanic' have too long been considered as exclusive and unique categories. Roman and barbarian legislation in the fifth and sixth centuries must be regarded not just as the laws of the schools or of the northern forests, but as expressions of the social and ideological flux of the society of late Antiquity. To a considerable degree *Germania* and the Germans were part and parcel of this world before the settlements; they would become increasingly so after. This approach will not explain completely all the provisions of the barbarian laws, but it is an avenue which at least promises to be fruitful; without exploring it, invocations of Germanic prehistory are without foundation.

Whatever else they are, the barbarian laws are not unadulterated Germanic custom, however that is conceived, though the idea of a homogeneous and pure strain of Germanic law is a misleading notion anyway and no more applicable to the period of Caesar than to that of Clovis. Despite all the problems, we can, within limits, have a fairly good idea of the legal elements lying behind the collections of the *regna*. These include more or less straight Roman and ecclesiastical law; vulgar law, or law already in a state of devolution, not to say decomposition, from norms which could be recognized as Roman; late Roman forms adapted, sometimes in distinctive ways, to the needs and ideas of the new settlers; law which is probably *sui generis* and custom which has been carried into the Empire and preserved. In particular instances some of these elements would have been long lived and have had an influential role in European legal history; some appear to have had no future whatsoever, but to have become moribund shortly after their recording. In dealing with *Lex Salica* we shall have occasion to consider examples of the diverse components of the *leges*. To recognize their existence, however, does not mean that one can always easily peel back and isolate layers, as if the collections were composed of undisturbed geological strata with a readily apparent history. While some elements remain relatively intact, others appear in inextricable combinations, transformed and adapted in new contexts. All of this is to say that in an abstract sense, if not always in detail – and herein lies one of the problems of their study – the *leges* in varying degrees are reflections of the diverse mixture of forms and ideas which make up the cultural and social realities of the post-invasion successor kingdoms.

From the point of view of the description of kinship structure and its varied application in the legal system, *Lex Salica* and its associated provisions hold a unique and invaluable position among the *leges barbarorum*, and, in fact, among the legal and narrative sources of the entire medieval period. The areas of medieval jurisprudence in which rights and obligations derived from kinship played an important role were diverse. They included not only the involvement of kinsmen in such realms as inheritance, guardianship, marriage and remarriage, but also the participation of kinship-based personal groups in the broad area of feud, the payment and receiving of compensation, responsibility for malefactors and wergeld debtors, and proof by means of oathhelpers or co-swearers. There can be no doubt that, in principle at any rate, the involvement of kin groups in legal and extra-legal procedure is an ancient and long-lived feature of European legal history in general, and of the northern barbarian peoples in particular. Yet it is only in the high and late Middle Ages that there emerges extensive documentation of the role of the kindred as a personal group in the legal system.[3] If we expect so ancient an institution to be thoroughly recorded in the *leges*, we face disappointment, for on the whole they are brief and ambiguous on the subject; whether this fact has sound sociological foundations in some cases, or is simply the result of the Roman law background of the collections and the discretion of the collectors is difficult to say. There is one exception, however, to this general state of affairs, namely *Lex Salica*, which combines an early date of first redaction with a significant body of material on the role of the kindred as a category and personal group.

A consensus of opinion would date the *Pactus Legis Salicae*, in its earliest redaction, to around the years 507-511. Although there is reason to question the precision of this date, its redaction in the early or mid-sixth century seems assured. This places it among the earliest of the *leges*: considerably younger than the fragmentary *Codex Euricianus*, it is true, but almost contemporary with the *Lex Burgundionum*, some of whose provisions, however, predate the Salic collection by several decades. The impressive number of documents illustrative of kinship structure in the *Pactus* are augmented by a related series of documents, including capitularies added to the original collection, independent royal statutes, succeeding redactions of the collection itself, and finally, in the late

---

[3] Surveyed by Bertha Phillpotts, *Kindred and Clan*.

Merovingian and Carolingian periods, *formulae*. On particulars, some of the *leges* provide more extensive information. The treatment of inheritance in the *Leges Visigothorum*, for instance, is unsurpassed even in many later documents. None, however, remotely approaches the scope and range of matters dealt with in the *Pactus*, and, most importantly, none treats lucidly of the participation of the kindred in the area of feud and compensation. This and the early date of first redaction make *Lex Salica* a unique source in western legal history. Unfortunately its importance is equalled by the magnitude of the problems surrounding a critical and historical understanding of the text of the law, and so it is to these problems we must address ourselves before proceeding to consider specific provisions.

II

Lex Salica has been aptly dubbed the "Schmerzenskind" of the *Monumenta Germaniae Historica*.[4] Originally Pertz in the 1820s and 1830s planned it as the first volume of the *Leges* series. *Lex Salica* never became the first volume, of course, nor the second, nor any succeeding volume, until 1962 and 1969 when a critical edition of the major redactions appeared under the hand of K. A. Eckhardt. The delay of well over a century was not due to lack of effort. Over the years, many of the scholarly lights connected with the *Monumenta* were involved in the problem. The crowning blow came near the end of the First World War when debate over the proposed edition of Mario Krammer led soon after to its being pulped on the eve of publication. In the meantime various editions of the Salic texts appeared, frequently based on what is now called the A redaction, and in particular upon manuscript A1, and often accompanied by extensive commentary.[5] As far as encompassing the variety of text forms was concerned, the most serviceable edition (and to some extent still a necessary accompaniment to *Lex Salica* studies) was that of J. H. Hessels, which printed the manuscripts of the various text families in parallel columns, and arranged the redactions chronologically in the order which corresponds to the most recent edition. None of these efforts, however, approached a critical edition in the sense originally conceived.

---

[4] On the rather complicated trials and tribulations of the *Monumenta* with *Lex Salica*, see K. A. Eckhardt, *Einführung*, pp. 53 ff., rpt. in *Pactus*, MGH LL, 1, IV, 1, pp. xxxv ff. (see below, nn. 7, 8) and S. Stein, "Lex Salica," *Speculum* 22 (1947) 113 ff.

[5] On the various editions of *Lex Salica*, see the two volumes of Eckhardt's edition (below, n. 8).

The reason for the difficulties is not hard to find. There was more or less general agreement that the original *Pactus Legis Salicae* went back to the years of Clovis I or even before. The problem arose in trying to determine the form and contents of Clovis' law and its relation to, and the worth of, succeeding redactions. The manuscripts preserving the texts of the Salic law all date centuries after the period of supposed first redaction. This in itself is not extraordinary, but what is particularly troublesome is that these manuscripts contain a variety of redactions and are all roughly contemporary in date, that is, late eighth and ninth centuries. Moreover, frequently the text of particular laws is plainly corrupt and the text often varies considerably from redaction to redaction and sometimes even from manuscript to manuscript within a particular family. This last difficulty is particularly acute in the A redaction, around which a consensus has grown that it represents the oldest form of the Salic law; in fact almost from the beginning of modern *Lex Salica* scholarship a large segment of opinion felt that in the A text was to be found the closest approximation to the original text of Clovis. However, agreement as to the primacy of the A text has never completely solved the problem of the history of *Lex Salica*, the relation and importance of the various redactions, the variety of readings, and the indefinite relations between manuscripts; neither has it dispelled the disquieting fact that forms of the different redactions were contemporary with one another for varying lengths of time and provided ample opportunity for contamination between various versions of the law. The problems were such that Wallace-Hadrill, writing in 1952, would say: "It seems that our chances of selecting, let alone re-constructing, the 'original' *Lex Salica* are remote indeed. Probably there never was an 'original' in the diplomatic sense."[6]

While these words were being written, K. A. Eckhardt was in the very process of reconstructing such an original. First in the series *Germanen-rechte*,[7] and then, in the sixties, in the *Leges* section of the *Monumenta*,[8]

---

[6] "Archbishop Hincmar and the Authorship of Lex Salica," *Revue d'Histoire du Droit* 20 (1952), rpt. in Wallace-Hadrill, *The Long-Haired Kings*, p. 119. These comments were made in his consideration of S. Stein's view that *Lex Salica* was a ninth-century forgery by Hincmar of Rheims (see especially "Lex Salica," 113-134 and 395-418). The argument of forgery never had much to recommend it, even apart from the fact that the earliest manuscript, A2, dates from the mid to late eighth century, but it is symptomatic of the difficulty in clearly tracing the history and transmission of the *Lex* much before the ninth century.

[7] *Pactus Legis Salicae*, I, 1: *Einführung und 80 Titel-Text* (1954) – henceforth referred to as *Einführung*; I, 2: *Systematischer Text* (1957); II, 1: *65 Titel-Text* (1955); II, 2: *Kapitulieren und 70 Titel-Text* (1956); Germanenrechte N.F. (Göttingen). And *Lex Salica, 100 Titel-Text*, Germanenrechte, N.F. (Weimar, 1953).

[8] *Pactus Legis Salicae*, MGH LL, 1, IV, 1 (Hanover, 1962), and *Lex Salica*, MGH LL, 1, IV,

he attempted to reconstruct the original texts of the major redactions of
Salic law, to date them precisely, to attribute authorship to them, and
to show their interrelation and devolution. Similarly, he tackled the reconstruction and dating of many of the capitularies found added to *Lex
Salica* in some manuscripts, as well as the reconstruction, dating and
attribution of the various prologues, and epilogues, likewise associated
with the text. In addition, he addressed himself to the problems arising
from the so-called Malberg glosses and the monetary system of the law. In
the process, he provided a more complete view of the various forms of
Lex Salica than was heretofore available, even though several volumes
often have to be juggled in order to make proper use of his researches.[9]
Yet the main thrust of his conclusions remains problematical, and there
are severe problems with the nature of his reconstructed text, the dating
and attribution of the various redactions, and indeed with the very
concept of the nature and devolution of the law. The magnitude of the
task completed by Eckhardt should not be minimized, nor can his
conclusions be ignored since they purport to solve almost every major
problem connected with the text of the law, but it is also clear that they
must not, by the uniqueness and authority of the edition, be accepted as
the authoritative statement on *Lex Salica*;[10] we must be careful not to
accept certainty simply for its own sake. After one hundred and fifty years
of modern scholarship the enigma of *Lex Salica* is still with us. The real
value of Eckhardt's work is to have gathered together for the first time the

---

2 (Hanover, 1969). All references to *Lex Salica* will be to these two volumes. The
redactions contained in each volume are indicated in the table of abbreviations. The term
Pactus Legis Salicae (A1, C5, K32) is not well attested, but with certain reservations I
would follow Eckhardt's distinction. Modern scholarship, most manuscripts, and external
references, call the law simply *Lex Salica*. Cf. Nehlsen, *Sklavenrecht*, pp. 257-258.

[9] The division of the redactions into two volumes was no doubt unavoidable. Far more
lamentable is the fact that none of the critical discussion and justification for the
reconstructed texts is included in the *Monumenta* editions, seemingly for copyright
reasons. Unless all is taken on faith, this material is absolutely essential for understanding
how Eckhardt has treated the redactions. To make matters worse, cross references to the
relevant "Germanenrechte" volumes are virtually non-existent, and they, in turn, have no
indices.

[10] On the whole, critical reaction seems to have been slight; cf. Schott, "Der Stand der
Leges Forschung," pp. 37-38 and Wormald's treatment of his conclusions, "Lex Scripta,"
p. 108. Useful reviews are those of R. Buchner, *Historische Zeitschrift* 182 (1956) 366 ff.,
and 191 (1960) 612 ff. An important critique of Eckhardt's approach to the law, and his
treatment of the so-called 'B' redaction is R. Schmidt-Wiegand, "Die kritische Ausgabe der
Lex Salica – noch immer ein Problem?" in zrg ga 76 (1959) 301-319. See also her "Lex
Salica," hrg 2: 1951-1953; and Nehlsen, *Sklavenrecht*, pp. 251-258 and 356.

material necessary for a critical and informed approach to the text and transmission of the Salic Law.

The following chapters naturally concern the evidence for kinship structure in Salic law and not the textual history of *Lex Salica* itself; they also primarily concern the evidence of the earliest form of the codification. But it will be apparent from the remarks above that the question cannot be divorced completely from the broader problems of the nature and transmission of *Lex Salica* as we now have it. This is particularly true for the provisions bearing upon kinship, since in places they display greatly divergent texts. Before proceeding, it will be worthwhile to outline briefly the major recensions of the law. In so doing we can appraise a number of specific features of Eckhardt's conclusions as they apply to the main body of *Lex Salica* and affect the reconstruction of the original text and our understanding of its devolution. This also will give us an opportunity to take into account the approach and methodology followed in succeeding chapters dealing with the evidence for kinship structure.

Lex Salica[11] is preserved in about eighty manuscripts, ranging in date from the latter half of the eighth century to the sixteenth century. The majority of them – about sixty – belong to the late Carolingian redaction. The manuscripts are distributed among some eight text classes or redactions. The most important of these classes for our purpose are labelled, according to the *Monumenta*, A, C, D, K, and H. This alphabetical arrangement is generally agreed to reflect the historical and chronological development of the text. In addition, Eckhardt claims to have found in the texts of these redactions clear traces of a B redaction, which is not preserved in any manuscript, and which he places chronologically between the A and C forms of the law.

The A redaction is preserved in four manuscripts (A1-A4): A1, dating from 800-814; A2, dating from 751-768; A3, ca. 800; and A4, second quarter of the ninth century. A2 is the oldest of all the *Lex Salica* manuscripts. Eckhardt shares the usual view that the A redaction, containing a text divided into sixty-five titles, represents the earliest form of the law.

According to Eckhardt, although the B redaction has not been preserved in any manuscript, traces can be found principally in A2 and in

---

[11] For the older views and literature, see Brunner, DRG 1: 427 ff.; for the more recent, R. Buchner, *Rechtsquellen*, pp. 15 ff., Schmidt-Wiegand, "Lex Salica," 1960-1962, and Schott, pp. 36-38.

Herold (which will be discussed below). He ascribes it to Theoderic I, between the years 511-533. He believes the B redaction to be derived from forms of the law which lie behind A4 and, in particular, A3.

The C redaction, which also contains a text of sixty-five titles, but with additions, is found in only two manuscripts (C5, C6), dating from the end of the eighth century and the second quarter of the ninth century respectively. Excerpts can be found in a third manuscript of the mid-sixteenth century. Eckhardt claims to be able to date this redaction to the years 567-593 under Guntram of Burgundy, or 593-596 under Childebert II, and he associates it with the referendary Asclipiodotus, whom he also regards as the author of the short prologue. He sees a B and an A form, from which A4 is also derived, lying behind the C redaction.

In Eckhardt's scheme these three redactions constitute the Merovingian *Pactus Legis Salicae*, and they form the first volume to the MGH edition along with the later K and H redactions, which resemble them closely. The D and E redactions constitute volume two of Eckhardt's edition, the Carolingian *Lex Salica*. D and E are formed of a text similar to the *Pactus* but divided into about one hundred titles.

As others have, Eckhardt associates the D redaction with Pepin and the date 763/764; he ascribes the redaction and the longer prologue to Baddilo. D is found in three manuscripts (D7-D9): the earliest, D9, dating from 793; D8 from soon after 813; and D7 around the first or second quarter of the ninth century. Eckhardt regards the redaction as drawn from an A, and principally B, form of the law.

The E redaction is generally thought to be an emended form of the D text. It is found in six manuscripts: E11-E15, dating through the course of the ninth century, and E16, from about the mid-tenth century. Eckhardt dates this redaction to 798 under Charlemagne and the editorship of Ercanbald. Somewhat confusingly, his designation of this text as *Emendata*, and the date he proposes, diverge from previous views which connected both name and date with the K redaction, since the date 798 is in fact associated with manuscripts of the K redaction.[12]

The K redaction, which is represented by the bulk of *Lex Salica* manuscripts, and which was recopied throughout the Middle Ages down to the sixteenth century, divides the text into seventy titles. The text itself is largely dependent on the C form of the law. Eckhardt dates it to 802/803 at Aachen under Charlemagne, and calls it the *Karolina*.

---

[12] See Buchner, *Rechtsquellen*, p. 17, and Hessels, vii. Eckhardt regards these dates as carried over to K from manuscripts of the E redaction.

The final redaction which is of concern to us[13] is the printed edition of Herold (H), published in 1557. It is divided into eighty titles. In this form it certainly does not represent a Merovingian or Carolingian text class. However, it has always seemed that Herold drew from manuscripts which have not been preserved. Eckhardt claims that these constituted principally two manuscripts of the lost B and C redactions respectively, once preserved at Fulda, so that Herold can be used as the primary source for the reconstruction of the sixth-century B class. Herold certainly also used manuscripts of the K redaction, and no doubt others. Many scholars have suggested that H gives a composite text.[14]

The main thrust of Eckhardt's conclusions is best summarized when he characterizes the results of his researches as showing that *Lex Salica* corresponds to a common south Germanic legal practice, and that the versions of the law embodied in manuscript represent successive official redactions under the auspices of the Frankish state. Even if this departs mightily from the opinion prevailing up to now (he concludes), it should surprise no one who is familiar with the other *Volksrechte* of the fifth to eighth centuries.[15]

A number of features of Eckhardt's presentation deserve further comment. The first concerns the absolute chronology of the redactions. There are serious difficulties with the absolute dating of all the major text classes, but for our purpose it is most important to consider the first three (A, B, C).[16]

---

[13] There is a ninth-century S class which is a systematic arrangement of the K redaction, and a V class also of the ninth century which is constituted of fragments of an OHG translation.

[14] Hessels, xxi; Brunner, DRG 1: 429-430; Schmidt-Wiegand, "Kritische Ausgabe," pp. 305-309. Her view that Herold had a D manuscript before him is almost certainly correct. Some B provisions reconstructed from H are clearly better regarded as D texts: cf., e.g., D 75.1, 2 and B 41.11a, 11b (= H).

[15] *Einführung*, p. 14. "Wir stehen also hier vor einer allgemeinen südgermanischen Rechtssitte. Sie auch für die salische Franke nachgewiesen zu haben, scheint mir, neben der Ausgabe also solcher, das wesentliche Ergebnis meiner Arbeit" (ibid.).

[16] The problems with the E and K redactions should be implicit in the discussion of these redactions above: in a number of K manuscripts after the longer prologue appears a statement to the effect that in 768 or 798 Charlemagne "hunc libellum tractati legis salicae scribere iussit."

The basis for dating the D redaction is found in this statement found in D7, once again after the prologue: "Anno ter xiii decimo regnante domino nostro Pipino gloriossissimo rege francorum. Amen." Much the same statement appears in D9 but with the name "Carolo rege" and the date 793, which must indicate simply the time at which the manuscript was written. The date in D7, however, cannot be the date when the manuscript was written because it contains material post-dating Pepin. But need this fact indicate that the date in question is one of redaction, or may it simply be the date of the copy of *Lex Salica* upon which D7 is based ? It is by no means certain that the D redaction

Eckhardt, like many other commentators, finally settles on the last years of Clovis' reign as the date for the original redaction of *Lex Salica*. But while there is little trouble in accepting a sixth-century date, even an early sixth-century date, the attribution to Clovis is a supposition, based more upon the weary hopes of scholars who have tackled the question than upon the evidence itself.[17] Moreover, in accepting an early sixth-century date of redaction, we should not with equanimity imagine that we have in the A manuscripts a simple, if deteriorated, transmission from this period. Quite apart from the fact that later dates have been suggested for individual provisions,[18] Eckhardt's consideration of the "fliegende Satzungen" makes it clear that the original redaction has undergone additions. The "fliegende Satzungen" are clauses or provisions which appear in different order, or are absent, in more than one of the A manuscripts. Eckhardt plausibly interprets them as originating as marginal glosses which have gradually been assimilated into the manuscript texts as we have them, but owing to their ambiguous placement, interpolated in slightly varying order. If from the point of view of textual criticism it is more difficult to prove in specific cases that the same kind of interpolation took place in regard to words, phrases, and passages within provisions, it is nevertheless certain that this kind of interpolation is also a factor in the A family. When we find a variety of readings within a family or a serious disturbance in its text, it is not enough to consider only the possibility of a breakdown in the manual transmission of the text, or a misunderstanding of its contents (which supposes that by comparing texts we can re-establish the prior form, fuller perhaps than any surviving); we must also keep in mind the possibility of later additions made to the text, whether through the incorporation of interpretations and glosses or amplifications of a revisor familiar with later

---

was drawn up under the orders of Pepin – and even if one were to accept this, nothing indicates the redaction was in any sense 'official'.

[17] See Eckhardt, *Einführung*, pp. 177 ff. and Buchner, *Rechtsquellen*, pp. 16-17, where the various views and evidence are considered. Arguments that the *Lex* presupposes a united kingdom and not a *Teilreich* are without any worth. A sign of an early date is the dearth of christian and ecclesiastical material. The references in the *Edictum Chilperici* and the *Pactus pro tenore pacis* of around mid-century to *lex salica* may very well refer to a written compilation, but it is well to remember that the *formulae* show instances where invocation of "Salic law" clearly does not refer to the written code: *FBig.* 6, for example.

[18] See Franz Beyerle, "Über Normtypen und Erweiterungen der Lex Salica," ZRG GA 44 (1924) 216-261; Buchner, *Rechtsquellen*, p. 16 and n. 55; and Nehlsen, *Sklavenrecht*, p. 357.

redactions.[19] This will be clearer when we go on to consider the fact that, at least by the eighth century, *Lex Salica* was in large part a literary and antiquarian document.

There is no evidence for the dating and attribution of the B redaction at all, but its chronological position is dependent on the supposition that it originates in Austrasia and must predate C. The dating of the C redaction is based on two considerations. The first concerns the inclusion in the C redaction of ʟs 13.11, which prohibits marriage with certain relatives. Much the same text appears in c. 22 of the Council of Tours of 567, where there is no mention of the Salic law, and without a doubt is borrowed from the *Lex Romana Visigothorum*. From this Eckhardt concludes that the C redaction must postdate 567 and is to be dated roughly in the same period, but before 596, when Childebert ɪɪ regulated much the same matter in a different fashion. It is impossible to endorse this line of reasoning. The dating after 567 seems likely, but Childebert ɪɪ's regulation, if it indicates anything, shows only that he was unfamiliar with this provision of the Salic law, since he saw fit to regulate essentially the same matter in his *Decretio* of 596. All that seems likely is that, probably at some point after 567, the law in question was added to the text in sixty-five titles on the basis of the Council of Tours which in turn was based on the *Lex Romana Visigothorum*. The second piece of evidence for the attribution of the C redaction to Guntram or Childebert is just as tenuous. Eckhardt connects the shorter prologue with the drafting of the C redaction. On the basis of supposed resemblances between this prologue and the treaty of Andelot of 587, presumed to be the work of the referendary Asclipiodotus, he attributes the prologue and the C text to the court of Guntram or Childebert. Once again the evidence will simply not bear this interpretation, even if we overlook the question of the association of C and the shorter prologue. The textual resemblances between the prologue and the treaty of Andelot cited by Eckhardt are minimal and commonplace and constitute not the slightest grounds for attributing both to the same author, Asclipiodotus.[20] The dating of the C

---

[19] Eckhardt himself has shown the interpolation of provisions of what he calls the B redaction into A2 and the borrowing by A4 (ʟs 1.3) of a passage from the Carolingian K redaction.

[20] Remarks by Buchner (*Hist. Zeitschr.*, 182: 372), who in some respects seems not unfavourable to the attribution, make this clear: "... aber E.s Zusammenstellung (I 171) weckt einen irrigen Eindruck von dem Ausmass der Übereinstimmung: er schiebt einzelne Worte, die wenig besagen, aus späteren Teilen des Vertrags in die (teilweise erheblich umgestellten !) Anfangssätze ... ein.... Was bleibt, scheint mir Verfassergleichheit nicht zu beweisen. Damit wird aber auch die Folgerung fraglich, dass der Prolog die authentische Vorrede einer Neuredaktion der Lex Salica sei, namlich der Textfassung C:

redaction must therefore remain problematical; there is no conclusive evidence for dating it relatively early or late.

This conclusion underscores that there is little point to Eckhardt's dating and attribution of the B redaction. But what are we to make of the claim to have isolated a B redaction in the first place? There are a number of distinct aspects to this problem: (1) the presence of B in A2; (2) its presence in Herold's text (H) and its role, along with a lost C manuscript, as the basis for H; (3) the chronological position of the B text – or texts; and finally (4) the practical consideration of extricating it from Herold in particular. As Buchner noted, the reconstruction of the B text is the most audacious and also the most assailable aspect of Eckhardt's edition.[21] That A2 contains readily perceptible interpolations from a text slightly different from what we now have preserved in the other manuscripts is quite correct; we can call this a B redaction without inferring anything as to its relative chronology.[22] It is also another matter to equate this text form with a lost manuscript used by Herold. Moreover, even if we accept Eckhardt's major conclusions, there can be no doubt that in the practical process of extricating the 'B' text from Herold Eckhardt has considerably exceeded his brief as editor. Particular attention will be paid in the appendices below to specific instances of Eckhardt's reconstruction of the B text on the basis of Herold. There considerable doubt is cast upon the idea that Herold transmits in an unadulterated form a sixth-century B (or C) version of the *Lex Salica*. What is important, and lamentable, is that this facet of Eckhardt's formulation necessarily influences his perception of the original A redaction, since he imagines the B redaction to have appeared hard on the heels of the so-called Clovis recension.

When the evidence for the dating and attribution of the various redactions is considered, it is clear that there is little substance to Eckhardt's claim to have established that the various forms of *Lex Salica* are the result of the continuing re-edition of the law by the Frankish state. On the contrary, rather than being proved, this is one of the prime suppositions of his reconstruction and fits well – it can be said, necessarily – with his acceptance of a relatively closed tradition among the

---

diese Deutung scheint mir möglich, aber nicht beweisbar, mindestens bisher nich voll bewiesen."

[21] *Hist. Zeitschr.* 191: 616.

[22] Interestingly enough, in the later of his reviews Buchner seems far less sure of the relative chronology of the B redaction (p. 619), although he does defend Eckhardt against the suggestion of Schmidt-Wiegand ("Kritische Ausgabe," pp. 301-319), that the 'B' is actually a better version of the D redaction.

various text classes. But if throughout the Merovingian and Carolingian period, *Lex Salica* was the official expression of the Frankish state, why is the evidence for its practical use in Frankish society so meagre? Why were so many divergent forms of the same law permitted to exist? Why were the earlier, and presumably out-of-date, redactions never abolished by any of the Carolingian or Merovingian kings? Why is there no statement of official status, even in the case of the later redactions, whose surviving manuscripts stand very near in time to the date of their origin? The absence in *Lex Salica* of the official bureaucratic apparatus of the chancery found in contemporary Visigothic, Lombard and Burgundian law, and its survival in many separate forms are precisely what has always suggested that it has had a different history. Whatever one thinks of its origins and the genesis of some of its redactions, *Lex Salica* should not be equated in its authority and implementation with the *leges* of the southern kingdoms. The question in part is, of course, what is meant by 'official'? That it owes at least some of its present form to the instigation and interest of the Frankish kings is not unlikely. It may even in origin have been a form of kingly literature. But we should not think that, in its various forms, *Lex Salica* represents a developed and developing living body of official law.

Recently the ideological and symbolical context of the *leges barbarorum* has been stressed, and we have been reminded that we make a mistake by associating too closely the northern and Frankish-based laws with the practical administration of justice.[23] Some time ago Wallace-Hadrill wrote of *Lex Salica* that it was a literary as well as a legal text conserved in and by ecclesiastical circles. "It is not surprising that in an antiquarian age, like the ninth century it should have enjoyed a sudden vogue and been disseminated in a variety of texts rich in sometimes meaningless emendations." To recognize the literary, ideological and, at least by the eighth and ninth centuries, antiquarian nature of *Lex Salica* gets us to the heart, I think, of the problem of the texts as we now have them. In the ninth century Lex Salica was an antiquarian document which symbolized the antiquity of the Frankish people and the legitimacy of the monarchy and Empire, a document which was frequently meaninglessly and corruptly copied, but which also, on occasion, was consulted and fixed up. So it was in the eighth century also. And for how long before that? To see *Lex Salica* in this way underscores that we need not always understand the variety of forms as resulting from external, official and

---

[23] Wormald, "*Lex Scripta*," esp. pp. 119-125, 135.

centrally directed attempts to update a body of living law, but rather as the result of an internal process of transmission, emendation, speculation, and contamination. So too, garbled passages need not always be viewed as the deteriorated remnants of a once full and coherent text. Signs of the antiquarian nature of *Lex Salica*, and the internal processes at work in it, are all over. The transformation of the sixth-century *De migrantibus* in the ninth-century interpretation of Louis the Pious has already been considered.[24] Other examples are worth noting from provisions which will be considered more fully in subsequent chapters.

De chrenecruda, which regulates a somewhat mysterious procedure concerning wergeld liability, was included in the A and C redactions. The D redactor likewise included it in all its confusing and confused detail; however he added in the rubric the comment that it was observed only in pagan times, indicating that, at least by the mid-eighth century, the law was considered a dead relic to be associated with legal procedure before Clovis' conversion. The succeeding E redactor recopied the rubric adding further comment, but left out the body of the text. However, in the K redaction, attributed to Charlemagne, the provision reappears in all its detail but without any hint of its obsolescence or abrogation. From here it passed on to an Austrasian systematically-arranged redaction (S) of the mid ninth century. If *De chrenecruda* was "Salic Law" to eighth- and ninth-century Franks, there was no question of their ever seeing it in their courts. Rather it was from their point of view ancient history.[25] It comes as no surprise, therefore, to find in this instance that the various text classes show a large number of textual variants. *De reipus* is another example of much the same phenomenon. Again like *De chrenecruda* one of the more puzzling entries, it regulates the procedure to be followed on a widow's remarriage. Its details are unlike anything we know from other barbarian or later Frankish law. All the redactions contain it, including the ninth-century systematized collection, in much the same detail. There is no commentary on the validity or application of the law. Once again, however, we can be sure that it was not law-in-practice of the eighth and ninth centuries. A capitulary attributed to Louis the Pious mentions the provision, stating that it is to be of no value but that the Franks are to continue to follow the custom of their ancestors, which bears no resemblance to the *De reipus* procedure. These provisions emphasize that we are not necessarily dealing with redactors who had any particular

---

[24] See Ch. 4, n. 19.
[25] Cf. also ls 69 (A17) and the various prologues and epilogues.

understanding of specific laws. But this is not really surprising when we consider that, no matter the dates of the redactions, the various texts are variations of the original text which goes back to the early sixth century.

The anachronism of the social and legal context of some of the provisions was only one problem faced by later redactors. Attempts undertaken before the Carolingian period to understand or fill out obscure provisions resulted in an internal process of emendation and contamination which had nothing to do with law-in-practice at any time or with substantive changes to the legal practices of the Franks. An example of this process is certainly to be found in the famous provision *De alodis*, LS 59, which lists the mother, brother and sister, and maternal aunt, as heirs to the estate of an individual who has died childless. The primary reason for this perplexing sequence of heirs was given some time ago by Heinrich Brunner who recognized that the law is only a partial statement of Frankish inheritance and presupposes a parallel or concurrent right of succession by the paternal relatives. This was also how the early redactor of the *Lex Ribvaria* understood his Salic model, for he inserted the paternal kin into the inheritance sequence as a concurrent category. This happy result was not repeated in the subsequent redactions of *Lex Salica* however, which, in attempting to account for the rights of the paternal kin, inserted the paternal aunt after the maternal aunt in consecutive sequence, at the same time instituting other changes which emphasized the paternal side of Frankish inheritance. The K redactor, facing a puzzle which made little sense, attempted to remedy the incongruous position of the maternal aunt among what was now a largely paternal category of relatives by reversing the sequence of the previous redactions and giving preference to the paternal aunt. Brunner, in making one of the first cogent attempts to interpret Frankish inheritance recognized that the confused and intractable sequence of all the later redactions could hardly accurately reflect the law-in-practice of Frankish inheritance but had clearly grown out of a process of haphazard interpolation and emendation. The confusion caused by the peculiar sequence of relatives in the original redaction of *De alodis* did not end with the provision itself. Long ago it was recognized that the designation of certain maternal relatives in most versions of *De chrenecruda*, LS 58, resulted from glosses drawn originally from the neighbouring *De alodis*. Again, the various ways in which the interpolation was carried out, and the resultant divergent and intractable texts, none of which agree with one another, testify not to the deterioration of official, valid, and coherent law, but rather to a process of speculation, misunderstanding, and contamination.

The nature of the provisions discussed up to this point, the uncomprehending attempts to make sense of their regulations by Carolingian redactors, the dating of all extant manuscripts to the late eighth, ninth, and later centuries, and the sudden diffusion of the text in the ninth century, all suggest that *Lex Salica* was to a large extent a novelty in the Carolingian period, even though the original version in sixty-five titles goes back to the sixth century. There is incidental confirmation of this view if we consider the phrase *lex salica*.

Before the Carolingians, mention of *lex salica* is a rare occurrence and its meaning ambiguous. It does appear in two capitularies of the sixth century. The *Pactus pro tenore pacis* of Chlotar and Childebert mentions procedures *quod lex salica habet*; the *Edictum Chilperici* refers to a certain principle of inheritance *sicut et lex salica habet*. These phrases have naturally been taken as incontrovertible proof that the Salic codification was already in existence in the sixth century. But the question should be asked: must *lex salica* always refer to a written law, to a specific code? A very notable historian of the Merovingians has stated that no compromise over nomenclature is possible, that *lex salica* means a particular code.[26] But a perusal of the *formulae* will show this to be a mistaken notion. The *Formulae Bignonianae* (no. 6) mention betrothal *per solido et denario*, that is betrothal accompanied by the payment of a solidus and a denarius. This procedure is said to be *secundum legem Salicam*. Yet there is no mention of this in the codification *Lex Salica*. We do know that such a procedure was peculiar to Frankish law from an epitome of the *Historia Francorum* where the legates of Clovis offer for the betrothal of Chrotechild a solidus and a denarius *ut mos erat Francorum*, as was the custom of the Franks.[27] Clearly, in the *Formulae Bignoniae*, *lex salica* refers to the national, largely unwritten, law of the Salic Franks, not a particular codification *Lex Salica*. This is pointed out not to deny that the *Pactus pro tenore pacis* and the *Edictum Chilperici* refer to the codification *Lex Salica* – they may, and in any case a sixth-century date for the original redaction seems to me assured – but to emphasize that we must be careful before assuming that the written law lies behind a reference to *lex salica*.[28] This situation should not be surprising. *Lex* can mean written law, but also custom, contract, privilege. Ernst Levy, among others, has pointed out that even the term *lex Romana* from the early sixth century does not always

---

[26] Wallace-Hadrill, *Long-Haired Kings*, p. 109.

[27] MGH LL 5, *Formulae*, n. 4, p. 230.

[28] The same is true of the *lex Alammannorum*. In general see Wormald, "*Lex Scripta*," pp. 121-123.

indicate a specific statute or codification but also includes the Vulgar law.[29]

In the Carolingian period there are clear and increasing references to the codification *Lex Salica*. The *Cartae Senonicae*, dating from around the years 768-775, contains a formula enabling a testator to get around that most distinctive of Salic provisions, the restriction upon the succession rights of daughters. There the testator refers to the limitation as being enshrined in the codification *Lex Salica: sicut lex Salica contenit*. It is instructive to compare this formula with a similar *epistola hereditaria* dating from the early part of the same century or from around the middle of the seventh century. Here there is no mention of *lex salica* but the restriction upon daughters' inheritance rights is referred to simply as a *diuturna sed impia consuetudo*, a long standing but impious custom. However, this formula was copied into a later Carolingian collection. Here the wording was slightly changed. The *diuturna sed impia consuetudo* was changed to the direct invocation of *lex Salica* as in the roughly contemporary *Cartae Senonicae*.[30] Even these Carolingian invocations of *Lex Salica* do not indicate a widespread implementation of the provisions of the codification, but they do show an awareness of the written text which was probably recent and which was part of a novel, and short-lived, attempt to stress the authority of written law.[31] Only in the Carolingian period did the concept of the written Salic law become a widespread part of the legal currency and only at that time was a serious, if failing, attempt made to equate the national law with the written code *Lex Salica*.

The picture of *Lex Salica* which has been presented here suggests, I hope, why the story of the Salic codification reveals itself so darkly. It seems clear too, that to the Carolingians it was a puzzle which they could not always penetrate and this no doubt helps explain the failure of Charles' attempt to reform the national laws of the Franks.[32] Yet it is

---

[29] *West Roman Vulgar Law*, p. 16, n. 69, with citations.

[30] *FSen*. 45; *FMarc*. 2.12; *FMerk*. 23; and see below, pp. 185-188.

[31] On the use of writing in the administration of justice, see F. L. Ganshof, *Recherches sur les capitulaires* (Paris, 1958) and *The Carolingians and the Frankish Monarchy*, trans. Janet Sondheimer (Ithaca, 1971), pp. 125-142. For the implications of Ganshof's conclusions for the 'schriftlose Zeit' of the *leges*, see Wormald, "*Lex Scripta*," pp. 123-124, and Schmidt-Wiegand, "Kritische Ausgabe," p. 315.

[32] Einhard suggests he only seriously undertook the task after he became emperor, but he makes no bones about the failure of the enterprise:

> Post susceptum imperiale nomen cum adverteret multa legibus populi sui deesse – nam Franci duas habent leges, in plurimis locis valde diversas – cogitavit quae deerant addere et discrepantia unire, prava quoque ac perperam prolata corrigere,

probably because of the Carolingian interest in this record of their ancient national law, and the attempts to utilize it as part of the corpus of the written law of the Empire, that we can still occasionally penetrate the legal and social conceptions of early sixth-century Gaul.

The nature of the problems confronting us concerning Frankish kinship, and indeed other aspects of the early Franks, cannot, therefore, be properly appreciated outside the question of the transmission of the *Pactus Legis Salicae*. The text may have suffered severely in the course of transmission; it may have been subject for a long time to all kinds of revisions, emendations and additions, some of considerable merit, others of none. Yet there can be no doubt that in the earliest redaction, whatever the circumstances and purpose of its compilation, one can still find a reflection of the living law of the early sixth century. If the difficulties are often gritty and the conclusions sometimes untidy, this does not mean that a considerable amount cannot be said about Frankish kinship. At the very least the issues need to be outlined and the material put upon a fresh foundation. This has not really been done since Heinrich Brunner, a long time ago, dealt in scattered fashion with the major kinship texts of the Salic law.

III

What remains to be done is to describe the method of presentation followed in the succeeding pages. Since obviously our major concern will be the earliest form of the law, the primary evidence will be the A redaction, which, despite some early opinion to the contrary,[33] is now agreed to contain a much older version of the law than that of the other redactions.

Whenever a law is cited, reference will be made in the apparatus to other redactions that assist the understanding of the A class or provide divergent readings indicating a devolution of the original text of the law. Notice will also be taken in this apparatus of reconstructions and interpretations by editors and commentators. Where necessary, fuller discussion will be found in the body of the text or in appendices.

---

sed de his nihil aliud ab eo factum est, nisi quod pauca capitula et ea imperfecta legibus addidit.

(*Vita Caroli*, ed. O. Holder-Egger, *MGH Scriptores Rerum Germanicarum in usum scholarum* 25, c. 29.) Cf. Boretius 1: nos. 39, 41.

[33] Pertz, the initiator of the *Monumenta* project, believed the C form to be the oldest. Initially this was followed by Krammer, who later switched his preference to D.

The A family itself, as has been indicated, is represented by four manuscripts (A1-A4). Little is gained and much lost by attempting to cite, and justify, an abstract reconstructed text.[34] If this means instead citing one of the A manuscripts, there is little doubt as to which one it should be: greater dependence, often a narrow dependence, on A1 has been almost universal among all those who have accepted the A redaction as the oldest, which is to say most editors.[35] It is also the text usually followed by commentators and legal historians. While Eckhardt's MGH edition is less dependent on A1 than those of many of his predecessors, its primary role is still apparent when one considers the form of the reconstructed text and, in cases of divergent readings, the prevalence of A1 over the other A manuscripts and the younger redactions when it agrees with another manuscript. Although Eckhardt himself does not draw the conclusion, his consideration of the "fliegende Satzungen," only emphasizes the conservative nature of A1; for it frequently lacks provisions which are considered to have originally been marginal glosses because of their varied positioning in other manuscripts of the A family. In the following discussion, therefore, the form of the law cited will be that of A1.

[34] There is also little point in trying to give a precise stemma of the A manuscripts. None is derived from the other, but their exact relationships are problematical. The attempts to define their relationship by Eckhardt involves the supposition of a considerable amount of contamination within the A manuscript tradition. On this see Buchner, *Hist. Zeitschr.*, 182: 369. Eckhardt prints no stemma in the MGH edition, but see the Germanenrechte *Pactus* II, 1, 45-47. What is clear generally is the greater similarity between A1 and A2, and between A3 and A4.

[35] So Pardessus, Waitz, Merkel, J. Behrend, J. H. Hessels, R. Behrend, Geffcken, K. A. Eckhardt and J. H. Eckhart. On the earlier editions see Eckhardt's introduction to his edition.

9

The Bilateral Kindred
as a Personal Group I:
Feud and Compensation

A. The Paying and Receiving of Compensation:
LS 62, *De conpositione homicidii*
and LS 68, *De homine ingenuo occiso*

In the early Middle Ages, and well beyond,[1] one of the most significant functions of kin groups and kinship-based groups, was their role in the judicial and extra-judicial process of feud and compensation. The intermingling of vengeance, compensation, kinship liability, and some form of judicial or quasi-judicial process, was by no means peculiar to the Germans; it can be found at some point among most European and many non-European peoples. Nevertheless, the judgment holds true for the most part that, in the area and period dealt with here, the bloodfeud was "the most undoubtedly Germanic of all barbarian institutions."[2] From this we should not conclude that, in the West, all features associated with feud and its accoutrements are the product only of long barbarian tradition rooted in a society with a rudimentary legal system: many can also be a natural response to the breakdown of public law, or result from changing conceptions of what constitutes public law.[3] When we find elements of the Roman population in the successor kingdoms taking to feud, we need

---

[1] In certain areas throughout the later Middle Ages and even into the early modern period; see Phillpotts, *Kindred and Clan*, especially on Scandinavia. Farther afield, the bloodfeud in Albania is well-documented for the nineteenth and twentieth centuries.

[2] Wallace-Hadrill, "The Bloodfeud of the Franks," in *The Long-Haired Kings*, p. 121.

[3] Cf. for instance the changing meaning of *vindicatio*: Levy, *West Roman Vulgar Law*, pp. 210-219.

not postulate barbarization; self-help does not have to be taught in order to be learned since it is an obvious means of coping with weak or ineffective public authority. Yet the general features surrounding feud process, and the compensation of homicide, as found in the north and in areas of heavy barbarian settlement, is of undoubtedly Germanic descent. Writing at a time when such self-help was alien to Roman law, Tacitus gave a description of customs among the first-century Germans which, in its general outline, is applicable to procedures found in the Romano-German kingdoms and throughout the Germanic (and non-Germanic) north at a later date. The system of feud and compensation mentioned by Tacitus, which involved to some extent a wider category of kinsmen, and which entailed the already established practice of the royal or public authority sharing in the *multa* in cases adjudicated in the assembly,[4] prefigures to a remarkable extent the general phenomenon of medieval feud process.

There are many problems connected with the relation of feud to the judicial and social structure of medieval society, particularly as regards the legality of vengeance and the active role and extent of kin groupings in it; the nature of the liability falling upon kinsmen in the compensation procedure; and the realities of distribution and payment when this entailed a fairly wide range of kinsmen. While vengeance was often recognized, it was at best extra-judicial and has left little trace in the laws touching on kin liability. It has been pointed out that the narrative evidence indicates that the vengeance-group was a small ad hoc force composed of the closest kin, and this feature has been linked to the "complexity" of the new social arrangements in the successor states and the dispersal of kin groups in the settlement.[5] The literary sources certainly suggest that it would be unwise to transfer the relative obligations falling upon distant and not so distant kinsmen in the compensation procedure into a gauge for measuring their role in vengeance. The relative who is legally or socially bound to participate in compensation may not be easily given over to ambushes or expeditions in the night; indeed the vengeance group when it appears is best seen not as a strict kin group at all but as a kindred-based group composed of interested relatives, friends, and dependants. The smallness and composition of these groupings, however, should not necessarily be seen as the result of the dispersal of kindreds and new conditions. Most feud was undoubtedly local feud and the more kindreds remained in the same localities, the more complex and interlocking

---

[4] Above, pp. 59-60.
[5] Wallace-Hadrill, "The Bloodfeud of the Franks," pp. 125-126.

became the kinship network; consequently the more likely reconciliation became, as kinsmen and affines with divided loyalties would be less inclined to take sides. For some time now it has been recognized that the interlocking network of relationship was an important factor conducive to compensation and reconciliation.[6] The same factor would also tend to limit the size of the vengeance group when violence broke out. The dynamics of kindred organization no doubt can take many forms but probably the impulse to reconciliation and the smallness of the vengeance group were inherent in the overlapping nature of bilateral kindred systems from the beginning and not particularly the result of new settlements and new civilization. What concerns us, then, is the configuration of the kin group involved in the paying and receiving of compensation and the divisions of that group, including the proportional obligations proper to its internal categories. This is the area in which the legal sources provide us with information, although this information has undoubtedly been subjected to a great deal of schematization.

Various aspects of the relation of wergeld and kinship categories occur together with sufficient frequency in many of the areas of Germanic settlement to permit a certain amount of generalization.[7] The kind of abstraction which can be drawn up from the later data is useful if we do not mistake similarity for uniformity in practice and detail, and if we remember that the resemblances in form can preside over divergent conditions and can persist throughout innumerable mutations which expand or contract the role of kinship in the process of compensation. Frequently, when a case of homicide was put to compensation, not merely the heirs of the deceased and the homicide himself were involved, but a more or less wide group of relatives of both parties. This necessitated a number of divisions of the wergild corresponding to the kin categories implicated in the receipt and payment. Looked at simply from the side of the deceased's kindred[8] we find a fundamental distinction between the

[6] Ibid. Wallace-Hadrill's fine analysis of Frankish feud practice *in situ* is probably expressed by him in terms of changes brought about by kin dispersal in the settlement and the complexity of Gallo-Roman society because he proceeds from a modified version of the traditional teaching on kinship structure, with its supposition of a prior coherence of the kin group and the role of agnates. But cf. more recent remarks in *Early Germanic Kingship*, pp. 41-43.

[7] "The first point to strike us in the wergild schemes of the various countries is their fundamental similarity" (Phillpotts, p. 265). For a summary and tabulation of most of this evidence, ibid., pp. 265 ff.

[8] The basic principle seems to be that the divisions on one side receive or make payment to their counterparts on the other side. How this worked in practice is difficult to say, particularly in cases when on one side or another a group was lacking. Saga evidence at least suggests a good deal of dickering. Phillpotts, p. 265.

portion which goes to the slain's heirs or very near relations and that
which falls to the wider kin. There is some variation in the proportions,
but the one most frequently encountered is 2:2 or 2:1; in the former case
one-half of the total wergeld fell to the heirs and the remaining half to the
wider kindred as a whole. The wider kin itself was not undifferentiated
and repeatedly the basic distinction was between patrilateral and matrilateral relations. Here too there is some variation in the proportions borne
by each, but by far the most prevalent one is 1:1, which is to say maternal
and paternal kinsmen were treated equally. Within each of these bilateral
divisions the amount claimed by an individual depended upon his degree
of relationship to the slain. The usual method of division was by halves,
but there is clear evidence also of a system of division by thirds, whereby
in succession each nearer group received two-thirds of the remaining
compensation.[9] In turning to consider in detail the compensation
provisions of *Lex Salica*, which gives in fact the earliest description of the
relative role of kinship categories in the process of compensation, we shall
find, despite some ambiguity in detail, a clear reflection of this general
pattern of compensation and kinship division.

In the earliest redaction of the Salic law there occurs the following
provision (LS 62) regulating the receipt of wergeld payment:[10]

> 1. Si cuiuscumque pater occisus fuerit medietate conpositionis filii col-
> legant et alia medietate parentes quae proximiores sunt tam de patre quam
> de matre inter se diuidant.
> 2. Quod si de una parte paterna seu materna nullus parens non fuerit, illo
> portio in fisco colligatur.

> 1. If anyone's father is killed let the sons collect half the compensation,
> and let the near relations from both the father's and the mother's side divide
> the other half between them.
> 2. But if there is no relative on one side, whether the paternal or maternal,
> let the portion pertaining thereto be collected by the fisc.[11]

---

[9] For convenience, see Phillpotts' summary, pp. 265-268.

[10] The basic interpretation of the Salic compensation regulations (LS 62, 68) is that of
Heinrich Brunner, "Sippe und Wergeld nach niederdeutschen Rechten," ZRG GA 3 (1882)
31 ff.

[11] *filii*, line 1: translated here literally as 'sons', since this is a compensation regulation,
although in the legal language of late Roman law and the *leges*, *filii* can equal 'children'.

de una parte, line 4: following Brunner ("Sippe," p. 31) and Eckhardt's reconstructed text this is an emendation in place of *de nulla* of A1, which is nonsensical as it
stands; cf. the texts in A2, A3 and the younger redactions. Clause 2 is missing in A4.

In A2 this provision has been entered twice. One entry is certainly an interpolation,
labelled by Eckhardt the B redaction. It is essentially the text of the D redaction without its

Further elaboration is found in a succeeding chapter, but as far as it goes the present regulation is quite straightforward and presents a number of the key elements of kinship participation in Frankish compensation procedure. At the core is a distinction between the deceased's nearest kin or heirs (*filii*) and the more distant kindred. This distinction corresponds to the common division of the wergeld in two equal parts, one half going to the heirs and the other to the wider group of relations. The latter includes maternal and paternal kin, the term *proximiores* being used to designate both patrilateral and matrilateral relatives.

The division between relations on the father's side and those on the mother's side is the second fundamental distinction of Salic procedure which is common to many wergeld schemes. It is a recurrent feature not only of Salic law but also of its derivative systems and is frequently applied, for instance, in later inheritance laws.[12] In the provision before us the claims of these two groups are independent to such an extent that, on the failure of one side, the portion of the wergeld pertaining to it does not pass to the other side but like *bona vacantia* is taken by the fisc.

The fact that paternal kin do not fall heir to the portion of the maternal kin and vice versa is not altogether surprising, especially if we do not start from the proposition that wergeld once pertained only to agnates: for both groups are linked by blood and interest only through the deceased and his descendants and both are, in reality, independent entities united momentarily through common injury. What is more surprising is that the *filii*, who are related by blood to the paternal and maternal kin, seem to be excluded from claiming the portions falling to the wider category of kinsmen. Such a fractionalization of the wergeld – or more accurately of the kinship categories who share in it, since from the point of view of this law, the wergeld as a whole is collected even if only through the intervention of the fisc – well illustrates the conception of the kindred as a temporary unit of divergent and autonomous groups, but the rigid circumscription of claims has the look of fiscal opportunism. One suspects that in arrangements made outside the purview of the fisc there was more give and take, and each party got away with what it was able.

It can be suggested, however, that the entry of the public authority into the network of claims[13] provided, apart from revenue, a means of forcing

---

regularized spelling and inflection. H, the principal source for Eckhardt's reconstruction of the B redaction, here does not give a 'B' (or C) text, but one derived from K.

[12] The so-called *Tochterrechte*; see Brunner, "Sippe," p. 32.

[13] While it is tempting to see this as the result of the enhanced prestige of the Frankish monarchy, it should be remembered that in the earliest reference to wergeld procedure in

the payment of the whole wergeld and of replacing the protection to life and honour normally afforded by a full kindred. On the face of it this is certainly not a blow at the principle of compensation and feud, but it can be seen as an attempt to regulate procedure, and discourage homicide, by fixing the indemnity and ensuring that the homicide and his party do not escape the full weight of compensation owing to a lack of relatives on the side of the deceased. Later additions which specify that the fisc may give its portion to whomever it pleases may indicate that the fisc would yield its gain to the plaintiff, heir, or widow.[14]

Further information on the principles of division among the wider kin is found in an addition (LS 68) to the original redaction of 65 titles.[15]

> Si quis hominem ingenuum occiderit et ille qui occiderit probatum fuerit, ad parentibus debeat secundum legem conponere. media conpositione filius habere debet. alia medietate exinde ei [= matri] debet ut ad quarta de leude illa adueniat. alia quarta pars parentibus propinquis debent, id est tres de
> 5 generatione patris et tres de generatione matris. si mater uiua non fuerit, media parte de leudae illi parentes inter se diuidant, hoc est tres de patre proximiores et tres de matre. ita tamen qui proximiores fuerit parentes de praedictis conditionibus prendant. et tres partes illis duabus diuidendam demittat. et nam et illis duabus ille qui proximior fuerit illa tertia parte duas
> 10 partes prendant, et tertia parte parenti suo demittat.

The text has clearly suffered from faulty transmission, but it seems to me questionable that its original condition was much better than at present. In any case problems of interpretation arise not from what the text says badly but from what is taken for granted and not said at all; the substance of the provision, if poorly worded, is quite intelligible:

> If anyone kills a freeman and the homicide has been adjudged, he must compensate the relatives of the deceased according to law. The son of the deceased must have one half of the compensation. Then one half of the remainder is owed to [his mother, i.e., the widow of the deceased] so that one quarter of the wergeld (leudis) goes to her. The other quarter is owed to

---

the *Germania* the *civitas* or *rex* receives part of the *multa*. Even if a sometime thing, the principle of the state's intercession in compensation is of considerable antiquity. Exacting a penalty from the homicide, though, is quite a different matter from claiming the share of deceased relatives.

[14] "portio ... in fisco collegatur aut cui fiscus uoluerit dare" (C5). This power, of course, is implicit in the initial provision.

[15] It occurs only in two manuscripts, A1 and A2: Eckhardt, LS 68; Hessels, c. 101. A1 is used above. A2 is in virtual agreement except for two large lacunae.

the near relatives, that is, three categories from the paternal kin and three categories from the maternal kin. If the mother [i.e. the widow of the deceased] is not alive, let the relatives, that is the three categories from the paternal and maternal side, divide the half portion of the wergeld between them. Provisions must be made that the category of relations nearest in degree take according to established conditions, [namely that on each side it take two thirds] and leave three parts to be divided between the remaining two; and also, of the remaining two, those who are the nearest take two thirds of that third part and leave a third part to their kinsman.[16]

The inclusion of the deceased's widow, which is not unknown in other compensation systems,[17] must be regarded as an innovation upon the older provision, or a reflection of regional custom.[18] Her portion, which amounts to one-quarter of the wergeld is large and comes out of the half portion which according to ts 62 went originally to the paternal and

[16] *alia ... debet*, line 3: there is undoubtedly a lacuna in the text at this point; that the recipient of the quarter portion of the wergeld ("ei") is the *mater* becomes apparent in lines 5 and 6; Brunner suggests that originally after "medietate" (line 3) the words "matri medietate" had stood in place of the manuscript's "ei" ("Sippe," p. 33); Eckhardt's reconstructed text reads "Alia medietas exinde (matr)i debet"; Joseph Balon would read, "exinde (uxor)i debet" (*Traité de droit salique: Étude d'exégèse et de sociologie juridiques*, Ius Medii Aevi, 3, Namur, 1965, 2: 468, n. 2611). Eckhardt regards the *mater* as the mother of the deceased (*Einführung*, p. 82, n. 134) but Brunner's suggestion that *mater* refers not to the mother of the deceased but the mother of the *filius* (line 2), i.e., the widow of the deceased, is almost certainly correct ("Sippe," pp. 33-34). I think this is even clearer if we consider that this provision is referring back to c. 62, where the slain man is designated *pater*, and his *filii* are the group with first claim. Thus the *mater* here is the wife of the slain and mother of the *filius*. See also the terminology of *LBai*. 15.7, 8.

tres, line 4: taken here to indicate three categories, not just three individuals: the possible nature of the groups will be discussed below, but even if simply proximity of degree is intended there clearly might be more than one relative of equal degree claiming each portion; thus the conflation of singular and plural subjects (lines 7-10).

tres partes, line 8: Brunner would read: "prendant (duas partes). Et tertia parte ... dimittat" (lines 8-9), emending *tres partes* to "tertia parte"; Eckhardt's reconstructed text, likewise, reads: "ter(tiam) parte(m) ... dimittat." These emendations are meant to reflect the principle that the first two categories successively take two thirds of the allotted portion. Now this principle certainly lies behind the provision because we can see it clearly in lines 9-10 where the second category takes two thirds out of the third left by the first group. But it is questionable if these alterations are necessary; the text as it stands would be understood by anyone familiar with the principle of division and the provision presumes this is well known; *tres partes* is not a mistake for "one third," but refers to the fact that the third which is left by the first category is constituted of thirds and must be divided again.

parenti suo, line 10: following Brunner ("Sippe," p. 33) and Eckhardt's reconstructed text this is an emendation in place of *patre suo* (A1) and *patri suo* (A2).

[17] E.g., cf. Phillpotts, p. 69.
[18] Brunner, "Sippe," p. 35.

maternal kin. This may be regarded as limiting the rights of these groups, but, in the absence of the widow, the situation envisaged by the earlier chapter continues to prevail and her portion is claimed and divided by the wider kin; as will be seen, within the wider kin on either side the division proceeded by a system of thirds. With the introduction of the widow, it is apparent that the system of halves has been adopted also. Thus the *filii* take one-half; and the next recipient, the widow, takes one-half of the remainder, that is, one-quarter, leaving one-quarter to the wider kin.

The patrilateral and matrilateral kin (*proximiores*) almost certainly divide their quarter or half portion equally.[19] This is clearly implied if not directly stated by both provisions. In addition, quite apart from the fact that such parity between paternal and maternal kin is a marked feature of later wergeld provisions generally and of the Frankish area in particular,[20] direct confirmation comes from the chapter *De chrenecruda*, found in the earliest redaction of Salic law: here the matrilateral and patrilateral kin may each be made responsible for half the sum owed by a wergeld debtor.[21]

LS 68 gives further information on the divisions within the bilateral groupings. On each side three categories of relatives are called. The apportionment proceeds by a system of thirds, whereby the first category takes two-thirds of the allotment, the second, two-thirds of the remaining third, and the last category the remainder. Proportionally this works out to a ratio of 6:2:1; translated into fractions of the entire wergeld in the case where the spouse was deceased or had no claim, on each side the *tres proximiores* take 6/36, 2/36 and 1/36 respectively.

There is an extraordinary resemblance, noted by Brunner,[22] between the divisions and proportions of Salic law and those of the *Keure* of Oudenarde in Flanders[23] dating from 1300. According to this late regulation, the eldest brother of the deceased as plaintiff (and his younger brothers) receive one-half of the wergeld. The remaining half falls to the wider kin. Patrilateral and matrilateral kin take equally. Each side is divided into three groups who take successively by a system of thirds in the ratio 6:2:1. These are basically the divisions and proportions of Salic law. The system of thirds is particularly striking, as, elsewhere, only

---

[19] So Brunner, ibid.
[20] Ibid.
[21] See below, pp. 144 ff.
[22] "Sippe," p. 35.
[23] For which see Phillpotts, pp. 173-174.

traces of such a method of division can be found in Norwegian schemes.[24] Oudenarde is located in the very heart of early Salian settlement; all of which indicates at least a regional continuity of the structure of the Frankish wergeld scheme. Where the Oudenarde and Salic provisions differ is in the fact that the Oudenarde plan ignores the descendants of the deceased and designates his brothers as recipients of the half portion. The three bilateral groups are the first, second and third cousins (*rechtzweers*, *anderzweers*, and *derdelingen*) which again resembles the Salic *tres proximiores*.

So far we have been able to proceed with assurance. In trying to better understand the nature and limit to the categories of the *tres proximiores*, however, we are faced with problems which cannot be solved directly by the text or by reference to evidence in any way contemporary. What is clear from the wording of the provision, and the system of apportionment, is that the *tres* represent three distinct categories of proximity, not the three nearest individuals who could, conceivably, be of the same degree; for example, three brothers or three uncles. It must be said that, from the text alone, the three classes could possibly be defined by simple proximity of degree. However, if we give any weight to the widespread practice of later wergeld systems, including those in old Frankish areas, and to common methods of reckoning kinship for other purposes, we must suppose that the three categories refer not to degree simply but to parentelae, lines, or stocks.[25] The problem does not end here. For, granted that some form of parentelic system is in use, what must be determined next is the point at which the first category starts. Put another way, is the kindred employed for wergeld purposes limited roughly to second or third cousins? Brunner, certainly with the later situation of Oudenarde in mind and citing *De chrenecruda*, in which the categories of wider kin appear to start with the parentela of the grandfather (that is, first cousins),[26] suggested that the first parentela is that of the grandfather, and thus the range envisioned is that of third cousins of the deceased. This is probably the best way of regarding the Salic regulations before us: the brothers of the deceased would then claim with the *filii*, who are the heirs and who are thought to be, in this instance, of sufficient maturity to prosecute the

---

[24] Phillpotts, p. 266.

[25] In the *leges* this problem is not limited to the provisions before us. In Lombard law for instance, see the inheritance regulation of Ro. 153. I accept the proposition that in the Salic and Lombard instances we are dealing with some form of lineal-gradual or parentelic system.

[26] "Sippe," pp. 34, 36. *De chrenecruda* is considered imminently.

case and represent the immediate family of their father. On the other hand, the range of the kindred may conceivably have varied according to who was plaintiff; in that case, with the sons as plaintiff, brothers, as both maternal and paternal kin, would claim as the first category of the wider kin, making the effective range of the kindred second cousins. The problem of the range of the kindred for compensation purposes largely results from the necessary schematization of the wergeld schemes, but unless we accept the unlikely possibility that the three bilateral categories of near kin were defined simply by proximity of degree, among the Franks the kindred for compensation purposes appears to have normally been a bilateral group of second or, more likely, third cousin range.[27] As will be seen at a later point, roughly the same extent of kinship participation is suggested by the evidence for oathhelping.

B. Compensation Liability: ls 58, *De chrenecruda*

Closely connected with the provisions for the receipt of wergeld is the title *De chrenecruda*, which also forms part of the earliest redaction of Salic law. Although it adds little information on the nature of the kinship divisions in compensation procedure, it is, nevertheless, significant for the respective roles and legal functions of these divisions. In the case where a homicide is too poor to raise the amount of compensation required by law, ls 58, *De chrenecruda* regulates the procedure whereby his liability for payment can be transferred to his near relations.

1. Si quis hominem occiderit et totam facultatem data non habuerit unde tota lege conpleat, xii iuratores donare debet nec super terram nec subtus terram plus facultatem non habeat quam iam donauit.
2. Et postea debet in casa sua introire et de quattuor angulos terrae in
5 pugno collegere et sic postea in duropullo, hoc est in limitare, stare debet intus in casa respiciens et sic de sinistra manum de illa terra trans scapulas suas iactare super illum quem proximiorem parentem habet.
3. Quod si iam pater et fratres solserunt, tunc super suos debet illa terra iactare, id est super tres de generatione matris et super tres de generatione
10 patris qui proximiores sunt.
4. Et sic postea in camisia discinctus discalcius palo in manu sepe sallire debet ut pro medietate quantum de conpositione diger est aut quantum lex

---

[27] Cf. the phrase *tres proximiores* with the later terminology of the Oudenarde provision and also with Scandinavian and continental designations of the third cousin as 'fourth man' and second cousin 'third man': Phillpotts, pp. 69, 79, 115.

addicat illi tres soluant; hoc et illi alii, qui de paterna generatione ueniunt, facere debent.

15 5. Si uero de illis quicumque proximior fuerit ut non habeat unde integrum debitum saluat, quicumque de illis plus habet iterum super illum chrenecruda ille qui pauperior est iactet ut ille tota lege soluat.

6. Quam si uero nec ipse habuerit unde tota persoluat, tunc illum qui homicidium fecit qui eum sub fidem habuit in mallo praesentare debent et 20 sic postea eum per quattuor mallos ad suam fidem tollant. Et si eum in conpositione nullus ad fidem tullerint, hoc est ut redimant de quod non persoluit, tunc de sua vita conponat.

1. If anyone kills a man and having given all his [moveable] property still does not have enough to fulfill the whole amount legally owed, he must offer twelve oathhelpers to swear to the effect that he has no more property, neither above the ground nor below it, than that which he has already given.

2. And then he must enter his house and gather in his hand earth from the four corners; then he must stand in the doorway, that is on the threshold, looking into the house and thus with his left hand throw dirt over his shoulders upon his next of kin.

3. But if his father and brothers have already paid, then he ought to throw the dirt upon his kinsmen, that is the three categories from the maternal kin and the three from the paternal who are near kinsmen.

4. And then in his shirt, without belt or shoes, and with a rod in hand, he must vault the hedge in order that the former three categories [i.e. the maternal kin] pay for one-half the amount of compensation which is lacking or which the law awards; likewise the other three categories, which come from the paternal kin, must pay the same amount.

5. But if there is any kinsman among them who does not have property enough to pay the whole amount of his debt, again let the poorer relation throw *chrenecruda* upon the richer to enable him to pay the full legal amount.

6. But if the homicide still does not have enough to pay the whole amount, then those who have been his sureties must present him in the assembly and thus act as his sureties for four assemblies. And if no one stands surety for him in respect to the compensation in order, that is, to redeem the debt he has not discharged, then let him compensate with his life.[28]

---

[28] As usual, the text followed is that of A1. The major textual considerations will be dealt with in Appendix I. Except for 58.3 there is not enough substantial variation to require much comment. The text is absent in the E redaction.

58.3: As regards this clause, A2 is largely in agreement with A1. A3, A4 and C in place of the father and brother list the mother, brother and mother's sister and her sons. D,

De chrenecruda is amongst the most debated of the Salic provisions,[29] and probably more than any other it has been seen as reflecting the social and judicial conditions of Frankish prehistory. Certainly later redactors of the Salic law connected it with their own long dead pagan past.[30] While we need not follow them in this, at any rate it seems likely that, in the new Frankish kingdom created by Clovis, its historic life was localized and most likely short-lived.[31] This would help to explain the substantial textual

---

K and H list the father in conjunction with the latter relatives. These *mater* and *soror matris* texts have resulted from an interpolation based on the following chapter 59, *De alodis*, where these relatives appear in the context of matrilateral inheritance. For a fuller discussion of the variation of this clause, see Appendix I.

suos, line 8: on this meaning of *sui* cf. the final clause (58.6) in K: "Et si eum per conpositionem nullus suorum uoluerit redimere de uita conponat."

pro medietate quantum ... diger est, line 12: each group pays for one half the deficit. The view that the one half refers to the complete obligation due to the kinship categories successively has nothing to recommend it. See comments by Brunner, "Sippe," p. 39 and Geffcken, pp. 220-222.

hoc et, line 13: along with just about everyone else, I have emended "hoc est" of A1 ("hoc est," A2, A3) to "hoc et." Both phrases are normally abbreviated and thus easily misconstrued. A4: "et"; C: "et illi ... hoc est et illi," where both elements are found; H: "hoc et"; K: "id est."

58.5, 6: missing in A4. 58.5 shows a large lacuna in A2 and A3.

de quod non persoluit, lines 21-22: following Eckhardt, an emendation in place of "de quo domino persoluit" (A1). Cf. A2: "que non solsit"; A3: "de hoc quod non persolsit."

[29] *De chrenecruda* has not been the subject of recent research, but it once excited great controversy. The various views and literature can be found in J. and R. Behrend's edition of *Lex Salica*, 2nd ed. (Weimar, 1897); Geffcken, pp. 217-222; H. Fehr, "Über den Titel 58 der Lex Salica," ZRG GA 27 (1906) 151 ff.; Emil Goldmann, *Chrenecruda: Studien zum Titel 58 der Lex Salica*, Heidelberg, 1931, Deutschrechtliche Beiträge 13, 1; and E. Kaufmann, "Chrenecruda," in HRG, 1: 611-613. See also E. Meyer's review of Goldmann in ZRG GA 52 (1932) 359 ff.; Eckhardt, *Einführung*, pp. 76 ff., and *100 Titel-Text*, pp. 58-59, and especially Brunner, "Sippe," pp. 37 ff.

[30] "De crene cruda quod paganorum tempus obseruabant" (D). The E redaction adds, "deinceps numquam ualeat, quia per ipsam cecidit multorum potestas." It is a little doubtful what this is supposed to mean, unless *potestas* is taken in the sense of 'wealth', the passage indicating impoverishment. Eckhardt would emend "multorum" to "multarum" (nom. sing. *multa*) although all the E manuscripts have "multorum." Although ingenious, it seems to me to make less sense.

[31] No further reference to it is ever found and the procedure it entails is unique in the *leges*. Since *De chrenecruda* involves the liability for homicide being distributed to various kinsmen, it has often been stated that Childebert II's *Decretio* of 596 finally abolished that institution: "De homicidiis vero ita iussimus observare, ut quicumque ausu temerario alium sine causa occiderit vitae periculum feriatur: nam non de precio redemptionis se redimat aut componat. Forsitan convenit ut ad solutionem quisque discendat, nullus de parentibus aut amicis ei quicquam adiuvet; nisi qui praesumpserit ei aliquid adiuvare, suum wergildum omnino componat; quia iustum est, ut qui novit occidere, discat morire"

variations found in the surviving manuscripts.[32] By the early Carolingian period at least, and probably earlier, it had become the subject of antiquarian speculation and interpretation which may have originated well outside the area of original Frankish settlement.

As to the procedure itself, there is much about its details which is obscure, but the general circumstances and function of the process are still fairly clear. A homicide has taken place. At the outset the slayer has already made partial payment, so he, and probably his relatives, must have made some arrangement with the kin of the slain for payment of compensation. Unable to meet his financial responsibility from his moveable property, the slayer must swear with his oathhelpers to his insolvency. Thereafter by the procedure of *chrenecruda*[33] he can transfer this liability to his relations. Pretty clearly the law envisages two *chrenecrudas* and two distinct circles of kinsmen. The first is over the slayer's immediate family, defined in the text given above as his father and brothers. If they are unable to contribute further, the second *chrenecruda* is thrown over his more distant kin, the *tres proximiores* on both his paternal and maternal side. In order to complete the ceremony which transmits his liability to his kinsmen, he must jump over the hedge around his house, in a state which may symbolize his complete poverty. If, in the end, this fails to raise enough to fulfill his debt, and no one can or will bear responsibility for completing payment, the homicide must pay with his life, which probably means that he is handed over to the kin of the deceased to be either slain or reduced to slavery.[34]

(Boretius, 1: 16). The operative phrase here, however, is *sine causa*, and if later analogy is any guide, killing with cause could be interpreted very widely indeed.

Also of interest is the *Edictum Chilperici* (561-584), c. 8 concerning the *malus homo*: "auferat [= offeratur] per tres mallus ante rachymburgiis ut eum, si voluerint, parentes aut de suis rebus redimant, aut se sciant, si noluerint in quarto mallo nobis presentibus veniant: nos ordinamus, cui malum fecit tradatur in manu et faciant exinde quod voluerint." (Boretius, 1: 10). It is hard to know exactly what constitutes the category *malus homo*, although for the procedure of the *Edict* to be carried out completely he, like the pauper in ʟѕ 58, "res non habet unde sua mala facta conponat." At any rate, in the case envisaged in Chilperic's edict, the procedure of *chrenecruda* seems to be excluded.

In an addition found in Herold – which Eckhardt prints as part of the B redaction, but whose provenance and date must be left open – there occurs the following indication of the obsolescence of the *chrenecruda* procedure: "At presentibus temporibus, si de suis propriis rebus non habuerit, unde transoluere, aut se de lege defensare possit, omnis caussa superius comprehensa, ad caput suum pertinet obseruare."

[32] See Appendix I.

[33] For possible meanings of the word see Eckhardt, "Wortregister" and "Glossar," s.v. and Fritz Kern, "Notes on Frankish Words in Lex Salica," in Hessels, c. 58.

[34] Cf. *Edictum Chilperici*, c. 8 (Boretius 1: 10).

As indicated, the provision adds little to what we have already seen of kinship structure in ɪs 62 and 68, yet it raises a number of problems which touch directly and indirectly upon Frankish kinship and upon other facets of social and legal history. Of some interest for our concerns is the generally held notion that the process of *chrenecruda* involved the conveyance of the homicide's real property or *casa* to his relatives. Although the symbolism of the text may suggest this, there is no real proof. Behind this idea are the suppositions first, that the homicide, and the Frankish freeman in general, is not simply a tenant, but that, in the last resort, the *casa* is his to dispose of; second, and that the homicide has already separated himself from the household of his father. If we follow out this line of reasoning and ask why the *casa* was not alienated in the first place in order to help make up the debt, we must suppose some right of pre-emption on the part of his kin, and this quickly involves both paternal and maternal categories, or else the absence of a suitable market.

Another problem concerns the nature of the kindred's liability in wergeld payment. In ɪs 62 and 68 we have seen various kin categories participating in the receipt of wergeld. Normally it could be expected that corresponding groups on the other side contributed to payment by the homicide. However, the obligations of the homicide's kin to contribute may be the first to fade, even while the kinsmen of the slain maintain their claims. It is sometimes assumed, therefore, that in ɪs 58 initially the homicide is legally responsible for the whole wergeld, in addition to any other penalties imposed, and that consequently the liability of his kin is secondary. Certainly the specific obligation imposed by *De chrenecruda* is secondary, but it is quite possible that the law envisages that the kin have already contributed as best they can their customary shares, and that the secondary liability transmitted by ɪs 58 refers principally to the homicide's portion of the wergeld;[35] this could be a considerable sum since, on the basis of ɪs 62, the homicide must pay one-half the total. Moreover, contributions to wergeld payments may have been the norm of Frankish customary law while, at the same time, kinsmen were reluctant to bail out notorious malefactors without the compulsion of the *chrenecruda* process.

In turning to consider the nature and role of the kin groupings in *De chrenecruda*, we can speak with a little more certainty on some matters at least. Even if ɪs 58 lacked a clear indication of being related to ɪs 62 and 68, we could expect a close correspondence between both sets of texts

---

[35] Brunner, "Sippe," pp. 44-45.

because they are part of the same process. *De chrenecruda* is just a means for the kin groups involved in compensation on the homicide's side to be legally brought into play. It will be remembered that, on the side of the deceased, the basic divisions among the kin were: first, the distinction between the immediate family and the wider kin; and second, among the wider kin, the distinction between patrilateral and matrilateral relatives. The same fundamental pattern is found in ls 58. The first group that must bear the liability of the homicide is the latter's immediate family, the parentela of his parents, or the original household of the homicide, designated in A1 as his father and brothers. If, like the homicide, they have contributed to the point of insolvency, the next group comes into play – the wider kin. Here again we meet the *tres proximiores* on the maternal and paternal side. Corresponding to the situation in ls 62 and 68, each of the bilateral categories is quite clearly liable for one-half the amount lacking, *pro medietate*. It follows that, among the wider kin, the liability is concurrent, that is, the paternal and maternal kin bear half the burden at the same time. What seems likely, in addition, is that the liability on one side is independent of that on the other and cannot be transferred. On the basis of the other correlations between *De chre-necruda* and the regulations for the receipt of wergeld, we might expect that the liability was distributed according to the system of thirds, rather than being borne in its entirety by the nearest kinsman on each side, a circumstance which might entail a crushing burden. In any case the poorer relation on each side could, by the expedient of *chrenecruda*, transfer his share of the debt to his richer kinsman.

Despite various ambiguities *De chrenecruda* is important, especially when considered with *De compositione homicidii* (ls 62) and *De homine ingenuo occiso* (ls 68), as a concrete illustration of the solidary aspects of Frankish kinship, and of the law's conception of the relationship of the individual to the network of blood relations surrounding him. In these provisions we find kin categories or groups, even if in a sense temporary and independent, brought together as legal units through common relationship with an individual. Despite the temporary and fluid nature of these groups they are no less legal entities for that fact; though they may never be required to act, may never have an actual legal existence, they always have the potential for such an existence and the considerable rights and obligations which bear upon it. This circumstance is what underscores the need for *De eum qui se de parentilla tollere uult*, and the necessity for an individual to withdraw himself from the legal burdens of kinship recognized by law and society.

C. The Abrogation of Relationship:
LS 60, *DE EUM QUI SE DE PARENTILLA TOLLERE UULT*

De eum qui se de parentilla tollere uult:

In mallo ante thunginum ambulare debet et ibi quattuor fustis alninus super caput suum frangere debet. et illos per quattuor partes in mallo iactare debet et ibi dicere debet quod iuramento et de hereditatem et totam
5   rationem illorum tollat. et sic postea aliquis de suis parentibus aut occidatur aut moriatur, nulla ad eum nec hereditas nec conpositio perteneat.

Whoever wishes to disassociate himself from a blood relationship must go into court before the *thunginus* and there he must break four alder rods over his head. And he must throw them to the four corners of the court and there he must say that he disassociates himself from oathhelping, inheritance, and all the affairs of those kinsmen. And thus if thereafter any of his kinsmen is killed or dies, let no inheritance or compensation pertain to him.[36]

The A archetype appears to have ended here; but at a later date an addition, which in varying forms is found in all succeeding redactions, was incorporated into the A family concerning the claim of the fisc:

Si uero illi aut moriatur aut occidatur conpositio aut hereditas ad fisco perueniat.

But if he either dies or is killed, let compensation or inheritance go to the fisc.[37]

---

[36] *parentilla*, line 1: "a blood relationship," or more concretely a "group of kinsmen"; from *ratio illorum*, line 5, it appears a number of kinsmen are meant. The word will be discussed further below. A3 reads *de parentibus*, which is found also in E and incorporated into D, although in the latter case *parentilla* is found in the rubric.

quattuor fustis, line 2: A1 reads "tres fustis," but all other manuscripts have *quattuor* or (IIII), which is generally accepted as correct (but cf. Balon, *Traité*, 2: 557). The four quarters of the mallus might seem to require four rods, but the problem is, in part, that we do not know what the alder branches symbolize (cf. n. 44). The practice of indicating numerals with strokes, and the resultant possibilities for miscopying easily explain the divergence.

iuramento, line 4: so also A2, A4; A3, "de iuramento." For the most part there is agreement that this is parallel to *de hereditatem*, and thus is not instrumental ("by oath"). In addition to A3 all the remaining redactions (C-K) read *de iuramento*, so it was certainly interpreted as indicating oathhelping.

[37] *Si ... perueniat*: as in Eckhardt's reconstructed text, this reading is based on A2 and A4. A2: "si uero solo moriatur aut occidatur, conposicio aut hereditas ad eis permaniat" (*permanere* regularly = *pertinere* in A2). A4: "Si uero illi aut moriatur aut hoccidatur. Conpositio ad fisco perueniat." Are these versions the result of sloppy transmission, or editorial comment? Cf. also C and D.

The passage is lacking in A3. A1 contains a text unrelated to A2 and A4, inserted without a break at the end of the final clause: "sed hereditatem ipsius fiscus adquirat."

This final clause, here reconstructed from A2 and A4, probably started out as a gloss set at the end of the original provision. The reason for thinking it an addition[38] is based on a comparison of A1 and A3 with A2 and A4. A2 and A4 both contain a text which is probably related despite the fact that A2 indicates that the *hereditas* still pertains to the deceased's kinsmen.[39] On the other hand, the clause stating the claim of the fisc is lacking in A3; an abbreviated text is not characteristic of A3, though it is sometimes of A4. Either the final clause has been expunged in A3 – presumably because of the nature of the claim – or else it was never in the archetype of the A manuscripts. Indication that the latter view is correct comes from A1. Here we have a text which is clearly unrelated to that of A2 and A4:

> sed hereditatem ipsius fiscus adquirat.

As Behrend noted long ago, this is certainly an addition.[40] There are other signs of this fact apart from the divergence from A2 and A4. The phrase *fiscus adquirat* in any context is unique not only to A1 but to all the A manuscripts. The usual expression to express this idea is *in fisco colligatur* (ls 62, 44), which has also been passed on to the C redaction. *Fiscus adquirat*, however, is characteristic of later texts, added to A1,[41] and is found also in the D and E redaction and in interpolations of the 'B' redaction inserted in A2 (ls 62). The final clause of A1, then, was clearly not found in the archetype of the A family but was added by a later editor possibly familiar with the fact that other manuscripts of the law contained a clause touching upon the claim of the fisc. This strongly suggests that clauses concerning the fisc in A2 and A4 are also additions. Other than supposing that a final clause was expunged in the traditions of A1 and A3, and then in substance later added to A1, we must accept that the archetype of the A family contained no clause dealing with the claim of the fisc. ls 60, therefore, as it is preserved in manuscript, can be divided into two parts: an original provision outlining the procedure by which an individual could dissolve a particular relationship; and a clause added to manuscripts of the A redaction at various times, and in two distinct forms, purporting to describe the rights of the fisc toward the abjuror in event of his death.

[38] Against Eckhardt, who considers it genuine. His reconstructed text is based upon A2 and, principally, A4. The dissimilar A1 reading is printed as if the phrase *Si uero ille aut moriatur aut occidatur* had fallen out.

[39] See n. 37.

[40] *Lex Salica*, p. 126.

[41] ls 98.1; 99.1; 100.1.

This regulation outlining the formal procedure whereby an individual was able to renounce the rights and obligations of kinship is unique in the *leges* and finds no echo in the literary sources of the period. The only analogy to it can be found in the thirteenth-century *fourjurements* found in the Hainault district and adjacent French regions, all set well within the old area of Salian settlement.[42] To understand the regulation we must first determine the circumstances which would require it as a formal part of Salian procedure. It has been noted from time to time that the practical interest behind the renunciation in ls 60 must be chiefly the avoidance of feud and wergeld liability.[43] Despite certain difficulties of interpretation which arise from it, this remains the most plausible explanation. One cannot help but recall that the same situation lies behind the later *fourjurements*. What we are dealing with in ls 60 is an individual who stands in the centre of a whole web of relationships, some of which are imposing upon him profound legal and social burdens. In order to rid himself of this situation, and in order to leave no doubt as to the legal and semi-legal results of his act, he proceeds on his own initiative to a formal and public abjuration in the *mallus*.

What is the nature of the group of kinsmen who are forsworn, and what is the extent of the fisc's claim to inheritance and compensation as it affects the rights normally limited to the kindred? The answers to these two questions are the central problems in interpreting the law. The abjuration has generally been taken to apply to the whole bilateral kindred (*parentilla*) of the individual concerned. Thereafter, according to the usual

[42] This is not the only time that this observation has been made concerning aspects of the Salic law (see above, pp. 143 f.). The *fourjurements* were public repudiations by a large number of kinsmen of a common relative. These are extraordinary documents. In two cases given by Phillpotts (*Kindred and Clan*, pp. 179 ff.) we find two men repudiated respectively by 129 and 67 of their patri- and matrilateral kin. The context of these late procedures is invariably feud. Unlike the Salic provisions, however, these *fourjurements* involve the repudiation of an individual by members of his kindred, not the other way around. From Clermont-en-Beauvoisis, however, comes indication that, by a *fourjure-ment*, an individual could also forswear his kinsmen. Beaumanoir tells us that in order to gain security from an opposing hostile kin group a man could in public court forswear his kinsmen (quoted in Phillpotts, p. 194). The same procedure is also found in the customal of the Flemish town of Ardenburg (Brunner, DRG, 1: 129).

[43] E.g. by, among others, Brunner, "Sippe," pp. 42-43. This interpretation was by no means new. Ducange had written: "Cur autem quis se *de parentela* tolleret, ea potissimum causa erat, ut a bellis familiaribus sese subduceret" (*Glossarium*, s.v. *parentela*). In the twelfth century, the author of the *Leges Henrici Primi* (ed. L. J. Downer [Oxford, 1972]), borrowed the Salic provision for his treatment of English law and linked it with the need to avoid feud: "Si quis propter faidam uel causam aliquam de parentela se uelit tollere et eam forisiurauerit..." (c. 88.13).

view, he is thought to be, in effect, kinless; only the fisc can lay claim to his inheritance and compensation: it is the sole recipient of the *compositio* and *hereditas* in event of his death.[44] This interpretation deserves careful scrutiny. Those who have considered its implications, however, have balked at including sons among those abjured, especially as regards inheritance.[45] We must ask if any other exceptions should be made to the fisc's claim to inheritance and compensation. A number of profound and inherent problems make an overriding claim of the fisc implausible, and suggest rather that the renunciation, and the consequent abrogation of mutual rights and obligations, does not apply to the whole kindred, but rather to specific named individuals within it, from whom the abjuror wishes to disassociate himself; consequently the claim of the fisc – to whatever extent it had any reality in actual Frankish practice – replaced only the rights of the specifically forsworn kinsmen and not the rights of every member of the abjuror's kindred. There are good reasons in the text and in the Salic compensation regulations to support this interpretation.

We must first be sure of the implications in the notion that the subject of LS 60 forswore his entire kindred in order to understand fully the need for an alternative. Let us consider the example of a man who, because his kinsmen are recalcitrantly embroiled in feud or perhaps in illegal criminal activities, has been exposed to retaliation from his kinsmen's enemies, is about to be entangled in the procedure of compensation, or may be required to vouch for his relatives in court. Understandably anxious to disassociate himself from their activities and the ensuing consequences he

[44] Brunner ("Sippe," p. 42, n. 3), following up a suggestion made earlier by von Amira ("Zur salfränkische Eideshilfe," *Germania* 20, N.F. 8 [1875] 59) was inclined to regard the alder branches which are broken as symbolizing the branches, i.e., the stocks, of the kindred. The fact that there are four, in his opinion, would likely refer to the *Vierteile* of the *Magschaft*; but see n. 45. The *Vierteile* refer to the four stocks descending from the four pairs of greatgrandparents, which constitutes a bilateral group of roughly second cousin range. Recently much the same explanation has been given by Balon, although since he accepts A1's reading of *tres fustes*, he seems to regard the branches as symbolizing the descendants of the three ascendent generations, which is still second cousin range (*Traité*, 2: 557). Less explicitly, others simply indicate that the subject of c. 60 renounces all rights and obligations appertaining to members of his kindred and that in future compensation and inheritance fall to the fisc. R. Hessler, "Entsippung," HRG, 1: 947-949.

[45] Cf. Brunner, DRG, 2: 94, n. 30; Geffcken, pp. 228-229 and Behrend, p. 127. Their views that the fisc's claim only pertained to moveables rest upon the notion that land belonged to the community. The idea of the fisc excluding heirs of the body also seems to have bothered the author of the *Leges Henrici Primi* (see n. 43) who concludes: "Si autem ipse moriatur uel occidatur, hereditas uel compositio filiis suis uel dominis suis iuste proueniat."

decides to undertake the procedure found in LS 60, and withdraw himself from all their affairs, abrogating in the process the mutual rights and obligations of oathhelping, inheritance, and compensation. Now these rights and obligations operated within the bilateral kindred and affected a large number of relations on both the maternal and paternal side. It is almost inconceivable, however, that all these kinsmen could be acting in concert in such a fashion and in such activities as would compel a man to renounce them all. All the members of his kindred are related to the abjuror, it is true, but many are unrelated to one another; only his siblings of the full blood would be likely to share exactly the same kindred as the abjuror. The kindred would act as a group only insofar as this activity is derived from common relationship with the individual at its focus. In other words, the normal cause of the abjuror's problems cannot be the kindred itself, but only a group of kinsmen within it. But must we suppose that, in order to disassociate himself from the legal and semi-legal difficulties of, say, his maternal uncle or cousins and whatever mutual relatives are involved with them, he must break all the legal ties of kinship binding him to all his other relatives, including those on the paternal side? This is a difficult proposition to accept.

In LS 60 the word *parentilla* does not indicate the entire body of the abjuror's kindred. The word can mean kindred, but this is only one meaning among many. When used in reference to all the relatives of an individual, *parentilla* may mean kindred roughly in the technical sense of the word, but it could also be used, and in fact is so used elsewhere in *Lex Salica*, to denote blood relationship, or more concretely various categories of relatives within the kindred with whom, for a variety of specific reasons, an individual was associated. All it means in LS 60 is a specific relationship or a certain number of *parentes*.[46] In the actual court procedure the kinsmen being forsworn would be individually named.

In these circumstances it is difficult to imagine that the fisc's claim to compensation and inheritance excluded all other relatives. If we accept the validity of the final clause we must understand it as saying: "But if the abjuror either dies or is killed, let whatever compensation or inheritance

---

[46] Analogous to the use of *parentilla* is our own use of the words 'kin' and 'kindred'. Cf. also the medieval French use of the word *lignage* to refer to various configurations of kinsmen including the kindred.

Cf. *De reipus* (below, ch. 11) where *parentilla* certainly does not refer to the kindred as a whole but rather to either the categories within it which we would call stocks or to relationship in the abstract. Cf. also LB 85: "Si mater tutelam suscipere voluerit nulla ei parentilla praeponatur" ("If the mother wishes to take up the guardianship of her child let no other blood relationship take precedence over her").

which might otherwise pertain to his forsworn relatives now pertain to the fisc." The fisc simply supplants the rights and obligations of the specific relatives forsworn, and would be entitled to claim only whatever inheritance or compensation the forsworn kinsmen formerly had a right to claim by reason of kinship. Along with his offspring, other relatives may still have had legally binding kinship ties with the abjuror; whether the fisc was to be sole heir would depend upon which kinsmen had been forsworn. Implicit in the procedure of the final clause is the idea that the relatives are not merely renounced but that the fisc steps in to take their place. The safety of the individual is assured not merely by the abjuration but also by the spectre of the fisc, standing behind him ready to press suit or claim its share of the compensation if he is slain. The possibility of the fisc, so to speak, replacing missing kinsmen and sharing the rights of kinship with others, is not otherwise foreign to ideas in the Salic law. An analogy to the situation described above occurs in the compensation procedure. When kinsmen were lacking on one side or another of the deceased, the fisc laid claim to their portion and collected alongside the other kinsmen receiving shares in the compensation.

10

The Bilateral Kindred as a Personal Group II: Oathhelping in *Lex Salica* and the *Formulae*

Among the rights and obligations given up by a person who withdrew from a blood relationship (*parentilla*) was the right to require the participation of his kinsmen in compurgation and the obligation for himself to perform the same for a kinsman brought before the court.[1] The procedure of the plaintiff or defendant supporting his claim with the aid of a given number of co-swearers is characteristic of many early legal systems.[2] It is a feature of the judicial process in the original text of 65 titles and the subject of additions to the written Salic law; as we have seen, the homicide in *De chrenecruda* had to support his oath of insolvency with twelve *iuratores*. In all the examples of oathhelping found in the *Pactus* and its early additions, no mention is made of the co-swearers being drawn from the kindred. That, at times at least, this was the case, indeed the requirement, seems clear from the explicit inclusion of oathhelping among the obligations abandoned by the individual abjuring his kinsmen. From the *formulae*, it appears that oathhelpers must be drawn from among the accused's kindred in cases of status; at any rate, only in these cases is such a requirement explicitly made.[3] If the accused has not the suitable categories of relatives from which to draw, he may simply present freemen in their place. Insofar as the *formulae* make any other requirement whatsoever, in other cases the accused must furnish *iuratores* from among his neighbours.[4]

---

[1] See above, LS 60, p. 150.

[2] Generally see Brunner, DRG, 2: 512 ff.; for the literature, R. Scheyhing, "Eideshelfer," HRG, 1: 870-872.

[3] In an addition to certain manuscripts of the A text, found also in H, LS 67, cases on status are included along with two other types of suits which are to be conducted with twelve oathhelpers. It is not clear that these must be drawn from the kindred: cf. Brunner, DRG, 2: 523, n. 65.

[4] *FAnd.* 28 and cf. 50a; see also LS 102.

In the context of our discussion of the structure of Frankish kinship,
a number of important questions arise in regard to cases where kinship participation was necessary or expected. What principles, if any,
determined the kinsmen called in to support their relative? Were there
defined categories from which the relatives were drawn, and if so, what
principles determined the proportional representation? To what extent
was the participation of relations automatic or dependent upon the choice
of the accused? Did the nature of the lawsuit affect the structure of
kinship participation? Some answers to these questions can be given as
regards suits *de statu* from the *formulae* and capitularies. With little
exception these various pieces of evidence are quite consistent with one
another.[5] Moreover, they clearly reflect the same method of kin grouping
found in the *Pactus Legis Salicae*, despite their somewhat later date.

The earliest of the *formulae* to define the kinsmen required for oathhelping occurs in the *Formulae Salicae Lindenbrogianae*, which
originated in the old Salian regions around the Scheld and lower Maas.[6] A
man is accused of being a *servus*, a claim made on the basis of the status of
his father, mother, and grandparents (*genitor vel genitrix aut avus vel
avia*). In order for him to clear himself "he must swear in such-and-such a
church with twelve freemen (*Franci*), six from his paternal side and six
from his maternal side, that according to Salic law he was freeborn on his
paternal and/or (*aut*) maternal side."[7] As in the compensation regulations,
we find here that the fundamental division of Frankish kinship structure is
the distinction between matrilateral and patrilateral kin. Again, both sides
bear equally the legal burden devolving from their common kinsman.
This is the principle embodied in the *formula* at any rate. We should not
infer, however, that an accusation of servile status based on descent from
either one side or the other automatically required oathhelpers drawn
equally from the paternal and maternal side. The hypothetical example of
the *formula* is ambiguous, probably intentionally so, as to whether the

---

[5] So Brunner, DRG, 2: 516 ff. For an alternate view, see K. von Amira, "Zur salfränkischen Eideshilfe," *Germania* 20, N.F. 8 (1875) 53-66.

[6] Buchner, *Rechtsquellen*, p. 53: dated to the late eighth century.

[7] "advocatus illius episcopi aliquem hominem nomine illo interpellabat, dum diceret,
eo quod de caput suum legibus esse servus ipsius eclesiae vel ipsius episcopi, et propter
hoc de ipso servitio neglegens atque iectivus adesse videretur, quod genitor suus vel
genetrix sua, aut avus suus vel avia sua, fecerunt. Sed ipse vir ... hanc causam in omnibus
denegabat ... eo quod de parte paterna aut materna secundum legem ingenuus esse
videretur. Sed ipsi scabini qui tunc ibidem aderant, taliter ei visi fuerunt iudicasse, ut
supra noctes 40 cum 12 Francos, sex de parte paterna et sex de materna, in ecclesia illa
iurare debuisset, ut de parte paterna aut de materna secundum legem Salicam ingenuus
esse videretur" (no. 21).

accusation is founded on descent from one side or from both. The principle it seeks to maintain is that, all things being equal, oathhelpers normally were drawn in the same proportions from both bilateral categories of kinsmen. These considerations should be clearer when we look at the other texts.

The *Formulae Senonenses Recentiores*[8] contain two instances of attempts to reclaim individuals to the colonate. In the first, although the accused claims free birth on both sides, the claim of servile status is made on the grounds that the accused's father had been a *colonus*. To prove his free status the defendant must give an oath "along with his near relations (*proximiores parentes*), eight on his father's side and four on his mother's, if they are not deceased, and if they are, along with twelve freemen (*Franci*)."[9] In the second example the same claim of servile status is made against a woman, based upon her descent from her father and grandfather, allegedly *coloni*. In her case as well, it is adjudged that she must give an oath as to her free status "along with twelve of her male relations (*homines parentes*), eight from the paternal and four from the maternal side, if they are not deceased, and if they are, with twelve suitable freemen (*Franci*)."[10] Some stress has been laid on the fact that in the first example the relatives are designated as *proximiores*. Possibly this indicates that relatives nearer in degree must be called before those less near,[11] but *proximiores* may just as easily designate a range of kinsmen – and a fairly

---

[8] This younger collection of Sens *formulae* dates from the reign of Louis the Pious (814-840) (Buchner, *Rechtsquellen*, p. 53).

[9] "Repetebat ei, dum diceret, eo quod genitor suus nomen ille colonus sancti illius de villa illa fuisset ... et ipse ... hoc fortiter denegabat et taliter dedit in suo responso, quod de patre Franco fuisset generatus et de matre Franca fuisset natus ... et taliter ei fuit iudicatum ut [h]ac causa apud proximiores parentes suos, octo de parte genitore suo et quattuor de parte genetricae suae, si fermortui non sunt, et si fermortui sunt, apud duodecim Francos tales ... debeat coniurare" (no. 2).

[10] "Repetebat ei, dum diceret, eo quod avus suus ... vel genitor suus ... coloni sancti illius ... fuissent et ipsa femina colona esse debebat ... ei fuit iudicatum, ut apud 12 homines parentes suos, octo de patre et quattuor de matre, si fermortui non sunt, et si fermortui sunt, apud 12 homines bene Francos Salicos ... coniurare debeat" (no. 5).

[11] From a text associated with the *Lex Salica* comes evidence that the plaintiff could require only the relatives nearest in degree: "Si autem tales [i.e., paternal and maternal oathhelpers] postquam produxerit, dicat qui eum ammallavit non recipio istos testes, quia proximiores habes qui tibi dicant testimonium, et si ille dixerit quia non habeo alios testes quam istos, tunc ille qui eum ammallavit det contra illum testimonia, qui sapiant eum propinquiores habere quos ad testimonium dicendum adducat" (*Extravagantia*, B, 2, Hessels, 421; Eckhardt, Germanenrechte *Pactus* II.2: 535). If the defendant denies the charge the fragmentary conclusion indicates the issue will be decided by duel. As will be discussed shortly, there is doubt, however, as to how much of this text reflects Salian practice.

wide range at that, since eight adult male coswearers are expected on one side – from which the oathhelpers are to be selected. As in the Lindenbruch formula, the *proximiores* are to be drawn from both paternal and maternal kin. The proportion of paternal to maternal kin in the Sens *formulae*, however, is not 2:2 but 2:1. On the face of it one may suppose that we have before us differing procedures; in this case, it should be noted that the chronologically older source, which originates from the old area of heavy Salian settlement, shows the same parity between paternal and maternal kin characteristic of the *Pactus*. In fact it is almost certain that what we have in the Lindenbruch and Sens *formulae* is a difference not in principle but merely in application. The Lindenbruch *formula* considers the issue of servile birth from the point of view of paternal and maternal descent; the Sens *formulae* deal with cases in which accusation is based upon descent only in the paternal line. What this suggests is that the side most touched by the allegation must offer the most support in clearing its fellow kinsman. Two capitularies roughly contemporaneous with the Sens *formulae* show clearly that this is the principle in operation.

In the more important of these it is provided that, when the accusation of servile descent is particularly strong, the accused must support his claim to free birth with the oaths of twelve relations, eight drawn "from the side on account of which the accusation is made, whether paternal or maternal, and four from the other side."[12] This is precisely the situation that prevails in the *formulae* if the Sens and Lindenbruch examples are read together.

This relatively clear picture is clouded somewhat by the so-called *Extravagantia* B.2. Originating in Italy sometime around the mid-ninth century or later, it is the latest of our sources.[13] We find the same parity between maternal and paternal kin characteristic of the other texts, and the same disproportionate representation when the accusation touches one side only of the accused's descent, but with an important difference: rather than that most of the *coniuratores* should come *ex ea parte unde pulsatur*,

---

[12] "homo de statu pulsatus, si is, qui eum pulsat, ad convincendum illum procinctum habuerit, adhibeat sibi octo coniuratores legitimos ex ea parte unde pulsatur, sive illa paterna sive materna sit, et quattuor aliunde non minus legitimos et iurando vindicet libertatem suam. Quod si procinctus defuerit, adsumat undecumque 12 liberos homines et iurando ingenuitatem suam defendat" (*Cap. incert.*, AD 810-841, Boretius, 1: 315). *Procinctus* indicates that along with oathhelpers the plaintiff has already sworn a preliminary oath; see Brunner, DRG, 2: 517, n. 23. In the *formulae* this procedure is not necessary to require the accused to draw his co-swearers exclusively from his kindred, nor is there any evidence of it in the *Extravagantia* considered below.

[13] For editions of the text, see n. 11.

the contrary principle prevails, namely that "the accused shall give the most witnesses from the side uncontaminated by the accusation."[14] Considering the origin of the text, this is not old Salian procedure;[15] but the significance of the differing procedures is not clear. Behind the proportions of the northern sources lies the supposition that those most affected by the accusation have an obligation to respond; it is recognized that, in effect, the accusation is made not only against the defendant but also against an antecedent who represents only one side of the defendant's kindred. In addition, the ability of the accused to produce eight co-swearers, who are themselves freemen, from a side allegedly tainted with servile descent would presumably speak highly of his claim to free descent. The reversal of the proportions in the Italian fragment may be, as Brunner suggests, an alleviation of the procedure,[16] but it is questionable whether this view corresponds to the spirit of the provision. The proportions may show, rather, an expectation on the part of the court of perjury from the affected side, whose own interests would be served by the acquittal of their kinsman. The *Extravagantia*'s requirement may be a tentative step toward objectivity within the traditional concept of the kindred's role in the legal procedure.

Although this consideration of the *formulae* and capitularies has led us afield from the period which saw the origin of the *Pactus*, the results are nevertheless of some importance for the nature of kinship grouping in the earlier period. The *formulae* largely confirm what might have been predicted on the basis of the text in sixty-five titles. The aid of relatives in compurgation was an expected or required feature of the early Salic law, but to what extent or in what cases remains uncertain. In the early period, wherever we find explicit mention of kin groups involved in the judicial process, their structure is based upon the distinction of patrilateral and matrilateral kin, each of which equally shares the rights and obligations of the kindred's participation. When in the *formulae* the same situation is found in compurgation cases *de statu*, it is fair to conclude that the essentials of the custom we are dealing with go back to the period of the

---

[14] "Et si (quis) ex paterna genealogia mallatur (ad servitium) adhibeat ex materna progenie (septem) testes qui proximiores sunt, et ex paterna quattuor, et sic se id(oneet). Quod si vero ex materna progenie mallatur, septem (testes) proximiores adhibeat (ex paterna) et quattuor ex materna progenie, et sic suam libertatem proport(et; ita ex q)ua parte mundior est, ex ipsa parte plus dabit testes" (the brackets indicate where the text is illegible).

[15] Cf. von Amira, "Zur salfr. Eideshilfe," p. 56, who thought it was, and Brunner, DRG, 2: 517.

[16] DRG, 2: 517, n. 23. See Geffcken's description of the entire procedure, pp. 284-286.

earlier Salic law. Apart from showing the bilateral nature of the oathhelping groups, the *formulae* indicate another important feature of Frankish kinship. As we have seen in dealing with the kindred's role in compensation procedure, the evidence can be interpreted as indicating a fairly wide range of kinship participation, but in fact it tells us very little explicitly about the extent of the kinship categories. Although the evidence on oathhelping likewise gives no precise information on the extent of kinship involved, nevertheless, it leaves no doubt that the range would be fairly wide: the accused is expected to be able to present from one side of his family seven or eight (free) adult male co-swearers. Now the *formulae* take into consideration the probably not rare circumstance that such relatives may already be deceased, but otherwise it is expected that they shall be known and presented. As a realistic requirement this must suppose the involvement of kinship in oathhelping to at least second or third cousins.

11

Kinship Categories I: ʟꜱ 44, *De reipus*

Like some of the other Salic enactments which touch upon kinship, ʟꜱ 44 has occasioned vigorous debate on almost every aspect of its contents.[1] It has been a primary source for those who believe that traces of a prior matrilineal system can still be found in the earliest antiquities of the Germanic peoples, while, on the contrary, one of the most perceptive critics of the law, and a firm advocate of the agnatic theory of Germanic kinship, has declared that the law is an argument against matriliny.[2] 'Curious' is an adjective frequently applied to the provision and the pattern of relationship which it contains. Somewhat ironically, *De reipus* is the one Salic article dealing with various categories of kinsmen that most clearly shows signs of being patterned on the late Roman and vulgar law models reflected in the *Breviary* and *Lex Burgundionum*.

The law provides for the procedure to be followed when a suitor seeks to marry a widow, and the payment, called *reipus* or *reipi*, which he must make to specified relatives.[3] Before taking the widow in marriage, the

---

[1] The major work of interpretation is H. Brunner's "Zu Lex Salica tit. 44: De reipus," originally published in *Sitzungsberichte der Berliner Akademia* (1894), rpt. in *Abhandlungen zur Rechtsgeschichte. Gesammelte Aufsätze von Heinrich Brunner*, ed. K. Rauch (Weimar, 1931), 2: 67-78. For the various literature on the law, see Brunner, p. 67, n. 1, and Geffcken, pp. 167-172. Since Brunner very little has been said on the law. See also J. Balon, *Traité*, 2: 518 ff.

[2] Brunner, "Zu Lex Salica tit. 44," p. 71. The literature of the matrilinealists is found in Brunner and Geffcken (see n. 1), to which add Chadwick, *Origins of the English Nation*, pp. 307 ff.

[3] Modern scholarship usually refers to *reipus* in the singular, but the A redaction almost invariably employs the plural: *reipi, reipus illus* (= acc. pl. *reipos illos*); also *reipe* (= *reipae*), A3. The exception is *reipus* (s.) in A1, line 13, below.

There is more or less complete agreement that the word is related to ᴏʜɢ *reif*, Goth. *raips*, ᴏɴ *reip*, and means 'ring' or 'circle'. Comparable to the ᴏɴ *baugr*, ᴏᴇ *beag*, 'ring' or 'money', it is taken, particularly in the plural, to mean 'money'. Attempts to see the word as symbolical of kin structure (Balon, *Traité*, 2: 532), are, to my mind, not convincing.

suitor must appear in the *mallus* before the *thunginus* or *centenarius*.[4] There his payment of three solidi and a denarius (*reipi*) must be examined for soundness by three men. If all is in order and the court is in agreement, he may then marry the widow.[5] If he marries her without proceeding in this way, he is liable to a penalty of 63s., payable to the person to whom the *reipi* are owed.[6] But if all is done in conformity to the law, he to whom the *reipi* are due is to accept the payment of 3s. and a denarius.[7] The law then lists the order of the *reipi* recipients:

4. Si nepus sororis filius fuerit senussimus, ipse eos accipiat.

5. Si neptus non fuerit, neptis filius senior reipus illus accipiat.

6. Si uero neptas filius non fuerit, consobrine filius qui ex maternae genere uenit illi eos accipiat.

5 7. Si uero nec consobrine filius fuerit, tunc auunculus frater matris reipus ille accipiat.

8. Si uero nec adhuc auunculus fuerit, tunc frater illius qui eam mulierem ante habuit si in hereditatem non est uenturus ipse eos reipus accipiat.

9. Et si nec ipse frater fuerit, qui proximior fuerit, extra superiores nomi-

---

[4] "Sicut adsolit homo moriens et uiduam dimiserit, qui eam uoluerit accipere, antequam sibi copulet ante thunginum aut centenario hoc est ut thunginus aut centenarius mallo indicant, et in ipso mallo scutum habere debet, et tres causas demandare debent." Cf. ʟʙ 24.1: "Si qua mulier ... post mariti mortem ad secundas aut tertias nuptias, ut adsolet fieri, fortasse transierit...."

[5] "Et tunc ille qui uiduam accipere debet tres sol. aeque pensantes et denario habere debet. Et tres erunt qui sol. illius pensare uel probare debent et hoc factum si eis conuenit accipiat."

[6] "Si uero istud non fecerit et sic eam acciperit, mal[lobergo] reipus nihil sinus hoc est, ɪɪᴍᴅ din. qui f[aciunt] sol. ʟxɪɪɪ [cui] reipi debentur exsoluere debet." "Cui" which the sense seems to require is supplied from A2-A4. *Sinus = solutio*, see Kern, "Notes on Frankish Words," in Hessels, c. 44.

[7] The text of this provision is in disarray throughout the A and C redactions. The fullest text, reflected above, is found in A2 and A3: "Si uero quod superius diximus omnis secundum legem impleuerit, iii solid. [*et denarius* is in A1, D, E, K] ille cui re[ipi] debentur accipiant" (A3). In A2 and A3 a succeeding clause introducing the *reipi* recipients (*hoc discernendum est cui reipi debentur*) may or may not have been part of the A archetype.

On the other hand, A1 reads "si uero quod superius diximus omnia secundum legem impleuerit, tres sol. et denario electo reipi debentur." Apart from "electo" this text has strong affinities to A4 and C5, whether through three coincidental cases of homeoteleuton or not. If the reading of "electo" is to have any value, it must reflect the Roman prototype of the law to be discussed below, where the choice of suitor by the court is called *electio*: "but if he [the suitor] has fulfilled all that we have said above let the 3 sol. and denarius be owed as *reipi* by him who has been selected by the court." Despite this parallel, however (and the lack in A1, A4 and C5 of accipiant, which is required if *ille cui* or *cui* – rather than "electo" – is part of the text) it seems hazardous at this point to accept the text of A1. "Electo" may be derived ultimately from *ille cui*; in which case *ille cui* is preferable to the *cui* of Eckhardt's reconstructed text.

10 natos qui singillatim secundum parentilla dicti sunt, usque ad sextum genuculum, si hereditatem illius mariti defuncti non accipiat, ille reipus illus accipiat.

10. Iam post sexto genuculum, si non fuerint, in fisco reipus ipse uel causa
quae exinde orta fuerit colligatur.

4. If there is a nephew who is the eldest son of a sister, let him receive the
reipi.

5. If there is no nephew, let the eldest son of a niece receive the *reipi*.

6. If there is no niece's son, let the son of a female collateral who comes
from the maternal kin receive the *reipi*.

7. If there is no son of a female collateral, then let the uncle who is the
mother's brother receive the *reipi*.

8. But if there is no uncle at this point, then let the brother of him who
previously had the woman receive the *reipi* provided he has not entered
into the inheritance.

9. And if there is no brother, let the next of kin, apart from those named
above who were each called according to line, [or their relationship],
receive the *reipi* up to the sixth degree, provided he does not receive the
inheritance of the dead husband.

10. If there in no one, henceforth after the sixth degree let the *reipus* or the
claim which arises therefrom be taken by the fisc.[8]

[8] *si uero neptas filius non fuerit, consobrine filius*, line 3: the other A codd. read
"consobrino" (A2), "consubrini" (A3), "consubrinus" (A4) *filius*. C has both *consobrini*
and *consobrino filius*; D and E give all these, *consobrinus, consobrini*, and *consobrinae
filius*; H, "consobrinus" and K, "consobrinae" *filius*. This amount of variation in the *Lex
Salica* is not particularly extraordinary, but Eckhardt believes it is accounted for by a
passage which has been dropped in all the codd. but which originally was found between
fuerit and *consobrine*: "consobrinus filius materterae ipse accipiat. Si uero nec consobrini
non fuerint." Some such reconstruction is perhaps possible – this means that it had
dropped out not only of the archetype of the A manuscripts, but also from the A tradition
behind other redactions – but there is not sufficient grounds, textual or otherwise, to
require it. *Consobrina* (in *consobrine filius*) probably indicates not just a female cousin but
any female near relative including aunts: cf. Eckhardt, in his "Wortregister," *Muhme*. Cf.
also LS 13.11, added in the C redaction, prohibiting incestuous marriages. Female blood
relations beyond sisters and their daughters are designated simply *alterius gradus
consobrinae*. This must also include aunts since the wives of uncles are explicitly
mentioned in the provision.

auunculus frater matris, line 5: not a superfluous repetition since *auunculus* already
seems to designate the maternal or paternal uncle. Cf. LS 13.11.

*proximior ... extra superiores nominatos ... si hereditatem illius mariti defuncti non
accipiat ... reipus illus accipiat*, lines 9-12: indicates that the *reipi* recipients were relatives
of the widow's deceased husband. Early discussion of the law centred around the question
whether initially the relatives of the widow or of the deceased husband received the *reipi*.
According to the former view the relations up to and including the *avunculus* were the
widow's. Thereafter, the husband's kin received the payment. In support of this it is asked
why it was necessary to designate the *frater* (line 7) as "illius qui eam mulierem

Neither the *formulae* not the literary sources of the period contain any reference to the *reipi*, but some brief notice of the procedure is found in later enactments. In a capitulary added to the earliest redaction of the Salic law, reference is made to the payment of the *reipi* (*reibus secundum legem donare*) along with the *achasius*.[9] The latter was an amount paid to her deceased husband's near kin on a widow's remarriage in order to free the *dos* and to gain 'peace' (*pax*) with the dead husband's immediate family.[10] The category of kin receiving the *achasius* consisted of the father, mother, brother and brother's son; beyond this category, which is conceived of as the deceased husband's original or existing household, the intervention of the fisc might be requested.[11] Except for a brief and ambiguous reference to *rebus* (i.e., most likely *reibus*, *reipus*) in the *Edictum Chilperici* (AD 561-584),[12] no further notice of the procedure is found until about AD 819. A

---

ante habuit." This seems to have been suggested by the previous designation of the uncle as *matris frater*; cf. LS 100.

    nominatos qui singillatim secundum parentilla dicti sunt, line 10: follows Eckhardt's reconstructed text based on A2-A4. A1: "qui proximior fuerit, extra superiores nominatos singillatim dicti, secundum parentilla usque ad sextum genuculum ... reipus illus accipiat." This seems to reflect the parentelic or lineal-gradual system of succession; cf. Ro. 153 ("Omnis parentilla usque in septimum geniculum nomeretur, ut parens parenti per gradum et parentillam heres succedat") where, it seems to me, *parentilla* clearly means 'stock' or 'line'. The "dicti" of A1, however, seems to require the "qui" and "sunt" of the other manuscripts. Although the *nominati* are called to the *reipi* by line, it is less clear this is what *parentilla* means in A2-A4. For the state of the question on the parentelic system and a critique of its application in medieval law, see Hans-Georg Mertens, "Überlegungen zur Herkunft des Parentelensystems," ZRG GA 90 (1973) 149-164, who, however, does not consider the law of Rothair.

  [9] "Si quis mulier uidua post mortem mariti sui ad alterum marito dare uoluerit, prius qui eam accipere uoluerit reibus secundum legem donet. Et postea mulier si de anteriore marito filios habet, parentes infantes suorum consiliare [debet]. Et si in dotis xxv sol. accipit, III sol. achasium parentibus qui proximiores sunt marito defuncto donet, hoc est si pater aut mater desunt, frater defuncti aut certe nepus fratris senioris filius ipsis achasius debetur. Et si isti non fuerint, tunc in mallo iudici, hoc est comite aut grafione, roget de eam in uerbum regis mittat. Et achasium quem parentibus mortui mariti dare debuerant parti fisci adquirat... (LS 100). On payment the widow may take her dower to her new marriage, provided she maintain it for the eventual succession of her children by her first husband. If childless she is permitted two-thirds of the dower. She also relinquishes a portion of the furnishings brought from her father's house (*de casa patris*).

    The *achasius* is approximately one-tenth the *dos*: 3s. for a *dos* of 25s., 6 for one of 62s. The spelling *reibus* of LS 100 has parallels in LS 44 (A2, A3).

  [10] "Omnis mihi testes scitis quia et achasium dedi ut pacem habeam parentum..." (LS 100).

  [11] In their absence the *achasius* may also have gone to other kin, since the calling in of the public authority seems to lie at the discretion of the suitor.

  [12] "Similiter conuenit ut rebus concederemus omnibus leodibus nostris ut per modicam rem scandalum non generetur in regione nostra" (Hessels, LS 78.2). This passage

capitulary of this period provides that the suitor of a widow shall not follow the procedure found written in *Lex Salica*, but simply wed her *cum parentorum consensu*, "as up to now their ancestors have done."[13] Seemingly, then, the *reipi* procedure had become a dead letter long before this time. That it required comment at all is to be explained by the proliferation of manuscripts of the various redactions of Salic law which took place at the turn of the ninth century under the impulse of antiquarianism[14] and Charlemagne's desire to codify the various national laws. It is testimony not only to the gulf between the customary law of the eighth century (and probably a good time before) and the written law of the *Pactus*, but also to efforts on the part of some to reconstruct and implement the ancient codification.

The purpose of the payment of the *reipi* is best seen as being analogous to the payment made at the *desponsatio* of a maiden. According to the *formulae* this traditionally amounted to 1s. and a denarius. On the basis of *De reipus*, it seems likely that the comparable amount for a widow was 3s. and a denarius,[15] which was paid to her deceased husband's relatives.

Among the husband's relatives the payment did not go to the nearest relatives and heirs as might be expected. It is the nature of the circle of relatives found in LS 44 and the order followed in receiving the *reipi* which has occasioned the most surprise and given rise to the greatest perplexity, at least among non-matrilinealists. It is possible to distinguish a number of distinct categories which receive the payment in turn. The first, comprising the deceased husband's sister's son and niece's son, constitutes

---

is often taken as indicating the abrogation of the *reipi* obligation. Brunner ("Zu Lex Salica tit. 44," p. 69) suggests that the removal was only partial and involved only a renunciation of the final claim of the fisc. Equally, it can be seen as referring to the maintenance (*concedere* = to grant) of the procedure among all the *leudes* of Chilperic's kingdom. See Geffcken, p. 269.

[13] "DE XLVI CAPITULO (i.e., LS 44, *De reipus*) id est qui viduam in coniugium accipere vult, iudicaverunt omnes ut non ita sicut in lege salica scriptum est eam accipiat, sed cum parentorum consensu et voluntate, velut usque nunc antecessores eorum fecerunt, in coniugium sibi eam sumat" (c. 8, Boretius 2: 293).

[14] Note the learned conceit of the compiler of an eleventh-century Lombard cartulary who, in considering the betrothal of a Frankish widow, inserted along with the *thunginus* and *centenarius*, a *reparius* who holds the *mundium* of the widow (*Cartularium* 16, "Qualiter vidua Salicha desponsetur," in *Leges Langobardorum*, MGH, LL, IV, 599). See also Brunner, "Zu Lex Salica tit. 44," p. 69.

[15] See Geffcken, p. 171; Chenon, *Histoire générale du droit français*, 1: 382; Louis Falletti, "De la condition de la femme pendant le haut moyen-âge," *Annali di Storia del Diritto, Rassegna Internazionale*, 10-11 (1966-1967), 96, n. 16 and 109, n. 67. These, and others, see the money as a symbolical payment for the purchase of the *mundium* or *tutela*. As a betrothal fee it precedes the *achasius* (see n. 9).

the line or parentela of the deceased's parents; although the second category is designated as maternal relations, it is uncertain in fact whether the first category is also composed of maternal kin succeeding by virtue of common relationship with the deceased's mother. The *reipi* go only to male offspring of female relatives. The second category is constituted of the deceased's maternal relations, namely the son of a *consobrina* and the mother's brother. Unlike the other male relatives the *avunculus* is designated not in terms of his maternity, but on the basis of his fraternal relation to the deceased's mother. The third category is that of the brother. There is no indication whether he succeeds by virtue of the maternal relationship or simply as the nearest collateral. Up to this point only collaterals have been called, both the descendants and ascendants of the deceased being excluded. Thereafter, seemingly, the nearest cognate is eligible for the *reipi*. The receipt of the *reipi* is conditional upon the recipient's not having entered into the deceased's inheritance. A number of features of this order are striking: the precedence given the offspring of female kin and female maternal kin; the fact that, in the first two categories, the *reipi* may often have gone to minor children; and the antithesis of *reipi* and inheritance.

Before discussing further the exact nature of the first two categories of kin in particular, it is well to consider the reasoning behind this singular classification of relatives. The best explanation thus far is certainly that of Brunner.[16] Brunner notes that a prevalent theme of some of the early and later national laws is that marrriage ought not to founder on the self-interest of the relatives.[17] Marriage involved a considerable property transaction; so did remarriage, since it might bring about the whole or partial loss to the parties involved of the morning gift, dower (*dos*), and whatever the girl had received from her father, and result in the limitation or abrogation of the inheritance rights of the relatives concerned.[18] Relatives were often unwilling to lose this interest, and the situation became particularly volatile when, as was commonly the case, inheritance rights, either to the deceased or to the widow, were held along with the right to betrothal. Brunner suggested that, in order to solve this problem, the Franks modeled their procedure on a constitution of Valentinian I of AD 371 (CT 3.7.1), contained in the *Lex Romana Visigothorum* (3.7.1), or upon the practice based on this constitution found among the Gallo-

---

[16] "Zu Lex Salica tit. 44."
[17] Ibid., p. 75.
[18] See nn. 9 and 10 on LS 100.

Romans.[19] The constitution provided that when a dispute arose between a widow under twenty-five and her near relatives over the choice of suitors, the relatives must convene in a judicial hearing (*iudiciara cognitio*). Lest the self-interest of relatives with an eye to the widow's inheritance should impede the marriage, the judgment of those relatives should prevail who cannot benefit from her inheritance: "eorum volumus auctoritatem iudiciumque succedere, ad quos, etiamsi fatalis sors intercessit, tamen hereditatis commodum pervenire non possit."[20] In two very important respects the constitution of Valentinian and LS 44 converge and show that one was patterned on the other: first, in that the betrothal right and the expectation of inheritance must not be lodged in the same relatives; and second, in the requirement of a judicial hearing "whereas otherwise the court has nothing to do with marriage in German law."[21] According to Brunner the peculiar sequence of relatives found in LS 44 was the result of an innovation which, in contrast to the older law, granted the betrothal right and payment to the maternal kin of the dead husband.[22]

The crux of Brunner's contention seems to me certainly correct. The procedure and rationale of LS 44 was patterned after the practice of Valentinian's constitution. In the case of a dispute between a widow and near relatives, the purpose of the judicial hearing in the Roman procedure

[19] "Zu Lex Salica tit. 44," pp. 74, 78.

[20] (The first part of the provision concerns the power of the father if he is still alive.) "1. Quod si in conditionis delectu mulieris voluntas certat sententiae propinquorum, placet admodum, ut in pupillarum coniunctionibus sanctum est, habendo examini auctoritatem quoque iudiciariae cognitionis adiungi, ut si pares sunt genere ac moribus petitores, is potior aestimetur quem sibi consulens mulier approbaverit. 2. Sed ne forte hi, qui gradu proximo ad viduarum successiones vocantur, etiam honestas nuptias impediant, si huius rei suspicio processerit, eorum volumus auctoritatem iudiciumque succedere, ad quos, etiamsi fatalis sors intercessit, tamen hereditatis commodum pervenire non possit." *Interpretatio*: "... Si vero patres mortui sunt, nec sic quoque ex suo singulariter arbitrio nubendi habeant potestatem, sed pro honestate coniunctionis iudicium sequendum est propinquorum. Quod si duo petitores exstiterint, consulendi sunt quidem parentes nec praetermittendus est iudex, qui voluntatem feminae pro honestiore duntaxat parte prospiciat. Nec illis tantum propinquis praestet assensum, qui suspicione hereditatis utuntur, qui forte dum nuptias differunt, pro successione hereditatis mulieris mortem exspectare videntur: sed illorum magis, si talis conditio intercedit, electio sequenda est, qui nihil possunt de ipsius hereditate conquirere."

Cf. the eighth-century *Scintilla sive Epitome* (found also in Haenel): "Quod si fortasse propinqui malevoli videantur aut si duo fuerint petitores, iudicis praesentia exspectetur, quae et mulieris electioni faveat et malevolos parentes excludat ut quandoque ad illos possit mulieris hereditas pervenire."

[21] "Hier wie dort finden wir eine gerichtliche Verhandlung, während sonst im deutschen Rechte das Gericht mit der Eheschliessung nichts zu tun hat" ("Zu Lex Salica tit. 44," p. 74; also pp. 75, 78).

[22] Ibid., p. 78.

was not merely to accept the wishes of the disinterested relatives, but, as in the pupillary procedure ("ut in pupillarum coniunctionibus sanctum est"), to ensure *honestas nuptias*. To do this, the court consults the wishes of the widow and her relatives, and on that basis determines what choice of suitors is fitting. Now in the Salic procedure there is little point in limiting the courts' role to weighing the money. Rather, to short-circuit the problems arising from the fact that the betrothal right lay with the first husband's relatives, the Franks required that initially the betrothal right and payment should belong to the houses of the nearest disinterested relatives and that the acceptance of the suitor should lie with the court guided by the judgment of these relations and no doubt the wishes of the widow. The *mallus*, then, along with the parties concerned, to ensure *honestas nuptias*, makes the choice and acceptance of the suitor. After the money has been weighed and the court is in agreement, the suitor as the choice of the court can pay the *reipi* to the relatives entitled to receive the money.[23]

Naturally the circumstances behind *De reipus* do not agree in all particulars with those of the Valentinian constitution. Much of this has to do with the different nature of marriage and of kinship among the Franks. *De reipus* is an adaptation. For instance in the Roman case the procedure applies only to the widow under twenty-five. Among the Franks, however, the right of betrothal held by relatives was not extinguished when the widow reached a certain age. Most importantly, from the point of view of the extent of the application of the court procedure, the Frankish betrothal right was held by the husband's relatives, not, as in Roman law, by the widow's.[24] Thus the Roman hearing was held only when dispute arose between the woman and her relatives. The potential for conflict in the Frankish cases, however, was much greater, and the possible results far more hazardous, so that, from the outset, the widow's remarriage was made the concern of the public *mallus*. As a comparison with the relatively unregulated procedure among the Lombards shows, the basis for dissension was considerable.[25] Not only was the woman's betrothal right in the hands of non-relatives whose proprietary interests

---

[23] For a different view of the origin and aim of the court procedure, cf. Balon, *Traité*, 2: 525 ff. He regards the procedure as an expression of Frankish clan structure, in which the clan, acting through the *mallus*, accepts a suitor from another clan.

[24] In Roman law, the affines – her dead husband's relatives – might have to be consulted, however. Note the phrase found at the beginning of the Valentinian constitution: "sed publice consulatur affinitas."

[25] Ro. 182, 183.

and concepts of family solidarity and honour might run counter to the widow's desire, but she was always liable to be subjected to a suitor chosen in the interest of her husband's family. Moreover, the widow's part was liable to be supported by her own relatives if her husband's relations mistreated her or obstructed her own wishes as to remarriage. As in the case of the other Salic kinship regulations, *De reipus* brings us around again to the broad area of feud. Chilperic's edict associated a widow's remarriage with the potential for *scandalum*.[26] In the capitulary dealing with the payment of the *achasius*, one of the expressed aims is *pacem habere parentum*.[27] By making the acceptance of the suitor the concern of the court guided by the advice of the husband's relatives, the aim of *De reipus* was to mitigate this potentially volatile situation from the beginning.

Another area in which the Roman and Frankish regulations differ is in the precedence given non-inheriting relatives. The constitution and the *Interpretatio* stipulate no order among the kinsmen and leave the determination to the court if suspicion of self-interest arises. In this case the consideration of the court is simply that the relatives whose opinion is to be regarded most highly must have no immediate hope of inheriting. Partially at least because an actual payment is involved, the Franks stipulate a statutory order to be followed in the choice of the *reipi* recipient. In both cases, it must not be supposed that the relations called by the court have no potential to inherit, but merely that there is little chance of this right being exercised. We know that in Roman law the *cognati* might ultimately inherit at least up to the sixth degree, and that in Frankish law maternal kin also had inheritance rights.[28] One way of ensuring that the inheritance rights of the relatives involved are merely token would be to grant the *reipi* to distant relatives. The Franks did not do this, but instead gave it initially to the nearest kinsmen possible, whose inheritance rights were nevertheless minimal, and whose ties to the deceased's heirs and the household of his parents and brothers were the least. This explains the pattern of relationship found in ls 44. Thus, in the parentela of the parents, the *reipi* go to the separate households of the married sisters and nieces. The original household of the deceased – his mother and father and brothers and their sons – who had the most to gain from keeping his wife a widow or hand picking her next husband, is

---

[26] Above, n. 12.

[27] Above, n. 10.

[28] For the Romans, see *Inst. Iust.* 3.5.5; for the Franks, below, Ch. 15 and ls 59, *De alodis*.

postponed. This is precisely the category involved with the *achasius*, the normal rate of which, 3s, was roughly equal in amount to the *reipi*. Among the wider group of collaterals preference in receiving the *reipi* is given first to the maternal relatives. Of the bilateral kin they have the least to gain as a category since they would be excluded completely from inheriting the *alodis patris*, the family property of the deceased which originally devolved from his paternal side, and which would be the basis of his household. Here too the female line (*consobrinae filius*) is given precedence, since the *avunculus'* inheritance rights among the maternal kin were the greatest and his ties to the deceased, his brothers, and mother, the strongest (see Fig. 1a).

What must now be considered is the nature of the kinship categories which recieve the *reipi*, specifically the preferred first four or five orders: (1) *sororis filius* (2) *neptis filius* (3) *consobrinae filius qui ex maternae genere venit* (4) *avunculus, frater matris* (5) *frater*. These kinsmen, particularly the first four, have been taken as indicating a pattern of matrilineal relationship.[29] This is a possibility, although clearly there are considerations at work other than strict matriliny, for otherwise the *avunculus* would not be called so late. If the pattern is matrilineal, it does not, of course, testify to a once encompassing system of matriliny among the Franks, not to say the Germans, nor to the influence of some pre-Indo-European substratum. The Franks may simply have used matriliny for the very specific and limited function of the *reipi*.[30] Brunner suggested that the pattern of relatives here was the result of innovation and that the betrothal right originally pertained to the husband's nearest male relatives and heirs. Without speculating on the precise nature of the betrothal procedure before LS 44, there are grounds for thinking that the pattern there is in fact new. There is, first of all, the model of the Valentinian constitution, which indicates that the Franks based their betrothal procedure on principles and ideas which derived from late Roman law. Moreover, nowhere else in *Lex Salica* is the order and pattern of relationship described so minutely, except for the provision in the expanded text of sixty-five titles dealing with prohibited marriages, which is itself innovative and based on Roman

[29] Most recently, Balon, *Traité*, 2: 528-529.

[30] Nor need it indicate the very rare system of double descent wherein a person was the member of his father's patrilineage and his mother's matrilineage. The reasons for not regarding the *reipi* recipients as a matrilineal category are outlined above, but it might also be noted that their counterparts, the *achasius* recipients, are not a unilineal (agnatic) category either, since they include the mother, who has very important inheritance rights to her son's property (see below, Chs. 14 and 15).

FIG. 1. – THE FIRST FIVE ORDERS OF *R EIPI* RECIPIENTS

(a) as cognatic and matrilateral category

(b) as matrilineal category

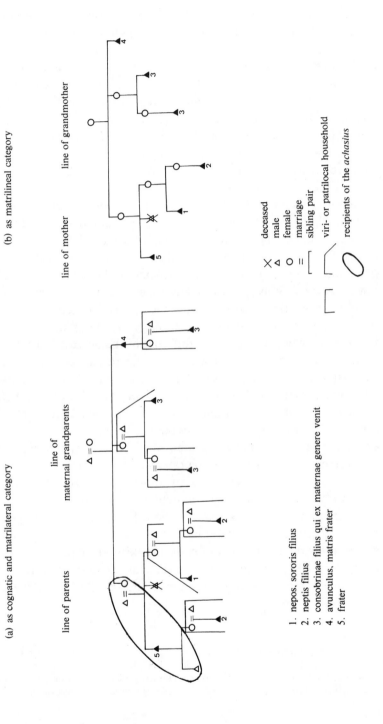

line of parents   line of maternal grandparents   line of mother   line of grandmother

1. nepos, sororis filius
2. neptis filius
3. consobrinae filius qui ex maternae genere venit
4. avunculus, matris frater
5. frater

×   deceased
△   male
○   female
=   marriage
    sibling pair

    viri- or patrilocal household

    recipients of the *achasius*

and ecclesiastical models.[31] In comparison with all the other provisions which we have dealt with touching kinship, little here is left to common knowledge.

However that may be, the claim that a matrilineal order can be found in *De reipus* is, in fact, only an inference. The text is seemingly very careful to specify the exact relationships involved, so that there will be no confusion: thus for instance, *nepos, sororis filius*, and *avunculus, matris frater*. But, in order to make the kinship pattern matrilineal, we must assume that the *neptis filius* applies only to the son of a sister's daughter's son, even though the term is equally applicable to a brother's daughter's son. In the same way, we must suppose that the *consobrinae filius* is related to the deceased only through females, that is, the maternal aunt and grandmother, although the term simply designates the son of any female cousin, or alternately, of any female collateral (See Fig. 1). It seems to me that this assumption of matriliny should not be made. The *neptis filius* and *consobrinae filius* are designated without further modification not because matriliny is assumed but because the terms are meant to apply simply to cognatic kinsmen who are the offspring of females. Thus in the line of the deceased's parents the *reipi* will go initially to males in households which are separate from that of the deceased, his parents, or brother. The sequence among the matrilateral category is designed to establish that male collaterals shall receive the *reipi*, but among them, the uncle must claim last: hence *consobrinarum filii* will be called before the *avunculus*. From the *Lex Romana Visigothorum* we have a good idea of the aims of *De reipus*. These would be amply satisfied simply by preferring married females and their offspring and matrilateral relatives. The principle behind the configuration of kinsmen in *de reipus* is not unilinealism but the avoidance of those with direct interest in the deceased's household and the widowhood of his wife.

De reipus not only has bearing upon the pattern of relationship and kinship structure, but it is also invaluable because it gives the only direct evidence for the legal extent of early Frankish kinship.[32] *Reipi* recipients are to be called up to the sixth degree. This range of relationship is also associated in the law with the right to inherit (*proximior ... si hereditatem*

---

[31] LS 13.11.

[32] The exaggerated proportions of the saying attributed to Guntram by Gregory of Tours (HF 7.21) do not merit serious consideration: "tunc rex iuravit omnibus optimatibus quod non modo ipsum [Eberulf] verum etiam progeniem eius in nonam generationem deleret, ut per horum necem consuetudo auferretur iniqua, ne reges amplius interfice-rentur."

non accipiat),[33] so that while the acceptance of *reipi* was denied to those who actually partook of the inheritance, it was also limited to the category of potential heirs.

The next aspect of Frankish kinship which must be considered is the nature of the kinship division within this category in the case of intestate succession.

---

[33] There is general agreement, but no explicit proof, that the 'Germanic' or 'Canonic' double count of degree computation is meant and not the Roman single count. When common relationship between two individuals was invoked, in the Roman system each step up to and down from the common ancestor was counted as a single degree: thus brothers were related in the second, first cousins in the fourth degree. By Germanic or Canonic count, each generation constituted a degree: thus brothers were related in the first degree, cousins in the second. The Germanic count is also further complicated by the fact that sometimes the point at which the count started varied.

12

Kinship Categories II:
An Introduction to Frankish Inheritance

A number of texts which deal with inheritance are the last significant body of evidence for the structure of kinship among the early Franks. At the time of the first redaction of their laws, the Franks practised a system of individual, or family ownership. This is indicated by the treatment of property in the Salic law,[1] and is also confirmed by the inheritance laws to be considered below. There are no clan holdings in the Frankish sources, nor any evidence at all for extensive lineage or clan structures among the population. As has been shown earlier,[2] the *vicini* and *migrantes* of the Frankish period tell us nothing about supposed primitive Germanic communities based on blood and descent, but reflect practices common to the late Empire. As far as the relationship of inheritance to kinship is concerned, therefore, we are dealing, not with corporate groups, but with categories of kinsmen who are called primarily as individuals to take up the effects of a deceased relative.

It is also worth noting that inheritance was just one element in the interrelated web of kinship obligations and rights, and by no means the most important, particularly as regards collateral relationship. If we limit ourselves, as we must, largely to the realm of law, the *Pactus* suggests that, outside the immediate family, which was the principle area of the devolution of property, kinship for most people primarily concerned feud and its related processes; for it was the threat of hostilities by kinsmen which frequently ensured redress for grievances ranging from homicide and personal injury to theft and marital infidelity. What, for instance, was more important to a pair of cousins: the vague and unlikely possibility that

---

[1] R. Latouche, *Birth of the Western Economy*, p. 81.
[2] Above, Ch. 4.

one might inherit part of the other's estate, or the realization that both might imminently be bound together in feud, compensation, and oath-helping procedure? It is because of the interrelation of kinship and feud that the *Pactus* gives us *De compositione homicidii*, *De eum qui se de parentilla tollere uult*, and *De chrenecruda*, and probably even the complications behind *De reipus*. From a legal and social viewpoint the solidary aspects of Frankish kinship are to be found not in inheritance but in feud and its related procedures. Yet the sequence of intestate succession is still one of the most concrete signs of the rights and obligations based on blood relationship, and potential heirs can often constitute an extensive category of kinsmen. What remains to be considered in the following pages is the nature and divisions of the Frankish inheritance category and the principles of relationship in operation.

The questions surrounding Frankish inheritance are as contentious as any of the interpretive problems of the Salic law. In part this results from the textual difficulties endemic to the study of *Lex Salica*. But the elliptical nature of the earliest provision also creates ambiguity, as does the fact that the inheritance sequence of most distant collaterals, as is true of a number of the *leges*, is left largely undefined, although certain rights of the immediate family are dealt with fairly fully. Since the work of late nineteenth-century scholars, in particular Brunner's interpretation of the important text ls 59,[3] a certain consensus is apparent, but (as in the case of the *Edictum Chilperici*) not all of it is justified by any means. Behind most interpretations of Frankish inheritance, whether in regard to particulars or to the broad outlines of its development, lies a theory of the development of private property. This is closely connected with ideas of kinship development which have been dealt with earlier; both are part and parcel of the nineteenth century's conception of the development of human societies, which has remained rooted in the literature up to the present. Put most simply, ideas of ownership, of both moveable and real property, were thought to have been originally collective or communal and to have eventually progressed to the kind of private ownership thought common to modern and Roman law. The problems of definition and comparative study here are immense, and initially more in the realm of anthropology than of law and history. It is neither intended or necessary to enter into them here. But, since the ideas referred to have persistently constituted much of the accepted implicit and explicit baggage of writings on Frankish kinship and inheritance, it is useful to consider briefly how this

---

[3] To be considered fully below, Ch. 15.

theory has been applied and how it has shaped interpretations of the evidence.

Two aspects of the traditional view are particularly important. The first involves the stark contrast frequently drawn between Roman ideas of absolute ownership, unity of succession, testament, and disposability of property on the one hand; and, on the other, the proprietal regimes thought to be prevalent among the Germanic invaders and in the successor kingdoms. Now while some of the contrast is justified, it is, nevertheless, clear that the Roman law which many observers have in mind is that of an ideal classical system. The corrective work of Ernst Levy on vulgar law, showing the vagueness of the idea of *dominium* in the late Empire, is now well known.[4] A perusal of late Roman legislation shows just how loosely phrases like *privato iure* could be used. Property so called could be bound over to public burdens, its owners forbidden to alienate it except to designated classes of heirs; and, as regards its inheritance, preference could be given to heirs liable to take up its public functions.[5] In the realm of inheritance, the kinds of distinctions common to the Frankish *formulae* – even the idea of ancestral property specially entailed by that fact – can be found in the *Theodosian Code*, although the precise nature and extent of their application is problematical.[6] The point being made here is not that the type of system sometimes thought characteristic of medieval attitudes to property, its ownership, and inheritance, was necessarily fully developed in late Antiquity, but that we can see clearly the tendency to explore a similar avenue. This aspect of the heritage of Antiquity was certainly passed on to the successor kingdoms.

A second feature of the traditional view concerns the development of proprietal forms among the Germans and increases the contrast with Roman ideas of property and inheritance. Property among the Franks, as also among the other Germanic peoples, is commonly thought to have gone through three stages: a collective or communistic stage before the period of invasions; familial at the time of the invasions; and afterwards an increasingly individual stage as a result of the confrontation with

---

[4] *West Roman Vulgar Law*. Published in 1951, it soon made a brief appearance in the traditional, if idiosyncratic, account of Balon, *Les Fondements du régime foncier au moyen âge* (1954), but its broad implications have only gradually begun to shape analysis of the legal foundations of the early Middle Ages; see Ch. 8, n. 2.

[5] See above, pp. 71 ff.

[6] Cf. CT 14.3.13, a. 369, where property acquired by a breadmaker by inheritance or gift, and thereafter included in the succession to his inheritance, is then considered part of the endowment (*dos*) and must be for the profit of the breadmaking establishment.

Roman law.[7] On the evidence of Caesar, the traditional interpretation supposed that the Germans did not possess the idea of private property in land but practised a system of agrarian communism. This regime is seen to be in evolution at the time of Tacitus, and it is thought probable that at this period the area around the homestead was held under private family ownership and subject to inheritance. Traces of the former collective system are said to be found in the *leges*, notably the *Edictum Chilperici*, but generally by the time of the invasions there was separate property as well as an intermediate system of family ownership, believed to be characterized by a lack of testament, alienation of real property only through the consent of family members, and succession to it only by male agnates.[8] Once the barbarians settled in the area of the Empire it is felt that the Germanic ideas of collective and familial property gave way before the Roman system,[9] although the Frankish idea of family property did not

---

[7] These ideas about Roman and German property can be found in all languages throughout the literature. The particulars of the account followed here are those of E. Chenon, *Histoire générale du droit français* (Paris, 1926-1929), 1: 412-419, which are by no means extreme. They are repeated by his successor, F. Olivier-Martin, *Histoire du droit français des origines à la Révolution* (Paris, 1948), pp. 3 ff., 17, and esp. 76 ff. Most of the same ideas are found in P. Ourliac and J. de Malafosse, *Histoire du droit privé*, 2nd ed. (Paris, 1968-1971), 2: 27 ff., 127 ff.; 3: 366 ff. Cf. also the earlier works of J. Brissaud, *History of French Private Law*, trans. R. Howell, The Continental Legal History Series, 3 (Boston, 1912), pp. 626 ff. and P. M. Viollet, *Histoire du droit civil français*, 3rd ed. (Paris, 1905), pp. 383 ff., 553 ff., 817 ff.

[8] The Thuringian law is frequently invoked as somehow preserving more purely the old Germanic system (*LTh.* 26-34). It gave preference to male agnates (*lancea*) over females and other cognates (*fusus*). This marks the earliest reference to the spear and spindle kin, which plays so prominent a role in traditional treatments of ancient Germanic kinship. In the initial stages of inheritance the daughter, mother, and sister had very minor rights to moveables. (The Thuringian law is not exclusively agnatic though: children inherit from their mother, the sons receiving the land and moveables, the daughters taking only the *spolia colli*; cognates eventually succeed after agnates; and certain female property, *ornamenta*, normally devolves from mother to daughter.) The law is from the early ninth century and it has long been recognized that it bears little resemblance to earlier Frankish practice. Cf. J. M. Pardessus, *Loi salique* (Paris, 1843), p. 697: "Quand on supposerait que les Francs saliques ont eu, dans l'origine, des usages semblables à ceux des Thuringiens, ces usages ont évidemment été modifiés." In fact the Thuringian law is the spectre which haunts most discussions of Frankish inheritance.

[9] As noted, the distinction between Roman individual and German family property is often pushed too far. If by family property is meant property which is not completely at the disposal of an individual, particularly by testamentary means, such a description is applicable to the situation found in the early Middle Ages. It is important to note, though, that at times we find broader and stricter limitations in later centuries than in earlier. (The point is well made by Bloch, *Feudal Society*, p. 141, with regard to the consent of near relatives to alienations.) On the other hand, the Roman situation was not the rampant individualism often implied and in some instances was stricter than barbarian practice. Quite apart from property bound by state restrictions, testators had to maintain statutory

completely decay, but continued in the distinction made between ancestral property and acquests.

As we have seen in *Part II*, the basis for much of this formulation is either tenuous or false; at its heart lie interpretations of Caesar and a series of texts from the early Middle Ages which can no longer be maintained. The evidence found in *Lex Salica* has been made to fit this framework and the later legal material made to show its evolution. Whatever truth may lie in the formulation is overshadowed by the fact that, as a whole, it tends to obfuscate texts rather than to explicate them, and casts a false light upon what must remain in dark or shadow. What is needed is a consideration of the relevant texts outside the traditional framework and the realization that there is a great deal we shall never know. In the following pages, the simple expedient will be tried of working back to the central crux of Frankish inheritance, LS 59, from later, better understood texts: first, the *formulae* which stand between the later customary law and the earlier *Lex Salica* and are quite clearly linked to both; and then, the sixth-century evidence, as found in the edicts of Childebert and Chilperic, and in Gregory of Tours.

---

portions for various classes of relatives, including ascendants and collaterals, if they would inherit on intestacy: generally, see W. W. Buckland, *A Text-Book of Roman Law*, 3rd ed., rev. by P. Stein (Cambridge, 1966), pp. 327 ff. and F. Schulz, *Classical Roman Law* (Oxford, 1951), pp. 275 ff.; cf. LRB 45.5, 6 and LRV 2.19.

13

Frankish Inheritance:
The Period of the *Formulae*

Along with charters, the single most extensive type of legal material from the Merovingian and early Carolingian period are the *formulae*. In view of their bulk, they tell us less about intestate inheritance than one would first imagine. In one respect, however, they are invaluable. We know that, from the earliest period, Frankish law in matters of intestate succession normally took into account considerations other than simple relationship. The sex of the recipient was a factor in the devolution of the inheritance, as was the nature and origin of the property to be inherited. As we shall see, these ideas are operative in ɪs 59, *De alodis*, the earliest statement of Frankish inheritance, but it is not until the period of the *formulae* that we find explicit illustration of the proprietal divisions.

In the *formulae* and other contemporary charter evidence, a distinction is commonly made between property inherited from one's parents, ancestral property, generally indicated by the expression *de alode parentum*, or in Ripuarian law, by the designation *aviatica*; and acquests, or properties acquired by some other means, such as gift or purchase, and said to be *de adtractu, conparato* or *conquesto*.[1] A mutual donation of

---

[1] See *FAnd.* 1.41; *Arv.* 3, 4, 6; *Marc.* 1.12, 20, 33; 2.4, 6, 7, 9-12, 14, among others. The distinction and its terminology thus is found already in the earliest of the *formulae*. *Alodis = hereditas* is the usually accepted thesis and most certainly correct. The classic statement of this fact with numerous examples and comparisons is that of N.-D. Fustel de Coulanges, *L'Alleu et le domaine rural*, Histoire des Institutions Politiques de l'Ancienne France, 4 (Paris, 1889), pp. 149-171, although he was by no means the first to make the equation (cf. Pardessus, *Loi salique*, pp. 691 ff.). See also Chenon, *Histoire*, 1: 419-420, with bibliography; and Geffcken, pp. 233-234. Various views on the word can also be found in Balon, *Les Fondements du régime foncier*, esp. pp. 47 ff. In this and succeeding works, however, he maintains the untenable view that *alodis* means "seigneurie allodiale," or "seigneurie salique," and refers to a peculiarly Germanic and Frankish regime.

That *alodis parentum* embraced inheritance from both parents is implicit in the phrase. Cf. the citations by Fustel, pp. 156-157: e.g., *Charta Ansberti*, "de alode parentum

usufruct made between childless spouses found in the *Marculfi formulae* (2.7) will illustrate this proprietal distinction and the meaning and use of the word *alodis*. The husband grants his wife, if she survives him, all his property (*omne corpus facultatis*) "tam de alode aut de conparatum vel qualibet adtractu." She will be permitted to make donations *pro anima* "de alode nostra." On her death, the remaining property reverts to the husband's *legitimi heredes*. Similarly the wife grants all her property "tam de hereditate parentum quam de conparatum." The husband too may make donations *pro anima* "de alode mea." On his death the remainder reverts to the wife's next of kin. This document succinctly illustrates that the meaning of *alodis* is *hereditas*. Indeed, the *formulae* frequently use the words interchangeably; another synonym is *successio*.[2] It is also apparent that the word *alodis* has two aspects depending upon the perspective from which the property of an individual is viewed. It first refers to all or any part of his property, from whatsoever source, whether inherited or acquired. It is his *hereditas* which will be passed on to his heirs or otherwise disposed of. Thus *Marc.* 2.9 refers to a case where sons acquire *omnis alodis* of their mother, which is explicitly stated to contain the *dos* granted to her by her husband. Second, it can refer to that part within an individual's estate which has come to him through inheritance and is thus distinguished from acquests gained by, for instance, gift, purchase or exchange.[3] In this sense *alodis* is the *hereditas* of the former owner. This context is usually quite clear, since *alodis* is then designated *alodis parentum (meorum)* or else as in the donation considered above, directly contrasted with the *adtractus*. When we come to ls 59 *De alodis*, it will be seen that the rubric corresponds to the first aspect of the word and means simply, "On inheritance."

Before dealing with the rather sparse evidence of the *formulae* for the intestate inheritance sequence and the application therein of the above

---

meorum tam de materno quam paterno"; and Pardessus, pp. 691 ff. There is also frequent reference to inheritance of specific properties from the *alodis paterna* or *materna*.

   Hereditas aviatica, in *LRib.* 57 (for the text, see below, Ch. 15, n. 11). It is also found in the charters as a synonym for *alodis parentum*: "quicquid de paterno materno vel de aviatico seu comparato ... ad nos legibus pervenit" (a. 788); "tam de aviatico quam de paterno sive de materno, sive de conparato" (a. 742); in Niermeyer, s.v. *aviaticus*. Its use in the *Decretio Childeberti* is slightly different; see further, below pp. 194-195.

   [2] Fustel, *L'Alleu*, pp. 149 ff., passim. In Charlemagne's time, the word, particularly in the form *allodium*, starts to indicate *patrimonium, terra propria*, land not held from anyone and thus, above all, heritable.

   [3] "res ... tam quod per regio munere ... quam et quod per vindictiones, donationes, cessiones, commutationes titulum vel de alodo parentum" (*FMarc.* 1.33).

proprietal distinctions, it is useful to touch briefly upon the situation prevailing in the later customary law. There, for the first time, we find extensive information about the sequence of inheritance. What is quite apparent is that the distinctions that have just been discussed between inherited and acquired property played an important role in the application of this sequence.[4] Despite some variation in details, the inheritance was divided generally into moveables and immoveables, a distinction barely perceptible in the *formulae*, but one which would be increasingly important in the customary law. The immoveables were then divided, in a manner directly derived from Frankish law, into *propres* (somewhat confusingly rendered as 'personal belongings') or *hereditas*, and acquests. The personal belongings were properties acquired by inheritance, while the acquests were properties otherwise obtained by the deceased in his lifetime. When the deceased left no descendants to inherit, the moveables and the acquests were grouped together and either inherited simply by the next of kin, or, as was often the case, divided equally between the paternal and maternal lines. In regard to the *hereditas*, the prevalent rule was *paterna paternis, materna maternis* (*ius recadentiae* or *revolutionis*). This meant that the property returned to the line from which it came: the paternal and maternal sides each retrieved that part of the estate which the deceased originally acquired from each by inheritance. The *ius recadentiae* prevailed in every county of the customary law in the feudal period and occasionally in areas of the written law.

If we return to the period of the *formulae* and look for indications of the details of the inheritance sequence and for the application of the proprietal distinctions in the succession, we find information only about the intestate inheritance of the deceased's descendants. Two *formulae* deal with the divisions of the inheritance and how these divisions relate to the succession of daughters; they are of some interest for our understanding of ʟs 59. The younger of the *formulae* is found in the *Cartae Senonicae*, which is dated around the years 768-775;[5] it is addressed to the testator's daughter:

---

[4] On inheritance in the customary law, see: Chenon, *Histoire*, 2: 229-243; Brissaud, *History of French Private Law*, pp. 642-651; E. Glasson, "Le Droit de succession au moyen âge," *Nouvelle Revue Historique de Droit Français et Étranger*, 16 (1892), esp. 698-706.

[5] Buchner, *Rechtsquellen*, p. 53.

It is well known to all that, as is contained in the *Salic Law*, you were unable to succeed to my property which came to me *ex alode parentum meorum* along with your brothers, my sons.

By means of this *epistola hereditaria* the testator proceeds to establish his daughter as an heir alongside her brothers to all his property, whether from the *alodis parentum* or the *contractum*.[6]

The older of the *formulae* appears in the collection of Marculf, which dates either from ca. 650 or 721-735.[7] It is called a *carta ut filia cum fratres in paterna succedat alode*. The testator addresses his daughter:

An ancient but impious custom prevails among us that sisters cannot have a share of the *terra paterna* along with their brothers.

The father then makes his daughter an equal heir along with her brothers to all his inheritance,

tam de alode paterna quam de conparatum[8]

The variation in terminology raises questions which will be considered below, yet there are points on which the *formulae* agree. First, on intestacy the deceased's daughters succeed equally alongside their brothers to at least part of the estate. This is identified with the *adtractus* in the Sens *formula*, and probably with the *conparatum* in Marculf, that is, property which the deceased acquired during his life. Second, to the property variously called *terra paterna* (*alodis paterna*) and *alodis parentum*, the daughters are postponed by their brothers unless expressly instituted as

[6] *FSen.* 45: "Dulcissima atque in omnibus amantissima filia mea illa, ego enim vir magnificus ille. Omnibus non habetur incognitum que, sicut lex Salica contenit, de res meas quod mihi ex alode parentum meorum obvenit apud germanos tuos, filios meos, minime in hereditate succidere potebas. Propterea mihi praepatuit plenissima et integra voluntas ut hanc epistolam hereditoria in te fieri et adfirmare rogavi ut, si mihi suprestitis in hunc seculo apparueris, in omnes res meas tam ex alode parentum meorum quam ex meum contractum mihi obvenit ... in hereditate apud germanos tuos, filios meos, succedas et equalentia inter vos exinde dividere vel exequare faciatis."

[7] Buchner, *Rechtsquellen*, pp. 51-52.

[8] *FMarc.* 2.12: "Carta ut filia cum fratres in paterna succedat alode. Dulcissima filia mea illa, illi [= ille]. Diuturna sed impia inter nos consuetudo tenetur ut de terra paterna sorores cum fratribus porcionem non habeant; sed ego perpendens hanc impietate sicut mihi a Deo aequales donati estis filii ita et a me setis aequaliter diligendi et de res meas post meum discessum aequaliter gratuletis. Ideoque per hanc epistolam te, dulcissima filia mea, contra germanos tuos, filios meos illos, in omni hereditate mea aequalem et legitimam esse constituo heredem ut tam de alode paterna quam de conparatum vel mancipia aut presidium nostrum vel quodcumque morientes relinquaeremus equo lante cum filiis meis, germanis tuis, dividere vel exequare debias et in nullo paenitus porcionem minorem qua ipse non accipias sed omnia vel ex omnibus inter vos dividere vel exaequare aequaliter debeatis."

heirs by means of an *epistola hereditaria*. It should be noted that they are not excluded from this part of the inheritance by any male agnate, as is often said; just as in the *Edictum Chilperici*, they are merely postponed if there are brothers ("sorores cum fratribus porcionem non habeant"; "apud germanos tuos, filios meos, minime ... succidere potebas") and are thus capable of inheriting the whole estate if there are none. These two features of Frankish inheritance account for the fact that daughters partook of the landed estate on the death of their father, as the *formulae* designed to offset the lack of representation clearly show.[9] These features also largely explain the great numbers of women who, in both the *formulae* and the charters, claim possession of their lands by virtue of inheritance from their parents, either mother or father, and why the number of women who appear as proprietors of landed property is, to use Fustel's word, incalculable.[10]

The final point on which the *formulae* agree is that the postponement of sisters by brothers is particularly characteristic of Salic law. As we have seen, the same fact is noted in the sixth-century *Edictum Chilperici*. The Sens *formula* clearly invokes the written Salic law: "sicut lex Salica contenit." The *Cartae Senonicae* in fact stem from the same period when

---

[9] Representation was not an accepted feature of Frankish law and without it grandchildren were postponed by the surviving children of the deceased. See further, below, pp. 193 ff.

FLin. 12: "Ego ... ille et coniux mea illa dilectissimis nepotibus nostris necnon et neptis nostris illis. Constat ... quod genitor vester, filius siquidem noster ... de hac luce visus est ante nos discessisse.... Ac igitur de causa conplacuit nobis atque convenit ut pro ipso proprietatis iure in quo genitor vester legitime succedere debuit post nostrum quoque discessum vos equalem partem contra avunculus vestros vel amitas vestras, filiis vel filiabus nostris ... accipere debeatis ... id est tam in terris quam in silvis, campis, pratis, pascuis, vineis, mancipiis, peculiis, pecoribus."

FMarc. 2.10, addressed to grandchildren by a deceased daughter (*nepotes ex filia*), permitting them to acquire, against their uncles, the portion due their mother if she had lived: "dum per lege cum filiis meis, abuncolis vestris, in alode mea accedere minime potueratis ... volo ut in omni alode mea ... hoc est in terris, domibus, [etc.] ... omnique suppellectile domus ... quicquid suprascribta genetrix vester si mihi suprestis fuisset de alode mea recipere potuerat, vos contra abunculos vestros ... prefato portione recipere faciatis."

[10] Fustel, *L'Alleu*, pp. 142-143, with examples. Cf., for instance, *FMerk.* 16: "dono tibi, dulcissima coniux mea illa ... rem meam ... quem ante hos dies de parte genitoris mei illius quondam mihi legibus obvenit, hoc est ... terris, domibus.... Simili modo et ego illa, dulcissimae iugalis meus ille, dono tibi rem meam ... que ante hos dies de parte genitoris mei illius quondam mihi legibus obvenit, hoc est ... terris, domibus."

Fustel, however, shared the view that according to Salic law women could not inherit land at all and that this was the rule which the Marculfian and Sens *formulae* were intended to circumvent (p. 140), although none of the evidence supports his view. He was led, then, to conclude in the case of the implications behind *FLin.* 12 (n. 9, above), for instance, that here "l'article de la Loi Salique paraît absolument oublié" (p. 142).

manuscript copies of *Lex Salica* began to be widely diffused. The phrase *inter nos consuetudo tenetur* used in the earlier collection of Marculf may possibly refer to the written law, but it seems more likely that, whether it refers to Frankish custom as a whole or to a local variation, it reflects conditions before the written *Lex* had become common currency to be dealt with by scribes and legislators. By the time the Marculfian *formula* was copied into the *Formulae Salicae Merkelianae* in the late eighth century, it was thought expedient to alter *consuetudo* to a more explicit connection with the Salic law: *secundum legem Salicam.*[11]

If we wish to know more precisely the nature of the property which sons inherited in preference to their sisters, we run into some difficulties, since this portion of the inheritance is variously designated.[12] The Sens *formula* calls it the property from the *alodis parentum meorum*, "the inheritance of my parents." A person inherited from both his father and mother, and the property from both these sources constituted the inherited portion of his estate, so frequently contrasted with the acquests. In typical fashion, the Sens *formula* goes on to designate the entire inheritance which the daughter now shares as composed of the *alodis parentum* and *contractum*. This is straightforward; the terminology is standard for the *formulae* and completely consistent within itself. Such is not the case in the Marculfian example: it designates the inheritance reserved for the sons as *terra paterna*; the rubric equates this with *alodis paterna*;[13] and, later, *alodis paterna* is contrasted with the *conparatum*. The terminology is unique. *Terra paterna, alodis paterna,* is never found in the sense of the

---

[11] No. 23 (see below, n. 15); the other alterations will be discussed shortly.

[12] Although it is difficult to find notice of this fact; "Les formules préparées au profit des filles sont d'une technique simple et nette" (H. Auffroy, *Évolution du testament en France des origines au xiiiᵉ siècle* [Paris, 1889], p. 213). Varying interpretations, however, underline the problems. Cf., for intance: Fustel (*L'Alleu*, pp. 140-141), who believed that the *formulae* show what is regarded as the old Salic rule that no woman could inherit land at all; Pardessus (*Loi salique*, p. 175), who regarded tham as indicating (rightly, I think), that the limitation applied not to "tous les immeubles delaissés par le père," but only to those which he held "par succession de ses père et mère, *aviatica*," an opinion which Chenon (*Histoire*, 1: cf. 444-445, 448-452) appears to share; and Heinrich Brunner ("Kritische Bemerkungen zur Geschichte des germanischen Weibererbrechts," zrg ga 21 (1900) 17, n. 1), who regarded the *formulae* as showing that the restriction applied only to property inherited by the testator from his father and corresponded to the *aviatica* of Ripuarian law; on the *aviatica*, see above, n. 1. Cf. also Bergengruen, *Adel und Grund-herrschaft im Merowingerreich* (Wiesbaden, 1958), p. 53.

[13] Conceivably the rubric could be understood more generally, in which case "cum fratres" = "equally with her brothers": "so that a daughter may succeed equally with her brothers to the paternal inheritance." But this does not account for the later contrast of the *alodis paterna* with the *contractum*.

comprehensive proprietal distinction between ancestral property and acquests: even in Marculf the usual expression to distinguish ancestral property is *alodis parentum*.[14] The *Formulae Salicae Merkelianae*, a collection roughly contemporary with the Sens *formulae*, which borrowed extensively from Marculf, also seems to have had trouble with the above terms. In its version of the formula in question, it replaces *terra paterna* with *portio paterna*. In the rubric it replaces *alodis paterna* with simply *portio*. It also drops altogether the confusing distinction *alodis paterna* and the *comparatum*, and instead simply notes that the daughter is hereafter established as an heir "in omni hereditate" so that she participates equally in the division of the *alodis paterna* with her brothers.[15]

This series of texts presents us with the classic dilemma of whether we are dealing with various perceptions of the same phenomenon or with substantially different procedures reflected in different language and terminology. The variety of terms raises a number of questions. Can the Sens *formula*, whose meaning seems clear, be reconciled with that of Marculf and its derivative the *Merkeliana*? Is the *terra paterna* of Marculf all the father's land or only ancestral land of some kind? Does *paterna* refer to the testator himself as *pater*, or does it indicate a previous ancestral origin for the property? There is no doubt that it is difficult to reconcile the various readings, if indeed they should be reconciled. The *leges*, in some cases, may have been meant to record or establish common law; at any rate, the nature and usual singularity of their evidence accustoms us to talking of them in this way. But as regards Frankish law, it is clear that, at the end of the Merovingian period and throughout the Carolingian period, there was a gulf, for whatever reason, between the provisions of *Lex Salica* and the law practised. It is impossible to tell to what extent there was regional variation in Salic law, but it is not unlikely that the diversity, particularly in details, characteristic of later customary law was also a feature of seventh and eighth-century legal practice. This is one way to consider the three *formulae* presented here. However, this

---

[14] *Alodis* (or *hereditas*) *paterna, materna, genitoris, genetricis*, of course is common enough in the *formulae* and charters indicating the inheritance of a particular parent or the origin of a particular piece of property inherited from that parent.

[15] No. 23: "Epistola per quam soror succedat in portionem cum fratribus. Dulcissima filia mea illa. Dum cognitum est qualiter secundum legem Salicam in portione paterna cum fratribus tuis, filiis meis, minime potes accedere.... Ideo per hanc aepistolam, dulcissima filia mea illa, contra germanos tuos, filios meos illos, in omni hereditate mea aequalem et legitimum esse constituo heredem ut de alode paterna quod morientes relinquerimus cum filiis meis, germanos tuos, dividere et exaequare facias...."

approach does not solve the problem that, even if the Marculfian *formula* is considered alone, it does not easily yield its meaning, since there are still internal inconsistencies to be resolved. In fact these are better seen in the context of the other *formulae*. When this is done it is apparent that there are a number of ways to reconcile the various texts.

At the outset we must eliminate the possibility that *Marc.* 2.12 – as it stands – refers to the postponement of the daughter in regard to all the land held by her father, *terra paterna*.[16] As will be seen, there is reason to think this was the case in the earliest redaction of the *Pactus*, but, quite apart from the testimony of the Sens *formula*, it is clear that in *Marc.* 2.12 *terra paterna* equals *alodis paterna* as it appears in the rubric and as later it is contrasted with the acquests. The *terra* then, is ancestral land, just as the *alodis parentum* of the Sens example is inherited property.[17] It is that part of the father's estate which he has inherited (*portio, portio paterna*, in the *Merkeliana*, i.e. his share in a previous inheritance). This, I think is the best reading of the *formula* as we now have it, and as it was incorporated into the Marculfian collection. However, if we give credence to the idea that originally the restriction applied to all the father's land, it is likely that the prototype of the Marculfian *formula* in fact gave the old rule and that the present version was an unhappy attempt to bring it up to date.

How, then, are we to understand *paterna*? Since the *carta* is addressed by a father to his daughter, it may simply reflect this fact by designating the portion in question of the testator's estate as 'paternal', which is common enough usage.[18] Otherwise there are two other suggestions which take *paterna* to refer to an antecedent of the testator, or *pater*, which deserve brief consideration, since they reconcile the inconsistencies

---

[16] So Fustel, *L'Alleu*, pp. 140-141, and recently U. Nonn, "Merowingische Testament: Studien zum Fortleben einer römischen Urkundenform im Frankreich," *Archiv für Diplomatik* 18 (1972) 52.

[17] And as is the *hereditas aviatica* of Ripuarian law.

[18] So apparently Fustel and Pardessus, above, n. 12. Then "tam de alode paterna quam de conparatum" = "both of the inherited portion of the paternal estate and the acquests."

In terms of the characteristic phraseology and expression of the *formulae*, we can compare the Marculfian "Diuturna sed impia inter nos consuetudo tenetur ut de terra paterna sorores cum fratribus porcionem non habeant; sed ego perpendens hanc impietate. ... Ideoque ... constituo ..." with this passage from the mid eighth-century collection from Tours, "Quicquid filiis vel nepotibus de facultate patris cognoscitur ordinasse voluntatem eius in omnibus lex Romana constringit adimplere. Ideoque ego ... ille ..." (*FTur.* 22). Both employ the same formula: a rhetorical and general statement of the nature and authority of the law in question, followed by the testator's disposition. In the Tours *formula* where the rhetorical invocation mentions *facultas patris*, in effect *pater* refers to the testator himself. In the corresponding phrase of the Marculfian formula, *terra paterna*, it looks simply as if *paterna* refers rhetorically to the testator as *pater*.

of *Marc.* 2.12. First, it should be noted that *paternus* in late Latin can mean 'ancestral' or 'family' and would be analogous to the *de alodo patrum nostrorum* found in a charter of the year 632 to designate inherited property.[19] The earlier treatment of oathhelping in the *formulae* also suggests a second way which makes sense of the text. It will be remembered that while one *formula* gave the general principle of parity of representation in cases *de statu*, another dealt with a limited and specific application. Fortunately we were in a position to reconcile the two *formulae* on the basis of a capitulary which explained the seemingly divergent texts. It is possible that much the same situation exists in the Sens and Marculfian inheritance *formulae*. The Sens text simply states the principle that sons are given preference to the inherited property (*alodis parentum*). The Marculfian example, on the other hand, starts from the specific instance where the testator is dealing only with property inherited from his father. Therefore the daughter can only be postponed from inheriting ancestral property from the paternal side (*terra paterna, alodis paterna*). This too could explain why the usual contrast between the *alodis* or *alodis parentum* and the acquests has been emended to one between the *alodis paterna* and the *conparatum*. In the model used for the Marculfian *formula* there simply was no *alodis materna* to be taken into consideration. Such specificity is common enough in the *formulae*. Details were meant to be changed, reduced, or expanded, to fit the circumstances.

The treatment of inheritance in the *formulae* is rather limited. Yet, despite the narrow concerns and the difficulties with *Marc.* 2.12, the collections present a fair picture of a number of features of Frankish inheritance in the later Merovingian and early Carolingian period which are of particular interest from the point of view of *Lex Salica*. The basic proprietal division was between ancestral property inherited from both sides of the family and acquests. In the later customary law we find this distinction applied widely in the inheritance of collaterals, but in the period of the *formulae* itself we only find notice of its application to the inheritance rights of the offspring of the deceased. On intestacy daughters were postponed by sons to the inheritance of the ancestral property and succeeded to it in the absence of their brothers. The acquests were inherited equally by the children regardless of sex. The *formulae* particularly associate this sequence with the Salic law. It, and other characteristic features of Frankish inheritance, will appear again when we go on to consider the evidence for the sixth century.

[19] Lewis and Short, s.v.; Pardessus, *Diplomata* (Paris, 1843-1849), 2: no. 256.

14

Frankish Inheritance: The Sixth Century

The *formulae* cannot be used as a sure illustration of early Frankish practice, not because the information they give is sparse, but because they are well removed in time from the period of the first redaction of Salic law. Fortunately before we have to deal with the text of LS 59 itself there is a body of evidence which allows us to see something of the inheritance procedures in the last half of the sixth century and which, though again dealing with a fairly narrow category of heirs, directly concerns the sequence of statutory succession.

A. DECRETIO CHILDEBERTI (596)

The Roman concept of representation, already found in Burgundian and Visigothic law,[1] was foreign to Frankish practice. In 596, however, Childebert II of Austrasia, shortly after his succession to the Burgundian kingdom, tried to introduce it into Frankish law in regard to the first parentela, that is, in the direct line.

> Conuenit ut nepotes ex filio uel filia, mortuo patre uel matre, ad auiaticas res cum auunculus uel amitas sic uenirent tamquam si mater aut pater uiui fuissent. De illos tamen nepotes istud placuit obseruari qui de filio uel filia nascuntur numquid de fratre uel sorore fuerint procreati.[2]

> It is agreed that grandchildren through a son or daughter, if their mother or father is deceased, are to succeed to the grandparents' property in place of

---

[1] LB 75.1; CE 327.

[2] According to Eckhardt (*Einführung*, pp. 139 ff., and the *MGH Lex Salica*, p. 174) the *Decretio Childeberti* survives in three redactions: two younger, associated with the D and E redactions of the Salic Law, and an older Merovingian redaction found in A1 and K17. (For the texts of each, see Eckhardt's editions, *Lex Salica* and *Pactus Legis Salicae*, respectively). The text used above follows A1 and K17, but in fact there is no variation in substance among the various versions. Cf. also Boretius, 1: 15.

their mother or father along with their uncles and aunts. This rule is to be followed with regard to the offspring of a son or daughter but not of a brother or sister.[3]

The success of the provision appears to have been extremely limited or at least localized. For according to the *formulae*, testamentary *epistolae hereditariae* were necessary for grandchildren, both *ex filio* and *ex filia*, to inherit alongside the siblings of their parents.[4] The provision suggests two things about the pattern of inheritance before the promulgation of the law: first, that daughters as well as sons were entitled to inherit the property of their parents, though, as the *formulae* and the other evidence to be considered indicates, they could only inherit a portion of the estate alongside their brothers; and second, since the provision is merely establishing representation, not the actual rights of *nepotes ex filia* to inherit, that grandchildren through a daughter had inheritance rights if there were no uncles and aunts to bar their succession.

The meaning of *aviaticae res* deserves some comment, since it has frequently been confounded with ancestral property and the *hereditas aviatica* of Ripuarian law.[5] Now there is little doubt that *aviatica here-*

---

[3] *auiaticas res*, lines 1-2: the meaning of *aviatica* in this context will be discussed shortly.

   tamquam ... fuissent, lines 2-3: lit.: "as if their mother or father had lived" to claim the inheritance.

   de illos ... procreati, lines 3-4: that is, representation is to be applicable in the direct line, but not the collateral.

[4] *FMarc.* 2.10; *Merk.* 24; *Lin.* 12. In this regard Chenon (*Histoire*, 1: 445) cites *FTur.* 22. However, the law prevailing there is, as the *formula* itself says, *lex Romana*. While representation was a feature of Roman law, the preference for agnates, still a part of the pre-Justinianic system, provided that *nepotes ex filia* succeed only to two-thirds of the estate their mother would have inherited. Cf. LRV 5.1.4. The Tours *formula* addressed to *nepotes ex filia* was intended to permit the grandchildren to claim the whole of their mother's share ("dum per legem cum filiis meis, avunculis vestris, in alode meo ad integrum minime succedere poteratis"). That this is Roman law was recognized by Fustel (*L'Alleu*, p. 140, n. 2), but he erred in ascribing the same source to the substance of *Marc.* 2.10 (see above, Ch. 13, n. 9). There the grandchildren were completely barred from their mother's portion ("dum per lege cum filiis meis, abuncolis vestris, in alode mea accedere minime potueratis"), that is, there was no representation at all without the *epistola*.

[5] E.g., Niermeyer, s.v. *aviaticus*; Fustel, *L'Alleu*, p. 140; Glasson, "Le Droit de succession dans les lois barbares," *Nouvelle Revue Historique de Droit Français et Étranger*, 9 (1885) 605, who, in discussing the *Decretio*, transforms the *aviaticae res* into the term *terra aviatica*; the last phrase makes a frequent enough appearance in modern scholarship on the analogy of *terra salica* but in fact there seems to be no documentary authority for it. (I would exclude from consideration LS 65c, whatever it means.) Cf. also Eckhardt's "Wortregister": *aviatica = nachgelassen*.

   On the other hand Bergengruen (*Adel und Grundherrschaft*, p. 55) has rightly pointed out that in the *Decretio* it means simply the "grandparents' inheritance." It is more

ditas in *LRib*. 57 means the inherited property of the deceased as opposed to the acquests. The reason for the terminology is simple enough. Since normally only property derived from a grandparent (*avus, avia*) through a parent was ancestral and consequently inherited by sons in preference to daughters, the original inheritance of the grandparent would have been the ancestral portion (*hereditas aviatica*) of the deceased parent's estate.[6] However, this is not the situation found in the *Decretio*. Here *res aviaticae* does not refer to ancestral property in opposition to the acquests but simply to the 'grandparent's property' from whatever source. This is clear enough when we consider that the law views the inheritance from the standpoint of the *nepotes* directly inheriting their grandparent's estate (*aviaticae res*)[7] and that there is no intervening inheritance by their parents. It is even clearer when we consider the law from the vantage point of representation. For certainly the entire estate, not just the ancestral portion, is being subjected to the principle of representation and, if we look at the *formulae*, we see that the lack of representation applied to the whole inheritance. Thus the provision implies nothing about proprietal distinctions and their application to the inheritance sequence within the first parentela.

B. *EDICTUM CHILPERICI* (561-584)

Despite the exceedingly poor state of the manuscript tradition, and despite being limited to the line of the deceased's parents, the *Edict of Chilperic* is one of the clearest statements of statutory inheritance to be found in any of the sources. Previously it was thought to be emending the inheritance sequence in favour of daughters and siblings by excluding the right of the *vicini*, but in light of the role of the *vicini* in Roman and Frankish law this can no longer be accepted.[8] Clearly enough the phrase "sicut et lex salica habet," whether or not it refers to LS 59, does not mean that what follows is new law: it is merely a counterpart to the expressions in the *formulae*

---

doubtful that it has the same meaning in *LRib*. 57 (see below Ch. 15, n. 11) as he suggests, because the text does not consider the succession simply from the viewpoint of the deceased's descendants.

[6] For example, A has property both inherited and acquired. On his death B, his son, inherits it. He in turn makes acquisitions. Thus his estate is composed of the *alodis patris* from his father and the acquests which he himself obtained. On his death the sons and daughters of B inherit. Now all the property of the grandfather, A, including his acquests, has become ancestral property and B's sons succeed to it, postponing their sisters.

[7] Cf. LRB 22.9, where *donationes avorum* is also rendered as *bona aviatica*.

[8] See above, Ch. 4.

which have already been considered, and refers to that characteristic
feature of Salic law – particularly as against Roman and Visigothic law –
whereby daughters were postponed by their brothers.

It will be remembered that the sequence of succession to the *terra* of the
deceased in the *Edictum* was as follows: initially, sons; then, daughters;
next, brothers; and, finally, sisters. This pattern illustrates three important
features of statutory inheritance which find confirmation in the other
sources. First, as we have noted, daughters were merely postponed by
their brothers, and not completely excluded by males of more distant
degree. This is what we found in the *formulae* and is also what we shall
find in the *Pactus*. Second, the postponement of females by their brothers
was not restricted to the direct line of the deceased, but was also a feature
of collateral inheritance. This too will be clearly seen in the *Pactus*. Third,
postponement was applicable not to the whole inheritance but only to part
of it. Again, this aspect of statutory succession is readily perceptible in the
formulae and the *Pactus*. However, the designation of this restricted
portion in the *Edictum* raises one of the most intractable, and in the end
probably insoluble, problems of Frankish inheritance. For, as we have
seen in the *formulae*, and also in Ripuarian law, this special part of the
inheritance is ancestral or inherited property, but in the *Edictum* it is
called simply *terra* or *terrae*, which, on the face of it, would imply all
land.[9] Similarly, in the *Pactus*, it is called in the earliest redaction *terra* or
tota terra; in the later redactions, however, it is designated *terra salica*, a
term which often is taken to mean ancestral land.[10] If, therefore, we accept
that *terra* in the *Edictum* and the *Pactus* refers to the landed property in
general, we must posit, in the interval between the late sixth century and
the redaction of the pertinent *formulae*, an emendation of Frankish
practice whereby the postponement of sisters was confined to ancestral
property of some kind. The possibility that some such development lies
behing the vagaries of *FMarc.* 2.12 has been discussed.[11]

Another somewhat puzzling feature of the *Edictum* is that, although it
mentions siblings as heirs, no notice is taken of the rights of ascendants.
The Roman, Visigothic, Burgundian, and Salian systems were all
characterized by the succession of the deceased's ascendants, specifically
his mother and father, if he had no heirs of the body. A likely explanation
for this lack in the *Edictum* is that, not being primarily an inheritance

---

[9] It has been suggested that the concluding portion of c. 3 in the *Edictum* refers to
acquests, but little can be said with any degree of certainty about this passage.

[10] Below, Ch. 15, n. 21.

[11] Above, pp. 187-190.

regulation, it is dealing quite ideally and schematically with the succession, and is principally trying to maintain the idea that the next of kin must precede the *vicini*, subject to the Salian provision that women are postponed by their brothers. It is possible also that the *requirement* that the next of kin succeed is being restricted to the descendant and collateral line.

C. Gregory of Tours' HF 9.33 and 10.12: The Inheritance Right of the Mother in Frankish Law

The final evidence for the second half of the sixth century is of a quite different nature from anything dealt with up to this point, since it is not a legal document but a narrative source, which illustrates the actual working of the inheritance and legal process. It concerns the dispute between Ingitrude and her daughter Berthegund around the year 589 taken before the court of Childebert II. These ladies were well-born, the mother being related to Guntram of Burgundy on the maternal side.[12]

The pertinent part of the dispute as told by Gregory of Tours concerns claims on the property of Bishop Bertram, the son of Ingitrude and the brother of Berthegund.[13] On his death, Bertram left as near relatives his mother Ingitrude, his sister Berthegund, and the children of a deceased brother, the *nepotes* of Ingitrude. Previously Bertram had been heir to the estate of his father. This inheritance (*res patris*) is the property under dispute: Ingitrude claimed all the property of her husband (*res viri*) which

---

[12] R. Buchner, ed., Gregorius *Zehn Bücher Geschichten* (Berlin, 1956), 2: 284, n. 3. The relationship was close enough for Guntram to claim the right, as *parens* of Berthegund, to punish her for any wrongdoing against her husband (HF 9.33); also Ingitrude was alleged to be privy to the intimate family matters of Clothar I (HF 7.36).

[13] "Interea defuncto apud Burdigalinsim urbem Bertechramno episcopo ... Tunc [Berthegundis] ... Pectavum pergit; voluitque eam mater retenere secum sed penitus non potuit. Ex hoc inimicitia orta, dum saepius regis praesentiam adeunt, et haec res patris defensare cupiens, haec viri, Berthegundis donationem Berthechramni germani sui ostendit, dicens quia: Haec et haec germanus meus mihi contulit. Sed mater eius non admittens donationem, omnia sibi vindicare cupiens, misit qui, effractum domum eius, omnes res illius cum haec donatione diriperit; unde se ipsam genetrix reddidit conprobatam, cum de rebus ipsis in sequenti filiae quaedam repetenti districta restituit. Sed cum saepius ego vel frater noster Maroveus episcopus acceptis regalibus epistulis ut eas pacificare deberemus, Berthegundis advenit Toronus in iudicio quoque accedens, coegimus eam in quantum potuimus rationem sequi: mater vero eius flecti non potuit. Tunc, accensa felle, ad regem abiit quasi filiam exhereditatura de facultate paterna. Tunc in praesentiam regis exponens causas, filia absente, iudicatum est ei ut, quartam partem filiae restitutam, tres cum nepotibus suis quos de filio uno habibat receperit. In qua causa Theutharius presbiter ... accessit ut hanc divisionem iuxta regis imperium celebraret. Sed, resistente filia, nec divisio facta nec scandalum resedatum est" (HF 9.33).

was now left by Bertram, while Berthegund offered a charter of donation (*donatio*) as proof that Bertram had conferred on her certain parts of her father's estate (*res patris*). But Ingitrude would not accept the charter and dispatched agents who broke into her daughter's house stealing both the charter and all her property, which Ingitrude later restored under suit of her daughter. After an attempt by Gregory at mediation, which was unsuccessful owing to the intransigence of Ingitrude, the mother proceeded to the royal court with the intention of disinheriting her daughter from the paternal property (*facultas paterna*), where in her daughter's absence she put her case before the king. The judgment was given that a quarter portion should be restored to the daughter and that Ingitrude, along with her grandchildren whom she had by a son, should receive three-quarters. The daughter resisted any attempt at division, however, and the matter lay unresolved. The end of the story takes place some five or six years later, on the death of Ingitrude at the age of eighty.[14] During this period Ingitrude had continued the enmity with her daughter because Berthegund had deprived her of her property (*res sua*); and she had instituted a granddaughter (presumably one of the children of the deceased son mentioned earlier) as abbess over her monastery. However, Berthegund arrived at Childebert's court to claim her mother's rule of the monastery, and King Childebert, forgetful of the judgment which he had given her mother, permitted Berthegund to take all the property which her mother and father had had ("res omnes quas mater vel pater habuerant"); although she did not get the monastery itself, Berthegund also received whatever her mother had left to the monastic foundation.

This story is of particular interest for understanding the nature of the mother's inheritance right in Salic practice. The salient feature in the order of events described by Gregory is that Ingitrude succeeded to the estate of her son Bertram – specifically to the *res patris* that Bertram himself had inherited from his father, Ingitrude's husband. For this reason Berthegund was forced to base her claim to her brother's inheritance on the donations made during his lifetime. This situation clearly reflects the rule of the

---

[14] "Ingytrudis vero religiosa ... cum aegrotare coepisset neptem suam abbatissam instituit. ... Haec vero, cum filia discordiam tenens pro eo quod res suas ei abstulirat, obtestavitque ut neque in monasterio quod instituit neque super sepulchrum eius permitteretur orare. Quae octuaginsimo, ut opinor, anno vitae obiit. ... Sed veniens filia eius Berthegundis Toronus, cum non fuisset excepta, ad Childeberthum regem abiit postulans ut ei licerit in locum matris suae monasterium regere. Rex vero, oblitus iudicii quod matri eius fecerat, huic aliam praeceptionem manus suae roboratam subscriptione largitus est, haec contenente ut res omnes quas mater vel pater eius habuerant suo dominio subiugeret et quicquid monasterio Ingytrudis reliquerit aufferetur" (HF 10.12).

Pactus Legis Salicae – which was a characteristic feature of Frankish inheritance – that a mother had inheritance rights to her deceased child's estate before any of the brothers or sisters.[15] The Ingitrude-Berthegund affair shows that this maternal inheritance right extended to ancestral property inherited by the child from the paternal side (*res patris*).

Roman, Visigothic, and Burgundian law took care in different ways that when a child died the property he had inherited from his father should also benefit the father's other descendants, even though the mother's close kinship tie with her child entitled her to an early right of inheritance: in Visigothic law, one means of protecting the rights of the other relatives of the deceased was to make the mother's right usufructuary.[16] The exact form of Ingitrude's proprietorship over the paternal property is never clearly stated but there are good reasons to suppose that it too was of a special kind. At one point the property is referred to as Ingitrude's (*res suae*), which it certainly was in the sense that she had the right to inherit it; elsewhere it is repeatedly, and pointedly, called *facultas paterna, res patris, res viri*. When Ingitrude obtained her son's estate she presumably took more than simply what came from her husband, yet the integrity of this portion of the inheritance was maintained. There is further indication of the special nature of Ingitrude's right over her late husband's property in her attempt to disinherit Berthegund. For the three-quarters was not granted to Ingitrude alone, but "cum nepotibus suis quos de filio uno habibat," that is, the property was to be maintained by Ingitrude for the eventual inheritance of her grandchildren. It is probable, therefore, that Ingitrude's right to the *res patris* or *res viri* was conditional on her preserving it for the descendants of her husband, in this case, the *nepotes ex filio* and (before the judgment made a settlement on her daughter) Berthegund and her children; and that the *res patris* had become a distinct entity among her other possessions.

It is useful here to try to piece together the legal and personal implications of Gregory's story. Gregory tells as a backdrop to the actual property dispute a number of events which had led to the strained relations between Berthegund and Ingitrude and the separation of Berthegund from her husband and children. In all her troubles the daughter had found refuge and support in her brother Bertram. At some point Bertram had become heir to his father's property. Realizing the probably perilous relations between Berthegund and her husband and mother, and aware that Ingitrude would be his heir on his death, Bertram

---

[15] See below, Ch. 15.
[16] See Appendix III.

sought to provide further for his sister by donating to her large portions of the paternal estate. When Ingitrude entered his inheritance she found a significant amount of her husband's property, over which she had a right which can be called usufructuary, had already been transferred to her daughter. After carrying off the proof of these donations, Ingitrude sought to have Berthegund disinherited completely from the paternal property. Not entirely successful, she did manage to receive a judgment from the court limiting her daughter's rights to a fourth; the remaining three-quarters were adjudged to Ingitrude to be maintained by her for the benefit of her grandchildren by a previously deceased son. But Berthe-gund was already in possession of an amount in excess of her quarter and so refused to accede to the division. Subsequently, on her mother's death, Berthegund appeared and, owing to what Gregory discreetly calls a lapse of memory on the part of Childebert, successfully claimed all the properties of her mother and father.

Gregory's account is useful for understanding the Frankish inheritance system and for filling out the bare and elliptical references in the *Pactus*. But its importance goes beyond this since the flesh it puts on these bones enables us to see the Salian system in the context of the other *leges*. As far as maternal inheritance is concerned, early Visigothic and Burgundian law were influenced in varying degrees by the late Roman pattern based on the *SC Tertullianum*. Unlike the somewhat later *Lex Burgundionum*, which more closely follows the Tertullian system, the *Codex Euricianus* already testifies to a radical divergence or devolution from the Roman norm. It is on these points of divergence – the postponement of all the deceased's collaterals by the mother and her usufructuary control of the *res patris* – that Visigothic and Frankish law agree. As we shall see, the divergence of Frankish maternal inheritance generally from the practices of the Gallo-Roman population is a worthwhile clue as to the reason for the inclusion of the perplexing sequence of heirs in ls 59, *De alodis*.

15

Frankish Inheritance: ʟs 59, *De alodis*

ʟs 59, *De alodis* and the *Edictum Chilperici* have always been regarded as
the pivotal texts for understanding the development of inheritance among
the Franks. Many have seen *De alodis* as a means of getting at the
primitive system of the Franks before the profound changes of the sixth
century thought to be perceptible in the *Edictum Chilperici*. Others, while
admitting these changes in the succession sequence, have suggested that
there were two basically distinct regimes prevailing in sixth-century
Frankish society: an older communal system reflecting ancient agrarian
society found in *De migrantibus* and the *Edictum*; and a more recent and,
by comparison, individualistic system represented by *De alodis*, which,
they thought, already shows adaptation of old Germanic ways to the
circumstances of the new surroundings.[1] Since, on almost any reading of
the text of *De alodis*, the results do not conform to the supposed ancient
system of the Germans, there was general agreement that the provision
showed signs of the new age, indeed that it too was intended to alter
traditional patterns, even though it was still largely thought to be founded
on the exclusion of women and their offspring from the landed
inheritance and a preference for male agnates of the lineage or clan. While
leaving room for varying interpretations of details, these ideas have
formed the basis for integrating the earliest evidence of Frankish
inheritance into the accepted framework of kinship and proprietal
development among the Germans.[2] Enough has been said in the above
pages to show that this framework is quite at variance with the sources of
the later sixth century and after, and that, in particular, the *Edictum*

---

[1] A variation on these ideas can be found throughout the recent work of Balon. Rather
than islands of collectivism surrounded by a Roman and Roman-influenced regime, he
suggests in place of the 'Roman' regime "un autre droit germanique, le domaine allodial"
(*Les Fondements*, p. 23).

[2] See above, Ch. 4, nn. 1 and 38; and below, n. 3.

Chilperici, so central to the traditional view, has been badly misunderstood. There is no evidence for the existence of a primitive Germanic communal regime or traces of lineage or clan ownership; none of the sources support the contentions that women were prohibited from inheriting (not to say owning) land, or that daughters and their offspring were excluded from inheriting land or ancestral property by male agnates; rather, in the *Edict of Chilperic* daughters inherit the *terra* after sons, and sisters inherit after brothers; in the *formulae*, daughters inherit ancestral property after sons; the offspring of daughters inherit their deceased mother's share in the inheritance; in other words, in no circumstances do we find the exclusion of women (and their offspring), but only postponement by their brothers in regard to certain types of property. What remains to be considered is *De alodis*. In turning to this provision we shall find not only that it runs counter to the accepted interpretation of Frankish inheritance but that, so far as its system can be seen, it too reflects the same general features found in the later sources.

De alodis as it appears in the A redaction of *Lex Salica* contains the earliest evidence for the lines and divisions of relationship that operated in the succession to an individual who died childless. Unique among all our sources, it alone gives details of the succession sequence as far as the third parentela, that is, the descendants of the deceased's grandparents. The primary and independent value of the first family of mansucripts must be emphasized. For the succeeding redactions, which range in time up to the late eighth century (and, if we include Herold, well beyond), contain an altered text. The value of the later texts is dubious and must be considered below, but it is sufficient to note here that commentators are largely agreed that any understanding of Frankish inheritance in the early sixth century must be based upon the A redaction. The variety of text forms, the extreme brevity of the chapter, and the seemingly peculiar order of the inheritance sequence contained in it has led *De alodis* to be considered one of the most perplexing entries in the Salic collection. As in the case of *De chrenecruda*, these features have resulted in much debate concerning the meaning and significance of the various forms of the text. As was the case with *De reipus*, the mention of maternal kin in the regulation has been taken by some as evidence of a prior matriliny among the Franks, while others have argued the patrilineal basis of Salic inheritance.

The most influential, and widely accepted, explanation of the intricacies of *De alodis* is that of Heinrich Brunner.[3] Prompted by the then growing

---

[3] "Kritische Bemerkungen zur Geschichte des germanischen Weibererbrechts," in zRG GA 21 (1900) 1-18, esp. 13-18. Implicitly and explicitly it lies behind succeeding non-

theory of an original Germanic *Mutterrecht*, espoused by scholars such as Dargun, Heusler, Opet, and Ficker,[4] and proceeding on the false assumption that a preference for men indicates a preference for the agnatic line,[5] Brunner wrote as a strong supporter of the patrilineal-basis of early Germanic kinship. It is important to note that, here as elsewhere, the problem was seen in terms only of the patrilineal/matrilineal distinction, and that extensive rights for women, or relationships through women, were regarded as supportive of the matrilineal viewpoint. One of the cornerstones of the matrilinealists was *De alodis*. Brunner's interpretation was both a forceful and lucid account of the chapter's obscurities. Yet there are serious problems with it, the proper explanation of which provides us with a better understanding of the provision. For this reason, after considering the text itself, we must deal more fully with the implications of Brunner's interpretation.

I

Although succeeding redactions display a divergent text, the manuscripts of the A redaction are virtually unanimous on their reading of LS 59. If anyone dies childless, his mother, if she is alive, succeeds to the inheritance. If there is no mother, the brother and sister of the deceased (*frater aut soror*) succeed. Then, if there is no brother and sister, the mother's sister (*soror matris*), that is, the maternal aunt of the deceased, succeeds. Thereafter, the next of kin on the maternal side (*de illis generationibus*) succeeds to the inheritance. Finally, the last clause states that the *hereditas* in land shall not go to a woman, but that all the land (*tota terra*) shall pertain to the male sex (*virilis sexus*) who are brothers (*fratres*).

De alodis

1. Si quis mortuus fuerit et filios non dimiserit, si mater sua superfuerit, ipsa in hereditatem succedat.

---

matrilinealist accounts of the provision. Cf. e.g. Brissaud, *History*, pp. 629-631; Chenon, *Histoire*, 1: 444-452; F. Beyerle and R. Buchner, *Lex Ribvaria*, MGH, LL, 1, III, 2 (Hanover, 1954), 157. For consideration of older views, see esp. Geffcken, pp. 222-228 and Behrend, pp. 124-125.

[4] To the older matrilinealist accounts of LS 59 can be added Chadwick, *Origins of the English Nation*, p. 308.

[5] "Kritische Bemerkungen," p. 1; in the following pages, all further references to Brunner's interpretation of LS 59 pertain to "Kritische Bemerkungen," pp. 13-18.

2. Si mater non fuerit, et fratrem aut sororem dimiserit, ipsi in hereditatem succedant.

5   3. Tunc si ipsi non fuerint, soror matris in hereditatem succedat.

4. Et inde de illis generationibus quicumque proximior fuerit, ille in hereditatem succedat.

5. De terra uero nulla in muliere hereditas non pertinebit sed ad virilem
9   secum qui fratres fuerint tota terra perteneunt.[6]

---

[6] *filios*, line 1: children, not simply sons. This is standard legal usage of the period and numerous examples can be found in the Theodosian, Visigothic and Burgundian collections. It is particularly clear in this case since the provision goes on to designate other female heirs without mentioning daughters.

   mater ... succedat, lines 1-2: so all the A codd. Succeeding redactions have added mention of the father; thus, e.g., C5: "si pater, si mater fuerit, ipsi in hereditatem succedat." This is an attempt to give both paternal and maternal kin. Cf. *LRib*. 57, below, n. 11.

   soror matris ... succedat, line 5: succeeding redactions C, D, E, H, then stipulate that if there is no *soror matris* the *soror patris* succeeds: "Si soror matris non fuerit, sic patris soror in hereditate succedat" (C6). Cf. *LRib*. 57, based upon LS 59: (after the brother and sister) "tunc soror matris patrisque succedant." It will be noted that the Salic additions have the paternal aunt succeeding *after* the maternal aunt, while the Ripuarian provision treats them as succeeding at the same time. These are attempts to give the order of inheritance of both paternal and maternal kin. Brunner, believing that the later Salic additions, unlike the Ripuarian redaction, were never in force, regarded the Ripuarian provision as a far more successful attempt at indicating the maternal and paternal succession. The problem for *Lex Salica* is compounded in the K redaction, where the order is reversed and the *soror matris* succeeds *after* the *soror patris*: "Si uero sorores patris non extiterint, sorores matris eius hereditatem uindicent." It seems clear that the singular order of the A redaction was as perplexing to later redactors as it has been to modern scholars and that attempts were made to integrate the paternal kin into its sequence with varying degrees of success.

   There is agreement that the *soror patris* clause was not part of the original A redaction. However, while A1, A3, A4 contain no reference to the father's sister, A2 does insert the *soror patris* passage even though the remainder of the chapter is virtually identical with the other A manuscripts. As we shall see, all the other redactions containing reference to the *soror patris* also give a succeeding text much altered from that found in all the A manuscripts. Brunner thought that A2 represented a kind of intermediate form between the A and C redactions. Eckhardt ascribes the clause to the influence of the B redaction. (The other characteristics of the B redaction's version of LS 59 as reconstructed by Eckhardt are lacking in A2. They are based on Herold, however, and in fact there is no foundation for their attribution to the B redaction at all. See Appendix II, below.)

   de illis generationibus ... proximior ... succedat, lines 6-7: there seems to be general agreement with Brunner that this refers to maternal kin, since the last mentioned relative is the *soror matris*.

   The succeeding redaction, C, and K, which was based upon it, after *succedat* add the proviso "qui ex paterno genere ueniunt" (C6); so too H. The same reading is also found in D7; D8, D9 have "ex parte genere"; Eckhardt's stemma makes acceptance of *paternum genus* as part of the D archetype doubtful. The E archetype clearly reads "ex parte istius generis." Brunner believed that the *paternum genus* was added because the *soror patris* was mentioned immediately before, and that consequently the *proximior* was then taken

Alodis in the rubric of LS 59 certainly means *hereditas* or *successio* and is best taken as referring to the whole body of the provision. This is the clear meaning of the word as we have found it in later sources and only this interpretation makes sense of the relation of the rubric to all the clauses of the provision. Where the *Codex Euricianus* and the *Lex Burgundionum* say *De successionibus*[7] the *Pactus Legis Salicae* says *De alodis*.[8]

---

to be on the paternal side. His view that these provisions had no particular validity but were the result of internal reconstruction by a later redaction is most certainly correct.

Cf. *LRib.* 57, where the next of kin after the *soror matris patrisque* is designated simply as *proximus*. Claimants in this category are allowed to the fifth degree.

De terra, line 8: succeeding redactions all designate the land as *terra salica*. See further below, n. 22. "De terra uero illa que muliere" of A2 has been seen as containing traces of a *salica* reading, but in light of the jumble of the last clause in A2 it must be regarded as reflecting *terra ... nulla* of the other A manuscripts. There is agreement that *salica* is an addition of succeeding redactions. Cf. *hereditas aviatica* of *LRib.* 57.

ad uirilem secum, lines 8-9: *sexum*, A3, A4; the jumble "ad uero exugu" of A2 derives from *ad uirelem sexum qui*. *Secum* of A1 is not a misspelling but the Latin variant *secus*, which in an indeclinable form is commonly found in the phrase *virile secus* and *muliebre secus*. Lewis and Short, s.v. *sexus*.

qui fratres fuerint, line 9: found throughout A and C, dropped in D, E, K, H, and *LRib.* 57.

Note: the final clause in Herold differs from all other redactions and contains an addition which is reflected nowhere else but in an addition to C6a, a manuscript of the mid-sixteenth century. On these texts, see Appendix II.

[7] CE 320; LB 14; and cf. LRB 38 and n. 20, below.

[8] "Le texte dit *hereditas*, la rubrique dit *alodis*; c'est manifestement la même chose. Il est impossible de traduire cette rubrique ... autrement que par 'de l'héritage' ou 'des successions'" (Fustel, *L'Alleu*, p. 154); so also, among others, Geffcken, p. 223; Chenon, *Histoire*, 1: 419.

On the other hand, cf. Beyerle and Buchner (*Lex Ribvaria*, p. 157) on the Salian and Ripuarian rubrics: "Das Rubrum *De alodibus* aus der Vorlage ist mit *hereditas aviatica*, ererbtes Land in Ribv 57, 4 sinngleich. In den Formulae ist *alodis* regelm. Gegensatz zu *adtractum* bzw. *conparatum*: Errungenschaft." The last statement of course is true as far as it goes, but the word regularly has a much broader connotation, and when it does mean the inherited portion of an inheritance it normally is either explicitly contrasted with the *adtractum* or else specified as *alodis parentum* (see above, pp. 183-184). Moreover, to take *alodis* in the sense intended by Beyerle and Buchner, while it helps reconcile the A redaction with the later evidence where the postponement of sisters is applied only to the inherited property, also means referring the rubric simply to the final clause (particularly as Beyerle and Buchner regard the *terra* as pertaining only to agnates). The result is to divorce the sense of the rubric from the main burden of the law, which, they agree, concerns matrilateral kin and the property which they are entitled to inherit. Cf. also Latouche (*Birth of Western Economy*, p. 80) whose account encapsulates the views on Germanic property outlined above in Ch. 12: "In the very beginning this word [*alodis*] stood for the ancestral home and its appendages. Subsequently it was extended to include the arable lands. The 'alleu' could be handed down only in the male line...." Other commentators (e.g., Niermeyer, s.v. 1) have mistakenly ascribed to *alodis*, as it is found in LS 59, the meaning "moveable property," believing this the only real *hereditas*, as the *terra* mentioned belongs to the "kindred" (by which is meant lineage or clan).

The preponderance of women in the inheritance sequence, the lack of mention of the father and, seemingly, paternal kin, the meaning of the term *fratres* for the recipients of the land, the nature of the proprietal distinctions which underlie the inheritance itself and the significance of later redactions of the law are all other points which need explanation. This is best accomplished by first following the gist of Brunner's interpretation of the provision, which is based upon three major considerations.

First, the lack of mention of the mother's brother, in Brunner's view, tells heavily against the idea that the provision is a remnant of matriliny, since the *avunculus* plays such a leading role in that theory and efforts to read *avunculus* into *soror matris* have been unsuccessful. He agreed, therefore, with the opponents of matriliny who regarded the passage as only a partial statement of inheritance, but not by supposing the father to have died, or the law to be concerned with female inheritance, since the inclusion of the brother makes that unlikely. Rather, clauses 1-4 are concerned with the deceased's maternal relatives; he believed that by *illae generationes* only the matrilateral kin (*Muttermagen*) can be meant, since this phrase is immediately preceded by mention of the *soror matris*. While full brothers and sisters are paternal kin, they are at the same time also maternal kin, and are included here along with half brothers and sisters of the same mother. The law therefore regulates the succession of maternal kin perhaps because of local variation or uncertainties surrounding their inheritance.[9]

Second, the maternal kin do not receive the whole inheritance but only moveables, and of these, only a part. Brunner noted that the distinction between *Muttermagen* and *Vatermagen* was already found in *Lex Salica* in matters of wergeld and would later occur in matters of oathhelping and guardianship. Noting, moreover, that later inheritance among the low Franks saw an equal division of the moveables between the patrilateral and matrilateral kin, he suggested that this was also the case in LS 59.

Unsuccessful attempts were made in later redactions, Brunner believed, to rectify the lack of mention of the paternal kin. This resulted in the insertion of the *pater* alongside the *mater*, the inclusion of the *soror patris* in successive sequence, and consequently the designation of the *illae generationes* as paternal kin. Brunner was doubtful about the legal reality of these changes;[10] but believed that the concurrent sequence in the

---

[9] Cf. Beyerle and Buchner (*Lex Ribvaria*, p. 157): "Zweck des [Salic] Gesetzes sei die Einführung und Reglung der Erbfolge im Weiberstamm."

[10] So also Beyerle and Buchner, *Lex Ribvaria*, p. 157. On the other hand, others have

provision of *Lex Ribvaria* based upon ʟs 59, was a successful attempt to combine the maternal and paternal kin.[11]

Third, Brunner regarded the inheritance of land (clause 5) as being restricted to male agnates. Noting that many think that *virilis sexus* refers to the sex of the heir (*Geschlecht des Erben*) and not the *Geschlecht des Stammes*, nevertheless, he proposed to take the expression as indicating the agnatic line, arguing that otherwise the added designation *qui fratres fuerint* was superfluous. The *fratres*, he believed, were not the sons of the deceased but (since the provisions presupposed childlessness) the brothers of the deceased by the same father.

On the basis of these considerations, Brunner's reconstruction of Frankish inheritance when there were no heirs of the body runs like this: the land goes only to male agnates; the moveables are divided, probably in half, one portion pertaining to the paternal kin, one to the maternal. Now Brunner regarded the succession of the maternal kin as an imitation of the paternal succession, a fact which, he believed, *LRib.* 57 and the efforts of later redactions of *Lex Salica* confirm. Thus the line of inheritance on the paternal side would be: first, the father, then the brothers and sisters of the same father; then the father's sister. The privilege of the *soror patris* to the moveables over her brother (the *patruus* of the deceased) indicated an original and complete postponement of daughters by brothers in the inheritance of the father of the *soror patris* and her brothers. This pattern at the same time was repeated on the maternal side: mother; brother and sister of the same mother; mother's sister. Why is the *avunculus* absent on the maternal side? Brunner believed that the special right of the mother's sister was derived from an imitation of the privilege of the *soror patris* among the paternal kin.

In a number of points Brunner's interpretation has much to recommend it. His denial of the matrilineal basis of ʟs 59 is certainly correct, although not really for the reason given by him, that is, the lack of mention of the *avunculus*. The most telling factor against matriliny is that the deceased's

---

seen the additions as marking real changes in the law in practice: e.g., Chenon, *Histoire*, 1: 448, 451-452. For details of the various changes to the A redaction, see n. 6 above.

[11] *LRib.* 57: "Si quis absque liberis defunctus fuerit, si pater, si mater, subrectis fuerint, in hereditatem succedant. 2. Si pater materque non fuerint, inter frater et soror succedant. 3. Sin autem nec eos habuerit, tunc soror matris patrisque succedant. Et deinceps usque quinto genuclo qui proximus fuerat in hereditatem succedat. 4. Sed cum uirilis sexus exteterit, femina in hereditate aviatica non succedat." Beyerle and Buchner drop *inter*: "Echt merow. ist *inter = insimul* in Ribv 57, 2 (Hss A1, A2) ... Gleichwohl kann es im Hinblick auf 57, 4 nicht dem Grundtext zugewiesen werden" (*Lex Ribvaria*, p. 157), but the reason given is beside the point.

children succeed first; their succession makes it exceedingly difficult to accept that the rest of the succession in c. 59 is a complete statement of the inheritance sequence and that this order is matrilineal. To do so would be to see matriliny in operation in the inheritance system only when there were no heirs of the body. Therefore we must consider the sequence as only partial. Brunner's suggestion that the order designates the succession of maternal kin and that this runs parallel to the paternal succession is most apt. So also is his view that the later redactions of the provision, with the exception of the *Lex Ribvaria*, are inept attempts to patch up the original and obscure provision of the A family.[12] This seems all the more likely for three reasons: the ease with which the A redaction and the law-in-practice of the Ripuarian provision can be read together; the difficulties and inconsistencies which arise when these are read alongside the later Salic redactions; and the presence in later redactions of law that had long ceased not only to be practised but also to be understood.[13]

A critical examination of Brunner's interpretation also reveals that there are serious flaws in his consideration of the landed estate, which involve his interpretation of *virilis sexus* and *fratres*, and his explanation of the exclusion of the *avunculus*. Properly interpreted, these points give us a better understanding of the law.

Virilis sexus as an equivalent of the male line is a possible explanation, though by no means necessary or even the most obvious, unless one starts with the assumption that all land could only devolve patrilineally. The correctness of the equation cannot really be argued. It is best to try first to interpret the law by taking clause 5 at its word and regarding *virilis sexus* as indicating the male sex. This seems all the more likely in view of the full phrase, *virilis sexus qui fratres fuerint*. In light of the texts from the eighth to the sixth century previously examined, it is hard to escape the conclusion that this phrase simply refers to that feature of Salic law whereby women were postponed by males of equal degree, namely their brothers, from part of the inheritance (and not excluded by male agnates). Accordingly, the final clause of LS 59 states in effect: although the preceding clauses specify certain females who shall succeed to the inheritance, the rule must be maintained that when women and men of equal degree inherit as brothers and sisters, the landed portion of the

---

[12] It should be noted too that these changes are accompanied by the addition of the designation *salica* to the simple term *terra* of the A redaction. On the possible connection of these factors see, below, n. 21.

[13] Above, p. 128 ff.

inheritance still must be reserved for the males, who postpone their sisters.[14]

Brunner's explanation of the complete exclusion of the *avunculus* is also open to serious objections. The absence of the *avunculus* is seen as simply a reflection of the exclusion of the *patruus* from the moveables on the paternal side. Since the reasons Brunner gave for this could only be applied with difficulty to the maternal kin, he had to suppose that the right of the *soror matris* must simply be imitative of the right of the *soror patris*. But there is no evidence which would support an original complete postponement of daughters by sons, and indeed the final clause of LS 59 (as well as the *formulae*) speak against such a supposition; it is also scarcely imaginable that the inheritance of maternal cognates was determined simply on the basis of symmetry with their paternal counterparts, and that maternal uncles permitted themselves to be shut out from their nephew's inheritance by their sister, because, on the paternal side, moveables went to the aunt. The crux of the matter, in fact, is already implicit in Brunner's reconstruction of succession on the paternal side, namely that, while the paternal aunt inherited moveables, the paternal uncle inherited the land. If we suppose, as I think we must, that the *avunculus* got something,[15] it becomes clear that, while his sister, the *soror matris*, inherited all or part of the moveables pertaining to the maternal side, he postponed his sister to the *terra* and succeeded to whatever land pertained to the maternal side. "Tunc ... soror matris in hereditatem succedat .... De terra uero nulla in muliere hereditas non pertinebit sed ad uirilem secum [= sexum] qui fratres fuerint tota terra perteneunt." Possibly the plural *fratres* is meant specifically to refer to the *frater* in clause 2 and the *avunculus*. At any rate

---

[14] In one form or another a view of considerable antiquity: see the citations in Geffcken, p. 227. Although Beyerle and Buchner (*Lex Ribvaria*, p. 157) accept that the land was reserved for the agnatic line, cf. their interpretation of *fratres*: "Das Nachbarerbrecht hatte in Neuster schon Chilperichs Ed. c. 3. zugunsten des Weibererbrechts in das Landlos bis zur 2. Parentel einschl. abgeschaft, doch nur im Sinne eines subsidiären Erbrechts hinter Brüdern. Vgl. Markulf II 12.... So ist wohl auch das *qui fratres fuerint* in Sal 59, 5 ... zu verstehen und dann vielleicht auch das *dum virilis sexus exteterit* in Ribv 57, 4."

Cf. LB 14: "Si quis filium non reliquerit, in loco filii filia in patris et matris suae hereditate succedat. Si ... nec filium nec filiam reliquerit, ad sorores vel propinquos parentes hereditas redeat"; and LA 57, *LBai*. 2.7; 15.9, 10, and *LSax*. 44, where also the daughter succeeds after her brother.

[15] Cf. Chenon (*Histoire*, 1: 448): "on ne peut s'expliquer cette lacune [i.e., of the paternal and maternal uncles] qu'en supposant que le droit des oncles étant incontesté, comme celui des frères, les deux lois frankes avaient jugé inutile d'en parler, tandis que le droit des tantes étant moins assuré, il convient de le mentionner expressément."

what is involved is the application of the Salic law principle that brothers postponed sisters to part of the inheritance. It is worthwhile noting that, by the time the *soror matris'* and *avunculus'* claim could arise, the deceased had already been heir to the moveable and landed inheritance of his mother, which he possessed independently of any property acquired on his own or received from the paternal side.

It is a central dogma of Frankish legal studies that the final clause of LS 59 indicates that women were completely excluded from inheriting land. In fact, it says only that sisters are postponed by brothers, which is also what is found in the later Frankish sources. The singular mention of the *soror matris* does not indicate that the *avunculus* was excluded, but rather is specific notice that the aunt is entitled, alongside her brother, to inherit that portion of the inheritance pertaining to the maternal side. Possibly this is the purpose of the provision: that the first two clauses beginning *Si* state the accepted order of matrilateral inheritance in the second parentela, and that the third clause, beginning *Tunc*, introduces into the third parentela the right of the aunt to succeed alongside her brother. However, it is more likely that the aunt has been carefully stipulated because she is the last female collateral to inherit alongside her brother. Thereafter the (male) next of kin, *proximior*, was called. *De alodis* does not give the extent of this category, but on the basis of *De reipus*, it appears to have extended to the sixth degree, however exactly that was counted.[16] The whole of LS 59 therefore concerns matrilateral inheritance.

Before we consider further the implications of the pattern of relationship and the proprietal divisions in LS 59, the major features of *De alodis* can be outlined with a great degree of certainty. The provision deals only with the inheritance of maternal kin when the deceased has left no children; since the pattern of succession is not matrilineal the sequence given is only a partial statement of Frankish inheritance and the inheritance itself was divided in some way between patrilateral and matrilateral kin. The provision displays what would be later called a peculiarly Salic principle – namely the postponement of women by their brothers as regards succession to part of the inheritance when both sexes were inheriting in the same degree. In *De alodis* the principle of postponement is applied to the landed portion of the deceased's estate. The pattern of succession to a childless individual in *De alodis* is as follows.

---

[16] Above, Ch. 11, n. 33. *LRib.* 57: "usque quinto genuclo qui proximus fuerat." The Salic and Ripuarian rules may be at variance here, as Beyerle and Buchner suggest (*Lex Ribvaria*, p. 157), but this is not certain since we cannot tell at which *parentela* each started the count.

The first of the maternal kin to succeed is the mother; she inherits both the landed and moveable estate since her brother, the *avunculus*, is not related to the deceased in the same degree as she is, and is called later; we know also from the story of Ingitrude in Gregory of Tours examined above [17] that in the late sixth century at least, if the father were dead, the mother inherited the entire inheritance of her child, postponing paternal and maternal kin, although the property the deceased had inherited from his father was held by her as a usufruct for the benefit of the other offspring of the marriage. Then the brother and sister of the deceased by the same mother succeed;[18] the sister is postponed by the brother in the succession to the landed inheritance (*terra*). Thereafter, the *avunculus* and the *soror matris* succeed;[19] again, as regards the landed inheritance, the uncle postpones the aunt; probably the *soror matris* was the last female collateral to succeed alongside her brother. Finally, the next of kin on the maternal side to the sixth degree succeeds; probably the male sex was given preference over the female to both the moveable and landed inheritance.

Why does *De alodis* give only a partial statement of Frankish inheritance? One must be careful in speculating why certain material is recorded in the *leges* and other material is not; this warning is particularly applicable to *Lex Salica* because of the obscure history of the compilation; nevertheless, the main points made by the provision about Frankish inheritance suggest the reason for the form of the law. LS 59 tells us the following: that the mother postpones the sister and brother; that the maternal kin succeed alongside the paternal by virtue of their maternal relationship; that, in the inheritance of the *terra*, males postpone their sisters when both succeed together; and that, among the primary relations called to the inheritance, females up to aunts inherit alongside their brothers. Each of these features is diametrically opposed to Roman practice. In Roman law the mother claimed after the brother and alongside the sister; there was no distinction between patrilateral and matrilateral kin but a distinction between agnates and cognates who claim successively; brothers and sisters entitled to claim shared equally; in the

---

[17] HF 9.33 (above, pp. 197 ff.).

[18] Not simply half-siblings of the deceased because full siblings would also be maternal kin.

[19] That is the descendants of the deceased's grandparents, or the third *parentela*. This order may be schematic, for possibly the line of the parents (including the descendants of the deceased's brother and sister) would have to be exhausted before the uncle and aunt were called.

primary category of collaterals (*agnati*) only females as far as sisters could claim with their brothers while other female agnates had to claim in the secondary group (*cognati*). *De alodis* appears to be a succinct statement of the major features which distinguished Salic law from the law of the Roman population; it is a statement of the peculiar "Frankishness" of Frankish inheritance.[20]

II

The idea that the maternal and paternal kin respectively have a largely independent claim to their portion of the inheritance is fundamental to the above interpretation and that of Brunner. As we have seen, the division between patrilateral and matrilateral kin lies at the basis of the Frankish wergeld and compensation scheme and is found in the oathhelping procedure. What this supposes for the succession sequence, and what is implicit in the order of LS 59, is that the inheritance was in some measure divided between the paternal and maternal kin. In which case, what lands could the maternal uncle claim ? Put another way, what was the nature of the respective rights of the paternal and maternal kin to the *terra* of the deceased ?[21]

---

[20] Whether, as Bergengruen suggested (*Adel und Grundherrschaft*, p. 52), a specific text resembling LRB 28, *De luctuosis hereditatem* served as a model for the form of *De alodis* is problematical.

[21] A brief comment is needed on the meaning of the word *terra* as found in the A redaction. The manuscripts of the A redaction are unanimous in designating the landed property reserved for the *fratres* as simply *terra* or *tota terra*. Succeeding redactions call it *terra salica*. This term has been much discussed; whatever precise meaning is given it there is much agreement that it must refer to ancestral land of some kind. As we have seen in the *formulae* and the *Lex Ribvaria*, the postponement of women applied only to the *hereditas aviatica* or *alodis parentum*. The question then arises how we should understand the *terra* of the A redaction. As only ancestral land ? Or land however acquired ? I think we must accept the latter solution. There is really no question of the earlier redaction having contained the term *salica*. The *Edictum Chilperici* similarly uses the simple *terra* or *terrae*. This suggests that the major change taking place in Frankish inheritance was the admission of women along with their brothers to the inheritance of acquests in land.

For bibliography and consideration of the various views on *terra salica* see Brissaud, *History*, p. 453, n. 2, and Balon, *Les Fondements*, pp. 59-84; cf. esp. Georg Frommhold, *Der altfränkische Erbhof. Ein Beitrag zur Erklärung des Begriffs der terra salica* (Breslau, 1938) and Bergengruen, *Adel und Grundherrschaft*, pp. 48-58. While most would see it as an equivalent in some sense of inherited property the precise meaning of the term in the context of *Lex Salica* is elusive. There are two main views. One would see *salica* as meaning 'Salian' or 'Salic', as in *Lex Salica*. But *terra salica* is not part of the original redaction, where it conceivably could have had this meaning, and it is fair to enquire where, outside of the younger redactions of the law, does *terra salica* (and its counterparts

A number of possibilities could be suggested. Most simply, for instance, the next of kin could be called to divide the inheritance. Or the ancestral and acquired property, which is to say the entire inheritance, could be divided, one portion being taken by the paternal kin and one by the maternal. But if the patrilateral/matrilateral distinction is to be applicable, and if we make the fair assumption that the proprietal distinctions of the *formulae* had a role to play in the collateral inheritance, two other possibilities seem likely. In the first, the inherited or ancestral property would go to one side, in this case the paternal, while the moveables and acquests in land were divided between the maternal and paternal kin. The second possibility also involves a division of the acquests and moveables between both bilateral categories. However, instead of all the inherited property returning to the paternal side, this part of the inheritance would be divided between the paternal and maternal kin on the basis of the principle that ancestral property should return to the side from which it came originally, that is *paterna paternis, materna maternis*, or *ius recadentiae*. It is worth remembering that by the time any property devolved upon collaterals beyond siblings, the deceased's inheritance normally would be constituted of property derived from both the paternal and maternal side. Property inherited by the deceased from or through his mother and father was intended for his benefit and that of his descendants. On his death without heirs of the body it was in the interest of the kin on both sides to claim the property originating from the respective sides lest it pass to relatives of the deceased unrelated to the original testator. Both possibilities outlined above are consistent with the clauses of *De alodis* and the *formulae*; there are good reasons, however, for thinking that the *ius*

---

terra Romana etc.) appear in this sense in a proprietal context? The documentary evidence which does show *salica* or *terra salica* in a proprietal context clearly suggests another etymology. The second, and prevailing view would connect the term with *sala*, house. Here *salica* basically means that which surrounds or pertains to the house. In support of this, in the mid eighth century, a large number of texts appear, mainly from the upper Rhine region, in which *salicus* means that which pertains to the chief manse or demesne: "Dono sala(m) mea(m) cum curtile ... et terram salicam," a. 763 (Niermeyer, s.v.). The latter view is more persuasive since there are complementary texts outside LS 59 itself to support it. Despite statements to the contrary (cf. Chenon, *Histoire*, 1: 449), however, it is difficult to relate this etymology with much satisfaction to the system of the *formulae* and the *Lex Ribvaria*. Two points are worth further consideration: (1) the relation between the succeeding redactions, particularly C, which first introduces *terra salica*, and the areas where this commonly appears as a term for the demesne or seigneurial manse; (2) the relation between the introduction of *terra salica* and the addition of the *pater, soror patris*, and *paternum genus* (C), since the home farm is a likely part of the deceased's estate to be reserved for sons, and among collaterals, the paternal kin.

recadentiae was a feature of early Frankish inheritance, and lies behind
LS 59.

As we have seen, as soon as we get a good view of inheritance within the wider group of collaterals in the later customary law, the *ius
recadentiae* is the prevailing principle in operation. While the bulk of
opinion has settled on a feudal origin for its appearance in the customary
law,[22] this is quite unjustified.[23] It could be pointed out that the proprietal
distinction between inherited property (*propres*) and acquests which lies at
the base of the principle was derived from Frankish law; or that late
Roman law already shows experimentation with the idea;[24] but the main
basis for suggesting a far earlier origin for the principle than the feudal
law is the *Leges Visigothorum*.

In the developed Visigothic law of the mid-seventh century, we find
that, when the wider group of ascendants was called to the succession, the
inheritance was divided into acquests and ancestral property. The former
was divided equally between the maternal and paternal kin. The ancestral
property was then claimed by both categories of kin on the basis of the
truncal principle (*troncalidad*), that is the *ius recadentiae*.[25] It is apparent

[22] Chenon, *Histoire*, 2: 239: "On a vu ... que les seigneurs, lorsqu'ils concédaient des
fiefs, tenures devenues héréditaires, les concédaient toujours, soit 'au vassal et à ses hoirs
de corps, nés de sa femme épousée', soit 'au vassal et à ses hoirs'; il résultait de là que les
descendants du vassal dans le premier cas, ses descendants et ses collatéraux dans le
second, étaient en quelque sorte 'substitués' d'avance dans le fief concédé; eux seuls
pouvaient y succéder. Les héritiers du *de cujus* qui ne se rattachaient pas au premier
'conquéreur' du fief se trouvaient forcément exclus: le fief ne pouvait donc être attribué
qu'à un héritier de sa *ligne*, à un 'lignager'."For the various views, see also Glasson, "Le
Droit de succession au moyen âge," p. 899, who, however, while admitting the influence
of feudal grants, saw the rule lying behind *Lex Salica* ("Le Droit de succession dans les
lois barbares," p. 608).

[23] Maitland, HEL, 2: 300: "Attempts have been made to represent *paterna paternis,
materna maternis* as a specifically feudal rule, one which takes us back to a time when
only the descendants of the original vassal could inherit; but such attempts seem to be
unnecessary; a rule whose main effect is that of keeping a woman's land in her own
family is not unnatural and may well be very ancient."

[24] The idea of a *ius recadentiae* was not altogether foreign to late Roman law. As early
as 339 it was established that property accruing by inheritance to a child under six on his
death reverted to the side from which it came, whether maternal or paternal, if there were
no siblings (CT 8.18.4). This rule was not included in the LRV and, so far as I am aware,
there is no other reference to it.

[25] LV 4.2.6: "Flavius Gloriosus Reccesvindus Rex. ... Quotiens qui moritur si avum
paternum aut maternum relinquat tam ad avum paternum quam ad avum maternum
hereditas mortui universa pertineat. Si autem qui moritur avum paternum et aviam
maternam reliquerit, equales capiant portiones. Ita quoque erit si paternam et maternam
aviam qui moritur relinquere videatur. Et hec quidem equitas portionis de illis rebus erit
que mortuus conquississe cognoscitur. De illis vero rebus que ab avis vel parentibus
habuit ad avos directa linea revocabunt." Zeumer comments in his edition: "Avis ius
statuitur quod dicimus revolutionis vel recadentiae."

that this long predates the feudal law and has nothing to do with fiefs. Moreover the proprietal distinction between acquests (*conquestum*) and ancestral property (*res ab avis vel parentibus*) which lies behind it is the same as that of the Frankish *formulae*. The *ius recadentiae* was not always a feature of Visigothic law but appears to have been introduced by Reccesvind sometime around mid-century. To understand its origins we must consider a particular feature of Visigothic and Hispanic legal development and the foundation of earlier Visigothic law upon the *Codex Euricianus*.

In recent years certain aspects of Spanish legal history have been reevaluated, and the recent rereading of the Eurician palimpsest has considerably augmented our understanding of the inheritance passages.[26] A striking feature of Visigothic law is that, in general, the later the legislation the more 'Germanic' is its outlook. The so-called Germanic elements have usually been seen as the reemergence of a popular Gothic law that had persisted under the layer of the Roman-based legislation of the royal court and that would reappear even more forcibly in later Hispanic customary law. But this view has been challenged; and in its place, it is proposed that the so-called Germanisms were the result of the increasing political and cultural dominance of the Franks, and that this is the context in which the introduction of the truncal principle into Visigothic law should be seen. Alvaro D'ors in his study of Eurician inheritance law notes that there is no trace of the *ius recadentiae* in the earliest Visigothic law and proposes that the efforts at introduction under Reccesvind should be considered the result of Frankish influence.[27]

This is an inference, of course, but in light of the development of Visigothic law and in light of the above discussion, it is one which makes much sense. The influence of Frankish law upon Visigothic law, the proprietal distinctions of the *formulae*, which when found in the customary and Reccesvinthian provisions are accompanied by the *ius recadentiae*, and the bilateral stamp of the earliest inheritance law of the *Pactus*, suggest that in some form the truncal principle lies behind the earliest redaction of *Lex Salica*.

[26] See Appendix III, n. 3.
[27] *El código de Eurico*. Cuadernos del Instituto Jurídico Español, 12. Estudios Visigóticos, 2 (Rome, 1960) pp. 265 f.; cf. Musset, *The Germanic Invasions*, pp. 209, 224 f.

16

The Structure of Frankish Kinship: Conclusion

It is clear from the present reexamination that many of the suppositions which have habitually been used to interpret Frankish texts from the early Middle Ages must be rejected on the grounds that they find no confirmation in the sources. In particular, the following notions must be excluded as a starting point for attempts to reconstruct kinship structure: that in origin Frankish kinship was wholly agnatic, and that this agnaticism stayed as the core of its structure; that agnaticism was still expressed through extensive lineage or clan organization which was associated with landholding and inheritance; and that, in inheritance, particularly as regards land, women and their descendants to a greater or lesser degree were excluded by all male agnates. We must be prepared also to question the assumptions that 'individualistic' forms of property holding and inheritance were the result of Roman influence, and conversely that 'familial' and 'corporate' rights and obligations must be a carryover of Germanic practices. These ideas never really found confirmation in the Frankish sources because they were drawn from a general theory on the social evolution of the Germanic peoples the credibility of which has steadily been eroded. This conclusion, though negative, is important, for the views contradicted here have previously determined our understanding of Frankish inheritance, property, and even social groupings, as well as kinship structure. They also appeared to offer a very clear model of the nature of change in the social and family institutions of Frankish Gaul.

What remains to be said positively about Frankish kinship structure? Much on particular points and as regards the near kin. If it is difficult to integrate all these points into a detailed picture, this is not a new dilemma; the prevalent view at its best always rested upon a small number of generalizations. Rather than attempting an extensive description here, which would be misleading unless accompanied by a continual and excessive refrain of qualification and supposition, in conclusion it is advisable to stick to the main features.

Since there is no trace of extensive corporate unilineal groups involved in landholding, inheritance or legal procedures, the basic kin group among the Franks would, therefore, appear to be the bilateral kindred. In the legal sphere of compensation and oathhelping, we find only the personal group, or kindred, with a bilateral stamp, drawing its members in the same proportions from both the paternal and maternal side. In oathhelping procedures concerned with status, the unequal representation which no doubt frequently resulted was due only to the unequal interest of the relatives touched by the accusation; this feature of recruitment illustrates that in a bilateral kindred various factors can influence the nature of the configuration of relatives called to exercise their rights or obligations. The legal extent of the Frankish kindred as a personal group cannot be given with complete assurance, but a range of second or third cousins is not an extreme estimate.

As far as the kinship categories of Frankish law are concerned, the various classes of relatives called to participate in inheritance and the receipt of *reipi* constituted a bilateral category to the sixth degree. As in the personal group, the distinction between the paternal and maternal kin was employed, but the sources do not tell us the nature of other internal divisions. However, it is clear that the laws on succession and remarriage are each also an attempt to balance notions of kinship with other, legitimate interests of the parties involved, and that these interests in part determined the classes and order of relations called to exercise their rights. In the law of remarriage, for instance, the *reipi* payment is only one element in a wider context which includes the *achasius* and the original proprietal exchanges at marriage, the need to ensure that the inheritance rights of the next of kin do no harm to the legitimate right of the widow to remarry, and the desire of the court to mitigate any pretence for disorder.

Important details of the inheritance sequence among near kinsmen and its relation to the proprietal regime of early Frankish society can also be reconstructed with much certainty when the sources are considered outside of the traditional interpretive framework of kinship and property holding. Moreover, *De alodis*, the central text for reconstructing the succession sequence, proves far less perplexing than is usually thought when it is realized that it is a succinct statement of those features of Frankish inheritance which distinguished it from the Roman system of the provincials. Without recapitulating the various suggestions made above about how the succession sequence probably worked, it is worth noting that its complexities appear to operate in a descent system with a markedly bilateral character. A number of aspects of the succession sequence emphasize this: the son and the daughter were the immediate heirs of their mother; the mother inherited from her children alongside or directly after the father; daughters and their offspring inherited alongside, and after, their brothers and their offspring; the maternal kin, including the mother's sister, had rights of inheritance which were exercised not after but concurrently with the paternal kin. These characteristics are hallmarks of bilateralism. They are worth stressing in conclusion because they run counter to so much that has been said about Frankish inheritance. In particular, the notion that women were excluded from inheriting land by male agnates of the lineage or the clan can no longer be maintained; nor can the view that the *Edictum Chilperici* marks a departure in the sequence of natural succession. In all of the sources we find only the postponement of women by their brothers to inheritance of the landed or ancestral property and their right to inherit that property if there were no brothers. The conclusions presented here do not mean, of course, that a degree of agnaticism was not also a feature of early Frankish inheritance; but this does not appear in the earlier sources possibly because they were concerned only with near kin and were intended as a counterpoint to the prevalent inheritance forms of the Gallo-Roman population.

De eum qui se de parentilla tollere uult speaks of the major rights and obligations of kinship as *compositio*, *iuramentum* and *hereditas*. Among the Franks the sphere in which these mutually dependent functions operated was an extensive web of bilateral relationship. Although it has its peculiarities, there is nothing particularly arcane about the Frankish kinship system. It does not reflect the hypothetical unilineal, clan and communal concerns thought to underpin ancient Germanic society. Without inferring a specific pattern of development or influence, we can say that, in the broad outlines of its structure, it looks both back to the Tacitean account of kinship in the society of the West Germans and forward to the prevalent forms of the high and later Middle Ages.

Conclusion

Central to understanding the creation of Western European civilization is the problem of the fusion and transformation of the historical culture of Antiquity and the preliterate cultures of northern Europe. The difficulties associated with the long centuries of birth are among the most profound confronting historians. If each step in the transformation of the heritage of Mediterranean Antiquity is not always clear, there is, at least, a trail to be followed, leading back not just to the Empire but to the historical cultures of the ancient world: sometimes the trail has been ignored, and sometimes assumed, but there is, in any case, a relative abundance of documents illustrating the cultural stops on the way. Looking in the other direction, from the standpoint of the history of the northern peoples and their acculturation, the view is quite different. Archaeology will continue to record the evidence of the material basis of society and even, to some extent, suggest inferences about social, economic, political, and institutional forms of the barbarian world, but the subtleties of these forms must depend upon a small number of classical sources and the after-the-fact testimony of the early Middle Ages and later. While this situation has been a severe limitation upon attempts to reconstruct prehistoric society and its transformation in late Antiquity and the early Middle Ages, it has also offered great scope for a formulation linking prehistoric and historic Westeren European society based more upon assumptions about the nature and development of primitive and barbarian societies than upon the evidence of texts. Because earlier scholars overestimated the 'primitiveness' of the Germans at the time of Caesar and underestimated the continuity between Antiquity and the early Middle Ages, they found the need for such a paradigm particularly compelling in order to make a tangible connection between *Germania* and the *regna*. Rightly noting the importance of kinship among the Germanic peoples, historians found in the idea of a particular form of kinship, namely the clan and extensive lineage and – what was thought to be its corollary – unilinealism, a means of understanding the forces shaping Germanic barbarian society; more than that, unilinealism, and the clan or lineage, were taken to be the keys for understanding the major social factors of the early Middle Ages and after. Not merely the structures of kinship and kin groups, but the legal, associational, and political conceptions of the Germanic peoples were thought to lead back to the clan and unilinealism. The clan was the germ of all social grouping. The continuation in attenuated form and, at the same time, the gradual disintegration of the clan and unilinealism explained the transformation of tribal society and polity from the time of Caesar to Charlemagne. As great a scholar as Marc Bloch believed that it was the vacuum and uncertainty created by this disintegration that created the need for feudalism. The twin assumptions of the clan, or lineage, and unilinealism were also used to explicate a whole host of texts from the early Middle Ages. As a consequence of the prevailing assumptions, many palpably inadequate and preliminary interpretations simply passed on to become accepted dogma.

What is surprising is that a theory of such profound import and dogged persistence in modern attempts to reconstruct the transition from Antiquity to the early Middle Ages should have so meagre a foundation after examination. On a theoretical level, it rests upon outmoded assumptions as to the nature of kinship forms and the development of human societies, and the evidence cited in its support fails to confirm any of its major tenets. The reexamination of the traditional view which has been undertaken in these studies has explored other ways of regarding kinship in Antiquity and the early Middle Ages and reevaluated a body of texts which have either been the major supports of the traditional theory, as is the case with the evidence adducing the clan as a landholding, settlement and military group, or else like the early Frankish legal sources, have been interpreted in light of its main assumptions. The failure of all of this evidence to bear the burden of the traditional view is important for our perception of early Germanic society, which now must be seen without recourse to constituent clans. Also, the failure of the traditional view allows the texts themselves to be read for fresh insight into the contribution they make to our understanding of the social and legal forms of Antiquity and the successor kingdoms.

The present rejection of traditional historiography's belief that early kinship was fundamentally different in structure from the prevalent forms of well-documented periods extends not only to the clan but also to the emphasis upon unilinealism (agnation) as the major structural feature of kinship. Since the clan and unilinealism were thought to be strongly linked, and one was more or less assumed to require the other, there was a tendency to treat cognation as a recent, weak or unstable factor in kinship systems. But no compelling evidence suggests that the predominantly cognatic systems of the Middle Ages resulted from a unilineal system in transition, or that the instances where medieval laws favoured unilineal categories were the weakened survivals of a once encompassing agnatic system, as traditional historiography believed. Probably Germanic society always displayed a variety of kinship forms, and various peoples developed systems to meet specific needs; varying degrees of emphasis upon agnatic categories are to be found in the well documented historical systems. Any comprehensive view of the development of kinship structure, nevertheless, should be based upon the notion of the bilateral kindred as the basic kin group of society, and upon the recognition of the antiquity and vitality of cognation. In these studies the examination of two of the major documents of Germanic antiquities, Tacitus' *Germania* and the *Lex Salica*, suggest largely cognatic societies with bilateral kindreds, and both texts are a severe stumbling block in any attempt to cast Germanic kinship structure as a whole in the mold of unilinealism. While it has long been recognized that systems with unilineal clans and lineages recognize cognatic relatives for limited functions, we have just begun to deal with bilateral societies without unilineal descent groups which admit unilineal principles for various ends. This development has produced results which are useful in understanding the society of the early Germans, but it may also be that study of the medieval systems themselves will help in understanding the structures and dynamics of cognatic societies.

However, it is well to recognize that in treating kinship in terms of descent and in the tripartite divisions of patrilineal, matrilineal and cognatic we have been dealing in fairly crude concepts with sometimes limited and formal applications in the full understanding of kinship systems as such. This approach has been dictated in part by the traditional way the question has been posed, but also by the nature of the evidence, for it is problematical how more than the broadest concepts and generalizations can ever be applied with certainty to the systems of ancient *Germania*. But from the general viewpoint of historical reconstruction the results of this necessarily restricted approach have been far from negligible. It has freed us from assumptions which have bedeviled attempts to reconstruct adequately society of the migration period and the successor kingdoms. It has told us something about kinship structure, the recruitment of kin groups, and a little about the heavy burden borne by kindreds in the legal framework of society. It has permitted the reinterpretation of important texts which illustrate the ancient world's view of barbarian society, and aspects of association, property-holding, inheritance and the legal rights of women, texts which have usually been taken as the starting point for discussions of historical development. It has allowed us to integrate the often isolated texts which were thought to support the traditional viewpoint into the prevailing contexts of the legal collections and the world of the narrative sources. We need no longer wonder, for instance, why Gregory of Tours, who shows interest in early Frankish history and the feuds and proprietal disputes of his contemporaries, failed to notice, even as remnants, the hypothetical patrilineal or matrilineal descent groups which modern scholars have attributed to the early Franks. Finally, the reevaluation of the sources has led us to diminish considerably the traditional dichotomy drawn between the so-called 'Germanic' and 'Roman' systems of the barbarian kingdoms, and allowed us to recognize the persistence of ancient social forms into the society of the early Middle Ages.

It was in the nature of the traditional teaching, its methodology and its view of the evolution of social and legal institutions that a comprehensive view could be offered of the passage of the Germanic peoples from prehistory to the historical period of the *regna* and beyond. The methodology and assumptions enabled scholars to argue back from historical (often late historical) documents to periods and situations lacking any documentation whatsoever and to reconstruct, in surprising detail, the institutions and social forms of ancient Germanic society. In rejecting the traditional assumptions we necessarily must raise many problems which the traditional view sought to solve. Put most simply, the main question is this: how do we explain Germanic society and its transformations without recourse to the clan and lineage? The answer depends upon what aspects of the social, economic, or political life of the Germans are under consideration; for if the lineage and clan, and the network of ideas associated with them, have been a convenient means of organizing reconstruction, they are by no means necessary. What must be recognized, however, is that the limitations on reconstruction are stricter than earlier scholars imagined. We simply cannot use comprehensive views of social evolution in place of documentation. As we have seen, to do so not only perverts the view of prehistory, but also the understanding of historical texts and the development of historical institutions. This may seem a late date to post such warnings, but the kinds of methodological misconceptions and the resulting misinterpretations of historical sources which have been dealt with in the above pages still permeate studies of ancient Germanic institutions even apart from those of kinship. Moreover, in emphasizing the need for conclusions based upon documentary sources rather than preconceived notions as to the nature of prehistoric society, we are, in effect, reiterating the necessity of exploring the social, legal, and ideological flux of late Antiquity. For the moment, at least, this is our primary hope for distinguishing the diverse elements and transformations of the *regna barbarorum*.

Appendix I

The *Mater* and *Soror matris* texts of ʟs 58.3

Following most commentators, I have quoted A1 (with which A2 substantially agrees), as the basis for ʟs 58.3. This lists the homicide's father and brother as his next-of-kin, and designates the wider kin simply as three categories of the maternal and paternal kin respectively. The gist of the text is straightforward and the general meaning clear; it is also in complete harmony with the rest of ʟs 58, particularly 58.4, and with what we know of compensation procedure from ʟs 62 and 68. It is important to stress that a good deal of harmony among the various provisions is to be expected because all regulate kinship participation in the same process of compensation; ʟs 58 simply deals with the problem of insolvency. If we leave ʟs 58.3 out of consideration for a moment, the various Salic provisions tell us a number of the characteristics of the structures of kinship participation in compensation procedure which we should expect to find reflected, or at least not contradicted, in ʟs 58.3. 1. According to ʟs 62 the right of plaintiff falls to a man's sons. We must then expect the father/son relationship to be primary as regards compensation obligation. Schematization may distort this feature, but any complete statement as to the participation of the nearest ascendants should include the principal role of the father. 2. According to ʟs 62 the rights of the two bilateral categories of the *tres proximiores* are concurrent and independent of one another, so much so that the fisc claims for a side that is defective. ʟs 58.4 confirms that each side is concerned with one half the amount. 3. ʟs 68 indicates that the *tres* are kinsmen of three distinct degrees or categories and not simply the three nearest kinsmen, possibly of the same degree. It is important to hold fast to these points in looking at the textual difficulties of ʟs 58.3.

There will be further discussion below of A1, A2 which conform to the pattern just outlined. The readings of A1, A2, however, have not been adopted by Eckhardt, whose reconstructed text of ʟs 58.3 is based upon A3 and A4, which show important similarities with the other redactions, including the seemingly next oldest form of the *Pactus*, C5 and C6. In

general these texts list the *mater* and *frater* as the homicide's next of kin
and indicate that the second *chrenecruda* is to be made "super sororem
matris aut super suos filios" (C6). The prevailing view of these *mater* and
soror matris texts, formulated by von Amira and supported by Brunner,[1]
regards them as contaminated by the immediately succeeding chapter 59,
De alodis, which deals with matrilateral inheritance. This view, I believe,
is certainly correct; but the implication of Eckhardt's reconstruction of ʟs
58.3 for our conception of Frankish kinship and the textual history of *Lex
Salica* requires that we consider a little more fully the *soror matris* texts,
particularly of the A redaction, and the editon of Herold (Eckhardt's B
redaction, ᴀᴅ 511-533). In the following pages it should be clear that the
problems of interpretation which arise from these readings, their internal
contradictions, and lack of agreement with the other Salic compensation
provisions, render the *soror matris* texts inadmissible.

I

A4 reads:

> quod si tam pro illo et mater et frater persoluerunt, tunc super sororem
> matris aut super suos filios debet illa terra iactare, quod si ille non fuerit, de
> [= debet: Eckhardt] illa terra iactate [= iactare: Eckhardt] id est super tres
> de generationem patris qui proximiores sunt.[2]

There are a number of very evident problems of interpretation of this text.
The first *chrenecruda* has been made upon the slayer's next of kin, his
mother and brother. From ʟs 62, however, we should expect at least the
inclusion of the *pater* in this list. The *chrenecruda* on the wider kin is
made first upon the *soror matris* and her sons; since this is a compensation
regulation, women are seen to participate through their menfolk: thus, the
frater for the mother and the cousins for the *soror matris*;[3] the relations so

---

[1] H. Brunner, "Sippe," p. 41; Eckhardt, *Einführung*, pp. 76 ff.

[2] A somewhat similar text appears in A3: "quod si iam proximior illo et mater et frater
solserint tunc superiorem sororem et matrem aut suos filios debet illa terra iactare id est
super tres de generatione patris qui proximores sunt." Since "superiorem sororem et
matrem" involves a repetition of *mater* we must assume that this is a confusion or
emendation of *super sororem matris*. Designating the *tres* as of the *generatio patris* only
makes sense if a phrase similar to "quod si ille non fuerit de(bet) illa terra iacta(re)" of A4
has dropped out. Cf. Eckhardt's reconstructed text, which seems to owe a lot to his belief
that Herold contains an unadulterated B text which followed hard upon the heels of the
so-called Clovis A text.

[3] Throughout c. 58 in all redactions the pronoun designation of the relatives involved
is masculine.

far listed could be interpreted as a matrilineal category.[4] In their absence, *chrenecruda* is then made upon the *tres proximiores* of the paternal kin; the mother's sister and her sons must, in conformity with the succeeding paragraph (58.4), constitute the *tres de generatione matris*. Again, there are difficulties with this sequence. While we know the participation of the wider kin in compensation was concurrent, A4 indicates that it was successive: the mother's sister and her sons shoulder the entire burden, and only in their absence is it transferred to the paternal side. In addition, we must expect the *tres* to be constituted of three distinct categories or degrees, but A4 indicates that the maternal wider kin consists of only the aunt and her sons. There is, however, a ready explanation for the appearance in ls 58.3 of the *mater, frater* and *soror matris* in this combination. For this sequence corresponds to the pattern given in ls 59, *De alodis*, for matrilateral inheritance, and may easily have been borrowed from there as a gloss for the maternal *tres*; there the matrilateral heirs are listed in succession *mater, frater et soror, soror matris*.[5] That this is in fact what happened seems certain, not only from the interpretative problems arising from the sequence but also from the inclusion in 58.3 of the phrase "quod si ille non fuerit." Now a similar phrase is regularly found throughout ls 59 and makes perfect sense in the context of inheritance, but is less than apt applied to wergeld and compensation procedure as it is found in ls 58.4, 62, and 68. Taken all together these considerations raise grave difficulties with the proposition that the *soror matris* readings form part of the original redaction of the Salic law. Their agreement in form and concept with the following chapter, *De alodis*, makes it far more likely that their original home was there and that they found their way into ls 58.3 as a result of interpolation.

In turn, the version of the C redaction differs from both A3 and A4. According to C,[6] the first *chrenecruda* is made upon the *mater* and *frater* as next of kin, and the second upon the *soror matris* and her sons, who are defined as the maternal *tres proximiores*. There is no mention of the paternal kin as in A3, A4 and there is no sign of the phrase "si ille non

[4] Where the narrative evidence explicitly refers to the participation of maternal kin in a claim for wergeld, this group is not matrilineal. See HF 3.31 where, according to Gregory, compensation is demanded for the death of Amalasuntha by her Merovingian kinsmen, who are her cognatic cousins on the maternal side.

[5] Incidentally the full sequence of later redactions of ls 59 (mother, brother and sister, mother's sister, then paternal side) also corresponds to A4's 58.3.

[6] "Quod si iam mater et frater solserunt tunc super sororem matris aut super suos filios debet de illa terra iactare id est super tres de generatione matris qui proximiores sunt" (C6); C5 gives much the same text.

fuerit." Internally at least, C makes some sense, since we could imagine that, immediately after the reference to *chrenecruda* being made on the next of kin in 58.2, the provision abruptly switches to considering the liability on the maternal side only. This still leaves the problems of trying to reconcile C with the *soror matris* texts of the earlier A redaction, and finding in C relatives representing three distinct categories of relationship.

The D redaction differs again from the earlier redactions. Clearly it has tried to weld together at least two versions: one containing the *pater* and another the *soror matris* texts.[7] The *pater* is also included in K, although, as is usual in other respects, it follows C.[8]

Finally, let us consider the text published by Herold in 1557. Herold's version of *Lex Salica* (H10) differs, sometimes considerably, from the other manuscripts, and it is principally in this that Eckhardt has found what he believes to be clear traces of a lost B redaction, which he dates to the years 511-533, and ascribes to Theuderic i. Eckhardt prints the divergent paragraph 3 of H10 as the early sixth-century B redaction:

> Quod si iam pater aut mater seu frater pro ipso soluerunt super sororem tunc matris aut super eius filios debet illam terram iactare; quod si isti non fuerunt, super tres de generatione patris et matris qui proximiores sunt.

It should be noted that H10 along with A4 contains the phrase, "quod si isti non fuerunt," but the meaning differs radically from A4 and all other redactions. The first *chrenecruda* occurs over the immediate family, defined aptly enough as the father, mother, and brother; the second, over the *soror matris* and her sons; finally, in their absence, a third *chrenecruda* can take place over the *tres proximiores* of the paternal and maternal kin. In this case, among the wider kin, the mother's sister and her sons do not constitute the *tres proximiores* on the maternal side but form a distinct group apart, which initially must bear the whole liability. Such a scheme, as we have seen, finds no support from the other compensation provisions. Among all the redactions, H is unique also in the relatives and categories of kin who are mentioned. Like A1 and A2, and D and K, it lists the *pater*, but unlike A1 and A2, it refers to the *soror matris* and *mater*. At the end of the paragraph, H describes the

---

[7] "Quod si iam pro illo pater aut mater uel fratris soluerint, tunc super sororis matris aut super suos filios debet illa terra iactare. Id est super generationis aut matris, qui proximioris sunt" (D7). So also D8, D9: "Generationis aut matris" indicates that originally *patris* came before the *aut*, but this was not in the D archetype.

[8] "Quod si iam pater aut mater uel frater soluerunt tunc super sororem matris aut super suos filios debet illam terram iactare id est super tres de generatione matris qui proximiores sunt."

proximiores as *tres de generatione patris et matris*. This is true also of A1 and A2; all other manuscripts list one group or the other but never both the paternal and maternal kin. However, rather than testifying to a separate redaction, these considerations of form and content suggest again that H is a composite or emended text. The variety of all these readings and the lack of agreement among redactions on the sequence and nature of the kinship categories simply underscores the unaptness of the glosses originally borrowed from *De alodis*.

II

Finally we must consider the text of A1 and A2. Both list the immediate family as *pater* and *fratres*.[9] There is no trace of the *mater* and *soror matris*, although there is mention of a "filius" in A2 not found in A1. As noted, acceptance of the reading of A1 has become prevalent. There can be no doubt, at least, that it has considerable antiquity. A2 is the oldest of *Lex Salica* manuscripts, dating from the 750s or 760s. The *pater* reading must predate this considerably since, according to Eckhardt, A1 and A2 were not derived from each other, nor from a common source.

But what are we to make of the "filius" reading in A2, which does not agree with A1 and, as it stands, seems to make little internal sense? The explanation given by von Amira,[10] who first supported the authority of A1, A2, was that a scribe finding *sui* mistakenly supplied a substantive, *filii*. This of course means reading *filius* as acc. pl., but in terms of the kinship terminology of *Lex Salica* there are good reasons to take "filius" at face value as a nom. singular: thus, "but if his father or brothers have paid, then the son must throw earth upon his kinsmen" etc. The homicide is called *filius* in relation to his father in the previous line. This usage is not peculiar if we consider the other wergeld provisions. There, since the first group to claim are the sons (*filii*), the deceased himself is designated, in terms of the *filii*, as *pater* (ls 62) and his wife, *mater* (ls 68). In neither case would we normally so indicate such relationships, but it is in fact an internally consistent system of kinship designation. In substance A1 and A2 are in agreement.

Given the inconsistency of the *soror matris* texts, both internally and externally, with ls 58.4, 62, and 68, and the ready source for these

---

[9] A2: "quod si iam pater aut fratris [= fratres] solserunt, tunc super suos filius debit illa terra iactare super iii de generacionem patris et de matris qui proximioris sunt."

[10] Eckhardt, *Einführung*, pp. 79-80.

readings in the succeeding chapter ʟs 59, we must firmly reject the originality of the versions of ʟs 58.3 found in A3, A4. The question is whether there is good reason to accept the originality of the reading of A1, A2. These readings are consistent precisely where A3, A4 are not, and, moreover, they are demonstrably of considerable antiquity. The agreement between A1, A2 is usually considered decisive, even by Eckhardt, against the readings of the other A manuscripts, and the younger redactions. Probably this is enough, but what is worth re-membering is that the firm ground in this sea of uncertainty remains 58.4, which is substantially the same in all versions. In conformity with what we could expect from ʟs 62 and 68, this indicates that each group of the *tres proximiores* from both the maternal and paternal side could be made responsible for one-half the liability.

Appendix II

Herold and C6a on ls 59

Herold's text of ls 59 contains a final clause differing from all other redactions:

> De terra vero salica, in mulierem nulla portio haereditatis transit, sed hoc uirilis sexus acquirit, hoc est, filii in ipsa haereditate succedunt. Sed ubi inter nepotes aut pronepotes, post longum tempus, de alode terrae contentio suscitatur, non per stirpes, sed per capita diuidantur. [Originally printed entirely in capitals.]

Two parts of the text are distinguishable: 1. *De terra ... succedunt*, corresponding to some extent to the content of the final clause in the other redactions; and, 2. *Sed ubi ... dividantur*, an addition reflected nowhere else except in C6a. C6a, a recently uncovered manuscript containing excerpts from *Lex Salica* dating – and this should be noted – from the mid-sixteenth century, appears to be a collation based, Eckhardt believes, upon the *Editio princeps* of Tilius. Under the rubric *De alodis* the following passage is noted:

> Vbi vero Alodis ad nepotes post Longum tempus euenit, vt ipsum diuidant non per stirpem sed per capita.

Much has been made of these texts for the reconstruction of early Frankish proprietal and inheritance forms. Seebohm, for instance, saw in Herold an indication that the early Franks practised ownership and division of the land among the heirs in a fashion similar to the system found among the Welsh lineages (*gwelyau*).[1] More recently, Balon has found in the word "Alodis" of C6a proof of his contention that *alodis* in the Frankish sources, including the rubric of ls 59 and the *formulae*, equals *terra salica*, that is the "seigneurie Salique" or "seigneurie allodiale."[2] The extent to which this theory pushes Latin syntax is

---

[1] *Tribal Custom*, pp. 150 ff.
[2] *Traité*, 2: 565.

apparent in his assertion that, in the phrase "de alode terrae contentio" of Herold's text, *alodis* is used adjectivally.[3] Eckhardt himself, in regarding Herold, part 1, as a B text, suggests that this B text introduced the much discussed term *terra salica* into the text-forms of the law; if his dating of the B text is followed, *terra salica* would then be a legal term of at least the early sixth century.

As the last example shows, great importance in the realm of textual criticism has also been attached to both texts.[4] As his reconstructed text of the final clause of LS 59 Eckhardt has printed part 1 of Herold as the distinctive text of the B redaction. The discovery of C6a meant that Herold part 2 could no longer be associated by Eckhardt with Herold's lost 'B' manuscript, and so it has been printed as a secondary addition to the C redaction along with C6a; however Herold part 2 has been emended in greater conformity to C6a. Eckhardt regards the texts of Herold, part 2, and C6a as pre-Carolingian in origin.[5]

The first conclusion that should be noted is that Herold has merged two distinct texts into one in his final clause. Two points about the origin and context of the passages being considered here also require some comment. In the first place there are clear Roman law parallels for Herold part 2 and C6a. Eckhardt cites two: LRV, Gaius 8, which he associated with C6a; and Justinian *Inst.* 3.1, 2, which he connects with Herold, part 2, and which obviously does not speak highly for its antiquity. Rightly suspicious of the editor's presence in Herold part 2, Eckhardt has emended the text in conformity with C6a which, if based on the LRV, could conceivably be Merovingian or Carolingian. Eckhardt concludes from all this that C6a finally proves that Herold had a manuscript source before him and not simply the Institutes. Perhaps it does but it also suggests some other conclusions about Herold's method of treating his texts which say little for the assumption that he transmits an unadulterated B or C text in his edition. In this context the acceptance of Herold part 1 as the accurate transmission of an early sixth-century B text, which on any account has little to recommend it, is firmly put beyond the pale.

[3] *Les Fondements*, p. 57.

[4] See the critique of Eckhardt's reconstruction by Schmidt-Wiegand, "Kritische Ausgabe," pp. 306-308.

[5] Little of the background to his treatments of the peculiar texts of Herold and C6a is given in the MGH edition, and the reconstructed text can only seem perplexing to the reader of this edition only. Cf. the discussion in *Einführung*, pp. 211-216 written prior to knowledge of C6a, and the Germanenrechte *Pactus* II, 1: 26-43 where an edition of all of C6a can also be found.

Another factor which renders Herold's text suspect, and which Eck-hardt himself emphasizes, is the concern jurists of the first half of the sixteenth century showed in the question of inheritance *per capita* and *per stirpes*; LS 59 was also the focus of contemporary interest in the so-called 'Salic law' of royal succession which preferred males and the male line – a juristic interest which, in fact, went back to the fourteenth century. This context surely accounts for Herold's extraordinary expedient of capitali-zing this one clause in his edition and again casts grave doubts upon the antiquity of the texts in question.

These doubts only increase when we consider the testimony of the score of manuscripts from the Carolingian period and all the redactions subsequent to A. For none reveal any of the peculiarities of style and content found in Herold's so-called B text of LS 59, which is indeed strange if, as Eckhardt suggests, the B redaction lay behind C (K) and D (E). This fact does not suggest, as Eckhardt believes, that subsequent redactors only appropriated "salica" from B, while maintaining the A pattern of the provision. Taken together with the other features of Herold's edition mentioned above, it only confirms that in the final clause of LS 59 Herold did not print a true text of the B or any other redaction for that matter. *Terra salica* still appears to be the innovation of the C redactor.

Whether C6a contains an early medieval addition is less important from the point of view of textual, legal and social history. In any case it is not part of the original redaction of C, since it is lacking in the two surviving Carolingian manuscripts (C5, C6) and in the Carolingian K redaction which is based closely on C. Its inclusion by a copyist at some point would not be extraordinary; A3 for instance adds clauses from the Burgundian law. Whether it is Merovingian or Carolingian, remains problematical. Arguing for its pre-Carolingian date, Eckhardt points to the early spelling *alodis*, not *allodium*, and the maintenance of the meaning "Erbschaft" not "Eigen." In fact it is not clear whether the intended meaning of *alodis* in C6a is *hereditas* or *patrimonium*. But neither the meaning nor the spelling is helpful for establishing a pre-Carolingian date. Carolingian formulae were familiar with the term *alodis* (not *allodium*) and the meaning 'inheritance'; moreover the early spelling was available to anyone who read the rubric of the provision.

Appendix III

The Succession Right of the Mother
in Roman, Visigothic and Burgundian Law

In the successor kingdoms of the fifth and sixth centuries a number of systems regulated the inheritance right of the mother. The provincial population continued to follow the classical system as emended in the imperial period and which, in varying degrees, influenced the Visigothic and Burgundian procedures. For most of the classical period Roman law had preserved the agnatic basis of the inheritance system by relegating the inheritance of mother to child and child to mother to the class *unde cognati*. Two *senatusconsulta* of the second century, the *SC Tertullianum* and *Orphitianum*, however, finally permitted mother and child to succeed to one another at the initial stages of intestate succession. This was the death blow to agnation, although the victim took a long time to finally expire. Most of the inheritance law of the later Empire can be seen as an attempt to juggle the principles of cognation, agnation, and *patria potestas*. The result was a complicated system[1] which Justinian, after halting attempts at reform, finally abolished. If we limit ourselves to the case of intestate succession to a deceased who had no descendants and whose father or *parens manumissor* had died, the sequence of heirs according to the *SC Tertullianum*, which regulated the succession of the mother, and the imperial constitutions, is this: first, the consanguineous brothers and sisters taking together, the brother postponing the mother; secondly, if there were no brothers, the mother and sisters together; third, if there were no sisters, the mother and the line of the paternal uncles together.[2]

---

[1] For instance, the extent of the mother's claim depended on whether she had the *ius liberorum*, that is, whether she had born three children by separate births if a freewoman and four if a freedwoman. Justinian abolished this completely even before *Nov.* 118 (CJ 8.50.2; *Inst.* 3.3.4). There is no trace of the *ius* in Burgundian and Visigothic law.

[2] Justinian outlines the historical development in *Inst.* 3.3.1-7. The major handbooks deal with this subject very inadequately and usually fail to mention that by CT 5.1.6 = LRV 5.1.1 ca. a. 320 and CT 5.1.7 = LRV 5.1.6 a. 426 the line of the paternal uncles claimed with the mother.

In the Visigothic law of Euric[3] the mother succeeded to her child's estate if there were no heirs in the descendant line.[4] In the pre-Eurician law, however, there is no doubt that the mother's inheritance right had corresponded to the late Roman Tertullian system in that the line of the paternal uncles had claimed with the mother if the father was deceased and the intestate had no siblings. In CE 327 Euric changed this and permitted the mother to succeed to all the property of her deceased child. Clearly the property included, and in many instances for all intents and purposes was composed only of, the paternal estate previously inherited from the deceased's father. Conditional to the mother's inheritance in the Eurician law, however, is the provision that she remain in widowhood,[5]

[3] We now are in a much better position to understand the *Codex Euricianus* (466-485) than heretofore. Preserved fragmentarily on a palimpsest, many of the surviving chapters have had to be reconstructed on the basis of later revisions and expansions in the *leges*. The poor state of preservation is particularly acute in the title *De successionibus*. Previously the basic edition was that of Zeumer (in *Leges Visigothorum*, MGH LL 1, 1), although other attempts at reconstruction have been made over the years. In 1960 a new edition and palingenesia was brought out by Alvaro D'Ors (*El código de Eurico*) who, with the aid of infra-red photography, has been able to offer greatly improved readings. These have considerably altered our perception of *De successionibus*. D'Ors' conclusion that the successorial regime *ab intestato* of the *Codex Euricianus* is not essentially distinct from the Roman tradition of the same period is largely sound. It will be clear that it is in the areas where there is a distinction or a devolution from the Roman rule that resemblances with Salian procedures are apparent.

[4] CE 336: "In hereditate illius qui moritur intestatus, si filii desunt, nepotibus debetur hereditas. Si nec nepotes fuerint, pronepotes vocantur ad hereditatem. Si vero qui moritur nec filios nec pronepotes reliquerit, pater aut mater hereditatem sibi vindicabit."

[5] CE 327: "In priori lege fuerat constitutum ut si patruus aut patrui filii cum matre --- vindicarentur. 2. Nos modo meliori ordinatione censuimus ut, patre defuncto, si filius decesserit, omnem facultatem eius sibi mater dibeat vindicare, quae tamen sit post obitum vidua. 3. Si vero qui moritur filios, nepotes, et pronepotes reliquerit, ipsi omnes habeant facultates..." (the rest of the law concerns representation among the *nepotes*). In the old Zeumer edition little of this is decipherable and the *patruus* is mistaken for the *pater* and the *mater* lost. There is still a lacuna of two lines and more in the first sentence. (The Zeumer edition is still necessary to see the spacing of the palimpsest, and occasionally, as in the case of this lacuna, it has some readings which have since disappeared, and which have not been printed by D'Ors in his text.)

Admitting the difficulties with the pertinent texts, D'Ors concludes from CE 327 that the rest of the sequence of Roman law was still in force in Eurician law; that is, the father postponed the brothers, the brothers postponed the mother, and the mother and sister took together (*El código*, p. 273). I think this raises more problems than it solves, for a number of reasons. 1. CE 336, as we have seen, after extensively listing the descendants, places the father and mother together as the next heirs. The use of *aut* probably means the father postponed the mother, but it makes it very difficult to accept that the *frater* also postponed her. 2. CE 327, above, takes great care to point out that certain classes of heirs completely postponed the mother and inherited all the property. Here again great-grandchildren, grandchildren, and even children (about whom there could hardly be any doubt) are listed, but not the *fratres*. 3. The mother's inheritance right in the *Codex Euricianus*, which is to say, her rights to the property are to be usufructuary.[6] If this requirement was called for against the paternal uncles it must also have prevailed when the mother inherited in place of her other surviving children (the siblings of the deceased), and indicates that, in return for inheriting all her child's property, she was required to maintain it for the eventual inheritance of the descendants of the marriage; CE 327 now extended this provision to the uncle's portion.

This brief consideration of Visigothic law shows that a number of the significant features of later Frankish maternal inheritance, insofar as they are perceptible in Salic law and in the Ingitrude-Berthegund story, can be found in Visigothic procedure of the last half of the fifth century. First, the mother inherits from her children before siblings. Second, the inheritance includes property which the deceased child had inherited from his father. Finally, the mother's rights over this property were usufructuary; she had to maintain it for the siblings and nephews of the deceased. It is problematical whether the Visigothic provision of widowhood indicates that Ingitrude's rights over the *res patris* or *res viri* too may have been

---

given the usufructuary condition, also in other respects differed from, and exceeded, that of Roman law. For instance, she succeeded alongside her children to her husband's property, provided she maintained her portion for the eventual inheritance of the children (CE 322). 4. In later Visigothic law the mother and father inherited their deceased child's property, postponing the siblings.

These considerations suggest that possibly (as D'Ors admits), the *frater* and *soror* were mentioned in the lacuna of c. 327; and that this law for the first time preferred the mother to all the other heirs of the Tertullian system if the father was dead. But it seems to me just as likely that even before the CE 327 the mother had inherited to the postponement of the brothers and sisters, and held the property in usufruct for their eventual inheritance. The expectant rights of the siblings would postpone the *patruus*. But if there were no siblings the uncle had had a right to claim with the mother, the mother's share now being held in full ownership as in Roman law. In CE 327 the same considerations which had been applied to the mother and the siblings were now applied to the mother and the *patruus*. She was permitted to inherit the whole amount on condition she preserve it intact for the eventual inheritance of the relatives whose rights had been deferred. As will be seen, the Burgundians were later to try the same expedient.

At any rate, the essential point is this: the Roman law right of a mother to a share in the inheritance, which was held in full ownership, in Visigothic law was being transformed into a right to the whole, which was held in usufruct. Both ideas are attempts to reconcile the contradictory feelings that, on the one hand, the closest of all kinship relations – that between mother and child – should entitle the mother to inherit her deceased child's property, and that, on the other hand, this property which had largely been inherited from the deceased's father should be for the benefit of the father's other descendants, or lacking them, his near kinsmen.

[6] See also CE 322, 321 where widow(er)hood is required to protect the entail of the descendants. Cf. CT 8.18. A later expansion of CE 327 maintains the usufructuary requirement for the benefit of descendants without the need of widowhood (LV 4.2.18).

conditional upon her remaining a widow, which she in fact did to the end of her life.

Two laws of the *Lex Burgundionum* consider maternal succession.[7] According to LB 24.3 a mother obtains a usufruct over all the *hereditas mariti vel filiorum* when her children die after their father. The provision is given in a title dealing with the remarriage of widows which shows one of the prime distinctions between Burgundian and Visigothic law. LB 24.3 quite clearly is considering the instance of deceased, young, childless heirs who have inherited their father's property; a *novella* (LB 53) added a short time later, which looks back on the provision refers to the heir as a *puer*. The paternal property which the mother takes in usufruct is to be preserved and not squandered. On her death it reverts to the statutory heirs. The *novella* designates them as paternal kin (*ex paterno genere*). As an amendment to the old law the *novella* henceforth permitted an equal division of the property between the mother and the husband's near relations provided there was no *puella*, that is to say, sister of the deceased and daughter of the mother. Thereafter the mother held her share in full ownership.

The mention that the division can take place only if there is no *puella* is important since it more clearly reveals the mother's position in the inheritance sequence and indicates the close relation of the Burgundian system to the *SC Tertullianum* and its amendments which were included,

---

[7] LB 24: "De mulieribus Burgundiis ad secundas aut tertias nuptias transeuntibus.... 3. Quod si forte nati fuerint filii et ut adsolet post mortem patris defuncti fuerint, ad matrem iubemus hereditatem mariti vel filiorum integram pertinere. Post mulieris autem obitum id quod de successione filiorum in usumfructum tenuit ad legitimos filiorum suorum heredes decernimus pertinere. Quod tamen intestatorum filiorum bonis praecipimus custodire."

LB 53: "Licet emissa iam pridem fuerit lege constitutum ut si defuncto patre intestatus obisset filius ac si mater eius rebus superfuisset humanis substantiam filii ita cunctis vitae suae temporibus possideret ut post transitum eius universa de quibus loquimur propinqui eiusdem pueri ex paterno genere venientes acciperent, sed postmodum cum obtimatibus populi nostri inpensius de causa tractantes advertimus speciem praedictae legis non minus dispendii ac litigii succedentibus exhibere quam commodi dum inter se diverso ambitionis iure disentiunt, quorum alterum tarditas adeundae hereditatis offendit, alterum proprietas amissa conturbat; ideoque rectius visum est ut sub eiusmodi temperamento praefatae conditionis vinculum laxaretur quo non reservari negotium placuit sed finiri.

Qua de re iubemus, sicut iam similis causa nostro est conclusa iudicio quotiens in hunc casum contraria fatum decreta vertuntur, continuo inter matrem defuncti pueri si tamen puella defuerit et propinquos quorum supra fecimus mentionem relictae facultatis divisio aequo iure et ordine celebretur ita ut unusquisque de medietate percepta faciendi quod voluerit ex lege habeat potestatem. Consultius nempe utilitatibus partium causae vestigio terminantur quam temporibus suspensa proficiunt."

among other places, in the *Lex Romana Burgundionum*.[8] According to the Roman procedure the brother postponed the mother and inherited with his sister. If there were no brother, the sister and mother inherited equally, postponing the paternal uncles. Almost certainly this is also the sequence in the *Lex Burgundionum* and explains why, in the *novella*, the presence of the *puella* would postpone the claim of the paternal kin.[9] Both Burgundian provisions presuppose that in order for the paternal kin's rights to be a question of contention there must be no siblings of the deceased.

If we compare the provisions of LB 24.3 and the *novella* it is apparent that the former provision marks a momentary divergence from the late Roman system, probably under Visigothic influence, which was soon rectified by the *novella*. As we have seen, Eurician law had already permitted the mother to postpone the rights of the *patruus* and his line provided she remained a widow and maintained the property for their eventual inheritance. Essentially the same requirement was introduced into Burgundian law by LB 24.3 which granted the mother all the property against the paternal kin provided she held it as a usufruct. But Burgundian law did not adopt the Visigothic requirement of widowhood; sticking more closely to Roman principles even while emending them, the Burgundian legislators allowed the mother to marry. Basing their provision on CT 3.8.2 (= LRV 3.8.2) a. 382, which required that a re-married widow's inheritance rights to the children of her former marriage should be usufructuary as long as other children of the marriage survived,[10] they simply extended this rule in the *Lex Burgundionum* to the *patruus* and his line because in Burgundian law his claim to inherit with the mother had been put in abeyance but not extinguished. When the

---

[8] LRB 10.5; 28; and see n. 2.

[9] Cf. Beyerle (*Gesetze der Burgunden*, pp. 167, 174) who places the mother after the siblings and uses LB 24.3 and 53 to illustrate the "germanische Sippeverfassung."

[10] On her death the property she had inherited from her deceased child returned to the surviving sisters. If there were none she could dispose of it by testament. It has long been recognized that the Burgundian lawmakers had knowledge of this constitution, since the matters of the preceding Burgundian chapters are also treated in the same Theodosian title; in addition to the edition of De Salis, see, before him, Bluhme, MGH LL, III (Hanover, 1863). However, it should be noted that the Burgundian law is quite distinct. In the first place, the benefit of reversion and usufruct is applied to the near kin of the husband. Secondly, the Roman stipulation of a usufruct is applicable only in case of remarriage. The *Lex Burgundionum* is not notable for its organization; it seems the order of the Theodosian title has suggested the inclusion at this point of LB 24.3. Much the same provision as CT 3.8.2 was reissued at Ravenna in 436 and again included in the LRV (CT 5.1.8 = LRV 5.1.8).

novella returned to a situation where the *patruus* and his line claimed along with the mother, once again in conformity with Roman law, there was no need for the mother's right to be usufructuary. The *Novella* which permitted a *divisio* between the mother and the husband's near kinsmen provided that afterward the mother's half share was to be held in full ownership ("unusquisque de medietate percepta faciendi quod voluerit ex lege habent potestatem"), which conformed again to the system of the *SC Tertullianum* as amended by Constantine and as found in the *Lex Romana Burgundionum*. The *Novella* itself purports to tell us why it was felt advisable to return to the old system prior to the amendments of LB 24.3: for the arrangements of this provision, it says, had pleased no one, since the paternal kin chafed at the delay of their rights and the mother was disturbed by the loss of full ownership (*proprietas amissa*) which she previously had over her half portion.[11]

This discussion enables us to get a good idea of Burgundian maternal succession, and lets us see it in relation to the Eurician and late Roman systems. In Burgundian law, if the deceased left no children and his father too had died, the following categories claimed the inheritance in this order. 1. The brother and the sister of the deceased; 2. the mother and the sister of the deceased. This corresponds to the Tertullian sequence. It also explains the much-discussed phrase of LB 14.2 describing intestate succession: "Si forte defunctus nec filium nec filiam reliquerit, ad sorores vel propinquos parentes hereditas redeat," since the sister claims with the brother and mother. In conformity with Roman law the mother doubtless held her portion in usufruct if she remarried and daughters survived. In Visigothic law she could claim all the child's inheritance provided she remained a widow and held it in usufruct. 3. The line of the *patruus* and the mother. Each held their portion in full ownership. This again is straight Roman law. It was reestablished after a brief flirtation with the Visigothic expedient of granting the mother prior claim but limiting it to a usufruct. Unlike the Visigothic case, however, the woman was not required to remain a widow.

Compared to the Visigothic law of Euric, Burgundian legislation appears to have stuck closer to the precedents of late Roman law. Although in Euric's collection there are clear traces of the former reliance on the Tertullian system of late imperial law, Visigothic procedure, as we

---

[11] The Constantinian provision fixed the mother's share at two-thirds if she had the *ius liberorum*, one-third if she did not. Since the Burgundians made no distinctions based on the *ius liberorum* they seem to have consequently settled on a straight division.

see it in the *Codex Euricianus*, was in a state of radical devolution from the Roman model. The complicated system of the *SC Tertullianum* and the imperial constitutions which owed its intricacies to the conservativeness of Roman jurisprudence and its foundation on a bedrock of agnation and *patria potestas* was considerably altered by the Visigoths. The mother was preferred to all the collaterals and the rights of the siblings and paternal uncles to the paternal inheritance were then protected by requiring the mother to remain a widow and hold the property in usufruct. The right in Roman law of the mother to share at an early point in the inheritance of her child, but to hold that share in full ownership, was being transformed in Visigothic law into a right to the whole which was to be held in usufruct. On the other hand Burgundian law of the late fifth and early sixth century was more firmly rooted in the *SC Tertullianum*. The mother was postponed by the brother and took with the sister. Some attempt had been made at simplification. As in Visigothic law there is no trace of the unnecessary complication of the Roman *ius liberorum* which Justinian would later abolish in the east. Owing to Visigothic influence the right of the *patruus* and his line had been put in abeyance before that of the mother, but the simplification not being fully carried out (as again Justinian would later do), the difficulties engendered resulted in a return to the system of the imperial constitutions.[12] Insofar as we are able to see both systems in operation, the result of the Visigothic development was to establish in the fifth century a system which, in its main outlines, we find later in sixth-century Salic law. Even the more conservative Romano-Burgundian procedure in a number of points resembled Salian practice as regards the care taken when the mother inherited lest the other descendants of the marriage should ultimately be defrauded of the inheritance of their deceased sibling and father. All this puts Frankish law, at least as regards the mother's inheritance of the *res patris*, firmly in the context of the legal experimentation and development of the west and east in the fifth and sixth centuries. Where the Visigothic-Salian system was distinctive, even in comparison to the radical reform of Justinian in the mid-sixth century, was in preferring the mother before the siblings of the deceased.

A long time ago Brunner suggested[13] that certain similarities of expression found among *Lex Salica* and a number of the *leges* go back to

[12] In 528 Justinian in the east decided to take what he called the *recta et simplex via*: permitting the mother to inherit along with the brothers and sisters and eliminating the right of the *patruus* and his line to share with the mother when there were no siblings (CJ 6.56.7; *Inst.* 3.3.5). This foreshadowed his far-reaching reforms in the *Novels*.

[13] In 1887; DRG, 2nd ed., 1: 438.

the common foundation of the fifth-century *Code of Euric*. This idea has been variously accepted and rejected.[14] What makes the problem so difficult is that the basis for affinity can transcend specific textual influences and overt borrowing. There can be little doubt of the influence of Eurician legal thinking on the *Lex Burgundionum*. LB 24.3, though placed in the Burgundian code where it is owing to imitation of the pattern of a Theodosian constitution, is introducing Visigothic law. Whether the substantial resemblances between Eurician and Salic procedures of maternal inheritance suggests that in this area the Franks too felt, in some way, the influence of a code which has been called the best legislative work of the fifth century[15] is an open question.

[14] For the older literature: ibid.; for the more recent: Eckhardt, *Einführung*, pp. 194-195. Buchner (*Rechtsquellen*, p. 17) accepts the Eurician influence in *Lex Salica*; Eckhardt, while admitting the fruitfulness of the idea for the other *leges*, denies it. Cf. Wallace-Hadrill (*Kingship*, p. 37): "The [barbarian laws] are a close knit group of texts deriving from a common source, Roman-Visigothic law."

[15] Ernst Levy, "Reflections on the First 'Reception' of Roman Law in Germanic States," *American Historical Review* 48 (1942) 28-29.

Bibliography

A. PRIMARY SOURCES

Die ältere Genesis. Ed. F. Holthausen. Alt- und mittel-englische Texte, 7. Heidelberg, 1914.

Aristotle. *Politics.* Trans. H. Rackham. The Loeb Classical Library. London, 1932.

Beowulf and the Fight at Finnsburg. Ed. Fr. Klaeber. 3rd ed. Boston, 1922.

Caesar, C. Julius. *Commentarii de Bello Gallico.* Ed. Fr. Kraner and W. Dittenberger. 20th ed. by H. Meusel. 3 vols. Berlin, 1964.

Capitularia Regum Francorum. MGH LL 2, I-II. Ed. A. Boretius. Hanover, 1883-1893.

Codex Theodosianus. Ed. Th. Mommsen. Berlin, 1905.

El código de Eurico. Ed. Alvaro D'Ors. Cuadernos del Instituto Juridico Español, 12. Estudios Visigóticos, 2. Rome, 1960.

Corpus Juris Civilis. Ed. P. Krueger et al. 3 vols. Berlin, 1872-1895.

Diplomata, Chartae, Epistolae, Leges Aliaque Instrumenta ad Res Gallo-Francicas Spectantia. Ed. J. M. Pardessus. 2 vols. Paris, 1843-1849.

Diodorus of Sicily. Trans. C. H. Oldfather et al. The Loeb Classical Library. 12 vols. Cambridge, 1939.

Einhardi Vita Karoli Magni. MGH, *Scriptores Rerum Germanicarum in Usum Scholarum.* Ed. O. Holder-Egger. Hanover, 1911.

Fontes Iuris Romani Antejustiniani. Ed. S. Riccobono et al. 2nd ed. 3 vols. Florence, 1940-1943.

Formulae Merowingici et Karolini Aevi. MGH LL 5. Ed. K. Zeumer. Hanover, 1886.

The Fourth Book of the Chronicle of Fredegar. Trans. J. M. Wallace-Hadrill. London, 1960.

Gaius. *Institutiones.* In *Fontes Iuris Romani Antejustiniani.* Ed. J. Baviera. 2nd ed. Florence, 1940. Vol. 2.

Gregory of Tours. *Libri Historiarum X.* MGH, *Scriptores Rerum Merovingicarum*, I, 1. Ed. B. Krusch and W. Levison. 2nd ed. Hanover, 1951.

——. *Zehn Bücher Geschichten.* Trans. R. Buchner. 2 vols. Berlin, 1956.

Herodotus. Trans. A. D. Godley. The Loeb Classical Library. 4 vols. London, 1926.

Leges:

    Gesetze Burgunden. Trans. F. Beyerle. Weimar, 1936.

    Leges Alamannorum. MGH LL 1, V, 1. Ed. K. Lehmann. Hanover, 1888.

    Leges Burgundionum. MGH LL 1, II, 1. Ed. L. R. von Salis. Hanover, 1892.

    Leges Henrici Primi. Trans. L. J. Downer. Oxford, 1972.

Leges Langobardorum. MGH LL, IV. Ed. F. Bluhme. Hanover, 1868.

Leges Visigothorum. MGH LL 1, I. Ed. K. Zeumer. Hanover, 1902.

Lex Angliorum Werinorum Hoc Est Thuringorum. In MGH LL, V. Ed. K. von Richtofen. Hanover, 1876-1889.

Lex Baiwariorum. MGH LL 1, V, 2. Ed. Ernst von Schwind. Hanover, 1926.

Lex Ribvaria. MGH LL 1, III, 2. Ed. F. Beyerle and R. Buchner. Hanover, 1954.

Lex Romana Visigothorum. Ed. G. Haenel. Berlin, 1849.

Lex Salica. Ed. J. Fr. and R. Behrend. 2nd ed. Weimar, 1897.

Lex Salica. MGH LL 1, IV, 2. Ed. K. A. Eckhardt. Hanover, 1969.

Lex Salica, 100 Titel-Text. Ed. K. A. Eckhardt. Germanenrechte, N.F. Weimar, 1953.

Lex Salica: The Ten Texts with Glosses and the Lex Emendata. Ed. J. H. Hessels. London, 1880.

Lex Salica zum akademischen Gebrauche. Ed. Heinrich Geffcken. Leipzig, 1898.

Lex Saxonum. In MGH LL, V. Ed. K. von Richtofen. Hanover, 1875-1889.

Loi salique ou recueil contenant les anciennes rédactions de cette loi et le texte connu sous le nom de Lex Emendata. Ed. J. M. Pardessus. Paris, 1843.

Pactus Legis Salicae I, 1: *Einführung und 80 Titel-Text*; I, 2: *Systematischer Text*; II, 1: *65 Titel-Text*; II, 2: *Kapitulieren und 70 Titel-Text.* Ed. K. A. Eckhardt. Germanenrechte N.F. Göttingen, 1954-1957.

Pactus Legis Salicae. MGH LL 1, IV, 1. Ed. K. A. Eckhardt. Hanover, 1962.

Leo VI Sapiens. *Tactica.* In J.-P. Migne. *Patrologiae Cursus Completus. Series Graeca.* 166 vols. Paris, 1857-1866. 107: 669-1120.

Marius of Avenches. *Chronica.* In MGH AA, XI, *Chronica Minora* II. Ed. Th. Mommsen. Berlin, 1894. Pp. 225-239.

Mauricius. *Arta Militara.* Ed. H. Mihaescu. Bucharest, 1970.

The Old English Version of the Heptateuch. Alfric's Treatise on the Old and New Testament and his Preface to Genesis. Ed. S. J. Crawford. Early English Text Society, Original Series, No. 160. Oxford, 1922.

Paul the Deacon. *Historia Langobardorum.* In MGH, *Scriptores Rerum Langobardicarum et Italicarum.* Ed. G. Waitz. Hanover, 1878.

Pauli Sententiae. In *Fontes Iuris Romani Antejustiniani.* Ed. J. Baviera. 2nd ed. Florence, 1940. Vol. 2.

Plato. *Laws.* Ed. R. G. Bury. The Loeb Classical Library. 2 vols. London, 1926.

Plutarch's Lives. Trans. B. Perrin. The Loeb Classical Library. 10 vols. London, 1914.

Polybius. *The Histories.* Trans. W. R. Paton. The Loeb Classical Library. 6 vols. London, 1922.

Strabo. *The Geography.* Trans. H. L. Jones. The Loeb Classical Library. 8 vols. London, 1917.

Tacitus. *Cornelii Taciti De Origine et Situ Germanorum.* Ed. J. G. C. Anderson. Oxford, 1938.

———. *Germania.* Ed. E. Fehrle and R. Hünnerkopf. Heidelberg, 1959.

——. *Germania.* Ed. J. Lindauer. Munich, 1967.

——. *Die Germania des Tacitus.* Ed. R. Much and H. Jankuhn. 3rd ed. Heidelberg, 1967.

——. *Die Germania des Tacitus.* Ed. K. Müllenhoff. Deutsche Altertumskunde, 4. Berlin, 1900.

——. *The Histories. The Annals.* Trans. C. Moore and J. Jackson. The Loeb Classical Library. 4 vols. London, 1931.

——. *Taciti De Origine et Situ Germanorum.* Ed. J. Forni and F. Galli. Rome, 1964.

The Theodosian Code. Trans. C. Pharr. Princeton, 1952.

Die Traditionen des Hochstifts Freising. Ed. T. Bitterauf. Quellen und Erörterungen zur bayerischen und deutschen Geschichte, N.F. 4, 5. 2 vols. Munich, 1905.

B. Secondary Works

Anderson, Perry. *Passages from Antiquity to Feudalism.* London, 1974.

Auffroy, H. *Évolution du testament en France des origines au XIIIᵉ siècle.* Paris, 1899.

Bachofen, J. J. *Das Mutterrecht.* Berlin, 1861.

Bader, K. S. *Dorfgenossenschaft und Dorfgemeinde.* Weimar, 1962.

Balon, Joseph. *Les Fondements du régime foncier au moyen âge depuis la chute de l'empire romain en Occident: Étude de dogmatique et d'histoire du droit.* Anciens Pays et Assemblées d'États, 7. Louvain, 1954.

——. *Traité de droit salique: Étude d'exégèse et de sociologie juridiques.* Ius Medii Aevi, 3. 4 vols. Namur, 1965.

Behrend. See *Lex Salica.*

Benveniste, Emile. *Indo-European Language and Society.* Trans. Elizabeth Palmer. London, 1973.

Bergengruen, Alexander. *Adel und Grundherrschaft im Merowingerreich.* Wiesbaden, 1958.

Beyerle, Franz. *Gesetze der Burgunden.* Weimar, 1936.

——. "Das Kulturporträt der beiden alamannischen Rechtstexte: Pactus und Lex Alamannorum." In *Hegau*, 1956. Rpt. in *Zur Geschichte des Alemanner.* Ed. W. Müller. Wege der Forschung C. 1975.

——. "Das legislative Werk Chilperichs I." ZRG GA 78 (1961) 1-38.

——. "Über Normtypen und Erweiterungen der Lex Salica." ZRG GA 44 (1924) 216-261.

Bloch, Marc. *Feudal Society.* Trans. L. A. Manyon. London, 1961.

——. "Une Mise au point: les invasions." *Annales d'Histoire Sociale*, 1 and 2 (1945). Rpt. in *Mélanges historiques.* Bibliothèque Générale de l'École Pratique des Hautes Études, sec. 6. Paris, 1963. 1: 110-154.

Bognetti, G. P. "L'Influsso delle istituzioni militari romane sulle istituzioni longobarde del secolo VI e la natura della 'fara'." *Atti del Congresso Inter-*

nazionale di Diritto Romano e di Storia de Diritto, 4 (1953). Rpt. in *L'età Longobarda*. Milan, 1967. 3: 3-46.

Bosl, Karl. "On Social Mobility in Medieval Society: Service, Freedom and Freedom of Movement as Means of Social Ascent." Trans. Sylvia L. Thrupp. In *Early Medieval Society*. Ed. Sylvia L. Thrupp. New York, 1967. Pp. 87-102.

Bosworth, J. and Toller, T. N. *An Anglo-Saxon Dictionary*. Oxford, 1898. *Supplement* by T. N. Toller. Oxford, 1921.

Brissaud, J. *History of French Private Law*. Trans. R. Howell. The Continental Legal History Series, 3. Boston, 1912.

Brunner, Heinrich. *Deutsche Rechtsgeschichte*. 2nd ed. Systematisches Handbuch der deutschen Rechtswissenschaft, 2, 1. 2 vols. Leipzig, 1906-1928.

——. "Kritische Bemerkungen zur Geschichte des germanischen Weibererbrechts." ZRG GA 21 (1900) 1-18.

——. "Sippe und Wergeld nach niederdeutschen Rechten." ZRG GA 3 (1882) 1-101.

——. "Zu Lex Salica tit. 44: De reipus." *Sitzungsberichte der Berliner Akademie* (1894). Rpt. in *Abhandlungen zur Rechtsgeschichte. Gesammelte Aufsätze von Heinrich Brunner*. Ed. K. Rauch. 2 vols. Weimar, 1931. 2: 67-78.

Buchner, Rudolf. *Die Rechtsquellen*. Supplement to W. Wattenbach and W. Levison, *Deutschlands Geschichtsquellen im Mittelalter: Vorzeit und Karolinger*. Weimar, 1953.

——. Review of *Pactus Legis Salicae* I, 1 and *Lex Salica: 100 Titel-Text*, ed. K. A. Eckhardt, Germanenrechte, N.F. *Historische Zeitschrift* 182 (1956) 366-375.

——. Review of *Pactus Legis Salicae*, I, 2; II, 1; II, 2, ed. K. A. Eckhardt, Germanenrechte, N.F. *Historische Zeitschrift* 191 (1960) 612-620.

Buckland, W. W. *A Text-Book of Roman Law*. 3rd ed., revised by P. Stein. Cambridge, 1966.

Bullough, Donald. "Early Medieval Social Groupings: The Terminology of Kinship." *Past and Present*, No. 45 (Nov., 1969), pp. 3-18.

Bury, J. B. *History of the Later Roman Empire from the Death of Theodosius I to the Death of Justinian*. 2 vols. 1889; rpt. Dover Publications, New York, 1958.

Chadwick, Hector Munro. *The Heroic Age*. Cambridge, 1912.

——. *The Origins of the English Nation*. Cambridge, 1907.

Charanis, Peter. "On the Social Structure of the Later Roman Empire." *Byzantion* 17 (1944-1945) 39-57.

Charles-Edwards, T. M. "Kinship, Status, and the Origins of the Hide." *Past and Present*, No. 56 (August, 1972), pp. 3-33.

Chenon, E. *Histoire générale du droit français public et privé des origines à 1815*. 2 vols. Paris, 1926-1929.

Childe, V. Gordon. *The Aryans*. New York, 1926.

Cole, Thomas. *Democritus and the Sources of Greek Anthropology*. American Philological Association Monographs 25. Western Reserve University, 1967.

Conrad, H. *Deutsche Rechtsgeschichte: Frühzeit und Mittelalter*. Karlsruhe, 1954.

Crossland, R. A. "Indo-European Origins: The Linguistic Evidence." *Past and Present*, No. 12 (Nov., 1957), pp. 16-46.

Dopsch, Alfons. *The Economic and Social Foundations of European Civilization*. Trans. M. G. Beard and N. Marshall, 1937; rpt. New York, 1969.

——. *Die wirtschaftlichen und sozialen Grundlagen der Europäischen Kulturent-wicklung*. 2nd ed. 2 vols. Vienna, 1923-1924.

Duby, Georges. *The Chivalrous Society*. Trans. Cynthia Postan. London, 1977.

Du Cange, Charles Du Fresne, Favre, L., et al. *Glossarium Mediae et Infimae Latinitatis*. 10 vols. Niort, 1883-1887.

Eckhardt. See *Leges: Lex Salica* and *Pactus Legis Salicae*.

Engels, Frederick. *The Origin of the Family, Private Property and the State*. New York, 1972.

Falletti, Louis. "De la condition de la femme pendant le haut moyen-âge." *Annali di Storia del Diritto: Rassegna Internationale*, 10-11 (1966-1967) 91-115.

Fehr, Hans. *Deutsche Rechtsgeschichte*. 6th ed. Lehrbücher und Grundrisse der Rechtswissenschaft, 10. Berlin, 1962.

——. "Über den Titel 58 der Lex Salica." ZRG GA 27 (1906) 151-172.

Fleckenstein, Josef. *Grundlagen und Beginn der deutschen Geschichte*. Deutsche Geschichte, 1. Göttingen, 1974. English translation by Bernard S. Smith. *Early Medieval Germany*. Amsterdam, 1978.

Fox, Robin. *Kinship and Marriage*. Penguin Books, 1967.

——. "Prolegomena to the Study of British Kinship." In *Penguin Survey of the Social Sciences*. Ed. J. Gould. Penguin Books, 1965. Pp. 128-143.

Freeman, J. D. "On the Concept of the Kindred." *Journal of the Royal Anthropological Institute* 91 (1961) 192-220.

Friedrich, P. "Proto-Indo-European Kinship." *Ethnology* 5 (1966) 1-23.

Frommhold, Georg. *Der altfränkische Erbhof. Ein Beitrag zur Erklärung des Begriffs der terra salica*. Breslau, 1938.

Fustel de Coulanges, N.-D. *L'Alleu et le domaine rural pendant l'époque mérovingienne*. Histoire des Institutions Politiques de l'Ancienne France, 4. Paris, 1889.

——. *La Monarchie franque*. 2nd ed. Histoire des Institutions Politiques de l'Ancienne France, 3. Paris: 1905.

——. "Recherches sur cette question: les Germains connaissaient-ils la propriété des terres?" In *Recherches sur quelques problèmes d'histoire*. Paris, 1885. Pp. 189-315.

——. "Recherches sur quelques points des lois barbares." In *Nouvelles recherches sur quelques problèmes d'histoire*. Paris, 1891. Pp. 279-413.

Galton, H. "The Indo-European Kinship Terminology." *Zeitschrift für Ethnologie* 82 (1957) 121-138.

Ganshof, F. L. *The Carolingians and the Frankish Monarchy*. Trans. Janet Sondheimer. Ithaca, 1971.

———. *Recherches sur les capitulaires*. Paris, 1958.

Gastroph, H. L. Günter. *Herrschaft und Gesellschaft in der Lex Baiuvariorum*. Miscellanea Bavarica Monacensia, 53. Munich, 1974.

Geffcken. See *Lex Salica*.

Genicot, Leopold. "The Nobility in Medieval *Francia*: Continuity, Break, or Evolution?" Trans. F. L. Cheyette. In *Lordship and Community*. Ed. F. L. Cheyette. New York, 1968. Pp. 128-135.

Genzmer, Felix. "Die germanische Sippe als Rechtsgebilde." ZRG GA 67 (1950) 34-49.

Ghurye, G. S. *Family and Kin in Indo-European Culture*. 2nd ed. Bombay, 1962.

Glasson, E. "Le Droit de succession au moyen âge." *Nouvelle Revue Historique de Droit Français et Étranger* 16 (1892) 343-601 and 698-796.

———. "Le Droit de succession dans les lois barbares." *Nouvelle Revue Historique de Droit Français et Étranger* 9 (1885) 585-683.

Goebel, V. J. *Felony and Misdemeanor: A Study in the History of English Criminal Procedure*. New York, 1937.

Goffart, Walter. *Caput and Colonate: Towards a History of Late Roman Taxation*. Toronto, 1974.

Goldmann, Emil. *Chrenecruda. Studien zum Titel 58 der Lex Salica*. Deutschrechtliche Beiträge 13, 1. Heidelberg, 1931.

Goody, J. "Indo-European Kinship." *Past and Present*, No. 16 (Nov., 1959), pp. 88-92.

Grimm, Jacob. *Deutsche Rechtsalterthümer*. 1828. 4th ed. 2 vols. Leipzig, 1899.

Hachmann, Rolf. *The Germanic Peoples*. Trans. James Hogarth. Archaeologia Mundi. Geneva, 1971.

Hachmann, Rolf, Kossack, G. and Kuhn, H. *Völker zwischen Germanen und Kelten*. Neumünster, 1962.

Haff, Karl. "Der umstrittene Sippebegriff und die Siedlungsprobleme." ZRG GA 70 (1953) 320-325.

Hagemann, H.-R. "Agnaten." In HRG, 1: 61-63.

Henning, R. "Die germanische fara und die faramanni." *Zeitschrift für deutsches Alterthum und deutsche Litteratur* 36 (1892) 316-326.

Herlihy, David. "Land, Family, and Women in Continental Europe, 701-1200." *Traditio* 18 (1962) 89-120.

Hessels. See *Lex Salica*.

Hessler, R. "Entsippung." In HRG, 1: 947-949.

Hintze, Otto. "The Nature of Feudalism." Trans. F. L. Cheyette. In *Lordship and Community in Medieval Europe*. Ed. F. L. Cheyette. New York, 1968. Pp. 22-31.

Hollister, C. Warren. *The Making of England*. Boston, 1966.

Huebner, Rudolf. *A History of Germanic Private Law*. Trans. F. S. Philbrick. The Continental Legal History Series, 4. Boston, 1918.

Jones, A. H. M. *The Decline of the Ancient World*. New York, 1966.

———. *The Later Roman Empire 284-602: A Social, Economic, and Administrative Survey*. 2 vols. 1964. Rpt. Oxford, 1973.

———. "The Roman Colonate." *Past and Present*, No. 13 (April, 1958), pp. 1-13.

Karayannopulos, Johannes. "Die kollektive Steuerantwortung in der frühbyzantinischen Zeit." *Vierteljahrschrift für Sozial- und Wirtschaftsgeschichte* 43 (1956) 289-322.

Kaser, Max. *Roman Private Law*. Trans. R. Dannenberg. Durban, 1968.

Kaufmann, E. "Chrenecruda." In HRG, 1: 611-613.

Keesing, Roger M. *Kin Groups and Social Structure*. New York, 1975.

Kemble, J. M. *The Saxons in England: A History of the English Commonwealth till the Period of the Norman Conquest*. 1849; rpt. London, 1876.

Kern, Fritz. "Notes on Frankish Words in Lex Salica." In Hessels, 427-564.

Klindt-Jensen, O. *Denmark Before the Vikings*. Ancient Peoples and Places, 4. New York, 1957.

Koebner, R. "The Settlement and Colonization of Europe." *Cambridge Economic History*. Ed. J. H. Clapham and E. Power. Cambridge, 1944. 1: 1-91.

Kroeschell, Karl. "Die Sippe im germanischen Recht." ZRG GA 77 (1960) 1-25.

Kunkel, Wolfgang. *An Introduction to Roman Legal and Constitutional History*. Trans. J. M. Kelly. Oxford, 1966.

Lacey, W. K. *The Family in Classical Greece*. London, 1968.

Lancaster, Lorraine. "Kinship in Anglo-Saxon Society." *British Journal of Sociology* 9 (1957) 230-250 and 359-377.

Latouche, Robert. *The Birth of Western Economy: Economic Aspects of the Dark Ages*. Trans. E. M. Wilkinson. 1961; rpt. Harper Torchbooks, New York, 1966.

Levy, Ernst. "Reflections on the First 'Reception' of Roman Law in Germanic States." *American Historical Review* 48 (1942) 20-29.

———. *West Roman Vulgar Law: The Law of Property*. Philadelphia, 1951.

Lewis, C. T. and C. Short. *A Latin Dictionary*. Oxford, 1879.

Leyser, K. "The German Aristocracy from the Ninth to the Early Twelfth Century. A Historical and Cultural Sketch." *Past and Present*, No. 41 (Dec., 1968), pp. 25-53.

———. "Maternal Kin in Early Medieval Germany. A Reply." *Past and Present*, No. 49 (Nov., 1970), pp. 126-134.

———. *Rule and Conflict in Early Medieval Society: Ottonian Saxony*. London, 1979.

Lovejoy, A. O. and Boas, G. *Primitivism and Related Ideas in Antiquity*. Documentary History of Primitivism and Related Ideas, 1. Baltimore, 1935.

Loyn, H. R. "Kinship in Anglo-Saxon England." *Anglo-Saxon England* 3 (1974) 197-209.

McLennan, J. J. *Primitive Marriage*. London, 1865.

Maitland, F. W. *Domesday Book and Beyond. Three Essays on the Early History of England*. 1897; rpt. London, Fontana Library, 1960.

——. For HEL see Pollock and Maitland.

Merguet, E. H. *Lexikon zu Schriften Cäsars*. Jena, 1886.

Mertens, Hans-Georg. "Überlegungen zur Herkunft des Parentelensystems." ZRG GA 90 (1973) 149-164.

Meyer, E. Review of E. Goldmann, *Chrenecruda-Studien zum Titel 58 der Lex Salica*, Heidelberg, 1931. ZRG GA 52 (1932) 358-369.

Mor, C. G. "Fara." In HRG, 1: 1074-1077.

Musset, Lucien. *Les Invasions: les vagues germaniques*. 2nd ed. Nouvelle Clio, L'Histoire et ses problèmes, 12. Paris, 1969. English translation by Edward and Columba James, *The Germanic Invasions*. University Park, Pennsylvania, 1975.

Needham, Rodney, ed. *Rethinking Kinship and Marriage*. A.S.A. Monographs, 11. London, 1971.

Nehlsen, Hermann. *Sklavenrecht zwischen Antike und Mittelalter: Germanisches und römisches Recht in den germanischen Rechtsaufzeichnungen*. Göttinger Studien zur Rechtsgeschichte, 7. Göttingen, 1972.

Nicholls, Kenneth. *Gaelic and Gaelicized Ireland in the Middle Ages*. The Gill History of Ireland, 4. Dublin, 1972.

Nonn, U. "Merowingische Testament: Studien zum Fortleben einer römischen Urkundenform im Frankreich." *Archiv für Diplomatik* 18 (1972) 1-129.

Norden, E. *Die germanische Urgeschichte in Tacitus Germania*. 4th ed. Stuttgart, 1959.

Olivier-Martin, F. *Histoire du droit français des origines à la Révolution*. Paris, 1948.

Ourliac, Paul and Malafosse, J. de. *Histoire du droit privé*. 2nd ed. Themis, Droit, 10-12. 3 vols. Paris, 1968-1971.

Pardessus. See *Leges: Loi salique*.

Peters, Edward. *Europe. The World of the Middle Ages*. Englewood Cliffs,1977.

Phillpotts, Bertha. *Kindred and Clan*. Cambridge, 1913.

Planitz, Hans and Eckhardt, K. A. *Deutsche Rechtsgeschichte*. 2nd ed. Graz, 1961.

Pollock, F. and Maitland, F. W. *The History of English Law*. 2nd ed. 2 vols. 1898; rpt. Cambridge, 1968.

Rabinowitz, J. J. "The Title *De Migrantibus* of the *Lex Salica* and the Jewish Herem Hayishub." *Speculum* 22 (1947) 46-50.

Radcliffe-Brown, A.-R. and Ford, Daryll, ed. *African Systems of Kinship and Marriage*. Oxford, 1950.

Reuter, Timothy, ed. *The Medieval Nobility: Studies on the Ruling Classes of France and Germany from the Sixth to the Twelfth Century*. Europe in the Middle Ages, Selected Studies, 14. Amsterdam, 1978.

Rietschel, R. "Sippe." In J. Hoops, *Reallexikon der germanischen Altertumskunde*. Strassburg, 1919. Vol. 4.

Ross, D. W. *The Early History of Land-Holding Among the Germans*. London, 1883.

Scheyhing, R. "Eideshelfer." HRG, 1: 870-872.

Schlesinger, Walter. "Lord and Follower in Germanic Institutional History." Trans. F. L. Cheyette. In *Lordship and Community in Medieval Europe*. Ed. F. L. Cheyette. New York, 1968. Pp. 64-99.

——. "Randbemerkungen zu drei Aufsätzen über Sippe, Gefolgschaft und Treue." In *Alteuropa und die moderne Gesellschaft: Festschrift für Otto Brunner*. 1963. Rpt. in *Beiträge zur deutschen Verfassungsgeschichte des Mittelalters*. Göttingen, 1963. 2: 286-334.

Schmid, Karl. "The Structure of the Nobility in the Earlier Middle Ages." Trans. Timothy Reuter. In *The Medieval Nobility*. Ed. Timothy Reuter. Amsterdam, 1978. Pp. 37-59.

Schmidt-Wiegand, Ruth. "Die kritische Ausgabe der Lex Salica − noch immer ein Problem?" ZRG GA 76 (1959) 301-319.

——. "Lex Salica." In HRG, 2: 1949-1962.

——. "Die volkssprachigen Wörter der Leges barbarorum als Ausdruck sprachlicher Interferenz." *Frühmittelalterliche Studien* 13 (1979) 56-87.

Schott, Clausdieter. "Der Stand der Leges Forschung." *Frühmittelalterliche Studien* 13 (1979) 29-55.

Schulz, F. *Classical Roman Law*. Oxford, 1951.

Schusky, Ernest L. *Variation in Kinship*. New York, 1974.

Seebohm, F. *Tribal Custom in Anglo-Saxon Law*. London, 1911.

Smith, Bernard S. *Early Medieval Germany*. Amsterdam, 1978.

Staab, Franz. *Untersuchungen zur Gesellschaft am Mittelrhein im Karolingerzeit*. Geschichtliche Landskunde, 11. Wiesbaden, 1975.

Stein, S. "Lex Salica." *Speculum* 22 (1947) 113-134, 395-418.

Stephenson, Carl. "The Common Man in Early Medieval Europe." *American Historical Review* 51 (1946) 419-438.

Störmer, W. *Adelsgruppen im früh- und hochmittelalterliche Bayern*. Munich, 1972.

Syme, R. *Tacitus*. 2 vols. Oxford, 1958.

Thibault, F. "Observations sur le titre 'De Migrantibus' de la loi salique." *Nouvelle Revue Historique du Droit Français et Étranger* 45 (1921) 448-458.

Thompson, E. A. "The Barbarian Kingdoms in Gaul and Spain." *Nottingham Medieval Studies* 7 (1963) 3-33.

——. *The Early Germans*. Oxford, 1965.

——. *The Goths in Spain*. Oxford, 1969.

——. "The Passio S. Sabae and Early Visigothic Society." *Historia* 4 (1955) 331-338.

——. *The Visigoths in the Time of Ulfilas*. Oxford, 1966.

Thomson, G. D. *Studies in Ancient Greek Society*. London, 1949.

Tierney, J. J. "The Celtic Ethnography of Posidonius." *Proceedings of the Royal Irish Academy* 60, sec. C (1959-1960) 189-275.

Todd, Malcolm. *Everyday Life of the Barbarians*. London, 1972.

——. *The Northern Barbarians 100 B.C. - A.D. 300*. London, 1975.

Van der Rhee, Florus. *Die germanischen Wörter in den langobardischen Gesetze*. Rotterdam, 1970.

Vinogradoff, Paul. *The Growth of the Manor*. London, 1911.

——. *Historical Jurisprudence*. 2 vols. Oxford, 1920-1922.

Violett, P. M. *Histoire du droit civil français*. 3rd ed. Paris, 1905.

von Amira, K. and Eckhardt, K. A. *Germanisches Recht*. 4th ed. Grundriss der germanischen Philologie, 5. Berlin, 1960.

von Amira, K. "Zur salfränkischen Eideshilfe." *Germania* 20, N.F. 8 (1875) 53-66.

Wallace-Hadrill, J. M. "Archbishop Hincmar and the Authorship of Lex Salica." In *The Long-Haired Kings and Other Studies in Frankish History*. London, 1962. Pp. 95-120.

——. *The Barbarian West A.D. 400-1000: The Early Middle Ages*. Harper Torchbooks. New York, 1962.

——. "The Bloodfeud of the Franks." In *The Long-Haired Kings and Other Studies in Frankish History*. London, 1962. Pp. 121-147.

——. *Early Germanic Kingship in England and on the Continent*. Oxford, 1971.

Walser, G. *Caesar und die Germanen. Studien zur politischen Tendenz römischer Feldzugsberichte*. Historia, Einzelschriften, Heft 1. Wiesbaden, 1956.

Watson, A. *The Law of Succession in the Later Roman Republic*. Oxford, 1971.

Wells, C. M. *The German Policy of Augustus*. Oxford, 1972.

Wemple, Suzanne Fonay. *Women in Frankish Society: Marriage and the Cloister. 500 to 900*. Philadelphia, 1981.

Wenskus, R. *Stammesbildung und Verfassung: das Werden der frühmittelalterlichen gentes*. Cologne, 1961.

Wormald, Patrick. "*Lex Scripta* and *Verbum Regis*: Legislation and Germanic Kingship, from Euric to Cnut." In *Early Medieval Kingship*. Ed. P. H. Sawyer and I. N. Wood. Leeds, 1977. Pp. 105-138.

Zachariä von Lingenthal, Karl E. *Geschichte des griechisch-romanischen Rechts*. 3rd ed. Wurttemberg, 1955.

Zöllner, E. "Die Herkunft der Agilofinger." *Mitteilungen des Instituts für Österreichische Geschichtsforschung* 59 (1951) 245-264.

Index

achasius 166, 171, 172, 218

Agilofings 99, 102

agnation, definition of 3. *See also* kinship, Germanic, traditional interpretations of

agri deserti 70-79

alodis 183-191, 233; *alodis parentum* 184; *alodis paterna* 184 n, 188-191 (see also *terra paterna*); in the rubric of LS **59**: 205

ancestor focus 4

Anniona 103

arimanni 90, 92 n

aristocracy, Carolingian 11. *See also* nobility

Aristotle 40

Arta Militara **11.4**: 53-54 n

associations, Roman 78

aviaticae res 194-195. See also *hereditas aviatica*

avunculate 56, 57, 60-64

avunculus: in Frankish inheritance 206-212; inheritance rights of, in *Germania* 57, 59; in LS **44**: 168, 172-174; in Merovingian Latin 165 n. *See also* avunculate

Balon, Joseph 201 n, 231-232

barbarian laws (*leges barbarorum*) 30, 35, 58, 115-118

Behrend, J. Fr. and R. 151

Bellum Gallicum. See Caesar, Julius

Beowulf 61-63 nn. 65, 68, 71.

Berthegund 197-200

betrothal 167; right of, and inheritance 168-170

Beyerle, Franz 84, 90-92

bilateral, as synonym for cognatic 3

bilateral kindred 5. *See also* kindred

bilinealism (or double descent) 29 n, 64 n, 172 n

Bloch, Marc 11-14, 15, 23, 89, 180 n

Bognetti, G.P. 90-91

Burgundaefarones 93

Brunner, Heinrich 15, 29, 130, 226; on LS **44**: 168-170; on LS **59**: 202-210

Buchner, R. 127

Caesar, Julius 7, 17, 19, 30, 36 , 38-50, 51, 52, 65, 109, 180

Capitula incerta (Boretius, **1**: 315) 160

categories, kinship: definition of 4; Frankish 163-219

Celts 48, 51

Chadwick, H.M. 23, 25-26

Charles-Edwards, T.M. 27

Cimbri 48, 51, 52

clan: definition of 4; in traditional historiography 5 (*see also* kinship, Germanic, traditional interpretations of). *See also* descent group; lineage

Codex Euricianus 118, 205, 215, 236-242

Codex Theodosianus **3.7.1**: 168-171; **5.14.30**: 74-75; **13.11.13**: 75, 81

cognatic clans 4

cognatic kindred 4-5. *See also* kindred, definition of

cognation: definition of 3-4; in early Middle Ages 11-12; in Frankish kinship 218-219 (*see also* categories, Frankish; kindred, Frankish); in Germanic kinship 8, 222-223; in the classification of kinship systems 6; in the traditional interpretation of Germanic kinship 17, 24, 30, 111, 222-223

comitatus 61

communism 40, 45, 49, 179

compensation 18, 59, 118, 119, 135-155, 178

concubinage 62

consensus omnium 77

consobrina in LS **44**: 168, 172, 174

consortes 104-105

constituent clans and lineages 7, 36, 64. *See also* group, universal or constituent; kinship, Germanic, traditional interpretations of

Council of Tours (AD 567) **c. 22**: 126

cum fara sua migrare 94

customary law 189, 214; inheritance in, 185, 214

Decretio Childeberti 126, 193-195

descent group: definition of 4; in the classification of kinship systems 6. *See also* clan; *genealogia*; group; lineage

deserta 99-100, 104

Ditmarschen 13, 29

domus 60

Dopsch, Alfons 68

D'Ors, Alvaro 215, 236-237 nn

double descent. *See* bilinealism

Drazza 102

Eckhardt, K.A.: and *Lex Salica* 119-128; on the reconstruction of LS **58**: 225-230; on LS **59**: 231-233

economy, Germanic 24, 42-50, 56, 99, 109

Edictum Chilperici 20, 125 n; **c. 2**: 166, 171; **c. 3**: 67-87, 130, 180, 195-197, 201, 202, 219; **c. 8**: 147 n

ego-focus 4

epibole 68, 71-72, 78

epistolae hereditariae 186-191; Roman and Frankish, 194

Eriching 104-105

ethnography, ancient 39-65; kinship in 40

Extravagantia **B 2**: 160-161; **B 11**: 75 n

Fagana 102, 104, 107

familiae et propinquitates 53

familia et penates 57

fara 7, 13, 20, 36, 65, 89-97, 110

faramanni 89, 90, 92

Farro 93

faru 91, 94 n

Ferings 104, 107

feud 20, 56, 57, 59, 64, 118, 119, 135-136, 152-153, 171, 177-178

feudalism 12, 13

filii 58, 204 n

fiscal units, Roman 71-72

formulae: *Bignonianae* **6**: 131; *Marculfi* **2.7**: 184; **2.9**: 184; **2.12**: 132, 185-191; *Merkelianae* **23**: 132, 188-191; *Patavienses* **5**: 105-106; *Salicae Lindenbrogianae* **21**: 158-160; *Senonenses Recentiores* **2** and **5**: 159-160; *Senonicae* **45**: 132, 185-191

fourjourement 152

fratres 59; in LS **59**: 203-212

Fredegar 63, 89, 93

Frisia 13

Fustel de Coulanges 93

Gauls 45

genealogia 7, 13, 19, 20, 36, 65, 99-108

genos 17

gens 13, 17, 27, 44

gentes cognationesque hominum 43-45

Genzmer, Felix 17, 20, 53

Germania: inheritance in 56-59; kinship in 42, 52-65; role of in the traditional interpretation of kinship 41. *See also* Tacitus

Grágás 20-21

Gregory of Tours 90, 93-94

group, definition of 4; personal 5; universal or constituent 5. *See also* descent group

gwelyau 231

Hahilinga 102

hereditas aviatica in *LRib.* **57**: 184 n, 194-195, 205

Herold: and LS **58.3**: 226, 228-229; and LS **59**: 231-233. See also *Lex Salica*, redactions of

Hessels, J.H. 119

homodoula 71

homokensa 71-72

honor 60-61

Hosi 102

hostages 56, 60, 64

Indo-Europeans. *See* kinship, Indo-European

in fara 94

Ingitrude 197-200

in heris generationis 54 n

inheritance communities 99 n, 100-102, 105, 107-108, 110

inheritance rights, Alamannian 100-101; female 108

——, Bavarian 100-101; female 108

——, Burgundian 199-200, 238-242; of mother 235, 238-242

——, Frankish 79-87, 130, 150, 152-155, 176-215, 218-219; and ancestral property 184-191, 194-195, 212-215; and representation 187, 193-194; female 68, 130, 132, 186-191, 196, 197-200, 202, 208-212, 219; in *Decretio Childeberti* 193-5; in *Edictum Chilperici* **c. 3**: 67-68, 79-87, 195-197; in *formulae* 185-191; in HF **9.33** and **10.12**: 197-200; in LS **59**, *De alodis*: 200-215, and reason for sequence of heirs, 200, 211-212, 218, compared with Roman law 211-212; of grandchildren, 193-195; theories of 67, 180, 187 n, 188 n, 201, 205 n, 210, 217, 231

——, Germanic 65; in the *Germania* 56-59; female 58

——, in customary law 185, 214

——, Roman 171, 199-200, 211-212, 235, 238-241; of associations 78; of grandchildren 194 n; of mother 235, 238-241

——, Thuringian 180 n

——, Visigothic 199-200, 214-215, 235-238, 240-242; of mother 235-238, 240-242

in vico et genealogia 105-106

ius liberorum 235 n, 241

ius recadentiae: in customary law 185; in Frankish and Visigothic law 213-215

Joseph, bishop of Freising 103

kindred: definition of 4; Frankish 135-162, 218, range of 143-144, 162, 174-175, 218; Germanic 223; in traditional historiography 16-19

kinship, Anglo-Saxon 11, 18, 26-27
——, Frankish 7; theories of, 67, 200, 217. *See also* categories, Frankish; kindred, Frankish; inheritance, Frankish
——, Germanic, traditional interpretations of 2-8, 11-32, 35-36, 89, 99, 109-111, 137, 201, 221-222, 224
——, Indo-European 14, 18, 20, 36-38
——, pre-Indo-European 24 n
kinship systems, classification of 6
Krammer, Mario 119
Kroeschell, Karl 21

landholding and ownership 18, 19, 24 n, 30, 36, 40, 42-50, 56, 58, 101, 110, 178-181. *See also* kinship, Germanic, traditional interpretations of; inheritance communities
——, Alamannian 100-101
——, Bavarian 100-101
——, Frankish 67, 176; ancestral property in 184-191; proprietal distinctions of 183-191; theories of 178-181, 201, 205 n, 217. *See also* inheritance, Frankish
——, Roman 179, 180 n
La Tène 46
leges barbarorum. See barbarian laws
Leges Visigothorum 119, 214. See also *Codex Euricianus*
Leo VI, emperor. See *Tactica*
leudes 93-94, 97
leudis 141
Levy, Ernst 117 n, 131
Lex Alamannorum **81**: 100, 106-107
Lex Baiwariorum **3**: 99, 102-103
Lex Burgundionum 118, 163, 205; LB **24.3** and **53**: 238-241; LB **54**: 89, 92
Lex Ribvaria **57**: 205 n, 206-207
Lex Romana Visigothorum 126, 163; LRV **3.7.1**: 168-171, 174
Lex Salica 7, 17, 2, 21, 25, 115-135; and antiquarianism 128-133, 146-147, 167; and Clovis 120, 125; and the MGH 119-122; and shorter prologue 126; LS **13.11**: 126, 174; LS **14.5,6**: 79; LS **44**, *De reipus*: 129, 163-175, 178, 218; LS **45**, *De migrantibus*: 67-87, 129, 201, and Jewish law 68 n; LS **46**: 84; LS **58**, *De chrenecruda*: 129, 130, 142, 144-149, 178; LS **59**, *De alodis*: 82, 84 n, 130, 178, 181, 183, 184, 201-215, 231-233, interpretation of 208-215, reason for sequence of heirs in 200, 211-212, 218; LS **60**, *De eum qui se de parentilla tollere uult*: 149-155, 178, 219; LS **62**, *De conpositione homicidii*: 135-144, 148-149, 178, 225-227, 230; LS **68**, *De*

homine ingenuo occiso: 135-144, 148-149, 225-227, 230; redactions of 119-134. *See also* Eckhardt, K.A.
Lex Thuringorum **26-34**: 180 n
liberi 58
lineage, definition of 4. *See also* clan; descent group
lineages, Welsh 231
Louis the Pius, capitulary of (Boretius, no. **142**): c. **8**: 167 n; c. **9**: 74 n, 129

Maitland, F.W. 27-28
Markgenossenschaft 19, 30, 45, 68 n
Marius of Avenches 89, 90
matrilateral, definition of 3
matriliny 12, 13, 14, 15, 22-26, 29, 57 n, 63, 163, 202-203, 206; definition of 3
Marxist historiography 15, 23
Mauricius. See *Arta Militara*
migrare 73
military organization, Germanic 19, 20, 21, 24, 36, 42, 53-56, 64, 65, 89, 95 n, 109-110
Möser, J. 45

nobility: German 11; French 12 n; Burgundian 93; Friuli 96; Bavarian 99, 102-103
Norden, E. 42

oathhelping 18, 118, 178; Frankish 147, 150, 157-162, 218

Pactus Alamannorum **2.45**: 54 n
Pactus Legis Salicae 121 n, 123. See also *Lex Salica*
Pactus Pro Tenore Pacis 17, 131
parentelic system, 143, 166 n, 211 n
parentilla 150 n, 154
participes 104-105, 107
participes villae 74
pastoralism 30, 40, 45, 49
paterna paternis, materna maternis. See ius recadentiae
patrilateral, definition of 3
patriliny, synonym for agnation 3
patrui 59
patruus 62-63
Paul the Deacon 89
peregrinus volens 75 n, 76
Phillpotts, Bertha 11, 21, 23-25
Plato 40, 47
political structures, Germanic 17, 18, 19, 26, 30, 31, 36, 56, 109
polygamy 62
Posidonius 47, 48, 51, 52

praecipuae prosapiae 96
private property. *See* landholding and ownership
propinquus 59, 61
proximiores 140, 142-3. See also *tres proximiores*

reipi, reipus 163. See also *Lex Salica*, LS **44**
religion, Germanic 47
remarriage. See *Lex Salica*, LS **44**
representation 187
Rothair **153**: 166 n; **177**: 89, 94, 97

Salic Law. See Lex Salica
"Salic Law" of royal succession 233
Scyths 47-49
Seebohm, F. 26, 231
settlement, Germanic 20, 79, 89, 91, 99-100, 103,
    106, 108-110
sicut et lex salica habet 67, 211-212
Sippe 16-23
sister's son. *See* avunculate
soror matris in LS **59**: 203-212
soror matris texts of LS **58**: 225-230
spearkin 13 n, 16, 180 n
spindlekin 13 n, 16, 27, 180 n
sponsorship 61
status, suits concerning 158-162, 218
stock 143, 153 n, 154 n, 166 n
Suebi 42, 46
super alterum 74-75
swordkin 16. *See also* spearkin

Tacitus 7, 19, 21, 25, 36, 38, 40-42, 47, 51-65,
    109, 136
Tactica **18**: 54 n
Tassilo, duke of Bavaria 103-104
terra paterna 188-191
terra salica 196, 208 n, 212 n, 231-233
Thompson, E.A. 23-24
tres proximiores 143-144, 147
truncal principle. See *ius recadentiae*

unilineal, definition of 3
unilineal systems 4
unilinealism. *See* kinship, Germanic, traditional
    interpretations of

vengeance 20, 136
veterans 70
vici 99
vicini 7, 20, 65, 67-87, 110, 176
vicus 105-106
villa 73-75, 101
Vinogradoff, Paul 26
virilis sexus in LS **59**: 203-205, 207-210
von Amira 226

Wallace-Hadrill, J.M. 120, 128, 136-137
Walser, G. 47
wergeld 18, 20, 99, 118, 137; divisions of
    137-138, Frankish 138-144
widow: remarriage of, see *Lex Salica*, LS **44**;
    right to compensation of 141